Researching the Paranormal

Researching the Paranormal

How to Find Reliable Information about Parapsychology, Ghosts, Astrology, Cryptozoology, Near-Death Experiences, and More

Courtney M. Block

ROWMAN & LITTLEFIELD
Lanham • Boulder • New York • London

Published by Rowman & Littlefield
An imprint of The Rowman & Littlefield Publishing Group, Inc.
4501 Forbes Boulevard, Suite 200, Lanham, Maryland 20706
www.rowman.com

86-90 Paul Street, London EC2A 4NE

Copyright © 2020 by Courtney M. Block
Paperback Edition 2024

All rights reserved. No part of this book may be reproduced in any form or by any electronic or mechanical means, including information storage and retrieval systems, without written permission from the publisher, except by a reviewer who may quote passages in a review.

British Library Cataloguing in Publication Information Available

Library of Congress Cataloging-in-Publication Data

Names: Block, Courtney M., 1986– author.
Title: Researching the paranormal : how to find reliable information about parapsychology, ghosts, astrology, cryptozoology, near-death experiences, and more / Courtney M. Block.
Description: Lanham : Rowman & Littlefield, 2020..| Includes bibliographical references and index. | Summary: "In this book, you'll find an assortment of resources that seriously examine various paranormal topics. You'll also learn how you can apply the components of credibility to find additional research as well as information on conducting your own paranormal investigations"—Provided by publisher.
Identifiers: LCCN 2020005398 (print) | LCCN 2020005399 (ebook)
Subjects: LCSH: Parapsychology.
Classification: LCC BF1029 .B56 2020 (print) | LCC BF1029 (ebook) | DDC 133.3—dc23
LC record available at https://lccn.loc.gov/2020005398
LC ebook record available at https://lccn.loc.gov/2020005399

ISBN: 978-1-5381-3144-2 (cloth : alk. paper)
ISBN: 978-1-5381-9217-7 (pbk : alk. paper)
ISBN: 978-1-5381-3145-9 (ebook)

For Christian

Aunt Courtney loves you more than she loves Bigfoot and Nessie.

Contents

Preface	xiii
Liminal Spaces: Where the Paranormal Intersects with Academia and How Liminality Challenges Our Critical Thinking	xiv
Notes	xvii
Acknowledgments	xix
Introduction	xxi
1 What Is the Paranormal?	1
Definitions and Traditional Understandings	1
Brief Outline of Paranormal Topics Discussed in This Book	6
Ghosts and Hauntings	6
Ufology	13
Parapsychology	19
Near-Death Experiences and Reincarnation	24
Cryptozoology	30
Astrology, Divination, and Mysticism	38
Occult and Magical Practices	40
A Note on Religion and Folklore	41
Notes	43
2 History of Paranormal Research and Seminal Figures	49
A Brief History of Paranormal Research	49
Brief Sketches of Key Figures in Paranormal Research	56
Contemporary Paranormal Scholars	59
Notes	63
3 Best Practices in Conducting and Gathering Paranormal Research	67

The Ins and Outs of Conducting Your Own Paranormal Research	68
Gathering and Seeking Out Paranormal Research	71
Note	81
4 Analyzing for Credibility in Paranormal Research	**83**
Sarah Blakeslee's CRAAP Test	90
Currency—When Was This Published/Created?	90
Relevancy—Is This on Topic?	90
Authority—Who Is the Author and What Is Their Experience?	91
Accuracy—Where Did This Information Come From?	91
Purpose—Why Was This Information Created?	92
Not All Credible Sources Are Scholarly, and That's OK	93
Notes	99
5 Universities, Professional Organizations, Associations, and Societies Engaged in Paranormal Research	**101**
Universities Engaged in Paranormal Research	102
Professional Organizations Conducting Paranormal Research	105
Associations and Societies Involved in the Paranormal	107
Information Is Everywhere	109
Notes	109
6 Primary Sources, Paranormal Museums, and Special Collections across the United States	**113**
Types of Paranormal Primary Sources	113
Museums with Paranormal Collections in the United States	115
Other Special Collections	119
The National Archives	121
Library of Congress	122
A Brief List of Notable Primary Paranormal Sources	122
Betty and Barney Hill Abduction Experience	123
A 1605 Publication on the Nature of Spirits	123
Spiritualism Periodical Published in 1882	124
May 2019 Article from the *New York Times* about Navy Investigations of UAPs	124
New York Times Article Highlighting the ESP Experiments of J. B. Rhine	125
The Heyday of Mesmerism	125
Witch Trial Documents from the University of Virginia	126
The Value of Holistic Research	126
Notes	127
7 Handbooks, Dictionaries, and Encyclopedias	**129**
Ghosts and Hauntings	130
Handbooks	130
Dictionaries	135

Encyclopedias	136
Parapsychology	139
Handbooks	139
Dictionaries	142
Encyclopedias	143
Cryptozoology	145
Handbooks	145
Dictionaries	145
Encyclopedias	146
Ufology	148
Handbooks	148
Encyclopedias	151
Reincarnation and Near-Death Experiences	154
Handbooks	154
Encyclopedias	155
Astrology, Divination, and Mysticism	156
Handbooks	156
Dictionaries	161
Encyclopedias	161
Occult and Other Paranormal	165
Dictionaries	165
Encyclopedias	166
Notes	171
8 Monographs	173
Ghosts and Hauntings	174
Parapsychology	179
Cryptozoology	188
Ufology	196
Reincarnation and Near-Death Experiences	203
Astrology, Divination, and Mysticism	208
Occult and Magical Practices	212
General Paranormal and Paranormal Philosophy	220
Notes	226
9 Journals and Databases for Finding Paranormal Resources, with a Selection of Relevant Journal Articles	227
Databases	232
Academic Search Premier	232
America: History and Life	233
BASE	233
Gale Primary Sources	234
Historical *New York Times*	234
MLA International Bibliography	235

Philosopher's Index	235
ProQuest Dissertations and Theses	236
PsycARTICLES	237
SocINDEX	237
Victorian Popular Culture	238
Scholarly and Peer-Reviewed Journals	239
British Journal of Psychology	239
Journal for Spiritual and Consciousness Studies	239
Journal of Abnormal Psychology	240
Journal of American Folklore	240
Journal of the American Society for Psychical Research	241
Journal of Near-Death Studies	242
Journal of Parapsychology	242
Journal of Scientific Exploration	243
Journal of the Society for Psychical Research	244
Paranthropology: Journal of Anthropological Approaches to the Paranormal	245
Sociology of Religion	245
Supernatural Studies	246
Popular Journals	246
Discover	247
Popular Science	248
Science	248
Sample Journal Articles on Paranormal Topics	249
Ghosts and Hauntings	250
Ufology	252
Parapsychology	256
Reincarnation and Near-Death Experiences	261
Cryptozoology	265
Astrology, Divination, and Magic	269
Occult and Other Paranormal	273
Notes	277
10 The UK's Intimate History with the Paranormal: Magic, Case Studies from the Society for Psychical Research, Special Collections, and Notable Paranormal Locations	**279**
The Modern World of Ghosts	280
A Brief Note regarding Magic in the UK	283
Fascinating Tales from the Scientific Pioneers	284
Universities, Organizations, and Collections	287
Notable Paranormal Locations in the UK	289
Notes	293
Bibliography	**295**

Index 305
About the Author 311

Preface

In the process of writing this book, many people asked me to describe it. I always hesitated a bit, trying to think of the perfect segue to begin answering that question. Most of the time I defaulted and said that it was merely a research guide to the paranormal. To be fair, part of it is a research guide. In the chapters that follow, for example, you can find loads of resources on various paranormal topics like ufology, cryptozoology, near-death experiences, ghosts, psychokinesis, and more. But it's actually more than just a research guide. Within these pages, I discuss the nuances of conducting your own paranormal investigation, offering tips and suggestions from my own personal experience. I also show you how to seek out and gather paranormal research—in other words, I show you the steps you need to take in order to locate scientific studies, articles, books, and more in your attempt to learn more about this wonderfully weird world. I provide an overview of what characteristics to look out for when questioning if something is a credible source. Credibility isn't just a concept relegated to students and professors—we all need to know how to ensure that the information we consume, reference, or use to inform ourselves about something is credible.

I do all of this to highlight the long history of paranormal research, which is something that I think many don't realize. In fact, I fear that some automatically assume that the paranormal has no history of scientific inquiry simply due to its nature. "It's all a bunch of hocus-pocus," I can hear them saying now, brushing off factoids like the labs at Duke University where scientists studied extrasensory perception, or the synchronicity theory proposed by the father of psychiatry, Carl Jung, after a series of his own mysterious encounters. I write this book to shine a light on this history of serious, academic research of the paranormal, and for the student or researcher who has even the tiniest interest in these topics. I especially write this for the students who are interested but who feel silly asking for help because they're afraid how professors or librarians will look at them when they mention they're interested in ghosts. I write this for those who are ensconced in academia but who feel like they can't discuss their interests for fear of not being taken seriously. I write this to illustrate that the world is a weird and wonderful place. I write this for those who revel in wonder.

LIMINAL SPACES: WHERE THE PARANORMAL INTERSECTS WITH ACADEMIA AND HOW LIMINALITY CHALLENGES OUR CRITICAL THINKING

Within the field of anthropology, there is a concept known as liminality. Popularized by researchers Arnold van Gennep and Victor Turner,[1] the notion of liminality refers to a transitional or in-between state that occurs during a ritual process—a stage in which the practitioner's understanding, identity, or role is in flux. To help us best understand this notion of liminality, I enjoy James Seale-Collazo's interpretation that tells us liminality refers to "a particular category of social situation in which structural constraints upon individuals are loosened or released and hierarchies blurred or held in abeyance."[2]

When we engage with the paranormal from a scientific or academic lens, we are holding in abeyance the structural constraints of accepted science and of our own preconceived notions of credibility. There are many who consider the phenomena that I discuss in this book as nothing more than pseudoscience—people who remain firmly rooted in a materialist framework that still dominates our institutions of learning and higher education. And then there are those of us who are comfortable stepping outside of that materialist framework and engaging with concepts and research that are still considered to be on the "fringe." Engaging with the paranormal within a materialist culture, then, creates a liminal space. It is liminal because even though it's not quite fully embraced by the scientific community, there are nevertheless highly credentialed and respected scientists who engage with this research and push the boundaries of our knowledge. Perhaps they are people who, like me, find comfort and a sense of belonging in these liminal spaces—who find a purpose in pushing back against the academic and scientific status quo. To dive even deeper into this argument, we can then posit that these researchers become liminal themselves, existing in an in-between world with one foot in academia and the other foot out—busy perhaps pushing back against dominant materialist philosophies.

Let's get back to the idea of holding credibility in abeyance. When I say that paranormal inquiry holds our preconceived notions of credibility in abeyance, I mean that it challenges us to expand our biases about what topics are and are not able to be researched in credible and scientific ways. Again, there are many who believe that no credible inquiry can be done on the topics mentioned in this book due simply to their nature. "There are no such things as ghosts," so therefore any scientific attempt at understanding this phenomenon is methodologically unsound. This is what some might say, and I'd argue that it's probably a larger group of people than we might realize. When you seek out paranormal research, then, you exist in a liminal space. Are you a serious researcher looking for serious information? How could you be if you are researching a topic that so many consider pseudoscientific? What does it mean to be someone who seriously investigates that which many don't take seriously at all? Herein rests the liminal space, and it's no small matter.

Another factor that creates this liminal space is unchallenged and untested notions of credibility. Students are constantly bombarded by professors or librarians who remind them to only seek out that which is credible. This is a good thing, don't mistake me here. However, underlying the notion of credibility are both personal and cultural assumptions regarding what is and isn't credible. I don't think it's a stretch to say that within academia there exists a culture of information hierarchy in which the academic, peer-reviewed resource is held as the top echelon of credibility. These resources are certainly deserving of that spot, but what sometimes happens is that we become blind to anything that isn't an academic, peer-reviewed item. Herein lies the danger of not challenging or questioning your ingrained biases of credibility. The role of authority comes into play here as well, as sometimes I worry that we also become blind to anything that wasn't created by an author with seven different credentials or degrees behind their name. Again, this isn't to say that we should be dismissive of authority and titles and experience; I simply raise this point to remind readers that just because an author doesn't have a certain title or degree, this doesn't inherently make their work any less credible. We get into trouble when we forget to have these conversations about credibility and when we forget to remind ourselves that credibility is a constantly evolving and contextual process. There is no black and white in credibility.

I'm not saying that credibility is a bad word or broken concept. I'm simply pointing out that we must challenge our assumptions regarding credible resources. For example, when conducting research, some students may disregard certain sources merely due to the medium in which they are published. In other words, a blog post may be disregarded outright before any real inquiry into its content, author, and message is done simply because it isn't an academic journal. Just like with authority, here is where we get into danger. When we allow assumptions about credibility to blind us to resources that may contain very credible and relevant information, we will miss out on certain perspectives and pieces of the puzzle. What becomes necessary, of course, is obtaining a balance of resources. You certainly wouldn't assume that you have comprehensive knowledge of near-death experiences based on blog posts alone. You would balance a blog post where someone outlines their firsthand experience of NDEs with a peer-reviewed article in which a psychologist or a neuroscientist tackles the topic of near-death experience. Intentionally combining vastly different types of resources to fill in the intellectual puzzle is a liminal act.

Furthermore, I would argue that the mere act of researching paranormal topics is a liminal act because it challenges the academic status quo. It challenges the notion that all paranormal research is pseudoscience, and it also challenges the notion of what it means to be an academic person. There is a long history of highly respected and credentialed academics who engage critically and scientifically with the paranormal, but for some reason this isn't very well known. In addition to simply not being well known, researchers' careers are sometimes attacked by those with dogged materialist agendas. I've read doctoral theses that contains notes on the author's fear of putting their paranormal research out into the world for fear of academic retribution or blacklisting. Why does this stigma happen? Could it be the way in which popular media represents paranormal inquiry? Could it be our rigid materialist philosophy that dominates our academic institutions? It's likely a whole range of reasons rolled into one, but nevertheless, paranormal research is a rebellious act that places the researcher in a liminal space.

It's good to be in the liminal spaces, however. The liminal spaces are where the status quos are questioned. It's where the assumptions surrounding what it means for both a topic and a person to be academic are turned upside down. It's where we challenge our personal biases about credibility, and it's where we will grow in leaps and bounds as consumers and researchers of information. Liminality allows us to critically engage with topics and research so often considered on the fringe and, through doing so, allows us to obtain deeper and more nuanced understandings of credibility, research, and the implications of being an academic who engages with the fringe. The liminal is where progress is made because you can't go back—you can only look forward to what's on the other side. The liminal is the place where ideas first flutter—where things are messy, unknown, and absolutely necessary for progress or change. Liminality, in other words, makes us better. It's where all of academia should be, in my opinion, but at the very least it is where our conversations about credibility and information literacy should be rooted. It's the entire impetus behind this work—to showcase and celebrate the work done by those who weren't afraid to step into this liminal realm. By reading this book you're entering a liminal space, and if you keep an open mind you may come through the other side a little different—I sure hope so.

NOTES

1. van Gennep, Arthur. (1960). *The rites of passage* Chicago, IL: University of Chicago Press; Turner, Victor. (1969). *The ritual process: Structure and anti-structure*. Chicago, IL: Aldine.

2. Seale-Collazo, James. (2012). Charisma, liminality, and freedom: Toward a theory of the everyday extraordinary. *Anthropology of Consciousness, 23*(2), 181.

Acknowledgments

I would like to first thank my parents for always championing my weirdness. Thanks for being my cheerleaders and for sharing an open-mindedness about the paranormal. Thank you to other members of my family, who are too numerous to list, but who have inquired about the book, asked questions, and offered encouragement and support—especially my three sisters who are probably not at all surprised that I wrote a book about weird stuff. Last, but certainly not least, thanks to each and every one of my friends and loved ones who checked in on me, asked questions, offered support, and served as cheerleaders throughout this process. I love you all.

Introduction

How uninspiring and colorless is that universe where there are no unknown corners, no panic-inducing moments, no hesitant hope-filled thoughts. Once everything is known, when all of the stars have been counted and their fires explained in every textbook, when the brain has finally been mapped and its minute seemingly incomprehensible workings mathematically and meticulously set down for all time, when the knowledge of "what comes next" has been reduced to "solved,"—I fear we will no longer exist in some wondrous mysterious world, but be trapped forever in a collective yawn of humanity. —John E. L. Tenney

Southern Indiana, circa 1994. My cousins and I gather around the campfire on one of our annual family camping trips. We take turns spinning tales about ghosts, goblins, and mysterious one-armed creatures. We revel in scaring ourselves to the point of walking two by two back to our tents, shining the flashlight at the nearby tree line and wondering what monsters lurked just beyond the reach of the beams. This is one of my earliest memories of being captivated by what I would later come to know as the paranormal. Back then, they were childhood urban legends, an entertaining activity used to thrill us and pass the time.

Shortly after this annual camping trip, I remember being in elementary school and devouring every title in the *Goosebumps* series. Shortly after that, in middle school, I would stay up well past my bedtime reading various editions of *Scary Stories to Tell in the Dark*. Any other scary story that my school library housed was fair game—I read them as quickly as I could get my hands on them. I remember watching *Unsolved Mysteries* with my mother, captivated by the paranormal tales that were featured. In junior high and high school (back in the days when you couldn't binge all available episodes of your favorite show), I counted down the days to each successive Sunday, eagerly anticipating the latest *X-Files* episode.

My love of and fascination with all things paranormal didn't stop there. In college, I continued reading various paranormal texts, having discovered by this time that there were very serious research endeavors being made in the field. When I was a freshman in college, it seemed that the floodgates of paranormal reality television shows poured open, and I devoured this influx, watching them with my mother and sisters. If there was a show even tangentially related to the paranormal, you could bet I watched it. Even to this day (and with much to owe to the invention of DVR), I schedule time to catch up on favorite paranormal shows with my mother. The paranormal has always felt like home.

In graduate school, I became fascinated with the lore and legends surrounding the Hoosier National Forest and the nearby Morgan-Monroe State Forest. Road trips with friends or solo excursions through these woods always made me wonder what was lying just out of sight, or perhaps hidden in plain view but only visible to those who knew what to look for.

Literature and paranormal reality shows haven't been my only brush with the paranormal, however. I vividly recall a moment when I was about ten or eleven years old. I was at a basketball game and, during a moment of sitting on the bench waiting to play, realized I had to go back to the locker room to retrieve something. I remember walking in and thinking that the room felt different. As I continued to walk deeper into the room, I heard someone call out my name. Thinking perhaps another player was in the locker room with me, I remember scanning the room to find who it was, looking behind doors and even getting on the floor to see if I could spy anyone's feet. I heard the voice call out for me again, but this time I turned and ran.

When I was in high school, I lived in a house nestled in the suburbs with my family. I recall on several occasions being home alone and hearing a loud crash. Convinced that a dresser, mirror, bookshelf, or other heavy object had fallen, I would scour the house only to find that everything was perfectly in place. In college, I took an evening tour of a historical county poor farm in Indiana and heard the distinct sound of footsteps one floor above us, when everyone was gathered on the ground floor. I convinced my family to go back with me one evening for a private investigation, and I experienced my first and only encounter with the phenomenon known as cold spots.

After graduate school, I took a trip to tour a historic home in Indiana and once again heard phantom footsteps. I went back to that same location with a paranormal investigation group and experienced what may have been psychokinetic behavior in an upstairs bedroom, during which an item moved of its own accord and in the direction that investigators prompted it to move. Perhaps one of the more frightening experiences I encountered was during a group investigation of an old rectory in Ohio. At the time of this visit, I had become a member of the Institute for the Study of Religious and Anomalous Experience (ISRAE). This group, based in Jeffersonville, Indiana, was appealing to me for a variety of reasons. Not only did a few newly made friends hold membership in this group, but it is a group dedicated to genuine scientific inquiry of the paranormal. Strict protocols and methods govern the way this group runs, and a hefty trial of training and investigations are required of all members before they are considered full members. It is a group of open-minded, kind individuals with a deep respect for the scientific method and a genuine curiosity to understand that which is not yet understood. I remain a member to this day.

After graduate school, having moved back near my family after accepting my first professional librarian post, I was spending the evening with my mother at my parents' home in Underwood, Indiana. I definitely got the paranormal curiosity gene from my mother, and that evening I was listening raptly while she was telling me about some of the strange occurrences that had been happening at their home—a house they had moved into only about six months prior. The things that had been happening in their home were minor—items being found in places they hadn't been left, lights and shadows in the corner of their eyes, a mysterious photo of strangers that seemed to appear from nowhere. As we were the only two home that evening, along with the family's faithful canine companion Suki, one of us suggested digging the cassette recorder out and conducting an EVP (electronic voice phenomena) session. For those new to the paranormal field, one theory is that audio recorders (of various types) are able to capture the sounds and voices of spirits and energy—sounds that we are unable to hear in real time with our own ears. Any readers who may have conducted similar sessions will know that there are many crackles and noises that recorders can capture, and that to qualify as a genuine EVP, the noise should be something that can easily and clearly be heard simply by pressing Replay, and without the use of any doctoring or editing. Sitting at the kitchen island, Suki lying quietly at our feet and watching us with curiosity, my mother and I began asking a series of questions. After about five or six minutes of asking questions, pausing to allow for potential replies, we rewound the brand-new tape to listen. Our heads leaned toward the recorder, listening intently, we both sprung back when, about halfway through, the clear and distinct sound of a small child singing or humming came through the speakers. To this day, we still wonder who or what we captured on the recording, as the house was empty save for me, my mother, and the family dog.

As mentioned above, my scariest encounter occurred during a trip with the paranormal investigation group ISRAE. We had traveled a few hours north to Ohio to investigate a defunct rectory nestled on the banks of the Ohio River. Three of us, including myself, went upstairs to investigate while the other members remained on watch silently at base camp. During a string of questions, the energy in the room felt like it was buzzing. Our eyes having become well accustomed to the dark at this point in the investigation, I remember seeing a shadow form on one of the walls of the room and rise to about four feet in height, where it stopped and remained still. Just as I asked the other investigators, "Does anyone else see this?" our colleagues at base camp began shouting wildly for us to come downstairs immediately. Responding to their shouts and walking quickly downstairs with our flashlights, we inquired what was wrong only to be met with the question, "Are you telling us you didn't hear someone pounding on the front door?" At the exact moment the mysterious shadow was inching its way up the wall, members at base camp reported hearing someone pounding on the front door of the rectory. Those of us upstairs had not heard a thing. The curious thing about this incident, however, is that we could hear our fellow teammates whispering one floor below at basecamp. How had all three of us been deaf to the sounds of someone whaling on the front door? Naturally, an outside scan of the perimeter revealed no mortal visitors, and we resumed our investigation.

More recently, on a trip to England, I stayed in an Airbnb in the lovely northern town of Sheffield. The room was perfect for the duration of my stay, during which I was attending a conference and giving a presentation. I remember sitting at the desk and putting some finishing touches on my Prezi when I heard what sounded like a breath behind me. It startled me so much that I dropped my pen and spun around in the chair to see who was behind me. The only thing that greeted me, however, was an empty room. Later that same evening, I awoke in the middle of the night to use the bathroom. Rolling over to one side, I flipped the switch on the bedside lamp only to have it pop and fizzle out. Thinking nothing of it, I rolled to the other side of the bed to switch on the other lamp, only to have it pop and fizzle as well. Lying alone in the dark, remembering the sound of the mysterious breath from earlier, it took a fair amount of time to build up the courage to slip out of bed and cross the room in the dark to turn on the main light switch.

While I have experienced a small number of mysterious experiences, this is by no means a qualifier for someone to have a genuine scientific curiosity in the paranormal. I mention these experiences simply to highlight how my curiosity has been piqued and the questions that they've raised in me. As thrilling and mysterious as the above experiences are (and though there may very well be scientific explanations for all of them), there is yet another way that my life has been intertwined with the paranormal. Being a librarian is intimately tied into my lifelong passion for the mysterious, because they pretty much grew up with one another—scouring library bookshelves for the latest *Goosebumps*; interlibrary loaning titles on Australian urban legends; having a free weekend between graduate school exams and loading up with bags full of books on reincarnation, parapsychology, mediums, and monsters; researching historical databases and newspapers for information on my own home or on local legends. More recently, as I've become a professional librarian, I regularly engage with patrons who are similarly interested in these topics and in learning more about them. Listening to their stories, connecting them with resources, ensuring that library collections have titles to fit their demands—these are all aspects of how my professional and personal lives are intertwined at the convergence of librarianship and paranormal studies.

Specifically, now, as I have transitioned from public to academic librarianship, I feel that these two aspects of my life are playing out in even stronger ways. As a reference librarian, I help field research questions from students. These research questions run the gamut from freshmen needing information for an introductory history class to graduate students needing help finding resources for their dissertations, and even expand to community patrons needing access to databases or various information. One of the singular greatest things about libraries, in my opinion, is that you never know what questions you're going to field on any given day. You must always be ready to connect a patron with resources suitable for their information needs. During these moments, however, an important part of librarianship is helping people develop the skills needed to continue research on their own. In my opinion, it is not beneficial to blindly serve people with the resources they need. Whenever possible, helping people develop critical information literacy skills can also help ensure that information is consumed (and shared) in ethical, responsible ways. That is why a chapter of this book is dedicated to the issue of analyzing sources for credibility. Helping people make the best-informed decisions about the information they consume is always a focus during any interaction.

About three years ago, I began a program where I offer one-on-one research assistance. Designed to facilitate a more in-depth, intensive session than students can usually get by stopping by the reference desk, it was through these one-on-one meetings that I started to really contemplate the nuances of helping university students navigate paranormal research. It has always been clear to me, as a librarian, that interest in the paranormal is a constant. Regardless of library, location, or life experiences, you will find people who have an interest in learning about the paranormal. The great thing about being a librarian is that you get to connect people with resources to satisfy and promote their curiosity. Promoting a person's natural curiosity is beneficial not simply as a way of validating a person's pursuits but also ensuring a research growth mind-set. Consider, for example, the confidence that a person would have if they set out to investigate a particular topic only to be mocked for being curious and/or being told before they even begin that there is no information on such topics. The effects would be tremendous and devastating, and it is a perpetual quandary to me why we are not more supportive of pursuits of information, even if they involve so-called fringe topics.

Promoting curiosity is an exact motivation for the book presented here. Research into the paranormal has a long history and is a valid endeavor, yet many students I meet with who express interest in paranormal topics seem to come to the table with one of two thoughts. They seem to have a slight assumption that they will not find any serious research on their chosen topic, or they fear pursuing a critical analysis of their topic for fear of not being taken seriously. It is troubling, to say the least, to witness a student have anxiety about pursuing genuine curiosities in institutes of higher education. While I attempt to dismantle some of the prejudices against scientific exploration or study of the paranormal, I would be remiss to not point out that very real opposition exists when it comes to these pursuits.

This book is instead designed to be a pathfinder for people who are interested, for any reason, in pursuing more information on various aspects of the paranormal. In an attempt to provide an avenue for people to become familiar with a large variety of work on various topics, I hope to also normalize the act of being openly curious about the paranormal. Readers should remember that although this work is by no means exhaustive, I have attempted to provide robust representation of various topics in the hope that it serves to connect people with credible sources of information regarding the paranormal. I hope, most of all, that it helps reduce stigma surrounding the academic pursuit of information on these topics. Through a detailed listing of sources, I believe that people will begin to understand the depth of scientific inquiry that is happening, and that has happened for quite some time. On that note, the sources listed here are sources that undertake a particular scientific or theoretical understanding of paranormal phenomena. This is not a compendium of scary stories à la *Scary Stories to Tell in the Dark* (though readers should find those and devour them because they are thrilling), but rather this work is a bibliographic listing of genuine attempts to understand the paranormal world around us.

The first chapter discusses what it means for something to be paranormal. Traditional understandings and definitions are presented, along with a brief overview of each paranormal topic. In chapter 2, I provide a brief historical outline of efforts into paranormal research, including information on seminal figures, studies, and associations and institutions engaged in paranormal research. In the third chapter, I discuss some best practices for engaging with paranormal research and some key issues to keep in mind. During this chapter, however, I primarily discuss my experiences conducting paranormal investigations and share my thoughts on how to effectively conduct your own investigations, from identifying potential sites to using and setting up equipment, to evidence review. This segues into chapter 4, which offers a conversation on the components of analyzing sources for credibility—an activity that any information consumer should keep in mind, but which particularly applies to subjects like the paranormal. The following five chapters present a bibliography of organizations, associations, books, periodicals, primary sources, databases, articles, and more regarding specific categories of paranormal inquiry. These chapters are designed to serve as pathfinders for people to begin their paranormal information gathering, and my hope is that it motivates people to continue feeding their curiosity. The last chapter discusses the magical history, special collections of paranormal resources, and paranormal hotspots of the United Kingdom. I also include case studies from the Society for Psychical Research.

Some readers may wonder which topics will be included in this resource. While there are many fields that fall under the general umbrella of the paranormal, this work primarily focuses on compiling resources that investigate the following topics: ghosts/hauntings, parapsychology, ufology, astrology/divination/mysticism, cryptozoology, near-death experiences/reincarnation, and the occult and magical practices. This resource can, then, be used in several ways. Readers can certainly browse to the sections they are most interested in if they wish to treat this resource as something akin to reference material, or they may choose to read it from cover to cover in the traditional way. Particular effort is made to include those sources that explore scientific inquiries into various paranormal topics. The purpose of this book, after all, is to outline the many credible and valid efforts that have been made to better understand the mysterious world around us.

On that note, some readers may question why certain categories like cryptozoology and ufology are included in a book claiming to be a compendium of scientific and intellectual pursuits of the paranormal. This is a fair question, and one worthy of discussion. Foremost, it is my hope that this work helps to redefine what it means for something to be worthy of academic or intellectual pursuit. Furthermore, some people may assume that no scholarly or serious literature exists about certain topics (like the aforementioned) simply because of the subject matter. However, there are many scholarly things to be learned from the vast amount of reported UFO sightings and even encounters with mysterious animals. At the very least, analyzing the collective experience regarding particular phenomena can yield greater understandings about how humans process information, how they react to and classify anomalous experience, and what these experiences may reveal about our current understandings of the world around us. If curiosity leads someone to conduct experiments that adhere to scientific methods, the subject under consideration shouldn't simply be the deciding factor when determining if such inquiry and research is valid. In other words, if we ensconce our curiosities (regardless if they are paranormal in nature or not) within a broader discussion of how to apply information literacy skills and how to employ scientific methods to any subject, then why should anyone be fixated on the worthiness of the topic at hand? Consider this—in a discussion with my mother recently, I learned that the health risks of cigarette smoking used to be so misunderstood that people could once openly smoke in doctors' offices and airplanes without anyone so much as batting an eye. Consider what society now knows about the risks of cigarettes, and we can quickly see that assumptions and ignorance can be deadly. Of course, I'm not saying that not scientifically understanding Bigfoot will kill anyone, but I am very clearly stating that we only stand to gain from our continued scientific pursuits of questioning that which we assume to be true.

I would like to make a note regarding access to the various sources listed in this work. Some of the works listed, particularly the journals, are not sources that are easily accessible to people via Amazon or eBooks. I strongly urge people to access items by using their local libraries. For example, many of the journals listed in this work will be available through academic libraries and possibly large public libraries. Most people understand that public libraries are free and open to the general community, but I'm not sure how many know that academic libraries are often wonderful resources for the community as well. Many academic libraries exist on state college campuses, which means that members of the community at large should be able to access those libraries as community members. And while access to journals and online resources may be limited to on-site usage, readers may still be able to access those resources free of charge. With regard to books, I urge people to check the catalog of their local public libraries and utilize a service known as interlibrary loan to obtain titles not owned by their home libraries. Most public libraries offer this service for free or for a small postage charge.

It is my hope that anyone interested in obtaining a deeper understanding about the paranormal as a serious field of study will benefit from this book. The language and terms used in this book will be friendly for even high schoolers interested in these topics, though certainly for adults of all ages as well, and for those from all backgrounds, regardless of your experiences with or understanding of the paranormal. In addition to general readership, those currently engaged in conducting paranormal research of their own will benefit from this work as it will serve as a tool to connect them with various resources that outline a wide variety of research methodologies and theories surrounding paranormal phenomena. I sincerely hope that all readers take from this book a renewed sense of how to approach research in a critical, ethical, and scholarly manner.

A brief introduction to the topics discussed in this book will be presented before including an annotated bibliography of resources so that readers, especially those new to the paranormal, will have a brief background understanding of the topics from which to build on before they dive into the sources. I believe this work differs from others on the paranormal since I focus mainly on scholarly, academic resources that investigate the paranormal. This not only brings the paranormal into the academic world, it also highlights to all readers the very real, very serious research that is being done in the field. Additionally, through a discussion of how to research paranormal topics yourself, and how to investigate the credibility of so-called fringe topics, I offer practical guidelines for compiling and conducting one's own research on these topics. These guidelines and skills have real-world implications. For example, it will help ensure that those interested in critically understanding the paranormal will have a solid, academic base of understanding from which to build, but it will also help readers join the scholarly conversation about these topics. As a professional librarian and an avid researcher of the paranormal, I bring these skills to this discussion to show others how they can become savvier researchers and more critical and ethical consumers of information. These are skills that can be applied to any topic, not simply the paranormal, and it is my hope that readers will understand how to evaluate information in a more critical manner. This is an important skill to have in an era that is inundated with information, in which it can be difficult to separate credible information from biased and inaccurate sources. Of course, it's all a balance, and my goal is that this book shines a light on how to achieve that balance.

I am eager to present this compilation of work in paranormal research because I hope to pay homage to an open-minded shift toward the importance of acknowledging and studying that which we do not yet fully understand. Recall, for a moment, that early American doctors once considered epilepsy a condition of being possessed. If it weren't for the pursuit of genuine scientific inquiry, how long would it have taken to discover epilepsy as a very real medical condition and to begin offering help for those who suffered under it? What range of wild superstition leading to suffering would still be prolific if it weren't for the genuine pursuits of investigation and study? In my opinion, we only stand to gain when we remain open minded about that which we do not fully understand.

While the pursuit of scientific inquiry and understanding is certainly beneficial, let us muse for a moment on keeping alive the spark of magic, mystery, and intrigue. It is my firm belief that the more we know about the paranormal, the more questions we unearth simultaneously. That's actually a great thing! How boring would life be if the total expanse of knowledge were known and absolute? What would drive us to learn more about the world around us? What would excite us simply because of the mystery surrounding it? Paranormal inquiry, while being a valid scientific pursuit to be sure, offers us a way to engage with the mysteries of the world around us and to stand humble before the fact that we don't have it all figured out. It offers a safe outlet for thrill and intrigue, and if in the process, we discover something about the world in which we live, how could that ever be a negative pursuit? As the quote provided at the beginning by John E. L. Tenney tells us, the world would be a much more boring place if we knew all there was to possibly know—the magic is in the wonder.

This book is not an attempt to alter anyone's faith or belief system. For some, like me, the paranormal can be intimately tied with one's own spiritual beliefs and behaviors; but this isn't an attempt to change anyone's mind. The goal of this work is to present, in an unbiased manner, a whole array of sources that have attempted to scientifically investigate various subfields of the paranormal. There is very real potential to be taken aback by some of the findings contained in these sources, but that is simply because, at least in the Western world, we have been conditioned to think that the paranormal is synonymous with superstition, folklore, and frivolity when nothing could be further from the truth. This book is for all people, of all faiths, and all beliefs. Choose the sources you'd like to learn more about—believe them, or don't believe them, but nothing presented herein is fake. They are all objects of genuine inquiry, and it is up to each reader to choose what they do or do not want to believe.

I would like to end on a personal note to readers coming to this work who have, like me, had paranormal curiosities since childhood. Your curiosity is valid, and your efforts at understanding the world around you are not in vain. Keep investigating, keep reading, and keep musing about the weirdness that consistently surrounds us. Take comfort and support in knowing that paranormal research has been around for quite some time and that it is a valid, if albeit underappreciated, intellectual pursuit. To those who are new to the paranormal, or even skeptical: you are appreciated and welcome here. The benefits of being an open-minded, critically thinking consumer of the strange and mysterious is far more beneficial than the effects of closed-mindedness or fear. I hope that you enjoy the many wonderful resources contained herein and that it inspires you to start, or continue, your paranormal journeys.

Chapter One

What Is the Paranormal?

DEFINITIONS AND TRADITIONAL UNDERSTANDINGS

To discuss the nuances of paranormal research, it is first beneficial to understand exactly what is meant by the word "paranormal." However, defining the paranormal is a curious endeavor and even the most basic source, the dictionary, reveals how vague definitions can be. *Merriam-Webster's Dictionary*, for example, defines the word "paranormal" as simply something that is "not scientifically explainable."[1] As this book hopefully illustrates, though, there are many valid scientific pursuits of understanding the paranormal, so this first definition is already problematic. Luckily, the *Oxford English Dictionary* gives us a more nuanced definition of the paranormal as that which "designat[es] supposed psychical events and phenomena such as clairvoyance or telekinesis whose operation is outside the scope of the known laws of nature or of normal scientific understanding; of or relating to such phenomena."[2] This definition is more specific, but it also only focuses on one type of paranormal phenomena: psychical events. How about UFOs? Cryptozoology? Astrology and divination? Magical practices? The occult? It's immediately apparent that the concept of the paranormal is not a static one. Further muddying the water is the fact that throughout human history various phenomena have been labeled paranormal simply because we lacked the ability to fully investigate or understand them. Take, for instance, the belief that what we now know is epilepsy was attributed to possession.

Getting back to traditional definitions, however, *Merriam-Webster* offers us a potential solution to defining this topic, and that is to consider instead the word "supernatural," which is defined as "of or relating to an order of existence beyond the visible observable universe," and/or, "departing from what is usual or normal especially so as to appear to transcend the laws of nature."[3] This definition strikes very near the true sense of the paranormal, in my opinion, and recognizes that there are things in our universe that exist beyond our current realities and understanding.

One of the proposed definitions of "paranormal" that I like best, though, comes to us from Marie D. Jones. In her 2007 book *PSIence*, Jones tells us that "the word *paranormal* means, simply, beyond normal, and includes any phenomena that can't be easily explained with a known law of science . . . these include angels and aliens, spaceships from other worlds, ghosts and mysterious creatures, ESP and psychokinesis, and remote viewing—places where the laws of physics are nullified and the center no longer holds."[4] What I find most refreshing about this definition is that it draws our attention to the fact that we only understand the world around us based on what we currently know and understand but that there exists a host of phenomena that cannot be easily explained. As I illustrate later in this book, scientists and researchers are uncovering new knowledge every day and experimenting with the paranormal, and Jones recognizes this when she writes, "Just because these phenomena occur beyond the range of normal experience and often defy scientific explanation doesn't mean they don't exist. And just because the basic law of cause and effect is tossed on its head by these events doesn't mean they can't possibly have their origin in the real world, the world of the normal."[5]

The above definitions help give a very clinical understanding of what we might mean when they use a particular word. What these definitions lack, however, is a contextual and etymologically historical understanding. Author Jeffrey Kripal tells us that the first occurrence of the word "paranormal" showed up in 1903, in the book *Les Phénomènes Psychiques (Psychic Phenomena)*, written by doctor and attorney Joseph Maxwell.[6] In his book, Maxwell uses the word "paranormal" to refer to certain psychic phenomena that were documented but not fully understood. In other words, people agreed that certain phenomena like precognition or telekinesis happened, but they weren't able to describe how—hence they were phenomena designated as "paranormal," or literally "beyond (para) the normal."[7] Kripal also reminds us, though, that the word "supernormal" appeared before "paranormal" and was coined by noted researcher Frederic Myers (more on him in chapter 2). Supernormal was "coined to describe our own almost total ignorance of all those fantastic phenomena that are a part of our human nature and the natural world but that we cannot yet model or explain within any adequate scientific framework."[8] These words, paranormal and supernormal, were not dripping with the connotations they seem to have today—connotations of fantasy, pseudoscience, and make-believe—but rather were used by highly educated and respected people to discuss those things they didn't yet know how to discuss. At some point in time, these words drifted drastically away from their original and intended meanings.

Of course, any attempt at sufficiently defining paranormal phenomena is tricky, because it is difficult to define that which you do not understand. One issue when discussing definition of the paranormal is that as Western readers we come to the paranormal table with a certain amount of cultural assumptions and biases about this topic. While it is outside the scope of this work to fully investigate the differences between Eastern and Western cultural assumptions of the paranormal, it is beneficial to note that our friends and colleagues in Eastern societies seem more open to many topics that may seem strange to their Western counterparts. Consider, for example, the Chinese practice of inscribing questions on bone, throwing them into a fire, and analyzing the cracks and fissures for answers—this is pure divination.[9] Even some Eastern medicinal practices illustrate the divide between Eastern and Western worldviews. To the Western patient, the idea of receiving any benefit from the insertion of needles in specific locations on the body may seem far-fetched. However, the Eastern practice of acupuncture, while steadily growing in popularity here in the West, is by no means a standard or universal routine of care, even though a Mayo Clinic Health Letter published in June of 2017 recommends acupuncture as a helpful treatment for chronic headaches.[10]

In terms of a more spiritual-religious exploration of the paranormal, researchers writing for the *Journal of Applied Social Psychology* discovered, when investigating links between spirituality and religion in China, that Buddhists and Taoists harbor exponentially more belief in the paranormal than do their Christian counterparts.[11] And while there are a fair amount of people identifying with Eastern religions here in the United States, we remain a country that is vastly dominated by people who identify with Christianity.

Of course, we cannot simply point to a difference in Eastern and Western worldviews when trying to define why modern American society seems sometimes to relegate the paranormal to nothing more than superstition or folklore. The Greeks, after all, regularly employed the use of an oracle, known as a Pythia, or priestess, who would consult with the gods and serve as messengers to priests and prominent leaders, as well as to Greek citizens.[12] Pythia would live out their days as messengers of the gods, often performing particular rituals when engaging in consultations. Their one-thousand-year employ ended when the Roman emperor Theodosius banned all pagan practices. Interestingly, the Greeks were not the only ones to engage in this particular activity, and in the Himalayas, this practice is still observed today. Known as Kumari, select young women serve in a capacity very similar to their ancient Pythia counterparts, offering consultations and advice to a select hierarchy of visitors, serving as direct messengers and embodiments of the goddesses Vajradevi and Durga.[13]

The intersection of gods, goddesses, and divination through oracles is a perfect segue to discuss the role that religion necessarily plays in any discussion of the paranormal. In fact, any person who has engaged in a religious practice or attended a religious service can understand that many religious events have paranormal connotations. Catholic services regularly invoke the "Holy Spirit" in prayers and offerings, and the sacrament known as communion asks followers to consume wine and bread that serves as symbols of the body and blood of Jesus Christ. Even the simple act of prayer—appealing to a higher, unseen power for support and guidance—carries with it a supernatural connotation. And let's not forget the thousands of reports from people who claim to have encountered angels. Core components of religion are actually quite paranormal when you think about them. How is the experience of someone claiming to see an angel any different from someone claiming to see an amorphous, wispy figure? Isn't an angel simply a particular type of entity?

Like religious experiences, paranormal encounters also carry with them a meaningful impact on the person who has experienced them, yet another way that religion and the paranormal are so intimately linked. Additionally, the lens of religion is one way that we can begin to analyze paranormal events and is, I think, one of the safer ways to embed paranormal inquiry without calling attention to the critics who are so eager to cry "pseudoscience" at every paranormal venture. Noted scholar Jeffrey Kripal, in fact, tells us that the "history of religion . . . has remained to this day a distinctly academic way of making sense of the foreign, the eccentric, and the strange."[14] More than being an academic endeavor, for some scholars of religion, critical inquiry can be a downright mystical and philosophical journey. Take, for instance, the words of kabbalah scholar Gershom Scholem who wrote once to a friend that, "for today's man, that mystic totality of 'truth,' whose existence disappears particularly when it is projected into historical time, can only become visible in the purest way in the legitimate discipline of commentary and in the singular mirror of philological criticism."[15] In other words, the veil between the mystical and science is simply an illusion, and all that is required to understand it is a willingness to critically engage.

Kripal also discusses how cultural biases shape the ways in which we view the paranormal. He specifically discusses how the Western researcher has been conditioned towards an inherent bias of the paranormal, and outlines it perfectly when he writes:

> The modern Western worldview has been dominated for the last century or so (a mere blink or wink in the bigger picture) by what has been called "instrumental reason" so named because it wants to turn everything into an instrument or technology. This worldview is materialistic and mechanistic, that is, it insists that all of reality is nothing but matter (that's the materialism part), and that this matter operates through machinelike mathematical laws (that's the mechanism part). The same worldview also commonly asserts that the *only* reliable way to know something about reality is through the scientific method

and, more specifically, through mathematics. If something cannot be turned into an object or "thing," replicated and controlled in a laboratory, and measured (that is, assigned a number or mathematical form), it cannot be considered real and so does not deserve our attention or respect. That is a bit of an exaggeration, but not much of one. The worldview of conventional science, technology, and instrumental reason, of course, is an extremely powerful and useful one. I am by no means against any of this. Quite the opposite. But what is useful is not at all the same thing as what is. Where things go wrong, then, is when individuals take this very modern and very practical way of knowing something about the world and assume that it represents the *whole* world.[16]

This quote from Kripal perfectly captures the consequences that can arise from being too singularly focused on specific methods, procedures, and physical outputs. When it comes to understanding traditional notions of the paranormal, it is important to understand the bias we carry with us before we even engage in a critical inquiry of this topic, and the importance of critically engaging with sources in an ethical and unbiased way will be further explored in chapter 3. Kripal urges us to be a bit more holistic and open minded in our pursuits of understanding that which we do not yet know and is a perfect segue back to our discussion of how to best define the paranormal.

The idea of the paranormal is an inherently large topic to consider because there is simply so much that falls under the umbrella of the larger category of "paranormal." If the basic definition of the paranormal is simply anything "whose operation is outside the scope of the known laws of nature or of normal scientific understanding," then it clearly has the capacity to encompass a wide variety of phenomena that is not yet completely, or even modestly, understood.

Below, I outline and introduce the paranormal concepts I include in this work. These sections merely serve to introduce a topic to the reader—they are by no means a comprehensive and exhaustive analysis. In fact, each category below could fill its own book, and many books have indeed been written on these subtopics. Many of the topics below can seamlessly flow into one another, so I don't want readers to assume that the paranormal fits into neat and tidy boxes—phenomena are actually quite fluid. I merely provide categories to help readers locate those categories in which they're most interested, and to provide a jumping-off point. I hope my discussions of each category paint an accurate picture and motivate readers to research more on their own.

BRIEF OUTLINE OF PARANORMAL TOPICS DISCUSSED IN THIS BOOK

Ghosts and Hauntings

At the most common and familiar entry point of the paranormal is, I believe, hauntings and ghost phenomena. Readers may not be familiar with the terms "parapsychology" or "cryptozoology," but everyone knows what you mean when you say "ghost." This is not to say, of course, that the matter is a simple and straightforward one, however, as there are a wide variety of reported ghostly phenomena and experiences. Adding to the complexity of this matter is the fact that each culture has its own worldviews on ghosts and hauntings and as such, definitions, beliefs, representations, and understandings about ghosts and hauntings vary widely. Regardless of your background or cultural history, however, these terms, in whatever language they may be expressed, are understood and experienced worldwide. Avery Gordon, in her book *Ghostly Matters*, gives us what I think is the most lyrical and nuanced understanding of ghosts and hauntings:

> If haunting describes how that which appears to be not there is often a seething presence, acting on and often meddling with taken-for-granted realities, the ghost is just the sign, or the empirical evidence if you like, that tells you a haunting is taking place. The ghost is not simply a dead or missing person, but a social figure, and investigating it can lead to that dense site where history and subjectivity make social life. The ghost or the apparition is one form by which something lost, or barely visible, or seemingly not there to our supposedly well-trained eyes, makes itself known or apparent to us, in its own way, of course. The way of the ghost is haunting, and haunting is a very particular way of knowing what has happened or is happening. Being haunted draws us affectively, sometimes against our will and always a bit magically, into the structure of feeling a reality we come to experience, not as cold knowledge, but as a transformative recognition.[17]

Gordon's manuscript is a fascinating, philosophical, and thought-provoking work on the relationship of ghosts and hauntings to social and political aspects of our lives, and while my purpose isn't necessarily to engage in such philosophical inquiries, I strongly urge interested readers to seek out this work. What Gordon provides us with (and why I think her work is extremely valuable) is a statement of ghosts and hauntings that illustrates how deeply interwoven the paranormal is into society and the very fabric of our lives.

While these experiences certainly come in myriad forms, ghost experiences include those moments when people witness either the image of someone deceased and/or the corporeal image of someone or something unknown. Encounters do not always have to take the form of human shape, as there have been many reports of mists, nonhuman shapes, and disembodied voices.

Artistic Rendering of a Ghostly Apparition. *Creative Commons/"Ghost 2" by Energetic Spirit is licensed under CC BY-SA 2.0*

The prevailing thought concerning ghosts is that their presence can be classified as either intelligent or residual. In the case of an intelligent haunting, an entity is thought to interact with and respond to the behaviors of the living and/or the environment. In the case of a residual haunting, it is thought that the haunting occurs like a video that has been set on loop—rather, that there is no intelligence but simply leftover energy playing on repeat. The haunting phenomena connotes a person or location afflicted or occupied by paranormal activity, but for purposes of this work, ghosts and hauntings will be classified together. Underneath the umbrella of ghosts and hauntings, you can include poltergeist phenomena, though one could just as likely argue that it would be more beneficial to include this under the aegis of parapsychology, and readers will understand why when we arrive at that topic.

While more information on the scientific pursuit of understanding ghostly phenomena will be included in further chapters, a look at some famous incidences of reported hauntings and ghostly phenomena here would be beneficial. One doesn't have to search far to come across tales of ghostly experiences. If you're like me, someone close to you may have experienced ghostly phenomena, or maybe you have experienced something yourself. Because I live very near the world's most well-known haunted tuberculosis hospital, let's start there.

The Waverly Hills Sanatorium was established in 1910 in Louisville, Kentucky—a time in which the city was suffering from a plague of tuberculosis and overwhelmed with afflicted persons. In fact, authors Roberta Simpson Brown and Lonnie Brown, in their book *Spookiest Stories Ever: Four Seasons of Kentucky Ghosts*,[18] tell us that Louisville had the highest mortality rate for tuberculosis in the nation, owing of course to the Ohio River valley and the bacteria and allergens that seem to thrive there. Still today, any native of this area (the author included) will tell you that allergies abound here but seem to be immediately resolved upon traveling outside the area. It makes complete sense that valleyed areas saw the highest mortality rates when it comes to tuberculosis.

Established in 1910, Waverly Hills was a very small, two-story establishment with a mere forty rooms, but it soon became evident that the facility needed to be significantly enlarged. Renovations began in 1924 and the new hospital was completed in 1926, equipped with five floors to manage and treat patients. It is estimated that thousands of people died at Waverly Hills since its inception. Tuberculosis was a devastating disease that plagued the nation during a time in which the antibiotic streptomycin had yet to be discovered, and medical advances simply weren't prepared to effectively combat and treat this condition—it's not surprising that thousands who were afflicted died there, but it is nonetheless a gruesome scene to envision. It certainly doesn't help that the physical appearance of Waverly Hills, with its sprawling, Gothic-like appearance nestled high on a hill in the woods adds to the macabre feeling that one gets today—it's the perfect breeding ground (pun intended) for ghost stories to abound.

Since its transition from hospital to geriatric home to private ownership, people have reported seeing shadow figures, hearing doors slamming shut, being stuck in rooms only to have someone come to their aid and open the door with ease, smelling fresh bread baking in the area once occupied by the kitchen, being touched by phantom hands, hearing voices whispering, seeing ghostly faces in the windows, and having rocks and debris thrown at them.[19] Countless paranormal investigations have occurred at Waverly Hills since it has been in private ownership, and chances are very likely that readers have either read about or seen this location portrayed in books, magazines, newspapers, or television shows. Its reputation as the world's most haunted tuberculosis sanatorium continues to thrive, and as long as there is a physical building to visit, it will continue drawing visitors eager to step back in time and perhaps experience something unexplainable.

Let's travel a bit farther south from Louisville now, to consider how the haunted history of a locale can imbue an entire city with the reputation of being haunted. Savannah, Georgia, is nestled on the banks of the Atlantic

Ocean in the far southeastern corner of Georgia. The sprawling architecture, Spanish moss, and square city blocks adorned with fountains paint quite a romantic picture of this historic port city. In June of 1732, King George II sent General James Oglethorpe and a crew of approximately 114 on the mission of establishing what would become Georgia, or the thirteenth colony of the United States.[20] Following Oglethorpe landing on the shores of present-day Savannah in 1733 and colonizing the area (even though it was already settled by the Native American tribe of Yamacraws) the history of this city continued to grow, and it became a key locale through the American Revolution and Civil War.[21]

It is clear that the city of Savannah has a rich and diverse history, but what about the ghostly underbelly of the city? It is nearly impossible to single out one lone incident of ghostly phenomena in Savannah as the city simply drips paranormal activity. In fact, Savannah has become a place famous for dark tourism, which as Tiya Miles reminds us, is tourism that "highlights violent and morbid subject matter by promoting visitation to sites of suffering, torture, murder, and death."[22] Such tourism is almost unavoidable in a city like Savannah, which has such a deep history that often includes the aforementioned subject matters. In fact, akin to walking the streets of Paris, tour guides often remind participants that at most given times, they are likely walking above an abandoned cemetery that was paved over as the city grew. Dark tourism is such a strong presence in Savannah, in fact, that more than half of tourists visiting the city take a ghost tour during their stay.[23] Some of the sites visited by tourists include the Sorrel-Weed Mansion, which was built in 1841 by Irish architect Charles Cluskey, and which became the first home in Georgia to be declared a state historical site in 1953.[24] It is said that the house is built above the graves of fallen soldiers from the battles of the American Revolution, and people have reported seeing shadow figures, hearing disembodied voices, and being touched when no one else is near.[25]

Yet another paranormal hot spot on Savannah's dark tourism circuit is the home and cemetery made famous by the book *Midnight in the Garden of Good and Evil*. The book centers on events that took place in the Mercer-Williams House in the mid-1990s. Construction on the Mercer-Williams House began in 1860 but was not completed until nearly ten years later due to the Civil War.[26] Jim Williams, a proponent of architectural preservation, purchased the home in the 1960s and is a key player in the infamous history of the home. Employing the services of Danny Hansford, Jim worked closely with Danny until an evening in 1981 when Danny was found shot to death in the house. Jim claimed self-defense and underwent lengthy trials until he was acquitted of murder in 1989. Jim's celebrations would be cut short, though, as he was found dead of reported complications from an underlying health condition a few months later, very near the same location that Danny's body was discovered.[27] Other untimely deaths in the home predate the demise of both Danny Hansford and Jim Williams, and visitors to the Mercer-Williams House have reported seeing apparitions, hearing phantom footsteps, being touched by unseen hands, and even walking by the unoccupied house to see all the rooms ablaze with light and the shadows of people having a party inside.[28]

The cemetery featured in the novel, Bonaventure Cemetery, has also played host to its own ghostly tales. Completed in 1846, Bonaventure was initially privately owned and known as Evergreen Cemetery. The city of Savannah purchased it in 1907, and it was expanded to more than one hundred acres.[29] Built in the Victorian tradition, with lots of trees and greenery and sloping sidewalks, the most famous spectral resident of the cemetery is six-year-old Gracie Watson, who died of pneumonia and whose tombstone is a seated, carved likeness of Gracie herself. Visitors have claimed to see the ghostly image of the girl near her tombstone, while other ghostly reports inside the cemetery include the sounds of a toddler's laughter, statues grimacing at passersby, and the disembodied snarls of packs of dogs.[30]

Savannah isn't the only city that can claim the unique characteristic of being holistically haunted, if you will. Let's now move a little farther to the east, to consider yet another coastal town and its spectral inhabitants—New Orleans. New Orleans is another city, much like Louisville, that witnessed tragic amounts of death. In this instance, though, the villain was yellow fever. Stanford professor Kathryn Olivarius, in an interview with NPR, helps describe the epidemic that occurred between 1817 and 1905, and which killed eight thousand people alone in 1853.[31] Professor Olivarius tell us that the disease killed nearly half of all who contracted it, and that its symptoms involved fever, convulsions, and delirium, among others. Most terrifying, however, is the way in which yellow fever was used to justify and promote slavery. Prominent New Orleans doctors spread the rumor that slaves were immune to yellow fever and that their labor saved others from exposure to the deadly disease.[32] We understand this to be an obvious falsehood, of course, but consider the cumulative weight of various evils that plagued New Orleans's history. It seems only logical that it has a notorious reputation as a haunted locale.

Specific instances of ghostly phenomena in New Orleans include such infamous buildings as the LaLaurie Mansion in the city's French Quarter. Author Alan Brown, in his book *Ghosts along the Mississippi River*, describes the history of the home, built in 1832 by Dr. Leonard LaLaurie and his wife Marie Delphine. The LaLauries quickly became eminent socialites of the New Orleans scene. Their prestige, however, took a dark turn on the evening of April 19, 1834, when emergency crews responded to reports of a fire at the LaLaurie Mansion. Upon arriving, they discovered the fire had been set by a female slave of the LaLauries to intentionally draw attention to the horrid conditions they were living in. The woman who set the blaze, for

The LaLaurie Mansion in New Orleans, Louisiana. *Creative Commons/"New Orleans-5631 Circa 1832" by MSMcCarthy Photography is licensed under CC BY-ND 2.0*

example, was chained to the stove itself. When the investigators searched the rest of the home, they discovered additional slaves shackled with chains in the attic and in serious stages of malnourishment. Rumors of gruesome experiments conducted by the LaLauries on their slaves abounded, and eventually a mob gathered in front of the home demanding justice be wrought upon the homeowners. The LaLauries somehow managed to escape, and while their fates are unknown, the sordid past of the home remains and seems to affect inhabitants to this day. Residents of the LaLaurie Mansion have reported being woken by screams and moans, while children have reported seeing the image of a woman running around the property with a whip. The mansion has been multiple enterprises through the years, including housing, a saloon, and a department store; it was even briefly owned by actor Nicolas Cage, though only for a year.[33] Today the house serves as luxury apartments, and while tourists cannot enter the building, it has been reported that passersby still hear the ghostly screams of those perhaps once tortured by the LaLauries.

While it is perhaps the building with the most gruesome history behind its haunted happenings, the LaLaurie Mansion is far from the only location in New Orleans that is host to mysterious events. Described as "one of the most magnificent of all the antebellum homes in New Orleans' Garden District,"[34] the Magnolia Mansion was built in 1857 as a gift to Elizabeth "Lizzie" Thompson from her husband. In 1921 the home was passed on to the daughter of the second owner of the mansion. Josephine Maginnis was heavily involved with the Red Cross and eventually donated the Magnolia Mansion to the Red Cross. It was used by that organization between 1939 and 1954, during which the home saw soldiers affected by both World War II and the Korean War, as well as victims seeking relief from floods, and which also served as a place for in-home care for the sick. It is rumored to be haunted by the ghost of a woman who tragically killed herself nearby, and who sought out spectral residence in the Magnolia Mansion after her home was torn down. Reports include doors slamming shut with so much force they sound like gunshots, strange oil-like substances dripping from the walls, phantom footsteps occurring between 2:00 and 3:00 a.m., misty shapes hovering above people, the image of a boy running through a dining room when no children were occupying the home, and one report of a woman being tucked into bed by an invisible presence.[35]

There are numerous other haunted locales in New Orleans (without even mentioning the vampire folklore of the area), but hopefully the two examples above give a good representation of the paranormal history of New Orleans. Let's continue to move west to visit the Stanley Hotel in Colorado, the hotel that was the inspiration for Stephen King's *The Shining*. King visited the Stanley, situated in the Rocky Mountains in the town of Estes Park, in 1973 when he was staying nearby in Boulder and decided to take a drive to nearby Estes Park at the suggestion of friends. After seeing the Stanley, King was inspired by its architecture and locale and even drafted portions of the novel in room 217 of the Stanley.[36] The Stanley Hotel was a beacon of paranormal activity long before being made famous by King's novel, however.[37] Construction of the four-hundred-plus-room hotel was completed in 1909 by F. O. Stanley, and since his death in 1940 his apparition has been seen by guests as they check in at the front desk. Sounds of a piano can be heard emanating from the empty former music room, while still other guests have reported seeing shadowy figures, hearing disembodied laughter, and witnessing items moving of their own accord. A more macabre event in the hotel's history occurred in the 1920s when room 217 exploded from an apparent gas leak, nearly killing then employee Elizabeth Wilson. She recovered and remained an employee until her death at the age of ninety, at which point guests in the hotel began reporting sightings of a floating chambermaid passing through doors.[38]

The examples listed above are by no means an attempt at exhaustively reporting the most famous ghostly cases in the United States—to do that, in fact, would require a work far lengthier than this one and which would need to be updated regularly. These brief examples hopefully illustrate the long and expansive history of reported ghostly phenomena in this country that cannot be defined by locale or time period. Incidents of ghosts and hauntings have not only been experienced in different locations and from different time periods, they have also become a key player in the tourism industry of many of these locations and cities. They are phenomena that deeply resonate with people, phenomena that attract people to certain locations, and phenomena whose lore and legend live on in eternity through collective memory and experience. Arguments of scientific validity aside, these experiences have very real anthropological merit.

Ufology

Another aspect of the paranormal that readers will likely already be familiar with is ufology, which is the specific study of unidentified flying objects. Marie Jones writes in her book *PSIence* that interest in UFOs blossomed in the 1940s. In 1947, in one of these early accounts, a pilot named Kenneth Arnold claimed to have seen nine mysterious aircraft he described as "pie plates skipping over the water," and the first appearance of the phrase "flying saucer" made its appearance in American news outlets.[39]

This was one of the earliest reported sightings, but the most famous UFO incident that occurred in North America was the crash at Roswell. In July of 1947, a memo sent to the FBI field office in Dallas begins, "Urgent. Flying disc, information concerning. [Redacted] headquarters, Eighth Air Force, telephonically advised this office that an object purporting to be a flying disc was recovered near Roswell, New Mexico, this date. The disc is hexagonal in shape and was suspended from a ballon [*sic*] by cable, which ballon [*sic*] was approximately twenty feet in diameter. [Redacted] further advised that the object found resembles a high-altitude weather balloon with a radar reflector, but that telephonic conversation between their office and Wright Field had not [redacted] borne out this belief. Disc and balloon being transported to Wright Field by special plane for examinati [*sic*] information provided this office because of national interest."[40]

In addition to the events reported above, there have been several other well-known UFO incidents. Perhaps the most prominent case aside from Roswell is the incident involving Betty and Barney Hill. On September 19, 1961, the Hills were driving back to their New Hampshire home from their vacation to Canada. While driving, they noticed a bright light in the sky above them and stopped their car to see if they could identify what was shining down upon them. Barney Hill, using binoculars, claims that he noticed window-like openings on some type of craft, through which figures were gazing at them.[41] The Hills fled back to their car to leave, only to later discover they had no memory of nearly two hours of that evening. Through hypnosis with a Boston-based psychiatrist, they recounted being led aboard an alien spacecraft and being examined by aliens. Betty even drew a detailed star map that she had recalled being shown.[42] Many others have discussed their beliefs and/or experiences about aliens or UFOs, including Presidents Jimmy Carter and Ronald Reagan, who claimed to have seen an unidentified flying object in 1969 and 1974, respectively.[43]

Another abduction experience, and one that is necessary to include in any discussion about UFOs, involves Travis Walton, whom some readers may recognize as the inspiration for the movie *Fire in the Sky*. Coined "one of the most controversial abduction cases of all time,"[44] Travis Walton and a crew of other forestry workers were traveling home one evening in eastern Arizona in 1975 when they claimed to have witnessed lights through the trees, eventually discovering a circular craft hovering approximately twenty feet above the roadway. Travis, curious about what he was seeing, exited his vehicle and approached the craft, at which point his fellow crew members reported seeing a beam of light erupt from the UFO, striking Travis and knocking him to the ground. The incident shook them so badly that they apparently fled, though they decided to return after they'd all calmed down. They were unable to find Travis anywhere. Local authorities were contacted and groups searched for Travis, but he was not located until five days later after phoning his brother in shock and asking for help. The tale that Travis told, however, was even more shocking than anything up to this point. He reported being taken aboard the craft and observing "three figures in orange suits who had huge, bald heads, huge eyes, and looked like fetuses."[45] He claimed to have lost consciousness after one of the creatures placed a mask over his face—the next thing he recalled, in fact, is waking up on the road twenty miles from where the incident first took place. While authorities suspected foul play or even an outright hoax, the interesting portion of this tale is that both Travis and his coworkers passed multiple lie detector tests as they recounted the details of their experiences.[46] These well-known personal experiences listed above are abbreviated here, of course, but I urge interested readers to look up more about them—some resources included later in this book, in fact, will be helpful for those curious for more.

The subject of UFOs isn't just restricted to tales of personal experience, however. There is a very lengthy history of government involvement with UFOs and UFO research. An October 14, 1979, article written in the *New York Times* details government investigations of UFO phenomena.[47] Reporter Patrick Huyghe explains that interest in reported UFO sightings stemmed from a fear that Russia had developed some type of new military weapon. However, Huyghe reminds us that "the Air Force's behind-the-scenes interest contrasted sharply with its public stance that the objects were products of misidentification and an imaginative populace."[48] In September 1947, Project Sign was established after the army chief of staff, Nathan Twining, sent a memo to the army air force commanding general that read, "The phenomenon reported is of something real and not visionary or fictitious," and that sighted craft appeared to be "controlled either manually, automatically, or remotely."[49] Project Sign found no evidence that reported sightings were Russian weaponry in origin, and it ended only to be replaced with Project Grudge. And while Grudge was only in operation for six months, having found no conclusive evidence of UFOs, it was nonetheless reopened a few short years later in 1951 after a "dramatic sighting of a U.F.O. at the Army Signal Corps radar center in Fort Monmouth, N.J."[50] In fact, Grudge would later be reclassified just one short year later in 1952 as Project Blue Book.

Project Blue Book was a program created by the air force to investigate UFO phenomena. Including Project Sign and Project Grudge in the scope of its purview, Project Blue Book ran from 1947 until it was officially ended on December 17, 1969. A January 15, 2019, article from the *New York Times* reports that during the tenure of this program, a total of 12,618 reports were made of flying objects, and of those, 701 remain unidentified.[51] Included here is an image lifted directly from the air force memos regarding the project and listing the number of sightings per year. At the core of this task force was J. Allen Hynek, a noted astronomer. Described as a skeptic of unidentified flying objects, Hynek "eventually concluded that they [UFOs] were a real phenomenon in dire need of scientific attention,"[52] and was even frustrated by some of the flippant rationales that were given as explanations for some sightings.[53]

Seven years after the formation of Project Blue Book, Cornell physicists Giuseppe Cocconi and Philip Morrison published an article in the journal *Nature*. In their article, Cocconi and Morrison are very clear in reminding readers that Earth is simply one planet out of many, and that there is still a vast amount that is unknown about fellow planets and galaxies. To quote them directly:

> Our environment suggests that stars . . . with a lifetime of many billions of years can possess planets, that of a small set of such planets two (Earth and very probably Mars) support life, that life on one such planet includes a society recently capable of considerable scientific investigation. The lifetime of such societies is not known; but it seems unwarranted to deny that among such societies some might maintain themselves for very long compared to the time of human history, perhaps for times comparable with geological time. It follows, then, that near some star rather like the Sun there are civilizations with scientific interests and with technical possibilities much greater than those now available to us.[54]

Marie Jones claims this article can be traced back as the inspiration behind the formation of the SETI Institute, or the Search for Extraterrestrial Intelligence.[55] Incorporated nearly thirty years after the publication of this article, SETI is an institute established to promote the scientific inquiry into

TOTAL UFO SIGHTINGS, 1947 - 1969

YEAR	TOTAL SIGHTINGS	UNIDENTIFIED
1947	122	12
1948	156	7
1949	186	22
1950	210	27
1951	169	22
1952	1,501	303
1953	509	42
1954	487	46
1955	545	24
1956	670	14
1957	1,006	14
1958	627	10
1959	390	12
1960	557	14
1961	591	13
1962	474	15
1963	399	14
1964	562	19
1965	887	16
1966	1,112	32
1967	937	19
1968	375	3
1969	146	1
TOTAL	12,618	701

Total UFO Sightings, 1947–1969. *FBI, Department of Justice/FBI Records: The Vault, Project Blue Book*

the study of life in the universe. Visitors to its website can learn that SETI "conducts research in a number of fields including astronomy and planetary sciences, chemical evolution, the origin of life, and biological and cultural evolution."[56] The institute specifically focuses on three key areas: investigating the presence or absence of life on other planets, regardless of how cellular or small that life may be; conducting experiments to see if sophisticated life forms can communicate via radio or light waves (this is what is traditionally understood as SETI); and keeping the general public informed and involved as to the research conducted.[57]

While no definitive proof of extraterrestrial life has been secured by SETI, the institute did nonetheless detect a strange anomaly at a partner lab in Ohio. In 1977, researchers at the Ohio State Radio Observatory picked up a strange signal—a signal that occurred at radio frequencies cited by the aforementioned Cocconi and Morrison as "the optimal signal that an ET might utilize and, therefore, we should focus on."[58] The significance of the strange signal, recorded at approximately 1420 megahertz, is explained in an NPR interview with Jerry Ehman, the astronomer who was woken from bed after being delivered the reading, analyzed it, and scribbled, "Wow!" in the margins, resulting in this anomalous signal being referred collectively as the Wow! signal. Ehman, after realizing the transmission picked up from outer space fell into the narrowband range, told NPR reporters that "narrowband signal would indicate intelligence . . . because in order to create a narrowband signal you have to have some electronics to handle that. It's not a natural phenomenon."[59] While the Wow! signal hasn't been detected since, many researchers still consider it one of the most compelling radio signals captured by a SETI project. Unfortunately, since it occurred merely once and hasn't occurred again, it isn't considered as proof of any communication with extraterrestrial intelligence. That doesn't deter researchers at SETI and elsewhere, though, as they continue their celestial searching.

In addition to SETI, volunteer researchers at the Mutual UFO Network, or MUFON, dedicate their time operating "the world's oldest and largest civilian UFO investigation and research organization."[60] Established in 1969, MUFON is entirely organized by volunteers and has been incorporated as a nonprofit organization. On their website, visitors can learn more about prominent UFO cases, can make reports of their own, and can also view others' reports via a "Live UFO Map" feature. Their website even features tutorials and software to determine if photos have been altered or faked. While MUFON is composed of volunteers and their website compiles a wide range of articles and news stories from many corners of the internet, it is indeed proof of something—people are fascinated by the celestial unknown and have been reporting unidentified flying objects for decades.

Interestingly, even with the vast array of personal accounts and the hundreds of publicly available government documents detailing interest in and research about UFOs, Greg Eghigian of Penn State University states that perhaps more so than any other paranormal field of inquiry, ufology has witnessed a very distinct struggle between skeptics and believers.[61] In fact, Eghigian tells us that "the public's relative curiosity about and openness to the notion of extraterrestrial visitation has stood in stark contrast to the views of scientists."[62] This is perhaps not any surprise to readers, as scientists may naturally be predisposed to harboring more intense focus on facts obtained via the scientific method. However, Eghigian goes on to tell us that there seems to exist a very real "UFO taboo" that actually exacerbates the reluctance of scientists to openly engage in any academic pursuit of investigating these phenomena. And even though, as a survey from the 1980s revealed, many ufologists believed that origins to UFOs weren't necessarily extraterrestrial, this group has continued to be shut out by the mainstream academic community.[63]

Also essential to this debate is the conversation, among anthropologists, of just how far one should "go native" in order to understand a particular phenomenon or widely reported events.[64] Many prominent academics and researchers who have, in the course of investigating UFO phenomena, claimed to now believe in the possibility of UFO phenomena and/or the existence of extraterrestrial life have been subject to scathing remarks and comments from the broader academic community. One prominent example is the Harvard University professor John Mack. Mack, who taught psychiatry, wrote a book titled *Abduction: Human Encounters with Aliens*, which has been coined "one of the most controversial books in the recent history of psychiatry" as in it, Mack claims to believe the stories recounted to him by his patients are not interpretations of psychiatric episodes, but are instead honest and accurate representations of real events.[65] Eghigian tells us that "the reaction of Mack's colleagues was decidedly negative, with many puzzled by the fact that someone they considered intelligent, affable, and so eminently reasonable could go down the proverbial rabbit hole."[66]

According to the academic community, or at least to the academic colleagues of John Mack, a willingness to believe in the existence of some type of paranormal explanation for UFO-related phenomena is akin to being unintelligent and unreasonable. When is it intellectually safe, then, to investigate aspects of the paranormal? Must we, as academics and researchers, always provide a caveat for ourselves as we engage with theories and potential advanced understandings of unexplained phenomena? Are we so entrenched in Western worldviews that tout science as absolute and all else as lazy logic that we are unwilling to admit that there are still mysteries in this world? To be sure, it is one thing to approach unexplained phenomena with an open yet skeptical mind and quite another to say that even entertaining the thought of such inquiry is unintelligent and unreasonable.

Even though the source of this noted struggle in ufology is unclear, there does seem to be a shifting tide in the public acceptance of potential UFO or extraterrestrial phenomena. For example, in a March 2019 article written in the *Orlando Sentinel*, reporter Chabeli Herrera wrote:

> In December 2017, *The New York Times* uncovered that the U.S. had gone so far as to fund a secret, $22 million, five-year project to study UFO claims. Since then, respected researchers, from the chairman of Harvard University's astronomy department to at least one scientist at NASA, have come out with theories, albeit controversial ones, that suggest closer study of the role extra-

terrestrials may play in certain phenomena. What's changed, said Robert Powell, an executive board member on the nonprofit Scientific Coalition for Ufology, is our understanding of the universe. As scientists have discovered more Earth-like exoplanets and begun to delve into the options for interstellar travel... the conversation has been shifting.[67]

Here we finally see some hope that we are lessening our hold on the materialistic Western worldview that seems to stifle inquiry with its clinical lens. Hopefully researchers will continue to allow themselves to be open minded while still upholding the spirit of genuine scientific inquiry—after all, how can the genuine pursuit of open-minded curiosity about the world around us lead us astray?

Parapsychology

> *We hardly need to be reminded that in a number of instances the scientific truths of yesterday are the relics of today. With scientific advances, theories, assumptions, and "facts" that were once unquestioningly accepted have come to be seen as erroneous and misleading, and it is the contention of those concerned with the study of the paranormal (parapsychologists) that there are—or may be—levels of complexity about the world and about human experience that we are now only just beginning to fathom.*[68]

Parapsychology is perhaps the largest and most scientific aspect of the paranormal, and while some readers may be familiar with this topic, I would guess that others may be hearing it for the first time. Readers may note that this topic contains the largest amount of bibliographic entries in this work, and this is due not only to the vast amount of topics that fall under the umbrella of parapsychology, but also because of the vast history of parapsychological research.

Parapsychology is quite simply "the scientific study of psychical phenomena" and is "sometimes used in place of 'psychical research.'"[69] In other words, parapsychology is "the study of mental phenomena which are excluded from or inexplicable by orthodox scientific psychology (such as hypnosis, telepathy, etc.)."[70] A term that is sometimes used in place of parapsychology is simply "psi," which was coined by two parapsychologists in the 1940s—R. H. Thouless and B. P. Wiesner.[71] One of my favorite definitions of parapsychology, which was offered to me by a friend who contributes to the scholarly discussion of it, is that parapsychologists acknowledge that the claims of paranormal activity people report are indeed happening but that we don't yet understand what is going on—in other words, there are potential scientific understandings to be had about these events, but we simply haven't uncovered them yet.[72] You can also consider it this way: the human mind interacts with the world around it in ways not yet fully understood.

Authors Robert M. Schoch and Logan Yonavjak, in their work *The Parapsychology Revolution*, tell us that there are four main categories of modern parapsychological research.[73] The first category concerns matters of extrasensory perception. Phenomena that fall under this category include "mind-to-mind . . . interactions and transmission of data through some means other than the normal senses such as vision, hearing, smell," and so forth.[74] This category also includes clairvoyance, defined by the authors as "the reception of information about objects, persons, and events by other than normal sensory means" that doesn't depend on any mind-to-mind communication but which rather is a result of a mental image, and is sometimes also described as second sight.[75] Precognition abilities are also subsumed under the umbrella of extrasensory perception. This is the specific insight of future events. On the other hand, retrocognition (which is another skill listed within this category) occurs when a person receives information about past events through unordinary means.[76]

The second category of abilities that qualify as parapsychological are those of a psychokinetic nature. Essentially, psychokinetic events (or, PK for short) involve an event in which "mental activity or consciousness alone can move or manipulate material objects."[77] The traditional notion of PK that most readers are likely familiar with is the idea of using one's mind to manipulate the movement of a spoon, for example. Telekinesis is sometimes used in place of PK, though it is a dated term. Psychokinesis is, I imagine, one of those paranormal traits that people often wish for in their daily lives—imagine the possibilities! Of course, PK doesn't just limit itself to mental impact on objects. One type of PK, known as direct mental interactions with living systems (DMILS), occurs when a mental act affects a person or biological entity in some type of physical manner—consider, for example, when people send out intense prayers of healing for friends or loved ones.[78]

The two remaining categories that Schoch and Yonavjak outline are materializations and survival studies. The authors define the former as the "materialization and dematerialization of objects and other entities, such as physical apparitions that have a physical energetic reality that can be recorded or detected."[79] The latter category concerns the question of human survival after death, the two main components of that topic being near-death and out-of-body experiences. For the purpose of this work, I have separated out these last two categories and given them consideration of their own. Materializations can be found here under "Ghosts and Hauntings," and survival studies can be found under "Reincarnation and Near-Death Experiences." The field of parapsychology, as may be illustrated here, can be overwhelming—after all, it includes all sorts of paranormal phenomena from ghostly apparitions to precognition to near-death experiences and much, much more. Hopefully readers will understand the utility of separating this larger category out a bit.

While the history of parapsychological research is found in later sections of this book, I will outline a brief overview of parapsychological research and notable issues here. The founding organization dedicated to studying psi events is the Society for Psychical Research (SPR), which was founded in Britain in 1882,[80] in order "to examine without prejudice or prepossession and in a scientific spirit those faculties of man, real or supposed, which appear to be inexplicable in terms of any generally recognized hypotheses."[81] Established with the goal of obtaining a scientific understanding about certain inexplicable (paranormal) occurrences, some of the earliest research done by the SPR included work on "thought reading" or "thought transference." One story in particular tells of a man who was struck with a vivid mental image of five eggs in a basket, two of them being rather oddly shaped. He came to discover later that his mother-in-law had, that very morning, delivered five such eggs to their household, the two oddly shaped ones having been set aside in a different room. Still other accounts tell of a woman who sensed the far-away death of a child; a young man's knowledge of his brother's undisclosed illness; and yet another young man who could always predict when his older sibling would be paying a visit.[82]

Author Renee Haynes, in her work on the history of this organization, explains that during the nineteenth century a belief in the "analogy between living processes and the mechanical triumphs of the industrial revolution" was in full force.[83] Because of this, there seemed to be an enhanced fervor of understanding all sorts of phenomena through the lens of academic, scientific study that was only further spurred on by the advancement of mechanical and technical inventions like railways, factories, and other such "automata" that resulted in the birth of a very mechanistic view of life.[84] It seems to make sense, then, that an organization like the SPR blossomed from an era that believed all progress and knowledge could be gained through detailed analysis and classification using advancing technologies. It was an era in which anything was possible.

The nineteenth century also saw the rise of spiritualism, which blossomed mainly due to the efforts of the infamous Fox sisters of New York.[85] The three Fox sisters, Margaret, Kate, and Leah, claimed to hear rappings, bangs, and the sound of furniture being dragged through their house in Hydesville. After working out a communication method in which they asked their supposed spirit to answer their questions through knocks (a sort of spectral Morse code, if you will), the sisters claimed that the noises were due to the antics of the spirit of a man buried in their cellar.[86] A group of people visited the house to determine the source of the noises themselves, and when they concluded that they could not determine any natural reasoning behind them, the popularity of the Fox sisters shot off like a rocket. They conducted seances throughout New York, and others soon followed their lead; "and soon other individuals and groups all over the country were producing similar phenomena, supplemented by the playing of musical instruments such as accordions and guitars."[87] In other words, spiritualism heralded in the era of paranormal as entertainment, and I would argue that portions of this movement could be viewed as providing the first "reality shows" of paranormal entertainment.

Researcher Andreas Sommer tells us that the popularity of spiritualism was a global phenomenon that helped to sharpen the opposition to paranormal inquiry from broader, scientific institutions.[88] The tension between those open to psi research and those who viewed it as pointless is best summed up by noted parapsychologist William Barrett who wrote, "There are others who, whilst not denying that the subject may possibly be a legitimate object of scientific investigation, prefer to give the whole matter a wide berth; contending either that it is a worthless will-o'-the-wisp, luring its victims, by an imaginary prospect of knowledge, into a miserable morass, or that it is distinctly forbidden by the Scriptures and condemned by the Church, so that its practice, and some would even add its investigation, is unlawful."[89] This quote illustrates the very real divide that existed between those engaging in psi research and certain other cultural institutions. It is a sentiment that I think still exists today, albeit perhaps not in quite a visceral way. Nonetheless, it is important to note that the field of parapsychology has always combatted resistance even though there is a wide swath of scientific literature that reveals to us some very mysterious things.

A more detailed historical outline of the field of parapsychology is provided in the next section, so let's jump ahead a bit. The Parapsychological Association is an organization that was established in June 1957 at the behest of well-known scientist J. B. Rhine of Duke University.[90] The first president and vice president of this organization were professors Dr. R. A. McConnell from the University of Pittsburgh and Dr. Gertrude R. Schmeidler from the City College of New York, respectively. Emphasizing both an international and professional focus, this association strives to advance the field of parapsychology while also communicating the research and science behind it to the public. On their website, they write that association "members use well-developed scientific methods to determine to what extent psi phenomena can be explained through presently understood processes—whether physical or psychological—and to what extent they may point to unknown forces and law, or necessitate a revised model of consciousness and its relation to the world."[91] As such, their research efforts focus on topics such as clairvoyance, telepathy, psychokinesis, and more.

Interestingly, author Marie Jones tells us that extrasensory perception (ESP) is the most frequently reported psi event. Of course, we know from the above discussion that ESP events include mental transmissions of information through means other than the known senses.[92] Dr. Paul Joire, a French scientist, coined this term in the 1880s during his research into hypnotism and the ability of patients "to sense things externally, without the use of the five ordinary senses."[93] The aforementioned J. B. Rhine, however, is the one responsible for making ESP a popular phenomenon to study in the United States. In the 1930s, Rhine and his colleague Dr. Karl Zener created a way to test ESP abilities and created what are now known as the Zener ESP cards. The cards contained common symbols like a circle or square, and Rhine and Zener used them to test if people could intuit what symbols were on the cards or if subjects could mentally transfer the images in front of them to another person. This experiment, while having been credited with its own faults, opened the door for further ESP research.

One of these later experiments involved sensory deprivation and is known as the Ganzfeld experiment. During these experiments, which require two subjects, one person is put into a state of sensory deprivation. What this means is that during the experiment they lose the ability of sight and sound, usually through the use of blindfolds and headphones. The other subject, known as the sender, then attempts to mentally transfer information to the receiver. The overarching theory behind the Ganzfeld experiment is that people put into a deep meditative or hypnotic state are more likely to have enhanced ESP abilities.[94] Another similar experiment involves a "sender" attempting to transfer mental imagery to a "receiver" as they are in REM sleep.[95]

Another psychical event that researchers study is precognition, a type of extrasensory perception (ESP) that involves the ability of a person to obtain information from the future. There have been multiple accounts of people with this ability, even some famous cases. Abraham Lincoln, for example, had a dream in which he died just three days prior to his assassination, and Mark Twain dreamed of his brother's passing before it happened.[96] Dreams, in fact, are often the subject of precognitive events. Researchers Julia Mossbridge and Dean Radin discuss, in a 2018 article from the *Psychology of Consciousness* journal, various experiments that study dreams and other forms of precognition and which seem to indicate that some subconscious element of our minds intuits information from the future.[97]

It may appear that psi experiments are only conducted by scientists in a lab, but it isn't just universities and scientists who are engaged in paranormal research. As some readers may know, and as was illustrated through our discussion of ufology, the government is intrigued by the paranormal and partakes in psi experiments. Specifically of interest is the phenomena of remote viewing, which is the ability to see something occurring at a distance not detectable by the field of human vision. Author Marie Jones tells us that "remote viewing has been at the heart of top-secret research funded by the CIA, NASA, the U.S. Navy, and U.S. Air Force since the early 1970s."[98] In

1972, for example, CIA officials funded a Stanford Research Institute experiment that was led by physicists Russell Targ and Hal Puthoff. During this experiment, remote viewers would be used to uncover locations and descriptions of government installations, and in one instance their experiment exhibited an instance of psychokinesis when one subject "was able to alter the output signal of a magnetometer by simply focusing his attention on the interior of the instrument."[99] In fact, Russell Targ wrote a number of books about his experience and has just recently released a documentary on this topic in conjunction with videographer Lance Mungia.

Parapsychology is the study of a wide range of psychical phenomena including telepathy, psychokinesis, remote viewing, precognition, and more. In this section, we learn that researchers, scientists, and even the government have been interested in studying these phenomena for many years. They are undoubtedly the phenomena that are most firmly entrenched within academia, due in large part to the work of the scholars mentioned in this section, but they are by no means the only topics worthy of academic inquiry. Let us turn now to an overview of reincarnation and the near-death experience.

Near-Death Experiences and Reincarnation

Many readers have likely read or heard stories about reincarnation and near-death experiences. Some may even have friends or family who have been through a near-death experience. And some readers may even have had a near-death experience (NDE) themselves. In this section, I will briefly discuss incidents of near-death experiences and reincarnation and introduce some of the studies surrounding these phenomena. As always, this section doesn't claim to be comprehensive, and more information can be found later in this book under the bibliographic entries for these topics.

To begin the exploration of these topics, let's consider Carol Zaleski's work titled *Otherworld Journeys: Accounts of Near-Death Experience in Medieval and Modern Times*. In her work, Zaleski reminds us that accounts of near-death experiences are nothing unique to the modern world. In fact, she believes that these experiences are just the modern manifestation of "otherworld journey narrations" that have existed in folklore from antiquity. She writes, "Eyewitness accounts of life after death can be found throughout the folklore and religious literature of the world. In Western culture, return-from-death stories developed within and alongside the apocalyptic traditions of late antiquity, flourished in the Middle Ages, declined during the Reformation, and reappeared in connection with some of the evangelical, separatist, and spiritualist movements of the nineteenth century. Today these tales have returned in full force in the form of 'near death' testimony first popularized in the early 1970s."[100] While I don't think that Zaleski is dismissing any person's account of enduring an NDE, I appreciate her work because it situates the idea of what she refers to as "return-from-death" experiences in the cultural, religious, and historical record. She illustrates perfectly that from almost the beginning of time humans have been obsessed with notions of death and specifically of rebirth. Understanding the ways in which paranormal aspects have played out culturally, religiously, and historically can only help to better understand the ways in which paranormal phenomena continue to play out today. Our long-standing fascination with "return-from-death" narrative and experience is certainly not irrelevant to understanding these phenomena today.

Focusing back toward a more scientific discussion of this topic, in 1998 radiation oncologist Jeffrey Long formed the Near-Death Experience Research Foundation after his extensive experience with patients and after reading about the phenomena in a 1984 medical journal article.[101] In the first ten years of the organization, which administers a survey to people who have experienced NDEs, Dr. Long captured more than thirteen hundred responses. Of these responses, 95 percent of people believed that their NDE was a real experience (not merely a vivid dream) and that it cemented within them a belief in life after death. Also intriguing is the fact that "the results of the [survey] clearly indicate remarkable consistency among NDE case studies . . . concepts [are] strikingly consistent across cultures, races, and creeds. Also, these discoveries are generally not what would have been expected from preexisting social beliefs, religious teachings, or any other source of earthly knowledge."[102] Dr. Long describes the impact that this research has had on him personally when he writes, "I long ago quit believing that death is the cessation of our existence. It took me a long time to reach this point. I was born into a scientific family. . . . I developed great respect for science. By scientifically studying the more than 1,300 cases, I believe that [the evidence] all converge on one central point: *There is life after death.*"[103]

From these descriptions alone, it is clear that NDEs are profound and mystifying experiences. Before digging into the work that Dr. Long and the Near Death Experience Research Foundation has done, however, let's examine the components of a near-death experience. The term "near-death experience" was first coined by Doctor Raymond Moody and "applies to the testimony of individuals who have revived from apparent death as well as those who have only come close to death."[104] Near-death experiences, as defined by Dr. Long, are "events that take place as a person is dying, or, indeed, is already clinically dead. People who have NDEs are called near-death experiencers (NDErs)."[105] It should be noted, however, that though these two definitions appear similar, there is some debate about accepted definitions of near death. For example, Dr. Long considers this attribute to be met if a patient is "so physically compromised that they would die if their condition did not improve."[106] This means, then, that a person must be very close to death and/or considered medically dead. That distinction, of course, means that you no longer have a heartbeat and/or are no longer breathing. The "experience" part of an NDE means that you have a vivid and lucid experience at or near the time of death.

The moment that cemented Dr. Long's fascination with NDEs occurred when he was a medical student at the University of Iowa. He discovered a rebuttal to an article in the *Journal of the American Medical Association*, a prominent research journal. The rebuttal was written by Dr. Michael Sabom in which he provided commentary on some recent research of his own. Dr. Sabom outlined that he had reviewed the NDEs of 107 patients and discovered that some patients reported out-of-body experiences that enabled them to report their operations in "distinct 'visual' detail."[107]

Researchers have concluded that there are twelve elements unique to an NDE, and while no two people experience the exact same thing, studies have shown that most or all of the following elements occur in sequential order: "out of body experience; heightened senses; intense and generally positive emotions or feelings; passing into or through a tunnel; encountering a mystical or brilliant light; encountering other beings (either mystical being or deceased relatives or friends); a sense of alteration of time or space; life review; encountering otherworldly realms; encountering or learning special knowledge; encountering a boundary or barrier; and a return to the body, either voluntary or involuntary."[108]

Dr. Long, in his research of more than thirteen hundred patients who have reported an NDE, points to several factors that indicate something paranormal occurs to these patients. His first point for proof is that patients exhibit lucidity after death. In his own words, "speaking both medically and logically, it is not possible to have a highly lucid experience while unconscious or clinically dead."[109] Dr. Long isn't simply referring to recounting vivid details of random experiences, but is rather pointing to the ability of patients to specifically describe and outline events that happened in the real world (often in their own operating room) after the moment in which they are technically clinically dead. In one instance, a man who was in a coma was visited by family and friends, who often left gifts. One of his gifts, a lavender candle, was placed in a drawer; when the man woke, he was able to inquire about the candle in the drawer before anyone had informed him.

The second factor that Dr. Long points to is that many patients report out-of-body experiences. What's most unique about these out-of-body experiences is not necessarily that they are a shared experience of NDErs, but that they provide a unique "point of consciousness."[110] They report not just seeing things from their corporeal body, but seeing themselves separate from their body and even being able to report accurately on items that could not have been in their corporeal field of vision. Another factor that Dr. Long points to as proof is the number of NDErs who are blind but report accurate visual reports after coming back from their NDE. One such report, in fact, came from a woman who had been blind since she was a few days old.[111] These are just a few of the factors that Dr. Long claims as proof that NDEs are events that indicate proof of consciousness after death.

What happens to NDErs after they come back from their experience? Two of the researchers listed above, Drs. Raymond Moody and Michael Sabom, were two founders of the International Association for Near-Death Studies, established in 1978, which not only provides information to people who have experienced NDEs and their loved ones, but also publishes the *Journal of Near-Death Studies*, a scholarly peer-reviewed journal that highlights NDE research.[112] Researcher P. M. H. Atwater, referenced on a home page of the association's website, published an article that was concerned with investigating the "aftereffects" of NDEs. What she found was that people who have NDEs reemerge not only with a renewed passion for life and a startling vision/encounter that cements a belief in life after death. She discovered that, along with those two characteristics, NDErs "[evidence] specific psychological and physiological differences on a scale never before faced by them."[113] In addition to exhibiting a renewed passion for life (which is a pretty obvious aftereffect for anyone who's had an NDE), NDErs also exhibit some very unique traits that they previously never exhibited. For example, Atwater's research discovered that it is common for NDErs to report psychic episodes in which they report seeing beings that they met in their NDE state, have out-of-body experiences, recall future events, and become sensitive to light and sound; in addition, electrical sensitivity occurs during which NDErs report their watches stop, their televisions change channels with no remote usage, telephone calls frequently drop, and computers regularly lose power.[114]

In a subsequent study on aftereffects, Atwater specifically studied the experiences of children who had encountered an NDE. Of the 277 children she interviewed, half of them claimed to remember their birth and provided their memories in such detail that it had to be verified by their parents. Furthermore, one-third of the children with NDEs indicated memories of events that happened before they were born, and which were determined again by consulting with the child's parents.[115] Most striking, however, was Atwater's focus on the brain development of children who have experienced an NDE. In her sample of children, 96 percent of those who experienced an NDE between birth and fifteen months tested at the genius level of intelligence. Eighty-one percent of those who experienced an NDE before they were six years old tested at the genius intelligence level as well.[116] Atwater posits that the difference between these two groups is a result of the brain development that occurs much more rapidly between birth and fifteen months. Additionally, she discovered that all children who endured an NDE came back with a reversed learning style. Most children, she reminds us, learn on a spectrum that goes from concrete to abstract. In other words, they learn details and facts before they grasp concepts. However, in her research, she has discovered that children who've had an NDE do better when learning abstract concepts before concrete details. Furthermore, after reading up on Atwater's research, Dr. Linda Silverman came forward to share some of her own research. Dr. Silverman examined the histories of gifted children with IQs in the genius level and found that 80 percent of her subjects with genius-level IQs suffered some sort of "birth trauma."[117] This overlapping of results is interesting since Dr. Silverman wasn't specifically studying NDEs, but rather the general characteristics of gifted children, and the fact that her research findings mirrored Atwater's reinforces her already credible research.

Now that we've covered NDEs in some detail, let's move on to another related aspect: reincarnation. Lumped in with NDEs because of its connection to death and rebirth, reincarnation is defined as "rebirth in new bodies or forms of life."[118] Reincarnation, or as it's often referred to in the literature as past-life experiences (PLEs), can happen in one of two ways: spontaneous or hypnotic.[119] Spontaneous occurrences of PLEs most often occur in children who remember facts about someone else's life and who sometimes also exhibit characteristics or personality traits of those people as well. Hypnotic PLEs are, of course, experienced when a person undergoes hypnosis to invoke past-life memories using a specific hypnotic technique known as past-life regression. Still other researchers have indicated that PLEs can occur in other situations, such as during the consumption of psychedelic drugs for recreation or medication, during deep meditative states, during sensory deprivation experiences, and even during dreaming.[120] Reincarnation is, as most readers may know, most closely affiliated in cultures that practice Hinduism, Buddhism, Taoism, and Jainism, but notions of reincarnation appear as far back as Egyptian times.[121]

The most well-known reincarnation researcher, Dr. Ian Stevenson, was a researcher at the University of Virginia, in the psychiatric medicine department.[122] After encountering a case in 1960 that piqued his interest in reincarnation, Dr. Stevenson researched nearly three thousand cases and went on to write hundreds of articles and handfuls of books on this topic. Dr. Stevenson focused specifically on researching cases of reincarnation in very young children and would investigate the veracity of each case through detailed interviews with these children. The children would recall and describe details of people in other towns or states and outline details of events they had no way of knowing. Quite often, Dr. Stevenson discovered that children between the ages of two and four experienced the most PLEs that then subsided between the ages of five to seven, or once the child began attending school.[123]

While reincarnation and PLEs have been more contested than near-death experiences, what is interesting about Dr. Stevenson's work is the high regard to which many view his methods. In fact, Stevenson helped pave the way for research parameters that could be used even in cases of respondents from different cultures and countries.[124] Some of the common research parameters included searching for birthmarks that might align with the deceased person's traumatic wounds, recognizing people that only the deceased would have recognized, talents unique to the deceased that are then displayed in the PLEr, and phobias displayed by the PLEr that were once possessed by the deceased and which the PLEr has no outwardly existing reason to harbor.[125] Since Dr. Stevenson was such a stickler for methods, he would obtain his data in very methodical ways. These methods included interviews with the subject as well as with friends, family members, teachers, and acquaintances, followed by interviews with the deceased person's friends and family when such person could be identified through reports given by the subject. He also gathered all pertinent documents including birth and death certificates as well as information such as criminal records, military records, and any other records that a person would generate in the course of a lifetime.[126] While not necessarily a factor required for reincarnation to occur, Dr. Stevenson investigated many more Asian cases of reincarnation than he did in North America. Interestingly, a key difference between his Asian and North American cases was that Asian children often had PLEs of people completely unknown and unrelated to them, whereas the majority of North American children who had PLEs exhibited traits and knowledge of those directly related to them such as a grandparent or aunt.[127] Similarities, though, that existed were the age at which both groups of children began displaying potential characteristics of PLEs and that the source of their PLE had passed in a violent manner.[128]

While Dr. Stevenson wasn't the only researcher of the PLE phenomena, he is mentioned in detail here because of his research standing on this topic. Interestingly, he never came out and directly expressed his personal belief in reincarnation, always using the opportunity to refer to what his research findings revealed. While Dr. Stevenson scientifically investigated the literal occurrences of reincarnation as we understand it here in North America, it is important to remember that reincarnation also plays a psychosocial role in certain cultures. The Esan people of Nigeria, for example, as author Isaac Ukpokolo tells us, use the notion of rebirth as a comfort when dealing with the loss of a loved one. It isn't Ukpokolo's goal to debate the scientific reality of reincarnation—he points that out specifically to his readers.[129] It is his goal, instead, to describe the ways in which reincarnation beliefs play out in important psychosocial ways in the modern world. Here is yet another way in which we see a connection between religion and the paranormal. In the Esan belief system, then, reincarnation is a very real thing and one that serves to advance the natural grieving process.

Cryptozoology

> Yet no age has been without its share of hidden creatures, and confirmation of purported species has been a vital and consciously debated issue among the collectors of human knowledge for thousands of years.[130]

So far, we've been introduced to the field of parapsychology, ufology, and near-death experiences, and even touched upon reincarnation episodes. One additional subtopic of the paranormal (and the author's favorite realm to consider) is cryptozoology. Cryptozoology is simply the scientific investigation into the existence of rumored but unverified creatures. Let's examine what sets cryptozoology apart from its parent field, zoology. Chad Arment, author and researcher, tells us that cryptozoology is "a targeted-search methodology for zoological discovery,"[131] and thereby ties it to this larger scientific field. However, the key difference is that cryptozoologists specifically search for mysterious or hidden animals (a.k.a. cryptids) that are *ethnoknown*. This characteristic is what differentiates a zoological discovery of a completely unknown and never-before-described species of fish, for example. To use another example, while we may not have any scientific evidence of the skunk ape of Florida, these creatures have been described and reported for many years. This unique quality of being described before obtaining concrete scientific discovery is at the core of cryptozoology. Arment boils it down for us when he writes, "Most collected species will be discovered and described without any prior knowledge of those species' existence. Ethnoknown species are those for which some prior contact with man has been communicated or documented. They may have solid standing within a people's belief system, or may have been a casual sighting scribbled into an explorer's journal."[132]

Researcher Peter Dendle, in an article written for *The Folklore Society*, helps situate the importance of cryptozoology in the historic record of mankind. He reminds us that pretty much every culture that has ever existed has had tales of mysterious creatures. Take, for example, the North American Bigfoot myths, Chupacabras of Hispanic cultures, a purported lake monster in Sweden's Lake Storsjön, medieval accounts of elves, Nessie in Scotland, and many more.[133] He points out, "The beliefs are sufficiently consistent across time and place that the question becomes inevitable: what do they mean? Why does humanity, as a whole, so consistently and ubiquitously populate its border spaces with fascinating and sometimes threatening creatures?"[134] Dendle posits, and I believe rightly so, that there is a very real emotional component to the field of folklore and specifically cryptozoology. A forefather of cryptozoological inquiry, Bernard Heuvelmans, believed this as well and considered "emotional response as a core feature of a cryptid."[135] In other words, Heuvelmans stated that in order for a creature to be classified as a cryptid, it has to have some sort of characteristic or trait that is upsetting, paradoxical, or overwhelmingly unique.

Let's investigate the contributions of Bernard Heuvelmans a bit more, as no discussion of cryptozoology would be complete without him. Heuvelmans was, in fact, the researcher who coined the very word "cryptozoology."[136] His seminal work, first published in French in 1955 and which in English translates to *On the Track of Unknown Animals*, is considered by many to be a founding work on the study of undiscovered creatures. Heuvelmans was a trained zoologist and the first scientist to devote his studies to cryptozoology;[137] he was also the president of the International Society of Cryptozoology, an organization that established the scientific journal *Cryptozoology*, a multidisciplinary publication aimed at understanding more about this field. In his own words, Heuvelmans writes:

> In the 1950s, I was an angry young zoologist, indignant at the ostracism imposed by official science . . . on those animals known only through the reports of isolated travellers, or through often fantastic native legends, or from simple but mysterious footprints. . . . I dreamed of delivering all of these condemned beasts from the ghetto in which they had so unjustly been confided, and to bring them to be received in the fold of zoology. It was to this perilous task which I set myself shortly before 1950, applying nonetheless all of the rigour which my scientific training imposed upon me.[138]

It was with this very spirit that Heuvelmans undertook his work at advancing the previously unnamed field of cryptozoology.

In his aforementioned book, *On the Track of Unknown Animals*, not only does Heuvelmans go in search of evidence for unknown animals, but he also illustrates the consequences of shutting oneself off to the possibilities of undiscovered creatures. In one particular example, he cites the case of the exploration of Madagascar by Admiral Etienne de Flacourt.[139] Many of Flacourt's observations and notations were dismissed as tall tales. In fact, in one instance he described a bird whose "eggs were enormous, eight times as large as an ostrich's, big enough for the natives to use as tanks for drinking-water."[140] Many people dismissed this account of such a bird, claiming that it was simply borrowed from Arabian tales of a large, mythical bird known as a roc that could carry unsuspecting seafarers off their ships. Flacourt published his accounts of the animals and landscape of Madagascar in 1658, which included descriptions of these enormous birds, but it wasn't until 1832 when Victor Sganzin, a French naturalist, traveled to Madagascar and witnessed locals drinking from an "enormous half-eggshell."[141] Sganzin wasn't able to take the eggshell back to France with him, but he nonetheless drew a detailed sketch of it, which was later examined by an ornithologist in Paris who concluded that it came from an ostrichlike creature. Still, it wasn't until 1851 that the existence of the fabled enormous bird was scientifically acknowledged when a sea captain "found three eggs and some fragmentary bones on the southwest coast of the island" and sent them to the Academy of Sciences in Paris. The eggs that the captain discovered could fit six ostrich eggs inside them, or in other words, could hold nearly two gallons of liquid.[142] It took over two hundred years for the scientific community to recognize the existence of these creatures. Of course, one factor at play here is the standards for determining concrete scientific discovery—after all, sketches are not physical evidence per se—but what I found to be a larger factor is what Heuvelmans describes as "intellectual deafness." He writes, "While they [scientists] remain obstinately deaf to rumors about unknown or supposedly fossil animals, these animals die out, some are already extinct, and we have lost the opportunity of studying them except as wretched remains."[143] If it took more than two hundred years to simply acknowledge the existence of the aepyornis, imagine the hurdles that must be in front of any number of other creatures.

This example of the trial of the aepyornis's discovery also reminds us that skepticism of undiscovered but ethnoknown creatures is not, by any means, a modern trend. I urge readers to let this point sink in, because I suspect that sometimes we assume that skeptical questioning is a result of the modern science–focused world we live in, when that would be quite far from the truth. While ancient societies may have more readily accepted myths as truth (in fact, Pliny the Great accepted the possibility of pretty much everything except werewolves),[144] there have always been those (dating as far back as antiquity) who were skeptical and claimed that tales of creatures were simply "optical illusions and tricks of the mind; exaggerated distortions of kernel truths," or that these tales came from "outright liars."[145]

Let's advance this brief overview of cryptozoology by examining the most prominent North American cryptid, collectively and popularly defined as "Bigfoot." Cryptozoological researcher Dr. Jeff Meldrum reminds us that the term "Sasquatch" is a more appropriate one that gives "deference to the Native American and First Nations terms," terms for these creatures (which have been reported long before the influx of European settlers to North America) that translate to "wildmen of the woods."[146] Dr. Meldrum goes even further, however, to say that even this term has been overly commercialized, which is why he most prefers to use the term "relict hominoid." He prefers this term not only because it is separated from pop culture but because it ensconces the cryptozoological pursuit of this creature more firmly in the realm of natural science.[147]

It is also worthwhile to keep in mind that North America doesn't hold claim as the only region in which cryptid sightings occur. After all, scientists first postulated the existence of large, hairy cryptids when people began reporting them in the Himalayas in the 1920s.[148] In 1951, traveler Eric Shipton and a crew of other mountaineers were hiking at an altitude of around nineteen thousand feet when they noticed large, strange footprints embedded in the snowy glacier they were traversing.[149] The noted traveler Sir Edmund Hillary was a member of this expedition; in an article written for the *New York Times*, he wrote that "I first accepted the fact that they [Yeti] existed in 1951" during the expedition in which Shipton photographed these prints and during which seasoned Sherpas recounted their sightings of the strange, hairy creatures to the group as they bunked together on their journey.[150]

Of course, hairy bipedal creatures aren't the only notable cryptids—they just happen to be the most well known in North America. Another prominent cryptid with a long history of reported sightings includes the Loch Ness Monster of Scotland. Decidedly different from Sasquatch, since Nessie (as it's collectively known and hereafter referred to as this) exists in water, the most famous reported sighting came from 1934 when London-based surgeon Dr. Robert Kenneth Wilson claimed to have captured four pictures of the mysterious creature raising its long, slender neck above the water. It is very likely that readers know the infamous photographs to which I'm referring, but did you know that earlier that same year four Benedictine monks residing at the nearby Fort Augustus Abbey also reported seeing the creature?[151]

We should begin our discussion of Nessie by mentioning the work titled *The Life of Saint Columba*, written by Saint Adamnan sometime around the early eighth century AD.[152] In this work (I accessed the version translated in 1905 by Wentworth Huyshe), there is a description of an event that occurred when Saint Columba needed to cross the River Ness and, having arrived

Views of Urquhart Castle on Loch Ness, Scotland. *Author photo*

there, came upon a scene of villagers burying a person who had just been attacked and killed by a river monster. Saint Columba ordered a man to swim across the river and retrieve a small fishing boat perched on the opposite bank. The man, named Lugne, believing that Saint Columba would keep him safe, obeyed and started to swim across the river. However, things went south quickly, as Huyshe translates for us: "The monster, which was lying in the river bed, and whose appetite was rather whetted for more prey than sated with what it already had, perceiving the surface of the water disturbed by the swimmer, suddenly comes up and moves toward the man as he swam in midstream, and with a great roar rushes on him with open mouth, while all who were there . . . were greatly terror-struck."[153] Luckily for Lugne, Saint Columba rushed in to save the day. Witnessing the monster about to devour poor, devout Lugne, Saint Columba charged forward and "after making the Salutary Sign of the Cross in the empty air with his holy hand upraised, and invoking the Name of God, commanded the ferocious monster, saying, 'Go thou no further, nor touch the man; go back at once.' Then, on hearing this word of the Saint, the monster was terrified, and fled away again more quickly than if it had been dragged off by ropes, though it had approached Lugne as he swam so closely that between man and monster there was no more than the length of one punt pole."[154]

Considered the oldest account of a brush with the infamous Nessie, it should become clear that the folklore surrounding sea monsters has been embedded in the Scottish memory since medieval times. We shouldn't assume, of course, the absolute veracity of Saint Adamnan's biography. In their book titled *Abominable Science!*, authors Daniel Loxton, Donald Prothero, and Michael Shermer point out that "there are good reasons to suspect that this encounter never occurred."[155] They point out that Saint Adamnan's work is a "hearsay-based biography" and that its author used second-, third-, and fourth-hand accounts as proof of real events. Furthermore, the figure of Saint Columba himself was a figure obscured by legend and lore, the authors claim, and the fact that the biography is packed with loads of other supernatural deeds of Saint Columba leads them to concur with other researchers that this biography is nothing more than a work of religious propaganda.[156] This shouldn't come as any surprise, of course. I think most readers understand that ancient texts were often used as allegories and influenced greatly by legends, superstitions, and using myths as moral guidelines.

It is clear that cryptids are a worldwide phenomenon, but let's refocus now on the North American Sasquatch. The term itself is Native American in origin, and "thought to be an Anglicized version of a Halkomelem Indian word meaning hairy giant."[157] The term "Sasquatch" itself didn't rise to popular prominence until the mid-twentieth century, when reports of bipedal creatures that came to be collectively referred to as Bigfoot began occurring, primarily in the Pacific Northwest. Specifically, the term "Bigfoot" arose

Loch Ness Centre, Drumnadrochit, Scotland. *Author photo*

from an incident in the Bluff Creek region of Northern California in August of 1958 when a construction crew working in the area kept finding large footprints near their worksite. When these footprints continued to occur over the course of a few weeks, the group began referring to the source as Bigfoot, and Jerry Crew (one of the workers) consulted a taxidermist to learn how to take a plaster cast in order to preserve evidence of these large footprints. After he successfully cast a mold of the footprints, he contacted journalist Andrew Genzoli, who ran a story about this creature coined by the construction workers as Bigfoot; the news story became so popular it was described as "loosening a single stone in an avalanche."[158] The Bluff Creek incident came approximately twenty years after Ralph Von Koenigswald, a German anthropologist, discovered proof of a previously unknown "very large extinct ape-like primate" that he dubbed *Gigantopithecus*.[159] In fact, it was Von Koenigswald's discovery that most people cited to explain that perhaps what people were witnessing was yet another unknown species related to *Gigantopithecus*. Unfortunately, it was revealed in 2002 that the Bluff Creek tracks were fabricated by a man named Ray Wallace—information that didn't come out until after Wallace's death in 2002.[160] Wallace, who was a logging crew member in 1958, is described by his children as a lifelong prankster, and while his pranks unfortunately revealed the Bluff Creek incident to be a hoax, cryptid researcher Jeff Meldrum doesn't let this one incident discredit all the others. In fact, Meldrum says, "Bluff Creek brought the idea into the public psyche and into the morning newspaper, but this thing has roots that go deeper than any isolated incident. . . . If I had come to the conclusion it was all a hoax, I would have washed my hands of it years ago."[161]

The most well-known report of a Bigfoot sighting came in 1967 when Roger Patterson and Bob Gimlin filmed what appears to be a large, hairy, bipedal creature walking along a creek bed in Northern California. In fact, their footage was filmed very near the same area of the now infamous Bluff Creek hoax. For this very reason (along with others that readers likely already know and/or can assume), there is great contention behind the authenticity of this footage, which is collectively referred to as simply the Patterson-Gimlin film.[162] Patterson, a documentary filmmaker who had been studying reports of Sasquatch sightings, set out with his friend Bob Gimlin to capture some footage for a documentary he hoped to create.[163] Riding on horseback, the two men were traversing the creek bed area when they rounded a bend and came upon "a Sasquatch crouching beside the creek to their left," which "reacted abruptly to the men's presence by standing up and walking away, from left to right, at a considerable angle . . . the initial confrontation was at a distance of less than 25 feet."[164] Patterson's horse became so spooked by the creature that he threw his rider to the ground. Luckily unhurt, Patterson grabbed his camera to begin filming the creature as it walked away. All in all, Patterson captured approximately two minutes of film, or 952 frames. His partner, Gimlin, remained on his horse throughout the incident, his hand on his rifle in the event that things went sour.[165] Once the creature disappeared out of sight, Patterson and Gimlin took casts of the footprints the creature had made, measuring its stride as well.

As readers can naturally imagine, Patterson was thrilled to present the film to scientists, thinking that it would be proof positive of the creature's existence. However, "only a few scientists were willing to even look at the film, and most of them promptly declared it to be a fake."[166] Perhaps not surprising, this footage has been the subject of an overwhelming amount of analysis and criticism; however, there are those in the scientific community who have acknowledged the importance of it. For example, two "respected experts in the biomechanics of human locomotion at prestigious institutions"[167] analyzed the footage and determined that the figure in the film could not have been a human in costume (the most often cited rebuttal to the film). The debate surrounding the film continues to this day, as many readers likely know. I can't help but make comparisons, though, between the Patterson-Gimlin footage and the Madagascar accounts of Flacourt in the seventeenth century. Nonetheless, the quest for Sasquatch continues.

In an event described as "a watershed moment in the study of anomalous primates,"[168] a group of Washington State residents were heading to a community garbage center close to the Canadian border, in the town of Bossburg. Once there, they discovered multiple footprints in the snow—however, this was November 1969, so naturally the group was perplexed about finding bare footprints in such weather. What's more curious is that these footprints measured approximately seventeen inches long.[169] Telling friends and colleagues about this curious sighting led to a small group of "amateur naturalists" to be formed, and when they scanned the woods surrounding Bossburg and the nearby town of Colville, they discovered approximately one thousand more strange footprints.[170] This incident caught the attention of Washington State University professor of anthropology Grover Krantz, an academic who had been researching these "anomalous primates" for years.[171] Although there has been much debate over the authenticity of the tracks, both Grover Krantz and John Napier, a scientist at the Smithsonian Institution, came to believe that the mysterious tracks were authentic.[172] This moment in 1969, however, cemented the event as watershed because for the first time, the experts weren't so quick to dismiss the novice. In fact, "the common narrative for discoveries of Sasquatch evidence was that amateurs claimed support for the beast's existence only to be dismissed by scientists interpreting the same evidence as a hoax or a misidentification. But not on this occasion. At Bossburg, the exact opposite occurred."[173]

Building on the novelty of that moment when scientists weren't so quick to be dismissive, researcher Brian Regal explores the dichotomy between scientist and "monster hunter." The latter term has been used to describe those who had little to no academic training in natural sciences but who harbored a passion for wilderness and an ambition to discover the hidden secrets of nature. However, he reminds us that before any formal academic systems existed to qualify discoveries, amateur naturalists, through their collection of specimens, formed the basis for what we currently know about nature in the United States. In fact, Regal tells us that "in the early part of North American history there were no professional scientists. There was a cadre of men of means . . . who roamed the countryside collecting and classifying the virtually endless array of new species that frolicked about the landscape of the New World. . . . Because of their efforts these amateur naturalists were the prime source of scientific knowledge about the North American continent."[174]

Regardless of the veracity of cryptids and regardless of the characteristics of those involved in studying them and questioning the truths behind the legends, tales of strange creatures and monsters have been and will continue to be embedded in the human psyche. Paleontologist Darren Naish offers an interesting perspective on why these creatures form a core subset of folklore worldwide when he says that creatures like Bigfoot are "the modern manifestation of a human-wide cultural concept, not a zoological reality."[175] Smithsonian writer Ben Crair helps elucidate Naish's comment by reminding us that "as so-called wild men, they hold a crude mirror up to our own species: what might Homo Sapiens be like if civilization had not removed it from nature?"[176] However, it is Gerald Durrell who, in his introduction to Heuvelmans's *On the Track of Unknown Animals*, describes to us the most significant reason why we should remain open to the field of cryptozoology:

> You would imagine by now that both [Bermuda and New Zealand] would have been pretty thoroughly explored and worked over by zoologists and ornithologists, and yet since the end of the war two supposedly extinct species have been rediscovered, in Bermuda the *cahow* and in New Zealand the *Notornis*. When you think that these birds have been living and breeding in little pockets, as it were, under the eyes of competent observers for so long without discovery, it is surely not straining credibility too far to imagine in the vast, sparely inhabited, or completely uninhabited areas of the world, such as the Congo forest, the great swamps of Africa, the Matto Grosso, the thick evergreen forests of Patagonia, or on the huge shining ramparts of the Himalayas, there may be found animals unknown to science.[177]

Astrology, Divination, and Mysticism

Author Roger Beck, in his book titled *A Brief History of Ancient Astrology*, describes astrology as part of the "cultural and intellectual history" of the Greeks and Romans through which they "searched for meaning and significance in the phenomena of the visible heavens."[178] Specifically, Beck tells us that the Greeks practiced four different types of astrology. One type is referred to as "genethlialogy" and is the specific relation of the constellations at either the moment of birth or the moment of conception and is used to "foretell an individual's fate, fortunes, and character."[179] Another form is "catarchic" astrology and is used to determine the best moment in time to undertake a particular venture. This is used, for example, to determine the best time to break ground on a new store or to travel. A third type of astrology the Greeks practiced is interrogatory astrology, which provides answers to questions based on the astronomical layout on that specific day—picture the daily horoscopes in newspapers and you've got the basic gist of this type. The fourth and last type of astrology is omen astrology, which was consulted during moments of celestial events like eclipses or thunderstorms and which meant different things depending on the season.[180] Many of these same astrological methods are practiced today.

Divination is "the action or practice of divining; the foretelling of future events or discovery of what is hidden or obscure by supernatural or magical means."[181] Divination is the art of foreseeing future events through some form of oracle. As we know from an earlier discussion, the Greeks consulted

Tarot Cards, an Example of a Divination Tool. *Creative Commons/"Tarot Cards Spread" by 2tarot.psychic is licensed under CC BY 2.0*

oracles in the form of people, the most famous being the Oracles of Delphi. Author Skye Alexander reminds us that tools such as tarot cards can also be considered oracles and are just one of many tools used in divination practices.[182] Ancient Egyptians practiced one form of divination known as hepatoscopy, which is "divining by inspection of the liver."[183] If you had a question in Egyptian times, you would seek the help of a seer, who would interpret the lines, etchings, and physical properties of the liver of a sacrificial animal to offer guidance related to your question. This is merely one of many divination practices that humankind has engaged in, but I like to include it as it firmly entrenches the art of divination in the ancient record. I include the topic of divination in with this general category alongside astrology and magic because of its intimate connection to magical practices and ritual.

Magic is defined as "the use of ritual activities or observances which are intended to influence the course of events or to manipulate the natural world, usually involving the use of an occult or secret body of knowledge."[184] Author and scholar Dean Radin reminds us that there is almost no topic of study that isn't influenced by magic—anthropologists study the ways in which cultures engage in ritual practices, psychologists study the reasons why people believe in magical thinking, and even historians scour magical texts (grimoires) to see what they can reveal about a certain place and time in the world. Dr. Radin also says that these scholarly inquiries are the very precedent for studying magic from a scientific lens, and he puts it quite eloquently when he writes, "I figured that if anthropologists can safely study the magical beliefs of what they used to call 'savages,' if psychologists are allowed to investigate why modern citizens still believe in magic, and if historians can survey the words used in ancient magical spells, then surely we're mature enough to examine the possibility of real magic without causing the world, or ourselves, to go berserk."[185] The point he makes is a very important one, because as Western scholars it is important to remember the cultural biases we bring to our own academic pursuits of certain topics.

Mysticism, as defined by Glenn Alexander Magee, editor of *The Cambridge Handbook of Western Mysticism and Esotericism*, "typically teaches that all finite things are connected; all are parts or aspects of a cosmic order," and that mystics are "concerned with the knowledge of the transcendent source of all being."[186] It is often expressed and experienced via an experience with the mysteries of our universe—a process in which someone's entire outlook on life is changed and which is referred to as gnosis. Many people who have a near-death experience frame it as a mystical experience in which their entire worldview is tilted on its axis. In terms of religion, mystical experiences may involve encounters with angels or other divine messages. It has also been closely linked with ritual practices, especially within Jewish mysticism.[187]

Some readers may still wonder why I include these topics. It's a fair question, and one that is important to address. These are topics that are deeply connected to issues of the paranormal, but they are also topics that are likely less familiar to the average Western reader, so introducing their place in the paranormal timeline will be helpful. Additionally, these topics are expressions of the mystical beliefs held by certain peoples, but more importantly to our discussion, they are practices that are rooted very firmly in the ancient, historical, and mystical timeline of humans. Understanding that these topics are related to the larger paranormal discussion will serve to ensure that those researching the paranormal have a more well-rounded understanding of not only the scientific inquiry of the paranormal but also of the cultural and sociological aspects of the paranormal as well. This point brings me to the last section of this chapter, which is a note regarding the inclusion of religious, mystical, and folklore sources.

Occult and Magical Practices

Any discussion of the paranormal would be remiss without mentioning the occult and magical practices. In most chapters of this book the occult is separated into its own category, but the chapter on monographs (or, books) includes the category of "Occult and Magical Practices" simply due to the fact that the most comprehensive treatment on the topic of magic I found is contained in monographs. In other chapters, however, magical practices is subsumed under the topic of "Astrology, Divination, and Mysticism" as these topics are so intimately connected to one another. You can find an abundance of monographs on the topic of magic and magical practices, so for this reason you see that distinction in the monographs chapter.

Readers have undoubtedly heard the terms "occult" and "magical practices." It may conjure images of Ouija boards, séances, or even the Satanic panic for some, perhaps due to the media's and pop culture's influence. The occult that I refer to here, though, refers to ritual or magical practices, such as those practiced by Hermeticists, folk magicians, cunning folk, or other ritual practitioners. It has its roots in antiquity and is often very closely related to divination and mysticism, so I try to keep these last two categories grouped together throughout the book. Occult practices are sometimes referred to as esotericism, and according to Glenn Alexander Magee, the four "sciences" of the occult (or esotericism) are "astrology, magic, alchemy, and spirit-seeing."[188] It has also been used to refer to all the discarded or rejected knowledge that usually occurs when ancient or native practices are usurped under religious control or dominion.

Occult and magical practices continue to this day, although perhaps to a lesser extent than they were once practiced—or, rather, maybe we just don't notice it. Nevertheless, the occult and magic communities make up a significant portion of the paranormal community, and for this reason it is important to include works that investigate these topics.

A Note on Religion and Folklore

> *The belief that everything in the universe, animate and inanimate, possesses an imperishable spiritual essence was once the global norm . . . today such animistic beliefs are no longer even regarded as primitive or foolish. Most of us simply think of them as wrong. Science has become the new story, rewriting the rule book for consciousness in a way that virtually eliminates the primordial question at the heart of all human experience up to the present age.* Who? *has now become* What?[189]

Religion and folklore are intimately linked with the paranormal. Particularly, religion and the paranormal are two topics firmly entwined with each other— the existence of one inherently validating the existence of the other. For example, Western Christian beliefs view God and angels as spectral entities (that is, noncorporeal), and belief in them exists without any visual or scientific proof. Understanding this, they don't seem much different than a person who harbors a belief in ghosts. Considering how the paranormal helps validate the religious, we can use the same example. Harboring a belief in ghosts as evidence of a sort of life beyond death is, I think, akin to harboring a belief in God as an entity proving that there is a higher power or meaning to life, which can be interpreted as life beyond death.

Folklore and urban legends are other categories very closely linked with the paranormal. We all have local legends about haunted houses or strange creatures or other paranormal phenomena. Our curiosity about the paranormal may stem from a story someone shares with us, or an urban legend we listen to around the campfire, asking ourselves, "What if" as we quickly walk back to our tents in the dark. These stories and urban legends are, of course, full of fantastic and paranormal elements that can influence our own personal understandings of, and beliefs in, the paranormal. They can even influence our experiences with paranormal phenomena as they serve to help us interpret that which we don't understand. For example, if someone experiences seeing a disembodied entity, they may filter that experience through the stories and images that they have associated with ghosts—in other words, folklore affects the way in which we view the world around us. In that regard, it is very important to understand and study the ways in which folklore and the collective imagination serve as filters for how we understand our own (and others') experiences.

It is important to note that these subjects are intimately linked with the paranormal, though it is beyond the scope of this work to analyze these two topics. The purpose of this book is to provide readers with a selection of annotated resources outlining the scholarly and credible research being done on scientifically understanding the paranormal. My goal is to show that the paranormal is a valid academic field of study, and to highlight the advancement of our understanding of paranormal phenomena. These topics—religion and folklore (while entirely worthy of their own academic pursuits)—are beyond the scope of my work here. And while there can be truths ferreted out from the origins of religion and folklore, the best thing about them is that they spark our imagination and creativity, stoke the fires of our curious inclinations, and help give us a way of interpreting the phenomena we encounter in the world.

Of course, studying the paranormal can also serve to shift one's own religious beliefs. Some topics discussed earlier include phenomena during which a person has a profound mystical experience. Consider near-death experiences. What else can a near-death experience be classified as if not mystical? After all, during an NDE many people claim to encounter a sense of life beyond death and an awareness of a deeper meaning—how can this not be considered a mystical and/or religious experience? If anything, it is difficult to draw an exact line dividing those topics that are or are *not* influenced by some topic of the paranormal, religious, and mystical. The more we understand through scientific inquiry of the paranormal, the more we produce new questions surrounding the reality and meaning of life as we attempt to fit that new knowledge into our current worldviews.

On another note, it is important to understand the role that organized religion has played in promoting a fear of the paranormal—a fear that has perhaps trickled down over the years to a disdain that some may harbor about the validity of paranormal research. I argue that organized religion has certainly helped propagate the idea that nonreligious paranormal beliefs are dangerous. Dean Radin, in his book *Real Magic*, outlines how the church has wielded power over communities to spread a fear of indigenous magical/religious practices when he writes, "Many orthodox religions have strictly banned magic, largely as a sociopolitical strategy. It would not do if infidels were allowed to worship anything not under the control of the proper ecclesiastic authorities. Like any struggle for political power, gaining the allegiance of the masses is much easier by inciting fear of the 'other' than by encouraging love and compassion."[190]

Readers likely understand that it's not possible to scientifically test the validity of a person's religious or faith-based beliefs. Faith is simply that—a belief in something that you consider an important part of your life, and for that reason, everyone's "truths" are vastly different. I urge readers to locate works on religion and folklore because they are topics that cannot be separated from the larger understanding of how we interact with the paranormal in society. Having a well-rounded understanding of all angles of an issue will simply help ensure that you have a more holistic understanding of that which you are studying. The next chapter deals with the historical timeline of paranormal research and highlights some key figures throughout paranormal history.

NOTES

1. Paranormal. (2019). In *Merriam-Webster*. Retrieved August 26, 2019, from https://www.merriam-webster.com/dictionary/paranormal

2. Paranormal. (2019). In *Oxford English Dictionary*. Oxford University Press. Retrieved August 26, 2019, from https://www.oed.com/view/Entry/137554?redirectedFrom=paranormal#eid#eid#eid

3. Supernatural. (2019). In *Merriam-Webster*. Retrieved August 26, 2019, from https://www.merriam-webster.com/dictionary/supernatural

4. Jones, Marie D. (2007). *PSIence: How new discoveries in quantum physics and new science may explain the existence of paranormal phenomena*. Franklin Lakes, NJ: New Page Books, 24–25.

5. Ibid., 25.

6. Kripal, Jeffrey J. (2019). *The flip: Epiphanies of mind and the future of knowledge*. New York, NY: Bellevue Literary Press, 23.

7. Ibid.

8. Ibid.

9. Combs, Allan, & Holland, Mark. (1990). *Synchronicity: Science, myth, and the trickster*. New York, NY: Paragon House, xv.

10. Headaches as you age. (2017, June 1). *Mayo Clinic Health Letter, 35*(6), 1–3.

11. Shiah, Yung-Jong, Chang, France, Tam, Wai-Cheong Carl, Chuang, Shen-Fa, & Yeh, Lun-Chang. (2013). I don't believe but I pray: Spirituality, instrumentality, or paranormal belief? *Journal of Applied Social Psychology, 43*(8), 1706. doi:10.1111/jasp.12125

12. Ruffle, Libby. (2017, May). Vessels of the gods. *History Today, 67*(5), 52.

13. Ibid., 58–60.

14. Kripal, Jeffrey J. (1999, Fall). "The visitation of the stranger": On some mystical dimensions of the history of religions. *Cross Currents, 49*(3), 368.

15. Ibid., 379.

16. Strieber, Whitley, & Kripal, Jeffrey J. (2016). *The super natural: Why the unexplained is real.* New York, NY: Jeremy P. Tarcher, 14.

17. Gordon, Avery F. (2008). *Ghostly matters: Haunting and the sociological imagination.* Minneapolis: University of Minnesota Press, 8. ProQuest eBook Central. Retrieved March 23, 2019.

18. Brown, Roberta S., Brown, Lonnie E., & Tucker, Elizabeth. (2010). *Spookiest stories ever: Four seasons of Kentucky ghosts.* Lexington: University of Kentucky Press, 151.

19. Ibid., 151–156.

20. Porter, Darwin, & Prince, Danforth. (2007). *Frommer's portable Savannah* (3rd ed.). Hoboken, NJ: Wiley, 9.

21. Ibid., 14–16.

22. Miles, Tiya. (2015). Goat bones in the basement: A case of race, gender, and haunting in old Savannah. *South Carolina Review, 47*(2), 25.

23. Gentry, Glenn W. (2007). Walking with the dead: The place of ghost walk tourism in Savannah, Georgia. *Southeastern Geographer, 47*(2), 222.

24. Visit Historic Savannah. (n.d.). Sorrel-Weed House. Retrieved January 6, 2020, from https://www.visit-historic-savannah.com/sorrel-weed-house.html

25. Haunted Savannah. (2020). Haunted Sorrel Weed House. Retrieved January 6, 2020, from http://savannahitc.com/haunted-savannah/haunted-savannah/haunted-sorrel-weed-house/

26. Ghost City. (2020). The haunted Mercer-Williams House. Retrieved January 6, 2020, from https://ghostcitytours.com/savannah/haunted-places/haunted-houses/mercer-williams-house/

27. Ibid.

28. Ibid.

29. Visit Savannah. (2020). Bonaventure Cemetery. Retrieved January 6, 2020, from https://www.visitsavannah.com/profile/bonaventure-cemetery/6129

30. Historic Tours of America. (2018). The most haunted cemeteries in Savannah. (2018). Retrieved January 6, 2020, from https://www.ghostsandgravestones.com/savannah/haunted-cemeteries

31. How yellow fever turned New Orleans into the city of death. (2018, October 31). [Interview with Kathryn Olivarius]. *All Things Considered.* NPR. Retrieved March 26, 2019, from Gale Literature Resource Center.

32. Ibid.

33. Brown, Alan. (2011). *Ghosts along the Mississippi River.* Jackson: University Press of Mississippi, 78–82.

34. Ibid., 64.

35. Ibid., 65–67.

36. Davenport, Jad. (2002, January–February). Rocky horror: The haunting legacy of Stephen King's *The Shining* looms over Colorado's Stanley Hotel. *Book*, p. 20. Retrieved from Gale Literature Resource Center.

37. Earls, Stephanie. (2016, October 31). Colorado's Stanley Hotel offers plenty of haunted tales: Reputation was earned before Stephen King's arrival. *The Gazette* [Colorado Springs, CO]. Retrieved March 26, 2019.

38. Ibid.

39. Jones, *PSIence*, 29.

40. FBI Records: The Vault. (1947, July 8). Roswell UFO: Part 1 of 1. Retrieved January 8, 2020, from https://vault.fbi.gov/Roswell%20UFO/Roswell%20UFO%20Part%201%20of%201/view

41. Steiger, Brad, & Steiger, Sherry. (2006). *Conspiracies and secret societies*. Detroit, MI: Visible Ink Press, 9.
42. Ibid.
43. Jones, *PSIence*, 31.
44. Lewis, James R. (2000). *UFOs and popular culture: An encyclopedia of contemporary myth*. Santa Barbara, CA: ABC-CLIO, 311.
45. Ibid., 311.
46. Ibid.
47. Huyghe, Patrick. (1979, October 14). U.F.O. files: The untold story. *The New York Times*. Retrieved March 27, 2019.
48. Ibid.
49. Ibid.
50. Ibid.
51. Blumenthal, Ralph, & Kean, Leslie. (2019, January 15). "Project Blue Book" is based on a true UFO story. This is it. *The New York Times*. Retrieved March 28, 2019, from https://www.nytimes.com/2019/01/15/arts/television/project-blue-book-history-true-story.html
52. Ibid.
53. Ibid.
54. Cocconi, Giuseppe, & Morrison, Philip. (1959, September 19). Searching for interstellar communications. *Nature*, p. 844.
55. Jones, *PSIence*, 33.
56. SETI Institute. (n.d.). FAQ: What is the SETI Institute? Retrieved April 2, 2019, from https://www.seti.org/faq#seti1
57. Ibid.
58. Schoch, Robert M. (2018, January 1). The Wow! Reconsidered signal. *Atlantis Rising Magazine*. Retrieved April 8, 2019, from EBSCOhost.
59. Aliens found in Ohio? The "Wow!" signal. (2010). *Weekend Edition Saturday*. NPR. Retrieved April 8, 2019, from Gale Literature Resource Center.
60. MUFON: Mutual UFO Network. (n.d.). Welcome to MUFON. Retrieved April 8, 2019, from https://www.mufon.com/
61. Eghigian, Greg. (2015, December 6). Making UFOs make sense: Ufology, science, and the history of their mutual mistrust. *Public Understanding of Science, 26*(5), 612–626. Retrieved April 8, 2019, from Sage Journals.
62. Ibid., 612.
63. Ibid.
64. Eghigian, Greg. (2014, November 13). The psychiatrist, the aliens, and "going native." *Psychiatric Times, 31*(11). Retrieved April 8, 2019, from EBSCOhost.
65. Ibid.
66. Ibid.
67. Herrera, Chabeli. (2019, March 19). The UFO community still believes: And science is starting to listen. *The Orlando Sentinel*. Retrieved March 26, 2019.
68. Carlton, Eric. (2000). *The Paranormal: Research and the Quest for Meaning*. Burlington, VT: Ashgate, 1.
69. Incorporated Society for Psychical Research. (2018). Glossary. Retrieved April 21, 2019, from https://www.spr.ac.uk/research/glossary
70. Parapsychology. (2019). In *Oxford English Dictionary*. Oxford University Press. Retrieved April 21, 2019, from https://en.oxforddictionaries.com/
71. Schoch, Robert M., & Yonavjak, Logan. (2008). *The parapsychology revolution: A concise anthology of paranormal and psychical research*. New York, NY: Penguin, 9.
72. Laythe, Brian. Personal communication, May 2019.
73. Schoch & Yonavjak, *Parapsychology revolution*, 5–14.
74. Ibid., 5.
75. Ibid., 6.
76. Ibid., 6–7.
77. Ibid., 8.
78. Ibid., 9.

79. Ibid., 10.
80. Ibid., 15–16.
81. Haynes, Renée. (1982). *The Society for Psychical Research 1882–1982: A history.* London, England: Macdonald, xiii.
82. Ibid., 25–28.
83. Ibid., xiii.
84. Ibid., xiii–1.
85. Ibid., 2.
86. Ibid.
87. Ibid.
88. Sommer, Andreas. (2014, December). Psychical research in the history and philosophy of science: An introduction and review. *Studies in History and Philosophy of Biological and Biomedical Sciences, 48*, 39.
89. Barrett, William F. (1917). *On the threshold of the unseen: An examination of the phenomena of spiritualism and of the evidence for survival after death* (2nd ed.) London, England: Kegan Paul, Trench, Trubner, 2.
90. Parapsychological Association. (2019). History of the Parapsychological Association. Retrieved April 22, 2019, from https://www.parapsych.org/articles/1/14/history_of_the_parapsychological.aspx
91. Parapsychological Association. (2019). What is the Parapsychological Association? Retrieved April 22, 2019, from https://www.parapsych.org/articles/1/1/what_is_the_parapsychological.aspx
92. Jones, *PSIence*, 80–81.
93. Ibid., 81.
94. Ibid., 81–82.
95. Ibid., 82.
96. Mossbridge, Julia A., & Radin, Dean. (2018). Precognition as a form of prospection: A review of the evidence. *Psychology of Consciousness: Theory, Research, and Practice, 5*(1), 79.
97. Ibid., 79–93.
98. Jones, *PSIence*, 83.
99. Ibid.
100. Zaleski, Carol. (1988). *Otherworld journeys: Accounts of near-death experience in medieval and modern times.* New York, NY: Oxford University Press, 5.
101. Long, Jeffrey, & Perry, Paul. (2010). *The science of near death experiences.* New York, NY: HarperCollins, 1.
102. Ibid., 3.
103. Ibid., 3–4.
104. Zaleski, *Otherworld journeys.*
105. Long & Perry, *Science of near death experiences*, 5.
106. Ibid.
107. Ibid., 22.
108. Ibid., 6–7.
109. Ibid., 53.
110. Ibid., 69–70.
111. Ibid., 82–85.
112. International Association for Near-Death Studies. (2019). About IANDS. Retrieved April 20, 2019, from https://iands.org/about/about-iands27.html
113. Atwater, P. M. H. (1998). Aftereffects of near-death states. International Association for Near-Death Studies. Retrieved April 20, 2019, from https://iands.org/ndes/about-ndes/common-aftereffects.html
114. Ibid.
115. Atwater, P. M. H. (2003). Our tiniest near-death experiencers: Startling evidence suggestive of a brain shift. *Journal of Religious and Psychical Research, 26*(2), 87–88. Retrieved April 20, 2019, from EBSCOhost.
116. Ibid., 88–89.

117. Ibid., 90.
118. Reincarnation. (n.d.). In *Merriam-Webster's Online Dictionary.* Retrieved April 21, 2019, from https://www.merriam-webster.com/dictionary/reincarnation
119. Slavoutski, Sergei. (2012). Is the reincarnation hypothesis advanced by Stevenson for spontaneous past-life experiences relevant for the understanding of the ontology of past-life phenomena? *International Journal of Transpersonal Studies, 31*(1), 84.
120. Ibid.
121. Ibid., 85.
122. Stafford, Betty. (2014). Is reincarnation true? The research of Ian Stevenson. *Journal for Spiritual and Consciousness Studies, 37*(1), 33–34.
123. Ibid., 33–34; Slavoutski, "Is the reincarnation hypothesis advanced," 84.
124. Ibid., 85.
125. Ibid.
126. Ibid.
127. Ibid., 87.
128. Ibid.
129. Ukpokolo, Isaac E. (2012). Memories in photography and rebirth: Toward a psychosocial therapy of the metaphysics of reincarnation among traditional Esan people of southern Nigeria. *Journal of Black Studies, 43*(3), 290. Retrieved April 21, 2019, from JSTOR.
130. Dendle, Peter. (2006). Cryptozoology in the medieval and modern worlds. *Folklore, 117*(2), 190–206. doi:10.1080/00155870600707888
131. Arment, Chad. (2004). *Cryptozoology: Science and speculation.* Landisville, PA: Coachwhip, 9.
132. Ibid.
133. Dendle, Cryptozoology, 190–191.
134. Ibid., 191.
135. Ibid.
136. Krantz, Grover S. (1992). *Big footprints: A scientific inquiry into the reality of Sasquatch.* Boulder, CO: Johnson Books, 1.
137. Ibid.
138. Heuvelmans, Bernard (1995). *On the track of unknown animals* (3rd ed.) (Richard Garnett, Trans.). London, England: Kegan Paul, xxiv.
139. Ibid., 601–603.
140. Ibid., 602.
141. Ibid.
142. Ibid., 604–606.
143. Ibid., 601.
144. Dendle, Cryptozoology, 192.
145. Ibid., 193.
146. Meldrum, Jeff. (2016). Sasquatch & other wildmen: The search for relict hominoids. *Journal of Scientific Exploration, 30*(3), 357.
147. Ibid.
148. Regal, Brian. (2016). Bigfoot or Sasquatch. In Christopher R. Fee & Jeffrey B. Webb (Eds.), *American myths, legends, & tall tales: An encyclopedia of American folklore. Vol. 1: A–F.* Santa Barbara, CA: ABC-CLIO, 113–114.
149. Hillary, Edmund. (1960, January 24). Abominable—and improbable? *The New York Times.* Retrieved April 14, 2019, from Historic *New York Times,* ProQuest.
150. Ibid.
151. Views of monster lessen skepticism. (1934, April 22). *The New York Times.* Retrieved April 14, 2019, from Historic *New York Times,* ProQuest.
152. Adamnan, Saint. (1905). *Life of Saint Columba (Columb-Kille) A.D. 521–597: Founder of the monastery of Iona and first Christian missionary to the pagan tribes of North Britain* (Wentworth Huyshe, Trans.). London, England: Routledge.
153. Ibid., 137.
154. Ibid.

155. Loxton, Daniel, Prothero, Donald R., & Shermer, Michael. (2013). *Abominable Science! Origins of the Yeti, Nessie, and other famous cryptids.* New York, NY: Columbia University Press, 135.
156. Ibid., 136–137.
157. Regal, Bigfoot or Sasquatch, 113–114.
158. Ibid., 113.
159. Ibid.
160. Crair, Ben. (2018). Call of the wild man. *Smithsonian, 49*(5), 12. Retrieved April 17, 2019, from EBSCOhost.
161. Martelle, Scott. (2002, December 6). Ray Wallace, 84, took Bigfoot secret to grave—Now his kids spill it. *Los Angeles Times.* Retrieved April 17, 2019, from https://www.latimes.com/archives/la-xpm-2002-dec-06-me-wallace6-story.html
162. Crair, Call of the wild man, 12.
163. Krantz, *Big footprints,* 87.
164. Ibid.
165. Ibid., 90–91.
166. Ibid., 91–92.
167. Ibid., 92.
168. Regal, Brian. (2008). Amateur versus professional: The search for Bigfoot. *Endeavor, (32)*2, 53.
169. Ibid.
170. Ibid., 53.
171. Ibid.
172. Ibid.
173. Ibid.
174. Ibid., 53–54.
175. Crair, Call of the wild man, 13.
176. Ibid.
177. Heuvelmans, introduction to *On the Track of Unknown Animals.*
178. Beck, Roger (2007). *A brief history of ancient astrology.* Malden, MA: Blackwell, 2.
179. Ibid., 9.
180. Ibid., 9–12.
181. Divination. (2019). In *Oxford English Dictionary.* Oxford University Press. Retrieved May 21, 2019, from https://www.oed.com/view/Entry/56121?redirectedFrom=divination#eid
182. Alexander, Skye. (2017). *The modern witchcraft book of tarot: Your complete guide to understanding the tarot.* Avon, MA: Adams Media, 18.
183. Aveni, Anthony. (1996). *Behind the crystal ball: Magic, science, and the occult from antiquity through the New Age.* New York, NY: Times Books, 20.
184. Magic. (2019). In *The Oxford English Dictionary.* Oxford University Press. Retrieved May 21, 2019, from https://www.oed.com/view/Entry/112186?redirectedFrom=magick#eid
185. Radin, Dean. (2018). *Real magic: Ancient wisdom, modern science, and a guide to the secret power of the universe.* New York, NY: Harmony Books, 17.
186. Magee, Glenn Alexander. (Ed.). (2016). *The Cambridge handbook of Western mysticism and esotericism.* New York, NY: Cambridge University Press, xvii.
187. Ibid., 63–65.
188. Ibid., xviii.
189. Strand, Clark. (2008). *Waking up to the dark.* New York, NY: Spiegel & Grau, 94.
190. Radin, *Real magic,* 23.

Chapter Two

History of Paranormal Research and Seminal Figures

> *Through education and experience, I've also come to appreciate that these [psi] experiences are not just curiosities. They're also responsible for most of the greatest inventions, artistic and scientific achievements, creative insights, and religious epiphanies throughout history. Understanding this realm of human experience thus offers more than academic interest—it touches upon the very best that the human intellect and spirit have had to offer.* [1]

A BRIEF HISTORY OF PARANORMAL RESEARCH

Now that you know the different paranormal topics that this book outlines, a discussion of the paranormal research timeline is helpful. As readers hopefully gathered from chapter 1, the paranormal has ancient roots and as such, is a presence interwoven with the history of humanity at large. In this chapter, I discuss the scientific efforts of studying the paranormal that blossomed after the sixteenth century. This was a century that saw "the foundations of modern science laid down by the rapid advancement in instrumentation and the art of measurement, along with the proliferation of scientific experimentation" alongside a "great religious transformation—away from idolatry and toward more abstract forms of supernatural belief."[2] In the grand scheme of human history, the scholarly study of the paranormal hasn't been around for very long. The inclusion of groups and prominent scholars in this chapter is by no means exhaustive. Any omission is merely my own human error. I'm also not suggesting that scholarly inquiry is the only valuable kind of inquiry into the paranormal, either. This chapter is not an attempt to prove any aspect of the paranormal but is moreover an attempt at highlighting the fact that various paranormal topics have drawn the interest of very serious and very highly credentialed peoples throughout history.

The word "proven" is quite problematic when it comes to the paranormal. Not only does it reduce phenomena to a very small box often dominated by a clinical Western worldview, it can be used as a dismissive tactic to reduce the paranormal to nothing more than (pun intended) hocus-pocus. It often seems that arguments surrounding the ability to prove or disprove something are used to rank and classify certain topics that are worthy of scholarly inquiry. A dogged focus on "proving" the paranormal while ignoring the scholarly inquiry that has been done delegitimizes entire cultural, personal, spiritual, religious, and magical experiences. Getting caught up in "proving" nearly any aspect of the paranormal will send one down a rabbit hole. This doesn't mean that some very interesting things haven't been cataloged and discovered when it comes to the paranormal, though. It simply means that as researchers and as consumers of information, we must always keep in mind that the more we learn about the paranormal, the more questions that will inevitably arise. Acknowledging that a phenomenon exists without being able to pinpoint how that phenomenon happens is not shoddy research. Take dreams, for example. We know that dreaming is a common human experience, but we do not yet know all the nuances of how dreaming occurs. However, we also do not let that stop us from continuing our research on dreams and dreaming. It's no different with the paranormal.

I suspect that there are a fair number of people who don't realize that the paranormal has been studied and taken seriously by a vast array of scholars and researchers. I see this repeatedly from students who seek help with researching a paranormal topic, and sometimes when engaging in conversation with those critical or suspicious of the paranormal. This work is an attempt to shine a light on the myriad research that has been done to better understand the paranormal in all its forms. By doing so, I hope it motivates readers to seek out additional resources on this topic or to perhaps conduct paranormal research of their own.

Since we're on the topic of problematic terminology, this brings me to another point. There are yet more problems with the words "scholar" and "researcher." I wonder how many of us conjure images of people in white lab coats bustling around a stark lab room when they think of the word "researcher"? Or perhaps envision a bespectacled person in a cardigan poring through dusty tomes in a quiet, high-ceilinged library when we think of the word "scholar." It's probably a very small percentage who picture *themselves* as a scholar or researcher, which is quite unfortunate, because there is absolutely nothing holding you back from becoming either of these categories. I suspect that we are starting to step away from the clinical notions of research, but there still exists a bias toward only certain types of research. I would argue that many in academia hold the peer-reviewed research article as the

History of Paranormal Research and Seminal Figures 51

pinnacle of credible research, and while these may certainly be wonderful resources, they are not the only credible sources on a given topic. My point here is that anyone has the potential to research the paranormal and produce information to share with others, and it is often through unique "fieldwork" that theories and understandings advance. It is with this understanding that I hope readers are motivated to conduct research themselves; chapter 3 discusses some techniques at jump-starting your own paranormal research. Understanding the limitations of how we talk about paranormal research is a good point to dive back into a historical outline of paranormal research.

Perhaps the best starting point for this discussion begins in 1882, with the founding of the Society for Psychical Research (SPR). The founding members, intellectuals and academics from London, were particularly interested in studying the idea that some aspects of the human body could survive after death.[3] It is important to note that the SPR (while a robust organization with many trailblazing researchers of paranormal studies) is by no means the first organization or body of individuals to set about on a serious inquiry of paranormal phenomena. The great poet Alfred Lord Tennyson himself cofounded the Metaphysical Society in Britain in 1868, a society that met to discuss issues of metaphysics and the paranormal and which published such papers as "The Soul before and after Death," "The Arguments for a Future Life," "On the Words Nature, Natural, and Supernatural," and "The Theory of a Soul."[4]

Nevertheless, the Society for Psychical Research is the most prominent early organization tasked with scientifically studying the paranormal. As we know, it was founded in 1882. The aims of this organization were "to examine without prejudice or prepossession and in a scientific spirit those faculties of man, real or supposed, which appear to be inexplicable in terms of any generally recognized hypotheses."[5] Some of the SPR's earliest research involved matters surrounding hypnosis and dowsing, and in fact author Renée Haynes credits the SPR specifically for helping to mainstream hypnosis into common medical practices.[6] In addition to focusing on serious scientific study, a significant portion of the society's early work also centered on ruling out cases of fraudulent behaviors and claims of the paranormal.[7] Whether outright fraud or simply a result of miscommunication, the task before the SPR was no insignificant one, as it became the first formal association dedicated to seriously studying these topics and attempting to sort fact from fiction. Of course, the paranormal commercialization of the spiritualist movement occurring at that time didn't help matters and is yet another reason why the task before them was paramount.

Several committees made up the SPR; some early examples include the Committee on Thought Transference, the Committee on Haunted Houses, and the Committee on Mesmerism. The very first publication produced by the SPR includes three reports on thought transference, a report on haunted houses, and two reports detailing studies on hypnotism.[8] The first large study done by the SPR was eventually published as *Phantasms of the Living*, and came on the heels of Eleanor Sidgwick's work and publication, *Phantasms of the Dead*.[9] Written in 1886, *Phantasms of the Living* compiles research on a wide variety of phenomena exhibited by people such as "thought-transference," telepathy, telepathic dreaming, hypnagogia and hallucinations, and disembodied voices, and is culled from more than seven hundred case studies of these aforementioned topics.[10]

The SPR's contribution to the academic understanding of the paranormal cannot be overestimated. Not only did they adhere to certain protocols and keep a keen eye out for instances of fraud and hoaxing, they amassed exceedingly large numbers of case studies, reports, surveys, and more. The SPR is still in existence today, and I urge readers to browse its website to see examples of its current research and modern activities.

Members of the SPR weren't the only people interested in the paranormal. In general, people have been (and continue to be) fascinated by such topics. Societal attitudes, though, have shifted and changed over the years, and Charles Richet helps us understand a brief historical timeline of dominant thoughts on the paranormal. Richet, a prominent French physiologist who was interested in hypnosis and became president of the SPR in 1905, lays out a brief history of metaphysics as he calls it (and what we can take to mean psychical research) in his 1923 work titled *Thirty Years of Psychical Research: Being a Treatise on Metaphysics*.[11] Richet notes that (as of 1923) there exist four distinct eras when it comes to dominant ideas of paranormal phenomena. He calls the first stage "The Mythical Stage," which he designates as the period from antiquity up to the year 1778, or more specifically, he tells us, up till the time of Franz Mesmer, the German scholar and doctor who coined the concept "mesmerism." Of course, this is a giant span of human history, but what Richet notes is that this period was dominated by the notion that paranormal phenomena were mostly indistinguishable from or relegated to the religious realm. To put it in his own words, "What can we build on stories that date back twenty centuries, transformed by ignorant and credulous priests? How, then, can we affirm anything concerning an improbable event said to have taken place two thousand years before. . . . Probably it is not entirely false; but we cannot discriminate between its falsehood and truth."[12] Richet tells us that this period of time is best digested as a historian would study the events and people of long ago, acknowledging that we will perhaps never have concrete answers to these phenomena but accepting that there is some truth to these events. Richet uses the telepathic examples of such prominent people as Socrates and Joan of Arc to illustrate this. Both received visions and/or visitations from some unknown source that made them privy to information that could not otherwise be known. In this first era of paranormal thought, then, Richet reminds us that at a certain point humanity simply accepted that these things occurred without necessarily being too concerned with ferreting out the root or cause because, at this point, the root was mystical in nature.

The notion of "animal magnetism" as proposed by German physician Franz Mesmer ushered in the next era of the paranormal timeline, which according to Richet, is roughly 1778–1847 when the Fox sisters arrived and ushered in the spiritualist scene. Richet refers to this second era as "The Magnetic Stage." In 1776, while Mesmer was studying at the University of Vienna, he wrote a dissertation on the ways in which planets have "physiological influences" on humans.[13] Mesmer claimed that "there was an invisible fluid found in the human body and throughout nature" that was affected by the gravitational pull of the planets and which furthermore was affected by the application of magnetic objects upon the body—a tactic Mesmer believed could cure disease.[14] Upon moving to Paris a few short years after his dissertation, Mesmer's theories and ideas were adopted by the Royal Society of Medicine and the Academy of Sciences, during which scholars at these institutions discovered "a certain psycho-physiological state which might sometimes be efficacious in the curing of disease."[15] A few scientists influenced by Mesmer's theory took the concept and created induced somnambulism (sleepwalking), and actually discovered that in this induced sleepwalking state, not only could they assist in curing certain ailments, but that patients displayed certain telepathic abilities. One such story involves a patient, whose eyes were physically held down by a doctor's hand, reciting lines verbatim from a textbook chosen at random and correctly identifying random objects placed in front of them.[16]

Some sources tend to overlook the impact of Mesmer and how his work eventually gave rise to the practice of hypnotism—a practice that is still used today and which some readers may even have experienced for themselves. While Mesmer's contribution is notable and, I think, fascinating to the realm of psychical phenomena, Richet tells us that in spite of the evidence of telepathic abilities, "the scepticism of official science prevailed. . . . [Reports were] disputed and then forgotten, and the metaphysic phenomena were taken up by novelists, denied or disdained by men of science."[17] Interestingly, though, Richet notes that some of this skepticism and dismissal was fueled by the presence of performers who exploited the tactics of mesmerism at fairs and events, charging people money as they "plied their dubious trade" among the masses,[18] which is actually a perfect segue to discuss the third era of paranormal ideology.

Richet's third identified era is "The Spiritist Stage" and is marked by the distinct rise of the spiritualist movement, especially in the United States. Circa 1847, a man living in Hydesville, New York, began hearing strange noises in his home. Upon investigating, he found no apparent reason for these strange noises, and eventually he sold his home to John Fox and his daughters Kate and Margaret.[19] Kate and Margaret (or Maggie) began hearing these noises too and, in their attempts at figuring out where the noises were coming from, claimed that the raps and bangs had an intelligence behind them. For example, the sisters would ask that a certain number of raps or knocks be given in correspondence with the age of a person and claimed to receive accurate replies.[20] At one point, Kate and Maggie left the Hydesville home to live with their older sister Leah in Rochester, but curious neighbor Isaac Post, fascinated by the girls' experiences, encouraged their curiosity by suggesting additional ways to communicate with the rapping, inviting them to discuss their experiences at dinner parties and even renting a large meeting hall in Rochester during which four hundred people attended to witness the abilities of the sisters who, by this point, had begun to manifest abilities themselves.[21]

Richet does remind us that many years later in 1888 Maggie and Kate claimed that their childhood experiences were nothing more than hoaxes, but they retracted *that* confession just a few short years later in 1892.[22] Regardless of the veracity of these events, a movement of raps and table tipping was born, and it took off with a bang, especially after the sisters drew the attention of popular spiritualist Andrew Jackson Davis, who further spread the hype of spiritualism.[23] Richet relays the boom that spiritualism set off when he writes, "A petition signed by fourteen thousand persons was presented to the Senate of the United States in 1852, asking for a scientific commission of enquiry. It had become a new religion; spiritualist circles and journals were numerous."[24]

The spiritualist craze blossomed in the United States, but those in Europe felt the effects as well. It drew the attention of the general public, to be sure, but it also drew the attention of scholars. One of these scholars was Dr. Robert Hare, a chemistry professor at Harvard who became so enthralled by spiritualist demonstrations that he "converted to Spiritualism and became a vociferous advocate of it as a science and a religion."[25] Dr. Hare was not simply a casual onlooker, though. He was a founding member of the American Association for the Advancement of Science, and he went on to write *Experimental Investigation of the Spirit Manifestations: Demonstrating the Existence of Spirits and Their Communion with Mortals* in 1855. Dr. Hare was not the only scholar who espoused the religious conviction of spiritism, the foundations of which were laid out by Allan Kardec (pseudonym for L. H. D. Rivail), a French educator and scholar. The crux of spiritism as a religious movement adhered to the belief that "the soul does not die; after death it becomes a spirit and seeks to manifest through certain privileged beings (mediums), capable of receiving directions and impulses from spirits."[26]

In 1869, the London Dialectical Society was formed with the specific goal of scientifically investigating phenomena inherent in the spiritualist movement. This ushers in the fourth era of the ideological paranormal timeline, which Richet refers to as "The Scientific Stage."[27] Richet notes that it is not merely the formation of this society that ushered in the scientific stage, but the fact that its work attracted the attention of noted British scientist William Crookes, hailed as "the first British scientist of note to engage in psychical research."[28] Crookes, dissatisfied with untested claims of spiritualism phenomena, took it upon himself to develop scientific experiments aimed directly at psychical phenomena and at one point wrote, "I do not say that these things are possible. I say that they exist."[29] This sentence indicates a clear shift toward science recognizing the presence of certain phenomena that are worthy of scientific exploration. Richet tells us that the message of this era was that "experiment is the path of progress, rather than religious or mystical speculation,"[30] but Richet also reminds us that this scientific focus was simply another lens through which to view the same phenomena: "[Crookes] said scarcely anything that had not already been stated by spiritualists. The novelty consisted in rigorous application of experimental method to phenomena till then imperfectly verified and only partially studied, and therefore given no place in science."[31] In other words, the scientific method didn't necessarily invalidate the untested experiences of paranormal phenomena, it simply helped embed the topic within the broader scientific community. In this era, too, we see the formation of the Society for Psychical Research, which I discuss above, and which I feel brings us full circle in our brief outline of the paranormal research timeline.

Richet ends his exposé on the eras of paranormal thought by musing that the paranormal may gain even more footing in the scientific community in the future. In certain ways, I think that Richet is right—since the publication of his work in 1923, interest in various subfields of the paranormal has only accelerated, and scholars of all backgrounds, skills, and credentials continue to research these phenomena. Additionally, since Richet's publication, wide subsets of additional phenomena have developed—for instance, cryptozoology, ufology, and near-death experiences. We only continue to add to our collective paranormal experience. Our culture does still seem to place higher value on that which can be expressed materialistically, which hinders some understanding of paranormal phenomena, but there is, I think, a large subset of citizen-scientists who are pushing the boundaries of what it means for something to be investigated scientifically. Coupled with traditional scholars who are still pursuing the paranormal in large degrees, paranormal research seems to be firmly embedded in the human experience and it doesn't seem to show any signs of slowing down.

Though this section only briefly touches upon the history of paranormal research and ideology, interested readers can find additional sources in the annotated bibliographies below. In addition to providing a brief collective timeline, I now introduce some key figures associated with the paranormal.

BRIEF SKETCHES OF KEY FIGURES IN PARANORMAL RESEARCH

This section highlights some key figures in both the historical and contemporary timelines of paranormal research. Hopefully the above section reinforces that not only is there a long, historical record of paranormal research but that an ongoing contemporary pursuit of understanding exists as well. While by no means a comprehensive list of all those who contribute to the timeline of paranormal research, I hope that this chapter illustrates the wide variety of scholars who have pursued the paranormal. I also hope that their stories inspire readers to take up the torch of intellectual paranormal pursuit themselves. I also hope that this section helps to break down stereotyped notions of what it means to be a scholar, as all that's really required to be a scholar is genuine curiosity, motivation, and dedication.

A brief biographical sketch of William Fletcher Barrett is a fruitful place to begin this discussion. Barrett was a noted Irish physicist, one of the founding members of the Society for Psychical Research (SPR),[32] and has been dubbed a "pioneer of psychical research."[33] After viewing the experiments of his friend and colleague John Wilson, a mesmerist (or hypnotist), Barrett began wondering about the power of the human mind and specifically "the discovery of unknown mental faculties."[34] Further inspired by the teachings of physicist John Tyndall, whom he worked closely with, Barrett went on to study sound and vibrations and at one point even documented the ways in which flame is affected by sound. His research eventually led him to become professor of experimental physics at the esteemed London Institution. A major contribution to psychical research, however, occurred when Barrett (along with others) founded the Dublin chapter of the SPR, which from its inception was primarily concerned with investigations into Ouija boards, automatic writing, and séances. Another major contribution of Barrett was his work documenting the practice of dowsing, as well as using physics to make the psychical more understandable.[35]

Another seminal figure in the timeline of paranormal research is Eleanor Sidgwick. Sidgwick, the principal of Newnham College, was a prominent member of the SPR and was, in fact, an eager student of psychical phenomena before the founding of the society. Working alongside other prominent researchers, such as Henry Sidgwick (her husband), Edmund Gurney, and Frederic W. H. Myers, Eleanor took part in séances of several purported mediums in the 1870s, including, among many others, the famed Kate Fox.[36] Eleanor was known for her deep involvement in analyzing reported cases of psychical activity, and she even presented research regarding her experiments on telepathy at the International Congress of Experimental Psychology in London. Eleanor was responsible for coming up with criteria that formed the foundation for serious inquiries into ghostly phenomena. After receiving a significant number of eyewitness testimonies and eliminating any that seemed to be affected by falsehoods, pranks, or exaggeration, the criteria that Sidgwick identified as necessary for *potential* proof of an encounter with a ghost or spirit are as follows:

> (a) whether the phantom or ghost communicated correct information previously unknown to the percipient; (b) whether there appeared to be some clearly defined purpose conveyed by the apparition; (c) whether the apparition of someone unknown was so vivid that the percipient could later identify the deceased from a portrait; (d) whether the phantom bore some distinct mark or identifying characteristic that the percipient had been previously unaware of; or (e) when two or more persons independently, and at different times, saw apparitions that were alike.[37]

As I mention above, Eleanor's husband Henry Sidgwick is also a seminal figure, and was in fact the first president of the Society for Psychical Research. Inspired by the experiments of the aforementioned William Fletcher Barrett, Henry Sidgwick and other colleagues founded the SPR in January 1882 with the specific interest of investigating the phenomena of "thought transference."[38] In just a few short years, the SPR had close to six hundred members, including many prominent citizens and scholars.[39] In addition to his work with the SPR, Sidgwick was a prominent philosopher, scientist, and educator at Cambridge University, a tenure during which he was a staunch advocate of curriculum reform and advanced opportunities in education for women.[40] Biographer Bart Schultz relates how Sidgwick had an ability to bring together divisive minds for the greater cause of knowledge: "To be sure, even at the start, the Society had its divisions, with the 'scientific' contingent on one side and the séance loving 'Spiritualists,' led by Stanton Moses, on the other side. One could safely say, however, that it was largely because of the comparative sobriety that Sidgwick early on brought to the society that their work enjoyed the long period of respectability that it did."[41] Though often described as having a skepticism that sometimes halted potential progress, Sidgwick was a firm believer in the reality of telepathy and other mind phenomena. Nevertheless, Sidgwick's focus on scientifically investigating the paranormal while separating one's own philosophical or theological opinions of the field helped set the groundwork for the vast research that came out of the SPR.[42]

A contemporary of the Sidgwicks and one of the founding members of the SPR was Frederic W. H. Myers, "a leading theoretician during the first generation of psychical research."[43] His interest in psychical phenomena was only deepened after an evening walk with his friend Henry Sidgwick, and as a result, he played a large role in the founding and work of the SPR. There are few issues of the society's proceedings that did *not* include an entry by Myers on some work in which he was involved. One of the earliest and most prominent works of the SPR was *Phantasms of the Living*, and it was this work in which the SPR classified the paranormal phenomena that they studied—an idea that is credited to Myers, who even coined the terms "telepathy" and "supernormal."[44] Myers's seminal work, published posthumously in 1903, is *Human Personality and Its Survival of Bodily Death*, a work that rested upon Myers's belief that there exists a core psychical self in each person that has abilities not restricted to the corporeal body. It was with this belief that Myers challenged the dominant philosophy that paranormal phenomena are a result of spirits of deceased people—in other words, ghosts.[45]

Yet another contemporary of the aforementioned scholars is Edmund Gurney, an English psychologist who became a psychical researcher with the SPR and who was particularly interested in studying hypnotism. Gurney was a keen observer of the spiritualist movement and had for a number of years been attending séances before his involvement with the SPR. Myers himself describes Gurney as the first English researcher who applied a critical psychological eye to the study of hypnotism. Gurney spent three years designing experiments solely focused on ferreting out the nuances of psychical phenomena that sometimes occur during hypnotism, and like Myers, friends and colleagues claimed to receive psychical messages from Gurney after his death.[46]

The final brief biographical sketch is that of William James, prominent psychologist and founder of the United States branch of the SPR. *The Encyclopedia of World Biography Online* described James as "America's major philosopher and one of the great psychologists of all times."[47] Growing up alongside his brother, the famed novelist Henry James, William eventually secured a position at Harvard teaching psychology. He firmly believed in the importance of studying altered states of consciousness and did not shy away from studying mysticism—in fact, he advocated for "mental healing" as a form of treatment for disease. In 1884, after a convincing experience with a medium, James was inspired to form the United States chapter of the SPR. James began a long career of studying mediums and acts of clairvoyance, becoming ultimately convinced that telepathy "pointed to a new kind of reality."[48]

There are many additional people affiliated with paranormal research (including a whole swath of notable mediums), but my goal is not to exhaustively expand upon each of them here. Rather, with this section, I highlight some key figures to show not only a timeline of paranormal research but also to inspire readers to uncover more in their own research. Sources that contain further information in this regard can be found in the annotated entries starting in chapter 7. Before I end this chapter, let's move now to a brief overview of some contemporary paranormal scholars.

CONTEMPORARY PARANORMAL SCHOLARS

A scientist on the cusp of the historical and contemporary divide of paranormal research is J. B. Rhine; no discussion of the paranormal would be complete without the inclusion of Rhine and his work. The next chapter contains much more detailed information on Rhine and his research, but he's also necessary to briefly include here. J. B. Rhine was a prominent parapsychologist who researched psychical phenomena such as telepathy and clairvoyance and is credited with coining the term "extrasensory perception."[49] Along with his colleagues from Duke University, he helped establish the Parapsychology Labs of Duke University, a research organization that existed well into the 1960s and which conducted more than ninety thousand experiments.[50] The work that Rhine and his associates did to advance the field of parapsychology cannot be overestimated, and I would recommend that interested readers consult Rhine's book *Encounters of the Mind* to learn more.

Readers interested in ufology or cryptozoology, and in particular the cryptids of West Virginia, may be familiar with the next contemporary paranormal researcher: John Keel. Keel was an avid researcher of ufology, and after finishing his military service in Frankfurt in the 1950s, he spent time traveling through the Middle East, supporting himself by writing articles for various publications.[51] When he returned to the United States in 1957, he was commissioned to write an article on UFOs that didn't actually end up getting published, but which was responsible for jump-starting his interest in this phenomenon. As a result, he ended up traveling across the country chasing UFO reports and interviewing witnesses—travels that eventually led him to the small town of Point Pleasant, West Virginia, in 1966. During that time, the small town was plagued by reports of a large, red-eyed, winged creature and mysterious men in black. Keel's visits to the town, interviews with people, and investigations during this time led him to publish *The Mothman Prophecies*.[52] Keel's other works include *Jadoo: The Astounding Story of One Man's Search into the Mysteries of Black Magic in the Orient*; *What We Really Know about Flying Saucers*; *Our Haunted Planet*; *The Complete Guide to Mysterious Beings*; and a chapter in *Phenomenon: From Flying Saucers to UFOs; Forty Years of Facts and Research*. Keel's legacy remains to this day one of the most prominent impacts of journalist-researchers to the field of the paranormal.

Since I mention Keel and his interest in ufology, I'll highlight another ufologist here—Coral Lorenzen. After an experience with a UFO sighting when she was nine years old, Lorenzen dedicated herself to the scientific understanding of UFO phenomena. In 1952, her experience and deep interest led her to create the Aerial Phenomena Research Organization (APRO) alongside her husband Jim.[53] Even though the APRO no longer exists, it did conduct research for almost three decades, and as author Mark O'Connell reminds us, "APRO proved to be a formidable force, boasting three thousand members at its peak."[54] In addition to their work with APRO, in which they interviewed eyewitnesses and investigated reports of UFO sightings, Coral and Jim went on to publish seven books on their experiences and research.[55]

Josef Allen Hynek is another prominent name in ufology. A noted astronomer and researcher who held positions at Ohio State University, the Smithsonian Astrophysics Observatory, and Northwestern University's Lindheimer Astronomical Research Center, Hynek is a name you inevitably stumble upon when researching UFOs. Hynek was the director of McMillin Observatory at the Ohio State University when the government solicited his help with investigating and debunking cases of UFO sightings. In the first year of this work, referred to as Project Sign, Hynek was involved in more than 230 cases of UFO reports, and discovered that of those, 20 percent were unexplainable. After Project Sign, he went on to work with Project Blue Book but was dissatisfied with the government's handling and motivation. As reporter Greg Daugherty tells us, "he chafed at what he perceived as the project's mandate to debunk UFO sightings. He was also critical of its procedures, judging the Blue Book staff 'grossly inadequate,' its communication with outside scientists 'appalling' and its statistical methods 'nothing less than a travesty.'" After researching a spate of incidents in Michigan and claiming they were the result of nothing more than swamp gas, Hynek became a figure that was scorned, at times, from both sides of the UFO spectrum—from the government to citizens alike. Hynek didn't let scorn keep him from his pursuits, however, and in 1972 he published *The UFO Experience*, a work in which Hynek himself coined the term "close encounter" and gave a system of categories for labeling reports and UFO incidents. As a result of his research and involvement in UFO phenomena, he established the Center for UFO Studies in 1973, an international organization that still operates today.[56]

Moving on from ufology to cryptozoology, any discussion would be remiss without mentioning both Bernard Heuvelmans and Loren Coleman. As readers know from earlier, Heuvelmans is considered the father of cryptozoology, but has also been given the title "Sherlock Holmes of zoology"[57] due to his vast research on the mysterious, undiscovered animals of the world. His two seminal works that helped advance the field of cryptozoology are *On the Track of Unknown Animals* and *In the Wake of the Sea-Serpents*. Heuvelmans not only scoured through vast amounts of resources and records to find information for both of these works, but he also conferred with other cryptozoologists from around the world. Loren Coleman, a modern-day cryptozoologist and friend of Heuvelmans, wrote in memory of his friend that "down through the years, without fanfare, Heuvelmans journeyed from the shores of Loch Ness to the jungles of Malaysia, from Africa to Indonesia, interviewing witnesses and examining the evidence for cryptids."[58] Coleman himself is a notable cryptozoologist who began his research in the 1960s; he has written seventeen books and countless articles on cryptids and is the founder of the International Cryptozoology Museum that readers can visit in Portland, Maine.[59]

Departing from the world of cryptozoology, another contemporary researcher of the paranormal is Dean Radin. Dr. Radin is the chief scientist at the Institute of Noetic Sciences, an organization whose mission "is to reveal the interconnected nature of reality through scientific exploration and personal discovery, creating a more compassionate, thriving, and sustainable world" and which is "inspired by the power of science to explain phenomena not previously understood."[60] He is also a professor at the California Institute of Integral Studies and has published four books and hundreds of journal articles on his work investigating psychical research. In his book *Real Magic*, Dr. Radin reminds us that while our current scientific advancements are wonderful, viewing the world strictly through science would mean missing out on wide swaths of other potential realities:

> First, there's no doubt that science is the most accurate lens on reality that humanity has developed so far. What we've collectively discovered about the nature of Nature over the last three or four centuries, from the quantum to the cosmological, is an awe-inspiring testament to our creativity and imagination. Technologies based on that knowledge provide proof that our discoveries are valid. So, when considering real magic, it would be foolish to just throw away what we've already learned. . . . But second, reality viewed through the lens of science is an exceedingly thin slice of the whole shebang. Science is tightly focused on the objective, measurable, physical world. That focus excludes the one and only thing you can ever know for sure—your *consciousness*, that inner spark of sentience that you call "me."[61]

In research from 2018, Dr. Radin and colleagues investigated the percentage of scientists and researchers who have had an "exceptional human experience" (EHE). Their hypothesis was that, as conventional scientists operating from a materialist worldview, they would be less likely to report and/or experience an EHE, defined by Dr. Radin and his colleagues by a list of twenty-five phenomena including things like creating fire without tools, observing people/places/things from an unobservable distance as it was happening, or receiving information about the past without any way of knowing it. They discovered that their hypothesis was abundantly wrong, with 93 percent of participating scientist and engineer respondents indicating that they had had some sort of EHE. Interestingly, scientists and engineers reported EHEs at often higher frequencies than another group of "general public" respondents. One of these EHEs, for example, was labeled as "known information about past events or an individual's past experiences without any possible way of you knowing it." Thirty-five percent of the general public respondents indicated that they had experienced this EHE, while 43 percent of scientists and engineers indicated that they had also experienced this phenomenon.[62] This is just one example of the research conducted by Dr. Radin; additional works will be presented in the annotated bibliographies in later chapters.

Dr. Jeffrey Kripal is another notable contemporary scholar of the paranormal and author of *The Flip*, published in 2019, in which he challenges readers to question the origin of their assumptions about spirituality, and by extension, the mystical world around us. Dr. Kripal is the associate dean of the School of Humanities at Rice University and also helped established the GEM Program, a doctoral program focusing on Gnosticism, esotericism, and mysticism. According to his website, "he specializes in . . . putting 'the impossible' back on the academic table."[63] In one of his prominent works, *The Super Natural*, coauthored with ufologist Whitley Strieber, Kripal argues that paranormal experiences are very real and profound aspects of the human experience. He also urges readers to think deeply about the religious and mystical implications that can be discovered through an intellectual inquiry of these phenomena. A profound scholar, Dr. Kripal uses a term that I find utterly fascinating when it comes to his belief in the paranormal, and that is "phenomenologically actual."[64] Dr. Kripal recognizes the deep impact that paranormal experience has not only on peoples but also on cultures, and he provides inspiring research and literature challenging us to reach beyond our own assumptions and stigmas about the paranormal.

Dr. James Houran, with an extensive background in psychological research, is yet another contemporary psychical researcher to keep in mind. A member of the Parapsychological Association, Dr. Houran has written well over a hundred articles on topics such as "transliminality, the phenomenology of ghosts, haunts, and poltergeists, as well as the . . . psychology of paranormal belief and experience."[65] Most recently, in a 2019 article published in the *Journal of Parapsychology*, Houran and a number of colleagues presented the need for a more updated way to measure and classify ghost/haunting phenomena to better assist in advancing theories and data gathering, as they argue that there is not currently a consistent data-gathering measure employed cohesively enough to allow theories to bloom.[66]

Dr. Julia Mossbridge is yet another prominent psychical researcher. Dr. Mossbridge, in addition to being a psi researcher, is also a neuroscientist who conducts research on precognition as well as presentiment effect. Presentiment effect, which she refers to as "predictive anticipatory activity," is the ability to anticipate an event prior to the event's occurrence. Her research has helped legitimize and create a standard of research on presentiment. As part of her work at the Institute of Noetic Sciences, she assisted with the development of the app Psi-Q, now referred to as Psi3, which tests three psychical traits through a series of "games": precognition, psychokinesis, and clairvoyance.[67] The app, available to the general public, was actually the first app developed by IONS to test psychical abilities on a large scale.[68]

In terms of scholars on ESP, and in particular Ganzfeld experiments, Deborah Delanoy is a contemporary psychical researcher who has amassed a large research portfolio investigating this phenomenon. Delanoy taught psychology at the University of Northampton, where she went on to become associate dean for the School of Social Sciences, and also director of the Centre for the Study of Anomalous Psychological Processes.[69] In an article published in the *Journal of Parapsychology* in 1996, Delanoy and fellow researchers set about to test a "new, improved approach to security measures within the Ganzfeld setting" that had been proposed and to offer their own suggestions on the future of Ganzfeld experiments of psychical phenomena.[70] Delanoy's research portfolio illustrates just how specific and nuanced contemporary paranormal research can be.

Dr. Etzel Cardeña is another noted parapsychologist. He is a psychology professor at Lund University in Sweden as well as the director of the Center for Research on Consciousness and Anomalous Psychology (CERCAP). His research includes inquiries on consciousness, hypnosis, meditation, and general parapsychology, and he has more than three hundred publications to his name. In a notable edited work, *Varieties of Anomalous Experience*, Dr. Cardeña and colleagues present a wide variety of articles that discuss research into and experiences about lucid dreaming, synesthesia, near-death experiences, past lives, and even alien abductions. His work will undoubtedly pop up in any psychical research you conduct.

The researchers in this section are but a drop in the bucket of contemporary paranormal researchers working today. I provide this list to highlight some of the notable people affiliated with the paranormal but also to shed light on the many diverse research paths that the paranormal can take—a trait that reinforces how the paranormal touches many aspects of our lives. The works of the researchers listed in this chapter (and more) are included in chapters 7–9. For readers interested in learning more about prominent parapsychologists in particular, be sure to check out the online resource *Psi Encyclopedia*, published by the Society for Psychical Research.

NOTES

1. Radin, Dean. (2019). Biography. Retrieved July 30, 2019, from http://www.deanradin.org/

2. Aveni, Anthony. (1996). *Behind the crystal ball: Magic, science, and the occult from antiquity through the New Age*. New York, NY: Times Books, 9.

3. Maher, Michaeleen. (2015). Ghosts and poltergeists: An eternal enigma. In Etzel Cardeña, John Palmer, & David Marcusson-Clavertz (Eds.), *Parapsychology: A handbook for the 21st century*. Jefferson, NC: McFarland, 327.

4. Hutton, R. H. (1885). The Metaphysical Society: A reminiscence. In *The Nineteenth Century*, the Huxley File compiled by C. Blinderman & D. Joyce from Clark University. Retrieved May 21, 2019, from https://mathcs.clarku.edu/huxley/comm/Hutton/Hut-Meta.html

5. Haynes, Renée. (1982). *The Society for Psychical Research 1882–1982: A history*. London, England: Macdonald, xiii.

6. Ibid., 15.

7. Ibid., 15–18.

8. Ibid., 25.

9. Ibid., 29–33.

10. Gurney, Edmund, Myers, Frederic W. H., & Podmore, Frank. (1886). *Phantasms of the living: Volume one*. London, England: Rooms of the Society for Psychical Research.

11. Richet, Charles. (1923). *Thirty years of psychical research: Being a treatise on metaphysics*. New York, NY: Macmillan, 15.

12. Ibid., 16.

13. Ibid., 21.; Franz Anton Mesmer. (2019, May 19). In *Encyclopaedia Britannica*. Retrieved August 13, 2019, from https://www.britannica.com/biography/Franz-Anton-Mesmer

14. Franz Anton Mesmer, in *Encyclopaedia Britannica*.

15. Richet, *Thirty years of psychical research*, 22.

16. Ibid., 23.

17. Ibid.

18. Ibid.

19. Ibid., 25.

20. Ibid; Abbott, Karen. (2012, October 30). The Fox sisters and the rap on spiritualism. Smithsonian.com. Retrieved August 13, 2019, from https://www.smithsonianmag.com/history/the-fox-sisters-and-the-rap-on-spiritualism-99663697/

21. Abbott, Fox sisters.

22. Richet, *Thirty years of psychical research*, 26.

23. Abbott, Fox sisters.

24. Richet, *Thirty years of psychical research*, 27.

25. Kneeland, Timothy W. (2008, July). Robert Hare: Politics, science, and spiritualism in the early republic. *Pennsylvania Magazine of History and Biography, 132*(3), 245.

26. Richet, *Thirty years of psychical research*, 29.

27. Ibid., 30.

28. Ibid; Alvarado, Carlos S. (2018, April 8). William Crookes. In *PSI encyclopedia*. Society for Psychical Research. Retrieved August 14, 2019, from https://psi-encyclopedia.spr.ac.uk/articles/william-crookes

29. Richet, *Thirty years of psychical research*, 31.

30. Ibid.

31. Ibid., 32.

32. McCorristine, Shane. (2011). William Fletcher Barrett, spiritualism, and psychical research in Edwardian Dublin. *Estudio Erlandeses, 6*(6), 39.

33. Noakes, Richard. (2004). The "bridge which is between physical and psychical research": William Fletcher Barrett, sensitive flames, and spiritualism. *History of Science, 42*(4), 419.

34. McCorristine, William Fletcher Barrett, 40.

35. Noakes, Richard. (2004). *Entry on William Fletcher Barrett*. Chicago, IL: Chicago University Press, 2. Retrieved July 31, 2019, from https://ore.exeter.ac.uk/repository/handle/10871/15939

36. Alvarado, Carlos S. (2018). Eleanor Sidgwick (1845–1936). *Journal of Parapsychology, 82*(2), 127.

37. Maher, Ghosts and poltergeists, 327.

38. Sidgwick, Arthur, & Sidgwick, Eleanor M. (1906). *Henry Sidgwick: A memoir*. London, England: Macmillan, 358.

39. Schultz, Bart. (2004). *Henry Sidgwick—Eye of the universe: An intellectual biography*. Cambridge, England: Cambridge University Press. 276.

40. Ibid., 1–2.

41. Ibid., 277.
42. Ibid., 277–280.
43. Frederic William Henry Myers. (2001). In *Encyclopedia of occultism and parapsychology*. Detroit, MI: Gale in Context: Biography. Retrieved August 14, 2019.
44. Ibid.
45. Ibid.
46. Edmund Gurney. (2001). In *Encyclopedia of occultism and parapsychology*. Detroit, MI: Gale in Context: Biography. Retrieved August 14, 2019.
47. William James. (1998). In *Encyclopedia of world biography online*. Detroit, MI: Gale in Context: Biography. Retrieved August 14, 2019.
48. Ibid.
49. J. B. Rhine: American Parapsychologist. (2019, February 16). In *Encyclopaedia Britannica*. Retrieved July 31, 2019, from https://www.britannica.com/biography/J-B-Rhine
50. Ibid.
51. Skinner, Doug. (n.d.). John A. Keel: A brief biography. Retrieved July 31, 2019, from https://www.johnkeel.com/?page_id=21
52. Ibid.
53. Coral Elsie Lorenzen. (2001). In *Contemporary Authors Online*. Detroit, MI: Gale in Context: Biography. Retrieved August 14, 2019; O'Connell, Mark. (2017). *The Close Encounters man: How one man made the world believe in UFOs*. New York, NY: HarperCollins, 101.
54. O'Connell, *Close Encounters man*, 101.
55. Coral Elsie Lorenzen, in *Contemporary Authors Online*.
56. Daugherty, Greg. (2019, June 5). Meet J. Allen Hynek, the astronomer who first classified UFO "close encounters." History.com. Retrieved August 15, 2019, from https://www.history.com/news/j-allen-hynek-ufos-project-blue-book
57. Bernard (Joseph Pierre) Heuvelmans. (2002). In *Contemporary Authors Online*. Detroit, MI: Gale in Context: Biography. Retrieved August 14, 2019.
58. Coleman, Loren. (2001). Bernard Heuvelmans (1916–2001). The Cryptozoologist: Loren Coleman. Retrieved August 14, 2019, from http://www.lorencoleman.com/bernard_heuvelmans_obituary.html
59. Cryptozoologist: Loren Coleman. (2012). Who is Loren Coleman? Retrieved August 14, 2019, from http://lorencoleman.com/who-is-loren-coleman/
60. Institute of Noetic Sciences. (2019). IONS: About. Retrieved July 30, 2019, from https://noetic.org/about/
61. Radin, Dean. (2018). *Real magic : Ancient wisdom, modern science, and a guide to the secret power of the universe*. New York, NY: Harmony Books, 2.
62. Wahbeh, Helané, Radin, Dean, Mossbridge, Julia, Vieten, Cassandra, & Delorme, Arnaud. (2018) Exceptional experiences reported by scientists and engineers. *Explore: The Journal of Science & Healing*, *14*(5), 329–341. doi:10.1016/j.explore.2018.05.002
63. Kripal, Jeffrey J. (2018). Jeffrey J. Kripal: Life. Retrieved August 15, 2019, from https://jeffreyj kripal.com/life/
64. Kripal, Jeffrey J. (2014). Better horrors: From terror to communion in Whitley Strieber's *Communion* (1987). *Social Research: An International Quarterly, 81*(4), 899.
65. Parapsychological Association. (2019). James Houran. Retrieved August 15, 2019, from https://parapsych.org/users/jhouran/profile.aspx
66. Houran, James, Laythe, Brian, O'Keeffe, Ciaran, Dagnall, Neil, Drinkwater, Kenneth, & Lange, Rense. (2019). Quantifying the phenomenology of ghostly episodes: Part I—Need for a standard operationalization. *Journal of Parapsychology, 67*(2), 35–37. doi:10.30891/jopar.2019.01.03
67. Duggan, M. (2020). Julia Mossbridge. In *Psi encyclopedia*. London, England: Society for Psychical Research. Retrieved January 8, 2020, from https://psi-encyclopedia.spr.ac.uk/articles/julia-mossbridge
68. Mossbridge, Julia. (2017, June 23). Do you wonder about your PsiQ? Institute of Noetic Sciences. Retrieved January 8, 2020, from https://noetic.org/blog/do-you-wonder-about-your-psiq/

69. Society for Psychical Research. (2018). Deborah Delanoy. Retrieved August 15, 2019, from https://www.spr.ac.uk/about/people/deborah-delanoy

70. Dalton, Kathy S., Morris, Robert L., & Delanoy, Deborah L. (1996). Security measures in an automated Ganzfeld system. *Journal of Parapsychology, 60*(2), 129–147.

Chapter Three

Best Practices in Conducting and Gathering Paranormal Research

Although the majority of this book serves as a bibliographic guide to researching the paranormal, I do want to include a brief section outlining some best practices when it comes to conducting paranormal research of your own. It makes sense that those interested in discovering more scientific literature concerning the paranormal may also be interested in learning more about conducting investigations and becoming involved with the paranormal on their own. After a discussion on how to ethically and scientifically conduct your own research, I will discuss the methods one should employ when seeking out and gathering others' research about the paranormal.

This chapter will be useful for those who are actively engaged in conducting their own paranormal research and/or those interested in learning how to get started. Additionally, this chapter will be useful to those interested in learning where to start in gathering primary or secondary research on a variety of paranormal topics. I will discuss how to begin thinking about paranormal research and will highlight collections and organizations that will be helpful for those interested in reading up on the scientific literature of the paranormal. After this discussion, in chapter 4, I will discuss the importance of gathering credible paranormal research, as once you understand how to think about the paranormal research process, it is important to understand how to apply components of credibility to sources you come across. This is no different from most information-gathering habits you have likely experienced. For example, how many of us have been guilty of googling the symptoms of a stomachache only to convince ourselves that we have contracted an obscure illness? (Yes, I'm raising my hand too—even librarians aren't perfect.)

I'm including this chapter to pay homage to those everyday paranormal investigators who, like me, are very much interested in this topic and who occasionally engage in investigative techniques. I hope that this chapter highlights that one does not need to be a PhD-holding scientist in order to engage in scientific pursuits of the paranormal. While the lay paranormal researcher will likely not be contributing to the vast body of scientific knowledge about this topic, that doesn't mean that paranormal investigation cannot be done respectfully and scientifically by the general public. Furthermore, engaging in paranormal investigation is simply downright fun. If you're like me and are interested in the prospect of touring historic or abandoned locations, interviewing homeowners who claim to experience paranormal phenomena, or simply sitting in the dark and letting the mysteries of the world unfold around us, you find all these strange endeavors scintillating.

THE INS AND OUTS OF CONDUCTING YOUR OWN PARANORMAL RESEARCH

In this section, I discuss some best practices for conducting your own paranormal research. I draw from methods used in the scientific literature as well as from the experience I've gathered as a paranormal investigator. Let me preface this section by reminding readers that no paranormal investigation should ever be conducted that violates lawful conduct. Therefore, efforts at securing permission to visit sites and/or conduct investigations on property should always be secured beforehand with those able to grant permission. Credible paranormal investigators don't break the law in the name of getting a few good stories. Equally as important, any evidence gathered during an unlawful activity will never be able to be publicly shared or discussed and is therefore of no value to the general body of knowledge about paranormal phenomena. I'm sure that readers understand the importance of being an ethical investigator, but it is important to include as a reminder nonetheless.

I would also like to remind readers that you don't have to have the fanciest, most expensive gadgets in order to be a credible paranormal investigator. The equipment that I use isn't anything revolutionary. What is most important is that investigators follow strict, scientific procedures using whatever tools they've decided to utilize. My best practices is really quite brief, as there are only some overarching guidelines that I think are "must-haves" and all else can be left to the discretion of the researcher. No two paranormal investigations look alike, and limiting oneself to the same methods can, I think, actually stifle creativity and innovation.

That being said, to get started with conducting paranormal research of your own, spend time seeking out some of the articles and sources listed in this book to get an idea of how other researchers have conducted experiments. You will quickly discover that there are a wide variety of methods that have been employed in investigating the paranormal, and these resources will not only explain their methods but also discuss the theories behind their methods, giving you as a researcher some background knowledge about how and why particular phenomena may occur. Immersing yourself in the scholarly literature beforehand can simply help you know what to look out for, but it may also help you design an experiment of your own. Researchers include information on their methods, after all, so that their experiments can be duplicated by others.

Once you have a specific paranormal target in mind, be it a location, an interview or observation with a person, or even an attempt to replicate an anomalous event, the most important thing when conducting paranormal research is to control your environment. What this means is that you should conduct your experiment with as little outside interference as possible. When investigating a location, for example, this could be quite challenging. After all, in this case, you cannot control much of the environment, but what you can do is thoroughly document your surroundings. Let's say you are investigating a local museum that is situated close to the road. If you have camera technology, it would be a good idea to have a camera pointed toward the street so that any passing vehicles will be noted along with a time stamp. If you don't have camera technology, this can still be done by placing an investigator outside who is responsible for noting the times when any vehicles pass by, any people pass by walking their dogs or perhaps smoking, or any other event that could potentially affect your research environment. Consider, for example, how the sound of a car passing by may result in an investigator situated in an upstairs bedroom claim that they just heard a sigh or whisper. Being able to refer to a time-stamped list of outside, uncontrolled factors will help ensure that nonparanormal factors don't get mistaken for the anomalous.

Just as outside influences should be documented via time stamp (whether it be digitally on a camera or written manually by an investigator), so too should any sensations, sounds, or observations by investigators be time-stamped as well. This means that all investigators should have some type of timekeeping apparatus that allows them to notate when they have noticed or experienced something strange. For example, if I note that at 12:45 a.m. I saw a strange light sweep across the room that I was investigating, I can cross-reference that to see if any vehicles, for example, drove past the house at that moment.

There are a number of ways that you can indicate time-stamped activity. You can certainly use the tried-and-true method of manually noting any event that occurs, or you can ensure that all technology used during the investigation is time-stamped together. To do this, you simply create a collective starting point for your devices. This can easily be done with items like handheld audio recorders. Simply gather your investigators and ensure that everyone hits Record at the same time, and note that time on a document. If you are using recording devices and they have been synced to a time stamp, investigators can simply state out loud when they experience something. These events will be picked up on the audio recording, and because it has been synced to a set time, a time stamp can be established. Cameras can be a bit trickier to time-stamp. If it is not possible to plug them in all at once, you can certainly use the time stamp on your DVR to sync your audio devices and label that time as the specific beginning moment of the investigation. If you are using separate camera and audio devices, syncing your audio recorders to the time stamp on the DVR is highly recommended.

Documentation is one of the most important things to adhere to in any investigation. Not only do you want to pay close attention to time-stamping events for cross-reference and analysis, you should also ensure that you've documented the time stamp so you know when the equipment was officially synced. Additionally, you also want to have a detailed outline of the equipment you have used, and where each unique piece of equipment has been placed in the location. For this reason, it's good practice to label your equipment so that you can easily note that "Recorder One" is in the kitchen while "Recorder Two" is in the upstairs hallway. Creating a blueprint of the location you are investigating and where all equipment resides will help in your later analysis but also helps ensure that you have adhered to strict documentation and recording.

Another way to control your environment is to keep a list of all investigators present and adhere to a set schedule of rotated investigation. In other words, if you have multiple investigators, you don't want one person investigating downstairs while simultaneously someone else investigates upstairs—this is a situation perfect for interference. If you're investigating downstairs, for example, moving around and asking questions, and perhaps shining a flashlight, all of these activities could potentially bleed through to the audio recorders and cameras in a different area of the location. What you've done is sabotage your own environment. For this reason, you should establish a schedule for investigators to follow so that when one group is investigating, another group could be quietly in another location reviewing cameras in real time or even outside noting any passing cars, people, animals, sounds, and so forth.

In terms of how to use technology such as audio recorders or cameras, it's always a good idea to place these items in fixed locations for the duration of your experiment so that you know where they are located at every moment. Honestly, this is nicer than having to carry a recorder or camera around with you. As an investigator, placing your technology in fixed locations ensures that you are unencumbered and free to observe. In terms of placing camera equipment, it's always best practice to try to cover any entrances or exits to a room. That way, if anything anomalous occurs, such as sound or movement, the camera will reveal if any person had entered the room at that moment. Essentially, by covering the entrances to rooms, you help eliminate the possibility that someone could have entered and tampered with the environment, whether knowingly or not.

Your paranormal research can be as complex or as simple as you'd like to make it. What is most important is controlling your environment, time-stamping equipment, and documenting everything. By doing these things, when you review your experiment you can more easily eliminate those moments that were a result of interference and identify those moments that are anomalous. After your review, you will likely gather an entirely different set of questions or theories that you can use when revisiting locations or tweaking experiments to continue your search into the unknown. I'd like to end this section by stressing that no two paranormal investigations are going to look the same, and that's a good thing. Creativity and outside-the-box thinking are wonderful attributes that can be applied to pursuits of the paranormal, and investigators should understand that as they continue their pursuits their methods will likely change and new questions will emerge—such is the nature of investigating that which we don't fully understand.

I'd like to point out that the methods above are all outlined from my personal experience researching ghost and haunting phenomena and from methods developed by Dr. Brian Laythe, the founder of ISRAE. As such, some of these specific methods may not be useful for every situation. However, as stated above, the most important things to remember (regardless of your topic of study) is to keep detailed notes/diagrams/images, and to control your environment as best as you can. Be empowered to conduct your investigations the way you want to conduct them; the goal is the same and the methods are many.

GATHERING AND SEEKING OUT PARANORMAL RESEARCH

When it comes to gathering paranormal research, there are some strategies I'd like to suggest now that can help you capture a comprehensive understanding of a particular topic. Earlier, you may have noticed that I used the phrase "primary or secondary research." Some readers may know the difference between the two, and I'd be willing to bet that any readers currently in college have heard their professors describe these in class. To give all readers an overview of these two different types of research, I will describe them here. Primary research is that which outlines the research endeavors of the authors themselves—in other words, some type of experiment or analysis was conducted that tested a particular hypothesis. For example, in one article that will be discussed later in this book, a researcher invited two groups of people to a reportedly haunted location. The first group of people included those who claimed to possess psychic abilities, and the second group consisted of people who had never claimed to hold any psychic prowess. The researcher asked each member of the "nonpsychic" group to walk through the location and make note of any particular areas in which they felt odd or frightened or otherwise uneasy. Then, the researcher asked each member of the psychic group to do the exact same thing in an effort to determine if there was any overlap between the two groups that perhaps could account for some sort of underlying environmental influence.[1] In other words, the author of this article conducted their own research, established an experiment, and tested a hypothesis, thereby establishing the report of their experiment as a primary research article. Quite often, primary research manuscripts will contain phrases such as "the authors tested" or "the authors conducted an experiment"—words and phrases that tell readers that some authoritative research method was employed.

On the other hand, secondary research occurs when an author or authors compile an analysis about primary research. To make this case clear, the book you are reading right now is an example of secondary research. I am not conducting any original research within these pages; I am merely outlining a topic, summarizing the work of others within my own discussion, commenting on those works, and presenting annotated lists of sources that may be useful to those interested in learning more about particular subtopics of the paranormal. Sometimes the line between these can be blurry, but a good rule of thumb is that secondary research sources don't make any claims that they've conducted any original research—they will not usually include a detailed methods section or contain a data analysis section. Within secondary research, in fact, the authors will refer directly to the original researchers they are discussing and say things like, "Anderson's research reveals . . ." or "Duchovny's data tells us . . ." On a side note, any fellow paranormal pop culture lovers who caught that reference should feel free to look me up and wax poetic about your favorite episode. Secondary research sources could also be discussing a topic in a professional and scholarly way. It isn't necessarily a requirement that any original research be referenced, but what's most important is that secondary research is a compilation of credible sources of and discussion surrounding some topic. The components of determining credibility, which is extremely important and necessary to be taken seriously as your own researcher, will be discussed in the next chapter.

This discussion about primary and secondary research isn't a discussion about one type of research being inherently better than the other. However, I would urge readers who are interested in researching the literature surrounding topics of the paranormal to ensure that you seek out sources that contain original research. If you find an article in which an author is describing the significance of a particular experiment surrounding psychokinesis, for example, it would be beneficial to then track down that original primary research source to delve into the experiment yourself. Whenever possible, it is always useful to track down the source of any discussion so that you, as a researcher, can come to your own intelligent decisions.

I imagine that some readers might be shaking their head and saying, "Um, this sounds an awful lot like a classroom lecture," and that would be a fair assessment. I bring these points up to not only remind readers about the importance of tracking down the original references in their sources, but also to set the stage for the many scholarly sources that will be discussed below. It is my suspicion (and I could be wrong) that there is a fair number of people who are unaware that the paranormal has a long and established place in the annals of scholarly research. Hopefully some of the discussion above has helped shed light on that fact, but I fear that those interested in learning about the paranormal don't ever go beyond a quick Amazon search. And that's certainly not a dig against Amazon (this librarian's bank statements would quickly reveal her to be a hypocrite on that matter); it's just that Amazon won't provide access to many of the scholarly research that is discussed below. Amazon will be a wonderful tool to gain access to some of the sources below, but my point here is that if you, as a person interested in learning more about the serious and scholarly side of the paranormal, limit yourself to only those sources available through Amazon, you will immediately be cutting yourself off from a large percentage of articles, manuscripts, and other sources.

While we're at it, let's examine this whole "Amazon-as-discovery-tool" discussion a bit further. While I enjoy using Amazon to purchase incense, beauty products, birthday presents, and the odd book or two (read twenty), I don't rely on Amazon to provide me with an exhaustive compilation of definitive resources on a topic that I wish to understand in a serious and scholarly way. This isn't to say that there are no serious sources to be accessed via Amazon—but there are some very real cautions to consider. First, I simply don't have the deep pockets to purchase everything I ever wish to read via Amazon. Secondly, and as mentioned above, Amazon doesn't provide access to a vast number of scholarly sources. And thirdly, I believe that we should curb our knee-jerk reaction to own every source we are curious about reading. It's great that we live in a book-loving world, but why do so many forget about the powers of their local libraries? Maybe it's because we live in an immediate gratification world—I'm certainly guilty of giving in to that every now and then. Maybe it's because of capitalism and the seduction of ownership as status—who knows? It isn't my goal to examine all the reasons we succumb to instant gratification, but it is worthy of our discussion here.

As stated above, limiting yourself to the Amazon catalog will not only ensure that you overlook a large number of sources, but it will very likely be vastly more expensive than all but a small percentage can afford—and that is simply because there is so much serious and credible research that has been done regarding the paranormal. Now, I understand that some people might feel a bit deflated by my suggestion not to start your serious research with Amazon. So, let me try to assuage some of that by describing the ways in which you can access the information presented below. Let me preface this discussion by saying that if you have a library card, you're already one step ahead of the rest.

Consulting your local libraries will tremendously boost your chances of locating many of the sources discussed in this book, and during the process you will save a small fortune. Not only do libraries offer access to information for free (let's not get into the taxpayer argument, please), but they also provide access to qualified researchers who can not only help you research topics but will also help track down sources that they may not individually hold at their respective libraries. Think of it this way—many libraries in the United States (and sometimes even the world) are connected via information-sharing services like interlibrary loan. This service means that you can ask your library to essentially borrow a book on your behalf. For example, if I wish to track down a particular title on parapsychology but my local library doesn't have it, I can ask if they will request it via interlibrary loan. During this process, a library that I'm not a member of will agree to loan the item to another library for a specific period of time, during which the library will then lend it to me. Some libraries offer this service for free, while others may charge a small fee to cover postage. The savings are tremendous, but equally as important is the fact that you will be able to access items not conveniently found in Amazon's array of items for sale. Items that you can obtain via this service can be traditional books, but they can also be journal articles—you'll note that there is a vast number of journal articles that are included later in this book.

Journal articles brings me to my next point regarding libraries. Some readers who are perhaps students, staff, or faculty at institutions of higher education may already be aware of this, but academic libraries offer many of these same services as well. In fact, many academic libraries in the United States situated on state university campuses are open to and serve members of the general public. I have discovered, based on my conversations with patrons at the academic library where I work, that it's not common knowledge that the public can freely access the academic library. It's understandable that this misconception exists—after all, the majority of a university exists to serve the needs of the students, and of course, private institutions are not often openly accessible to the public. Nonetheless, I would urge readers to investigate the accessibility of the academic libraries surrounding them for a number of reasons. First, academic libraries, due to their target audience of students, scholars, and researchers, will have subscriptions to pricey scholarly databases that may include many of the journals and/or journal articles presented in this book. While some very large public libraries may also subscribe to one or two of these databases as well, it's not very common for public libraries to maintain subscriptions to scholarly databases, and certainly not upwards of five hundred databases, such is the number at my academic library. And to put it into perspective, my academic library is situated on a regional campus of a flagship university, so if you are near one of the flagship universities, you may likely find double or triple the number of databases available. Of course, the major drawback for accessing electronic resources like databases at the academic library is that off-site access is usually restricted to students and faculty. What does that mean? It means that if you visit the library as a community or in-state member, you will likely only be able to access the online databases while physically inside the library. It's understandable that this might be inconvenient; however, access to these sources is still attainable. My point here is that no reader should assume that they won't be able to access any of the works listed below through some manner of assistance from local public and academic libraries.

So now we know that different types of libraries can help you learn more about the paranormal. Now that we understand that these libraries can help you locate resources, let's outline what some of these resources might be, and how best to locate them. There are many types of resources that contain information about the paranormal. This discussion of resource types isn't unique to the topic of the paranormal, so I urge readers to remember this for any intellectual pursuit. Perhaps the most obvious type of resource is books; some readers may already be familiar with some of the books listed below. In order to locate books, one can simply browse the library's online catalog on their personal device or computer. One of the great things about the digital world we live in is that you can find lots of information without even leaving the comfort of your home. And while these books may not be readable online, you should be able to determine if your local library has a copy of a specific title or on certain topics. This reminds me—when searching for books, it isn't necessary to know the title of a work beforehand—you can simply search for topics or even people that you are interested in. For example, if I'm curious if my local library has any works by Dean Radin, I can certainly just type his name and see what happens.

In terms of locating relevant books, it is important to keep in mind the practice of what I like to call "going from specific to general." In other words, I always advise searching as specifically as possible for an item you are interested in. For example, if I wanted to know if my local library specifically had *Harry Potter and the Sorcerer's Stone*, I wouldn't search for "wizards" and just hope for the best. Think specific first. Sometimes, however, this tactic leads you to a brick wall and makes it appear as if there are no resources when in actuality there are. Let's imagine a scenario to illustrate this. Let's say you are interested in finding resources on mediums. In this scenario, you know the topic that you are interested in, but you don't yet know of any specific titles. You pull up the library's catalog, type in "medium," and it tells you there are no results. You think to yourself that that's the end. And it may have been the end if you didn't remember that you can also go from specific to general. After you type in "medium," you think for a moment and type in "parapsychology," only to discover a handful of books on that topic located in your library. Once locating those items and browsing through the table of contents and/or the index, you discover that there are a few pages of information on mediums in one or two of those works—your tactic of going from specific to general has yielded results. This tactic is often useful because catalogs of information display results based on how those sources are classified and which keywords or terms are affiliated with them. Researchers often have to contemplate synonyms for their search terms or consider the larger field that their issue is affiliated with (in this example, mediumship is subsumed under parapsychology). It's not a perfect system; in other words, thinking creatively can often yield results.

Speaking of keywords, this brings me to an important point on doing any research. Keywords are exactly what they sound like—they are those "key" words or phrases that you use when searching for information. We are all used to using search phrases on a daily basis. When we say, "Hey Alexa, tell me when Stephen King was born," that is essentially a research question—in other words, it is your research need. When attempting to locate information in library catalogs (and even Google Scholar, so don't assume this is library specific), it is most beneficial to break your research question down into "key" words. In the case above, our keywords would be "Stephen King" and "birth date." However, an important thing to remember about keywords is that there are always several different ways to say the exact same thing, right? In the example above, then, we can just as usefully change our keywords to "Stephen King" and "birth" or "birthday" or "date of birth." Understanding the usefulness of always considering synonyms will keep you from overlooking potentially relevant sources when conducting research.

Aside from books, other information about the paranormal can be found in journals. Journals are compilations of articles that are published on a regular, periodic basis. For purposes of this book, we are separating journals from other periodically published items like newspapers. This is because journals usually contain articles that concern a specific topic or discipline. Newspapers, as many readers know, contain a wide variety of information on all types of topics and disciplines, and will be discussed directly afterward. Journals can be a great place to find information about the paranormal, and as readers will see, there is an entire section devoted to journals that cover a variety of topics in the paranormal. Journals can be one of two types: scholarly or popular. Scholarly journals contain articles that have gone through the "peer-review" process. This process, as indicated quite mysteriously by its name, is a process by which a researcher's work is reviewed by their peers to determine accuracy, quality, comprehensiveness, and several other items to ensure that it is of the highest academic standard of research and/or discussion. For example, if I was a Chupacabra expert and I decided to write an article for a scholarly journal outlining my research or theories on Chupacabras, my article would be sent to a handful of my peers. In this case, it would be sent to fellow Chupacabra experts in the country and perhaps even the world. My peers would analyze my paper and give me feedback regarding the quality of my paper. This could include giving suggestions on previous seminal Chupacabra research I failed to mention, advice on which sections to elucidate further, and any other comments they think would make my article stronger. Quite often what happens is that my peer reviewers will do one of two things: they will recommend that I make changes and resubmit the article or they may simply say that the article is dismissed entirely. If the latter is the case, I can submit my article to another journal or I can scrap my article and start over from the beginning. By going through the peer-review process, a journal ensures that its articles meet the standards of the greater academic community on that particular topic—in other words, it helps ensure that articles at that point in time are the most accurate and up-to-date representation of the topic at hand. Scholarly and peer reviewed are often used interchangeably, and scholarly is frequently held at the top of the totem pole of academic information. Scholarly journals contain articles written by experts in that particular field, and they often contain jargon or advanced technical language. The audience for these articles is usually fellow researchers; they quite often contain charts and data and are not found through a quick Google search—in fact, access to these articles is usually limited to expensive, subscription-based access that only institutions have the budgets to pay for.

The other type of journal is the popular one. In this case popular doesn't mean that it hangs out with all the cool kids. Popular journals are those journals that are likely more familiar to readers. *National Geographic* , *Nature*, *Popular Science*, *Discovery*, and *Time* are all examples of popular journals. These journals don't usually go through the peer-review process, they are written in more layperson-friendly language, they often contain multiple images, and they're often written by nonexperts who instead simply investigate a certain issue and report them for consumption by the general public. Popular journal articles can be a great way to begin learning about a topic for these very reasons. One of the key differences in terms of accessing these journals is that public libraries will very likely have subscriptions to vastly more popular journals than they do scholarly journals. Likewise, academic libraries will provide access to popular journals as well, though some may find it entirely accurate that their local public library contains more subscriptions to popular journals than their local academic library counterpart. The key to remember, again, is that that there are many institutions from which you should consider gathering information.

As discussed above, I would recommend investigating the availability of journals at an academic library near you. You can often browse an alphabetical list of journal titles, but you can also browse journal titles by typing in certain keywords. For instance, if I'm curious if an academic library provides access to any journals on the topic of mysticism or religious experiences, I could use the words "mysticism" or "religion" or even "religious" as keywords to generate a list of journal titles that include any of those words. From there, I can browse the issues of those journals or even search within them for specific topics I might be interested in.

You don't have to identify specific journals before searching for articles, however. Some academic libraries may have a feature that allows you to search the entire bank of databases, and you can start your search there. Of course, like I mentioned above, most academic libraries have a plenitude of databases, so searching all of them at once may yield an overwhelming number of search results. However, you can certainly modify your results by limiting perhaps to only books, or only articles written in the last ten years, or only articles written in newspapers, and/or articles written only in scholarly journals.

A key issue that I'd like to raise before we discuss newspapers is that this outline of sources to consult for paranormal information isn't a discussion of "better than, worse than." Just because I mention books first doesn't mean that I'm claiming they are the best source to begin with. They are simply the most familiar to people, and in my opinion that made them the friendliest to begin with. Of course, all types of information have pros and cons. Pros of scholarly journals are that they are vetted by scholar communities and represent the highest rigor of academic writing, but a con is that access to these journals won't be as easy as accessing a popular journal like *National Geographic*. A benefit of books is that they will contain a wealth of information and cover more ground, but a downside is that they take longer to publish and so you may not find as updated information in a book as you may in a journal. These sources of information exist on a spectrum, in which they all serve to enhance and add to each other. In fact, it's hard to get a comprehensive and holistic understanding of a particular issue if you limit yourself to one type of information. Scholarly articles, for example, will outline experiments and scientific understandings of paranormal phenomena, whereas books may likely do the same a bit more comprehensively or report on multiple projects and topics at once, whereas popular journal articles may outline recent, current events. In other words, don't limit your research to one type of information due to a misguided notion that one type of information is better than the rest.

Now that we understand that all information exists on a spectrum centered on your specific research need, let's not forget to mention the importance of newspaper articles. The greatest thing about newspaper articles is that they are amazing primary sources. Don't confuse this with the term "primary research" that was used above. A primary source is simply a source that was created at the time under investigation. In other words, *The Diary of Anne Frank* can be considered a primary source as it was written during the time in which you might be investigating. Photographs can serve as primary sources. For example, if you were doing a report on presidential inaugurations, a photograph of Barack Obama's first inauguration would qualify as a primary source. If you were researching the civil rights movement, then Martin Luther King Jr.'s "I Have a Dream" speech would be considered a primary source. Hopefully this illustrates what primary sources are. They can reveal loads of information about a particular moment in time (from photographic evidence to direct quotes of people involved), and newspapers are perfect resources to find such primary sources. For example, you can consult archives of newspapers to find the original news reports of the Roswell incident. In these articles you will see press photos of military personnel with supposed UFO debris in their hands, and you will also read direct quotes from the people involved in the early days of the incident. Newspaper articles can also help you establish a timeline of events and/or trace a story back to its first mention. Newspaper articles are wonderful sources for learning about reports of phenomena as paranormal and anomalous events often get captured in the public eye. Many public libraries may have archived copies of local newspapers—these archives copies may be physical editions and/or digitized versions that you can view online or through the use of a microfilm reader. Academic libraries as well may offer digitized access to local or statewide newspapers, and sometimes even the website for the newspaper itself (if it's still in print) may provide access to a certain portion of archived editions.

Newspapers, as we can see, serve as wonderful sources for historical information. There are additional resources you can use to gather historical information. Government websites, for example, can be helpful. The FBI's website contains links to a large amount of information on UFO-related research. Census Bureau records, many of which can be accessed through libraries, can provide information on former residents of certain addresses. Local history books found at the library can also reveal information about events in a town's history, former residents, births and deaths, marriages, and more.

Of course, institutional websites can be a good place to find paranormal information as well. For example, the website of SETI (Search for Extraterrestrial Intelligence) provides loads of information on research that they have conducted at their labs, and all the organizations listed above in chapter 1 have a web presence. Of course, searching for paranormal organizations on Google will provide links to a huge number of amateur groups engaging in various paranormal activities that may or may not be credible, so resorting to conducting your paranormal research on Google isn't the best place to start. And even though I said above that this discussion wasn't a matter of which type of information is better than the rest, I do urge readers to resist the urge to simply consult Google for their paranormal information needs—simply because there is no organizational or vetting process at play on the web at large. It also ties into the strategy described above as going from specific to general. Just like searching by specific titles or keywords, you should strive to start your research at specific sources already aimed at helping you find credible information such as library catalogs, journals, newspaper articles, and local history sources.

Hopefully this section has revealed helpful avenues to consider when searching for paranormal information. Overviews of each source were discussed as well as tips on how to use the majority of these resources through a specific focus on the keywords surrounding your paranormal research need. Don't forget that while Amazon and bookstores are certainly wonderful institutions, libraries (both public and academic) can offer vast amounts of paranormal research that are not available elsewhere. Additionally, libraries employ information professionals who enjoy helping students and researchers of all types not only find the information they need but learn how to effectively think about information and identify appropriate sources. Knowing what types of resources exist and where to find those resources is simply the first step of the process, however. What is even more important is understanding how to analyze those sources for credibility once you find them. You can't blindly trust that a source is credible without putting it through a series of tests; this is especially important for topics (like the paranormal) that are controversial to begin with. Chapter 4 will highlight ways in which you can determine the credibility of the paranormal resources you may find from consulting the sources listed in this chapter. Once you know how to both locate material and then analyze it for credibility, you will be on your way to becoming an ethical information consumer.

Did you also know that libraries can be valuable tools in conducting your own paranormal research? Libraries are not only helpful tools when seeking out paranormal research that others have done. They can also help you in the pursuits of your own paranormal investigations. For example, many public libraries have "local history" or "genealogy" sections that may contain items such as birth/death records, old yearbooks, newspaper clippings, cemetery listings, and much more. Additionally, you will find that many public libraries also have microfilmed copies of old, local newspapers. With just a few quick minutes of learning how to operate a microfilm reader (they're not as archaic and scary as they sound, I promise), you will find yourself digging through decades' and even centuries' worth of news and local reports. Many libraries also have access to maps of the areas, including those known as plat maps, which show land ownership, making families traceable via the land they once owned. The ways in which this information can be used are endless. A show that does a great job of highlighting the ways in which library and historical center records can be useful is the Discovery Channel's show *Kindred Spirits*. Some readers are likely familiar with this show, but for those who aren't, I would urge you to watch a few episodes. Not only are they quite well done, but they also show the investigators visiting and digging through information found in local public libraries, archives, and historical centers. It highlights the research process that should be included in an actual, ethical paranormal investigation.

Hopefully this chapter has shed some light on how to begin thinking about paranormal research. If you've conducted investigations or research of your own, hopefully it has contributed some helpful tips for continuing your work. There's certainly nothing wrong with interacting with the paranormal in casual and fun ways, but if you find yourself wishing to dig a little deeper or conduct yourself a little more scientifically, I hope that this chapter can help you chart that path. In addition, I hope that readers have started to see that there is a wide variety of scholarly literature on the paranormal, and that they can easily access these resources and more. Because the resources listed later in this work are by no means a comprehensive report of sources available on the paranormal, it is important for readers to not only understand where to go to locate serious, intellectual resources, but how to evaluate sources for credibility. After all, there is an overwhelming amount of information (on any topic) that isn't credible. One only has to consider the era of "fake news" that we are living in to understand this. The next chapter will help readers focus on specific traits of information to analyze that can help them determine if resources can be considered serious and scholarly. Knowing how to analyze information for credibility will allow readers to continue their intellectual pursuit of the paranormal (and truly any topic) on their own and for years to come.

NOTE

1. Maher, Michaeleen C., & Hansen, George P. (1992). Quantitative investigation of a reported haunting using several detection techniques. *Journal of the American Society for Psychical Research, 86*(4), 347–374.

Chapter Four

Analyzing for Credibility in Paranormal Research

This is coming from scientists. MENSA material. Brainiacs. Intellectuals. People with Ph.D.'s! What the hell is going on here?[1]

When it comes to finding research on any topic, you want to make sure that you consult credible sources. This might seem like common sense, and some readers may even be nodding their head and thinking, "Of course. We all know credibility is important." The topic of credibility, however, isn't one that is so easily navigable. We know deep down that credibility is an important thing, but it's likely something that many don't take the time to really investigate. It makes sense that it sometimes falls by the wayside—after all, with the influx of information swirling constantly around us, credibility can be easy to overlook. Sometimes sifting through resources and arriving at a seemingly relevant source of information is so relieving that we throw all concerns about credibility out the window, eager to simply trust that the author knows what they're talking about and that the quality of information contained therein is substantial.

Some people might think that credibility is something only students and academics are concerned with. Think about it: How many times have you googled something only to trust the first page of results that you stumble upon without digging further? After reading that first page or two of results, how often have you shared something you've learned or discussed it with friends without ever giving a second thought to the nuances of credibility? I can't recall hearing someone talk about the importance of analyzing information for credibility outside the confines of a classroom, and it is my hope that this chapter helps shine a light on how important this ability is, regardless of situation or topic. It's actually quite unfortunate that the issue of credibility isn't discussed beyond the classroom more often. The most we hear in general society and popular media are reports bemoaning the overabundance of "fake news," when in reality, these are issues that librarians have been talking about for decades.

Analyzing information to determine credibility is an important skill to have when consuming information on any topic, but it is particularly important when it comes to the paranormal. Why? The answer is a bit complex. First, there is an overwhelming number of urban legends and superstitions that get circulated repeatedly until you find yourself playing the world's biggest game of "paranormal telephone." The paranormal is a hot topic. Many people enjoy talking about it—and that's not necessarily a bad thing. It's clear that there's something about the paranormal that captures our imagination and interest, and it seems like every other person has a personal paranormal experience to share these days. Because of the popularity, however, it can be hard to sift through information to find sources that critically examine aspects of the paranormal.

Of course, popularity and the ubiquitous nature of the paranormal isn't the only factor muddying credibility. Because of the immense amount of information, there is not only a wide variety of types of information, but also a large variety of authors with all levels of varying backgrounds. For example, there is a multitude of podcasts, websites, magazine articles, YouTube clips, and newspaper articles about the paranormal. In chapter 3, I discuss four types of resources that can be used to find scholarly information about the paranormal—books, peer-reviewed or scholarly journals, popular journals, and newspapers. I'll note here that these aren't the only sources one can limit oneself to when scouring for credible information on the paranormal. However, they are primarily the sources outlined later in this book simply because these four types of resources provide a sound starting point for dissecting the paranormal from a more scholarly angle.

This brings me to my first point: let's not confuse the words "scholarly" and "credible." For something to be considered scholarly, it has gone through a peer-reviewed process, which I discussed earlier. Credible sources, on the other hand, are those sources that are accurate and trustworthy, and which contribute to the general conversation surrounding a topic. A piece of information doesn't have to be scholarly for it to be credible. Scholarly sources are, of course, certainly beneficial to include in your research, but there is a large amount of information that isn't scholarly but is still very credible.

Let's consider this example using the paranormal as our basis: You are researching the paranormal and specifically want to learn more about psychic abilities. You begin your search like most other people by going to Google. You enter the phrase "proof of psychic abilities." One of the first results is a link titled "The Reality of ESP: A Physicist's Proof of Psychic Abilities."[2] The title seems relevant, and your curiosity is piqued by the inclusion of the word "physicist," so you decide to investigate this link a bit further. Clicking on this link takes you to an article published in 2015 in a magazine called *Watkins Mind, Body, Spirit*. So far, everything seems good—the article has recently been published and it's been published in a magazine. You can't determine yet, though, if the article is credible for your research. At this point, taking a look at the author's credentials and the publisher's reputation is a worthwhile endeavor. Oftentimes you can simply skim the page for information on the author, though other times you may have to perform a web search for them. In this instance, you scroll to the bottom of the article and learn that Russell Targ is a NASA Award–winning laser physicist who helped found an investigation program at the Stanford Research Institute. Those are some pretty impressive author credentials. Those credentials alone, however, don't necessarily reveal that he is an authority on psychic abilities, so you have to investigate more. Some ways to do this are to independently search the author online or read the article for some clues to this question.

Before reading the article, however, it is also important to investigate the publication for authority and reputation. Ask yourself, "Who is the publisher and what agenda or bias might they have?" When you are looking at a web-based source, you can often find an "About" section located somewhere on the screen. In this case, the "About" section is located conveniently at the top of the page; reading through it reveals that *Watkins Mind, Body, Spirit* has been around since 1893 and is published by Watkins Books in London. The "About" page further reveals that this company is "one of the oldest and leading independent bookstores specialising in esoterica."[3] Continue to read about the organization to determine any biases they may have. In this case, it appears that you can confidently assume they are well poised to present on this topic in an unbiased manner.

The next step is to analyze the contents of the article—in other words, read through it. Throughout the article, there are multiple references to other studies and experiments done by institutions like the Stanford Research Institute, Princeton University, and Cornell University. These are pretty impressive references! Included in the discussion are the names of the researchers, meaning that these experiments can be cross-referenced to help determine the credibility of the current article under consideration. Additionally, reading through the resource will not only help ensure that it actually discusses the topic you are researching, but it can give you hints about the author's background knowledge and experience.

You have read through the article and have determined that the author, Russell Targ, lays out a pretty interesting case for the science behind psychic abilities. There are a number of other experiments referenced that you can (and should) track down, and the information is well written without typos and in a coherent, easy-to-understand manner. Your next step should be to analyze the credentials of the author themselves. If you are reading a digital source, sometimes the author's name will be hyperlinked, and you can click to view other sources by them and/or information on them. Other publications, especially books and journal articles, will provide some information about the authors themselves, such as their affiliated institutions or a bit of their background. However, a tactic that I would always recommend is to do an online search for the author to see what you can find. In this case, Russell Targ's name is not hyperlinked, but at the bottom of the article, there is a link to a book he's written. You can choose to start there, and view the book on Amazon, but let's see what happens when you type his name into Google. A quick search of his name reveals his background as a physicist and confirms the magazine article's claim of his involvement with the Stanford Research Institute. You also discover a link to what appears to be Targ's professional and personal website; here is where you learn that he has advanced degrees from Queens College and Columbia University, along with careers working at Lockheed Missiles and Space Company.[4] You also learn that he has published in such venues as *Nature* and the *Proceedings of the American Association of the Advancement of Science*. If you aren't familiar with these publications, then you can perform a search for their websites in exactly the same manner you search for the author—doing this reveals their stature as scholarly, credible organizations attempting to advance the understanding of science and the world around us. At this point you feel pretty confident about Targ's ability to not only serve as an authority on this topic but that the magazine, *Watkins Mind, Body, Spirit*, has presented the information in an unbiased and credible way.

At this point, you have considered the author's credentials and background, the reputation of the publisher, as well as scoured the contents of the article to determine its relevancy to our research question. You've also noted the publication date to see how current and/or outdated the information is. Unfortunately, there is no "References" or "Works Cited" on the original magazine article, so you will have to rely on locating those sources and experiments that Targ discusses in the article in order to verify that his information is correct. Even though Targ doesn't provide a handy list of sources at the end of his article, there is in-text information that can point you to additional sources that can verify or contradict what Targ writes. At this point, you need to ask yourself what purpose Targ has in writing this article. This is perhaps the most important step in analyzing a source because during this stage you analyze for the presence or absence of bias. In other words, did Targ write this article to persuade you to his point of view; to sell a product; to entertain you with some story or scintillating tidbits; or did he present the information in an attempt to spread awareness about and add to the general conversation about a particular topic? In this case, you decide that Targ's purpose is to spread awareness and have a conversation.

Ultimately, you decide that this source is good to include in your paper on the science behind psychic abilities. However, this source alone isn't enough for a balanced investigation of your topic. Think of it this way: You want to prepare a salad. A salad that only contains lettuce is pretty bland, while one that contains lettuce, tomatoes, carrots, croutons, cheese, egg, and dressing is much better. (You can pause here for a snack break if you'd like—the conversation about creating a balanced set of references continues below.)

Just like recipes don't require one ingredient for a successful dish, any good research will contain a variety of sources on your topic. Let's continue with this example to illustrate my point. You have one source currently—a recent magazine article written by a reputable publication from an author with some impressive credentials and a direct background on the topic. Now is a good time to seek out any scholarly, peer-reviewed publications on this topic. You can do this by going to Google Scholar and/or your library's list of databases. If you are researching at home and do not have credentials to log in into a library's set of databases, you can conduct a search using Google Scholar, but you can also seek out information from open-source scholarly databases on the internet—consider starting with BASE, https://www.base-search.net. Regardless of which route you take, your goal now is to find a scholarly, peer-reviewed article. You decide to head to the library's website and type the keyword phrase "psychic abilities and parapsychology" into a database. You know from earlier discussions that keyword strategies are important and that you shouldn't only just type the same phrase into different tools. You also know that psychic abilities are classified as parapsychology, so you decide to combine these terms. After browsing the search results for a few moments, you find an article titled "Individual Difference Correlates of Psi Performance in Forced-Choice Precognition Experiments: A Meta-Analysis (1945–2016)."[5]

This is a very different title from the first source, and some of these terms you may not even quite understand, but that's OK. From here, you engage in the same analysis you did with Russell Targ's magazine article, though there are some unique tactics to employ since this is quite different from a magazine article. From brief scrolling, you quickly see that this scholarly article is much longer than the magazine article—almost twenty-five pages, in fact. A good tactic to use when analyzing a scholarly article (or any source that is longer than a few pages) is to skim certain key areas of those sources. For a scholarly article, you will want to begin by reading the abstract. The abstract is that portion of the article that provides an overview or summary of what the article discusses. Once you do that, you should have a better idea of the contents of the article and if it actually fits into your research question—after all, titles can be confusing and/or misleading, and they certainly aren't long enough to reveal the nuances of the article in its entirety. Once you read the abstract, a good starting point is to skim certain key sections of the article.

Scholarly articles often have headings throughout—headings like "Introduction," "Method(s)," "Findings," and "Discussion" or "Conclusion." Navigating to certain sections and skimming them can give you a good idea of the overall message and usefulness of the article.

For instance, briefly skimming the introduction to this article reveals that the authors' goal is investigating and compiling other studies that specifically focus on forced-choice precognition experiments that analyze for certain individual personality traits as influencing success factors.[6] The introduction alone reveals to you that there are many types of psychic abilities, such as precognition and telepathy. Immediately, you are presented with some new information that wasn't explicit in your first source. Your understanding of the issue begins to grow. Remember, though, that there are other sections of the article. After skimming the introduction, you skip over the "Method" section and go directly to the "Results" section where you read some of the specific traits that the authors identify as influencing factors in the success of forced-choice precognition experiments.[7] If this section seems overwhelming to you, that's OK. Skip now to the "Discussion" section to see how the authors summarize their analysis. Right away, you discover that the authors claim some individual traits affecting psi abilities have not been studied extensively, even though they appear to affect psi significantly. As you continue to skim, you learn that certain individual traits appear to influence precognition more than others, and they discuss the need for replication studies to investigate these potential relationships further.[8]

As you skim the various sections of the article, you discover that the language used in this article is very different from the language used in *Watkins Mind, Body, Spirit*. Don't let that be a deterrent. If you don't understand one section of the article, skip to the "discussion" or conclusion, which often contains summarizing language that is a bit friendlier to digest than earlier sections of the paper. If you need to, read some sections twice and/or consult a dictionary to help you understand the lingo as you go. If the article contains such an overwhelming amount of scientific jargon that it's too difficult for you to read, then simply go back to the search results and find another article. At some point, the technical language surrounding this issue will begin to make more sense, especially if you are new to a topic or just beginning to research the issue. Nobody is an expert overnight, so don't consider it a sign of failure or weakness if you have trouble reading through these peer-reviewed scholarly articles. In fact, if you haven't used scholarly databases and/or Google Scholar much before, it might be a good tactic to begin by compiling magazine/newspaper articles, websites, and trade publications on your topic to build up your understanding of the vocabulary associated with your topic. Regardless of how and where you begin, though, remember that the research process is a constantly evolving practice and that you'll get better at it the more you do it.

At this point, you determine that the scholarly article is a good source to include for your paper as well. It outlines some specific types of psychic abilities and it discusses personality traits that might be influential. It also points out some of the weaknesses and limitations of psi research, and while this may initially seem discouraging, it is actually quite a positive thing. Understanding the limitations and/or weaknesses of the research you engage with is an ethical endeavor. For example, you may have chosen to research psychic abilities because you believe in psychics and enjoy reading about that topic. However, you cannot let your interest blind you to the limitations inherent in your sources. It isn't ethical to overlook those sections that disappoint you. For that matter, it is also important to intentionally seek out sources that argue the opposite of what you are researching. As a researcher, you also have implicit bias and should remain aware of how that affects your research process. If you intentionally choose to exclude an article because you disagree with the researchers, you are engaging in unethical tactics.

At this point, you have unearthed two sources that you consider credible enough to include in your research: an online magazine article and a scholarly publication. From here, you simply continue researching your topic using a variety of different tools like Google Scholar, library databases, book catalogs, or even websites. Whatever form the information comes packaged in is less important than if it meets the components of credibility. This is important to understand so that you don't begin to think that certain types of information are inherently useless. For example, there is just as much to learn from someone's personal blog post outlining their near-death experience as there is a neurologist's scientific report on their study of the effects of NDEs on the brain.

It is important to keep in mind that your research question will not be answered by one convenient, magical source. It is only through the combination of multiple sources and perspectives that you will begin to gather a holistic answer to your research question. It is just as important to understand that credibility exists on a spectrum. You may find a source that doesn't have any references listed (like the magazine article in the example above) but the other components of credibility are met. When combined with other sources, that small weakness of the magazine article suddenly doesn't seem so bad.

Hopefully this example illustrates how the various components of credibility work together. I'll now review these components in a step-by-step manner. A necessary caveat, however, is the reminder that credibility exists on a continuous spectrum—it is not something that fits neatly into check-marked boxes, and it is a task that must be engaged in each time you encounter a new piece of information. It may seem daunting, but once you begin to understand the various components of credibility, you will start to become a savvy consumer of information, and you'll be able to more effectively sort through the vast amount of information that is at our fingertips.

SARAH BLAKESLEE'S CRAAP TEST

In 2004, Sarah Blakeslee of California State University published an article titled "The CRAAP Test" in *Loex Quarterly*.[9] To develop a handy acronym for students to critically engage with the components of credibility, she created this wholly memorable term. The CRAAP test is an acronym that stands for: currency, relevancy, authority, accuracy, and purpose. It is a test that can be applied repeatedly to measure the credibility of a particular source. One should remember, however, that these traits exist on a spectrum, and a source doesn't necessarily have to fit all five components to be considered credible. The first component, currency, can help illustrate this point.

Currency—When Was This Published/Created?

Currency is the first component of the CRAAP test. Referring to the date that something was published, currency of an information source is important to consider. If you were researching the latest advancements in quantum theory, for example, you wouldn't want all your books or articles to come from the 1960s. Why not? The answer is very likely obvious to most readers—publication date matters because information changes and new discoveries and theories are constantly made. This doesn't mean that you can't have a source or two from the 1960s; it simply means that you should ensure that among your sources are those that are current, and which represent the latest scientific advancements in quantum theories. But remember, a source from the 1960s can still be useful as it may help you develop a historical timeline of your topic and/or help illustrate a particularly poignant person or event. Just because it's not the most up to date, then, doesn't mean that it should be discarded outright—this is the credibility spectrum.

Relevancy—Is This on Topic?

The next component of the CRAAP test is relevancy. Titles can sometimes be misleading, making you think they will be discussing one topic only to discover that it's really about something else entirely. To help you determine the relevancy of a particular source, try browsing key areas first. If you stumble across a book, skim the book jacket and table of contents. If it's still not entirely clear to you, read the first couple of pages of the introduction to gain a firm grasp of the scope of the work. If you are consulting a journal article, read the abstract, which is the summary often provided at the beginning of an article. Newspapers, magazines, and internet articles can often be scanned in their entirety to analyze for relevancy. What you're looking for here is confirmation that the work actually represents the topic that you are interested in—however you browse to determine that is fine.

Authority—Who Is the Author and What Is Their Experience?

The third component of the CRAAP test is authority. In other words, who is the author or authors, and what credentials or experience do they have surrounding the topic at hand? This does not necessarily mean that just because the author is a PhD-holding researcher that the source is credible by default. It's not just the mere presence of any advanced knowledge that determines authority. Authority refers to the connection of specific skills or expertise to the topic in the source. For example, a college professor who holds a PhD in molecular biology may have written an article about the particular stresses of first-year college professors. They don't hold a PhD in psychology (which one might consider an expert rank to discuss stress), but they do have first-hand knowledge about the first-year college professor experience, and that is what qualifies them as an authority on this topic. The nice thing about online sources is that authors are often hyperlinked, so one click can facilitate learning the expertise and background of authors. Likewise, a simple Google search can reveal pertinent information on authors. Sometimes, however, as is the case with newspapers, authors aren't listed. In this case, you can certainly investigate the reputation of the newspaper itself to determine how they select and publish articles. This can also be the case with websites that don't list specific people as authors, and which instead publish broadly as the organization. In those cases where organizations or publications are listed as the author, you will simply have to rely on what you know about that organization as well as the quality of the four other components of the CRAAP test.

Accuracy—Where Did This Information Come From?

The fourth component of the acronym is accuracy. What you ask here is, "Does the information presented in this source accurately represent this topic?" While this may seem like an obvious component—of course you want to consult sources that only accurately represent a topic—it is easy to overlook. The easiest way to scan for accuracy is to determine if the source lists a bibliography, reference page, or works cited page. In other words, do they provide a list of sources that they consulted in order to come to their conclusions or to present their information? If they do, make sure to scan the lists to get a sense for the types of information they consulted. As we are hopefully learning after all, the mere presence of such a list isn't an immediate qualifier for accuracy. If there isn't a separate reference page, maybe there are footnotes embedded in the text indicating where information was obtained. Sometimes, however, sources don't provide handy lists of references. Take newspaper articles, for example. Newspaper articles rarely, if at all, provide a list of references at their conclusion, so how can readers analyze for accuracy? Reading the article itself could reveal quotes or references to sources, which you can then track down to determine if it exists and/or was used appropriately. Accuracy also applies when data is presented—if there are charts or graphs, for example, do they explain how they arrived at their data? If you are consulting a journal article, this information is quite often found in the section labeled "Methods," making it easy to point to and determine if appropriate methodologies were employed. For example, if you unearth an article that shows a chart of the number of near-death experiences encountered by children between the ages of ten and fifteen sorted by geographic region, you should make sure that at some point in the article the author has outlined how they came by that information. Either they compiled it themselves or they got it from another source. If they compiled it themselves, they should have a detailed description of how they gathered all of that data, and if they found it from another source, it should be listed in the references.

Purpose—Why Was This Information Created?

Last but certainly not least, we arrive at the fifth and final component—purpose. This is perhaps the most important component of all. When analyzing a source for purpose, you ask yourself why this source was created in the first place. We may not consciously think about it, but information is created for all sorts of reasons. Let's contemplate presidential elections. All candidates publish information on their respective websites and in various handouts, pamphlets, newsletters, and so forth. During this period of time, potential voters are bombarded with all manner of figures, data, and statistics that claim to represent various issues or key talking points of each candidate. Pause for a moment to consider the authors' ultimate purpose—do they wish to inform us about a topic? Do they wish to sell us something? Are they trying to entertain us? Or do they want to persuade us to a particular point of view? Of course, we can all agree that the purpose in this example is to persuade consumers to vote a certain way. In these instances, the authors have a very clear and present bias. Understanding the potential biases that authors have can help you determine if a source is credible or if it is too tainted by its underlying bias.

On the flip side of questioning the bias of authors, we must also consider our own biases as researchers. This bias could play out in a number of ways. Let's consider that you are agnostic. In your research, you come across an article written in the *Christian Scholar's Review*. You may initially skip it because you assume it doesn't align with your personal convictions, but in doing so you are actually engaging your own bias. In terms of the paranormal, let's say you are researching haunting phenomena in a geographic area—it's an area you grew up in and that you've been fascinated by for years. You find an article written by a geologist that proposes a natural explanation for the seemingly paranormal phenomena that you've been so fascinated by. Not liking the author's conclusion, you ignore the article and continue your search for information. You've just engaged in bias. Part of research is a dedication to ethically investigate a topic, which means being aware not only of the bias inside your research, but the bias inherent in yourself as well.

When it comes to paranormal research, the components of credibility can help you sift through the endless number of sources that exist. And even though the above examples mention books, journal articles, newspaper, and magazines, they are components that can be applied to any piece of information in whatever format it appears. The key takeaway here is that these components must be balanced together to get a complete picture of credibility or lack thereof. And although you will find that some sources are more credible than others, those less credible sources are still beneficial to use. For example, you may find two sources that have some shortcomings but when used together represent a more accurate picture of the topic at hand. Ultimately, it is up to the individual researcher to determine credibility using the traits above as guidelines.

NOT ALL CREDIBLE SOURCES ARE SCHOLARLY, AND THAT'S OK

Let's transition back to the conversation about sources being scholarly versus credible. Sometimes it seems that there is a palpable disdain toward scientific pursuits of the paranormal. To be fair, there are many researchers, scientists, educators, and professional folks who value the pursuits of paranormal research, but there still seems to exist a certain outright disregard for these topics. Presenting information that is credible and/or scholarly can help combat this perception of the paranormal as nothing more than thrill-inducing folklore shared around campfires. Shining a light on the many sources of information that seek to critically question and investigate the paranormal can help elevate the status of this field. It can also help ensure that you, as a presenter of paranormal research, appear as an ethical and serious researcher.

A key point to keep in mind is the fact that information can be credible even if it's not scholarly. As we know, a scholarly source is something that has undergone the peer-review process. However, there is a wealth of information out there and not all of it is scholarly—thank god for that, actually, because quite a lot of scholarly information is expensive and/or can only be accessed through databases. Since we now understand the basic components of credibility, readers can hopefully understand that information credibility exists on a spectrum and isn't solely determined by the type of information that something is.

Perhaps the best way to understand the nuances of credibility as it pertains to the paranormal is to outline the research process. Before we begin, though, it is important to dispel some myths about research. Quite often, research is driven by the simple fact that we are curious about something we've overheard or read. We all engage in research daily, but we are probably not used to thinking of it in that way. If you are curious what time the local coffee shop opens, you know to pull out your phone and enter a quick Google search to arrive at your answer. If you are working and a customer asks for directions to the nearest gas station, you draw upon your expertise as a local and provide directions. In both instances, you have used different tools and methods to satisfy an information need. I know this might sound quite simplistic, but I raise these points to highlight the fact that research does not have to be a complicated matter and that it is a skill anyone can master.

This brings me to my next point. You don't need to be a college student, professor, or scientist to research a topic in a scholarly way. Even though I'm using words like "database," "scholarly," and "library," this doesn't mean that these methods are restricted to a certain class of people—in fact, it's quite the opposite. Anyone can employ these methods of research, and I would argue it's important that more people outside of academia begin to understand research in these ways. In this discussion, I will not only outline how to begin thinking differently about information, but I will also outline strategies of accessing information. We are all so used to consulting Google for answers to our questions, but there is an entire world of research beyond Google that is waiting for our perusal—and it's a world that's been right under our noses this entire time.

I presented one real-world research scenario above; now I include another to really drive these points home. In this example, I outline recommended strategies, talk about the importance of understanding your research need, and take a bit more of an-depth exploration of the research process. Hopefully, after working through both examples, readers will have a holistic understanding of the various skills and nuances involved with seeking out credible information.

To begin any research, you must first understand what your research question is. Your question could be as simple as "I want to know more about divination practices," or it could be more nuanced. Maybe you want to learn more about divination practices only in a certain part of the world or during a particular period. Sometimes you're not sure what your research question is, or maybe you feel like you don't know enough about a topic to consider where to start. For example, on your drive to work you listen to a podcast that discusses the Ganzfeld experiment. From listening to the podcast, you understand that it has something to do with the paranormal, and you want to learn more.

There are a couple of ways to begin your research on Ganzfeld experiments. Let's assume that you don't know very much about this topic other than what you just heard on the podcast. One tactic that I find quite effective is simply entering that topic into Google (or whatever internet browser you prefer) and finding some basic background information on that subject. Even though Wikipedia gets a bad rap from academics and scholars, I find that the problem is really that Wikipedia is misused. Citing Wikipedia as *the* source of your information isn't recommended—most wiki pages, after all, can be edited by anyone at any time, which immediately calls into question the "authority" and "accuracy" components of the CRAAP test outlined above. However, Wikipedia is great at providing references. Throughout the entry, you'll notice that there are little numerical superscripts that point you to a list of references at the bottom of each entry. *These* sources are the ones that you would end up citing if you found something credible listed therein.

Let's continue with our Ganzfeld experiment example. On the Wikipedia entry for "Ganzfeld Experiment,"[10] there are forty-six references listed at the bottom of the entry. Among these forty-six are citations that point readers to sources from the *Psychological Bulletin*, the *Journal of the American Society for Psychical Research*, the *Journal of Parapsychology*, and books from Cambridge University Press and Wiley-Blackwell—all sources that publish serious scholarly and academic publications. These sources are also often hyperlinked, which means that you can navigate directly to them. For this reason alone, Wikipedia is a great tool to help you start your research. Not only will it provide an immediate reference list for you to peruse, reading through the Wikipedia entry can help give you more background knowledge on your topic. As you know from chapter 3, part of researching anything is knowing the terms and keywords associated with that topic. In this example, associated keywords might include "psychology," "telepathy," "experimental psychology," "sensory deprivation," and "Charles Honorton." These keywords that you mine from the article can then be used to find even more information on your topic—indeed, keywords are the very building blocks of conducting research to begin with.

Once you start to understand the background information on a topic, one strategy that I find helpful is creating a keyword cloud. You can create this cloud in any matter you'd like—using a Word document, pen and paper, typing notes into your phone—however you want to capture your keyword cloud is perfectly fine. To do this activity, you simply take the core concept of your research question and write it in the middle of your page (if you prefer to instead create a list, that is fine too—there's no wrong way of organizing this). Draw a circle around the main concept and then simply write down all associated keywords and/or those topics you are curious about. Once you've brainstormed for a while, your keyword cloud may look something like the following figure.

Once you've exhausted everything you can think of, keep this keyword cloud handy as it will help you decide which keywords to pop into a database search. You can also continue adding keywords to this document as you begin your research and more questions arise.

Another place to start your research is by going directly to a database. Depending on how much you already know about a topic, you could have enough background information to bypass a Google search and jump right in. To help define things a bit, a database is simply a collection of information that has been compiled and organized into one accessible arena. There are some databases that cover many disciplines, such as Academic Search Premier (ASP). In this database, you could easily search for information from a wide array of subject areas like sociology, psychology, religion, the humanities, business management, and many more. It's not unique to any one subject area. Then there are databases that contain very specific sets of information, such as Chemical Abstracts Service. You would consult this database

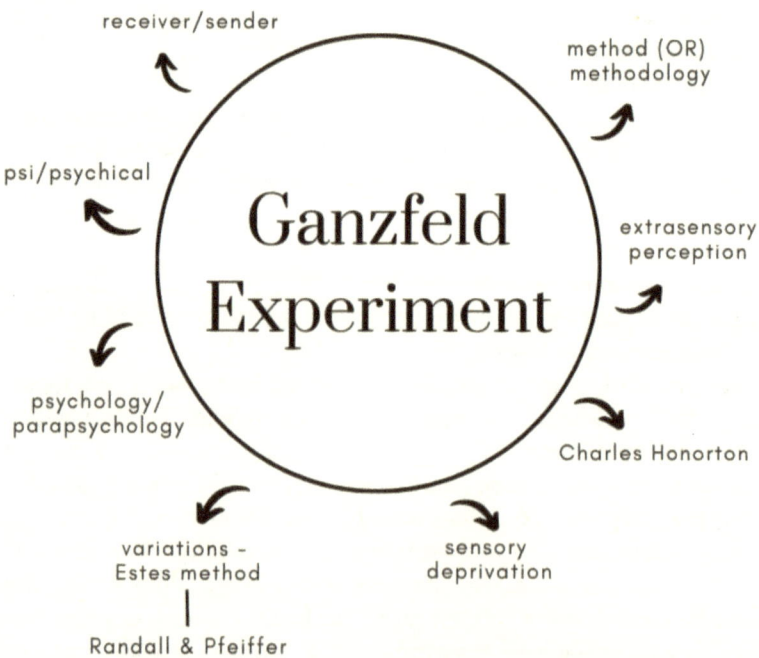

Example of a Keyword Cloud When Brainstorming Topics. *Author design*

if you were interested in learning about chemicals and chemistry but not if you needed information about the latest advancements in parapsychological research.

Accessibility is the first hurdle when using databases. As mentioned above, there are different types of libraries, and for purposes of this book, I focus on public and academic. Anyone can, of course, visit public libraries to browse their databases and collections, but most public universities also allow the general public to access library resources. It is important to keep this in mind because while performing a Google search is free (even though it may take you to sources you have to pay for), many databases are subscription based and don't allow open access to even search their contents. Because database access often requires subscriptions and fees, this isn't something the average person would be able to afford, which is why organizations like libraries pay these fees to provide access to their communities. What you can do to prepare, though, is visit the website of your local libraries to browse the databases that they provide access to; even though you may not be able to remotely access the contents of the databases, you can usually view a list of what databases the library provides and a brief description of those databases.

Not all databases are subscription based. There are those that are freely and openly accessible online, and Wikipedia provides a handy list outlining these open databases. This list is also hyperlinked, so you can quickly learn more about these databases. Fortunately, we are entering a period that welcomes the benefits of open access information. Open access simply means that information is freely and openly accessible to anyone visiting that site— no subscription needed. Open access not only benefits researchers who aren't affiliated with institutions to get free off-site access, but it also benefits institutions like libraries in reducing the often exorbitant costs of subscription databases. In other words, the crux of this movement is to reduce barriers to information to allow for unfettered access to scholarly information. One open access database is Paperity, which can be accessed by simply searching online. Paperity, in its own words, is "the first multi-disciplinary aggregator of Open Access journals and papers."[11] Paperity sums up its mission (and the goal of open access) when it writes, "Scholarly communication wants to be open, because openness is not about cost, it is about freedom of scientific investigation."[12]

Using Paperity as an example of what can be found on an open access database, 616 sources are found when typing in the keyword "paranormal." This is a rather broad search, of course, so let's try another. When you search for "parapsychology," you receive 175 results and while most of them are in English, there are some that are in French, German, and Turkish, proving that open access databases are friendly even for the international researcher. Another open access database, referred to as BASE (Bielefeld Academic Search

Engine), was created by the Bielefeld University Library in Germany. Using this database, I was able to retrieve seventy-eight results when searching "Ganzfeld experiment."

The great thing about open access databases is that you can conduct research in your pajamas if you'd like. All that's required is an internet connection, so you can research from any location. The downside is that there is still a lot of information locked behind subscription services. However, do you remember our conversation about publicly accessible libraries from earlier? If a library near you subscribes to a certain database, you can visit that library and conduct research on location. Sure, it's not as convenient as being able to research in any location at whatever time you'd like, but it can still be done without requiring anything more than the ability it takes to get there. What those folks sitting at home in their pajamas don't have at their disposal is a building full of library professionals who can help them with their research. I might be a little biased here, but I think that's a pretty great trade-off.

By now we understand some of the initial stages of the research process. The first step is outlining your research need—what are you curious about and what are the keywords associated with that topic? If you don't know enough background information about the topic, do a quick Google search and spend time reading up on it. Once you feel like you've gathered enough background information and have brainstormed some relevant keywords, the next step is entering those keywords into a relevant database. At this point, we are now firmly entrenched in the middle stages of the research process. At this point, researchers will have to apply the components of credibility to each source to determine if it will be useful. If a source doesn't meet your criteria of credibility, toss it aside and move forward. If you think a source might be credible, bookmark it for further inquiry when you have time to devote to reading that source in its entirety. A quick way to scan a source for relevancy and credibility is to browse certain sections: the summary or abstract, a table of contents (if any), the introduction, the methods, and the conclusion. Of course, not all items will have each of these components, but browsing certain key areas of a source can help you quickly judge if it will be worth reading exhaustively. What you don't want to do is read an entire source from beginning to end each time simply to judge the likelihood that it is relevant to your research. Tackle your research in stages.

Once you've consulted databases, browsed online, and even scanned library catalogs for relevant books, you end up with a certain number of sources you've determined may be useful. At this point, we are nearing the later stages of the research process; now you get to spend time reading, annotating, and making notes. During this stage you may realize that some sources you selected aren't actually useful, and that's OK. Set those sources aside and move on to the next. Once you've consumed those sources, this may be the end of the research process for you. Maybe you satisfied your curiosity. Maybe you're writing a paper for a class or giving a presentation. If that's the case, you now get to take what you've learned and present it in your own words to an audience. Remember that in order to be an ethical information consumer, you should give proper credit to all sources you've consulted. Regardless if you are researching for personal or professional reasons, holding steady to the tenets of credibility will simply make you a more informed consumer, and fewer people will be able to attack your stance because you've vetted your sources efficiently. People can certainly disagree with you, but if you keep credibility in mind, they won't be able to accuse you of sloppy scholarship.

Hopefully readers understand that access to scholarly and credible resources is readily available to anyone at pretty much any time. Sure, you constantly adjust how you previously thought about information and research, but the takeaway here is that there are resources available to anyone interested in finding credible paranormal research and information. Using any one of the methods listed above connects you with troves of information on various topics. And once you know where to go, all you must remember are the core components of credibility. I sometimes remind people that essentially, it's all CRAAP: currency, relevancy, authority, accuracy, and purpose.

NOTES

1. Jones, Marie. (2007). *PSIence: How new discoveries in quantum physics and new science may explain the existence of paranormal phenomena.* Franklin Lakes, NJ: New Page Books, 21.

2. Targ, Russell. (2015, April 14). The reality of ESP: A physicist's proof of psychic abilities. *Watkins Mind, Body, Spirit.* Retrieved May 28, 2019, from https://www.watkinsmagazine.com/the-reality-of-esp-a-physicists-proof-of-psychic-abilities

3. *Watkins Mind, Body, Spirit.* (2016). About. Retrieved May 29, 2019, from https://www.watkinsmagazine.com/about

4. Targ, Russell. (2014). Russell Targ: Brief bio. Retrieved June 4, 2019, from http://www.espresearch.com/russell/

5. Zdrenka, Marco, & Wilson, Marc Stewart. (2017, Spring). Individual difference correlates of psi performance in forced-choice precognition experiments: A meta-analysis (1945–2016). *Journal of Parapsychology, 81*(1), 9–32. Retrieved June 4, 2019, from EBSCOhost.

6. Ibid., 9–10.

7. Ibid., 13–22.

8. Ibid., 23–24.

9. Blakeslee, Sarah. (2004). The CRAAP test. *Loex Quarterly, 31*(3), 6–7. Retrieved May 13, 2019, from https://commons.emich.edu/cgi/viewcontent.cgi?article=1009&context=loexquarterly

10. Ganzfeld experiment. (n.d.). In *Wikipedia.* Retrieved May 14, 2019, from https://en.wikipedia.org/wiki/Ganzfeld_experiment

11. Paperity. (n.d.). About. Retrieved May 14, 2019, from https://paperity.org/about/

12. Ibid.

Chapter Five

Universities, Professional Organizations, Associations, and Societies Engaged in Paranormal Research

This chapter provides an overview of the universities, organizations, associations, and societies that engage in paranormal research. I hope this chapter reinforces the reality that paranormal inquiry is a valid and popular field of study, while also highlighting the fact that it isn't just solo researchers or small paranormal groups that are involved in advancing the field. You could be a member of some of the groups listed in this chapter one day. I will note that this chapter is not an exhaustive compilation of all societies and organizations affiliated with the paranormal (as that would truly be an epic endeavor) but rather serves as an overview of a handful of institutions dedicated to researching the paranormal. In this regard, this chapter is bibliographic in nature, outlining organizations that can be helpful in advancing one's own understanding of paranormal topics. It also reinforces the notion that not all worthy and valuable information is locked behind subscriptions to expensive academic journals. You can find loads of information from the organizations I discuss in this chapter.

Some of the information you may find from these organizations might not match your personal paranormal beliefs, and that's OK. This is something all researchers come up against at some point, and it's an important point to consider. You must always be aware of your own bias as a researcher and ensure that it doesn't keep you from evaluating relevant information simply because you don't like the conclusions. *This doesn't mean that you must abandon your personal beliefs or convictions anytime you come across infor-*

mation refuting your beliefs. *It doesn't mean that any paranormal experience you may have had is any less valid or real. It doesn't mean that your curiosity about the paranormal is not a valid one.* It simply means that in order to be an ethical researcher, you should be aware of information that is contrary to that which supports your beliefs. Knowledge is power, ultimately, and being aware of all sides of the issue is never a bad thing. Think of it this way: if you are a paranormal investigator who conducts research and publishes your findings, you may wish to be aware of the criticisms of your methods. For example, you can use these criticisms (if they are valid, of course) to help adjust your methods and potentially make your evidence stronger. Knowing the arguments against your point of view can also help motivate you to research particular topics or phenomena. I want to reinforce that being aware of both sides of an issue doesn't mean that you shouldn't feel empowered to stand by your convictions and to speak your truths.

With this caveat in mind, I now outline some of the universities, organizations, associations, and societies involved with paranormal studies.

UNIVERSITIES ENGAGED IN PARANORMAL RESEARCH

Since the crux of this book highlights research surrounding the paranormal, let's begin with a brief overview of universities engaged in paranormal research. Perhaps the most well-known higher education institute associated with the paranormal is the Rhine Education Center, which was first founded in 1930 at Duke University in North Carolina under the name Duke Parapsychology Labs.[1] Established by noted parapsychologist Joseph B. Rhine and three other members of the psychology department (William McDougall, Dr. Helge Lundholm, and Dr. Karl Zener), this is the earliest North American institute dedicated entirely to psi research in a higher education setting.[2] The Rhine Education Center also created the *Journal of Parapsychology*, which saw its first publication in 1937.[3] Upon its establishment in 1930, there were no other universities engaged in psi research, let alone psychology departments conducting targeted experiments on topics like precognition and telepathy.

In J. B. Rhine's own words, the research conducted "in our laboratory at Duke University were undertaken with the express purpose of cornering the problem of whether anything enters the mind by a route other than the recognized senses."[4] J. B. Rhine was particularly motivated by the curious habit of people (especially his highly credentialed colleagues and professors) to dismiss unexplainable occurrences as mere coincidence. He recalled one professor who recounted to Rhine, then a student, a moment that occurred when that professor was a young boy. A neighbor's wife had a disturbing dream about her brother, and it bothered the woman so much that her husband rushed over to the professor's house to borrow the horse and buggy in order to check in on the brother. Once they arrived at the brother's home, they found him lying in the loft of the barn, dead from a self-inflicted gunshot wound—which was exactly how the wife described her dream to the husband, down to the exact location of the incident.[5] What most impressed Rhine, however, wasn't necessarily the story itself. He was most concerned by the fact that his professor, a renowned and respected researcher motivated by the academic pursuit of knowledge, dismissed this story entirely as coincidence. Instead of being motivated by this story and investigating the untapped potential of the human mind and anything that might be learned from that endeavor, the professor had already convinced himself that no new knowledge could come from it because it was simply not explainable.

The earliest experiments conducted by the Duke Parapsychology Labs concerned hypnotism—in particular, whether students in a posthypnotic state performed better on telepathic endeavors than those in nonhypnotic states. While the early research to that aim did not find any conclusive effect, the lab moved toward experiments of extrasensory perception (ESP) in conjunction with a researcher from the Society for Psychical Research, Dr. Karl Zener.[6] As we covered briefly in chapter 1, Zener and the Duke researchers created a set of cards marked with symbols (circles, squares, stars, wavy lines, etc.) that were used to test the ESP abilities of subjects; these experiments revealed some of their first significant findings.[7] During these experiments, two people would meet in a room furnished only with a table and two chairs. The deck of cards would be shuffled and placed on the table between them—neither the researcher nor the subject knew what order the cards were in. The subject would focus their attention on the top card, and then after a moment of time they would call out what symbol they believed was on that card while the researcher noted their choice and removed the top card, revealing another card that would allow the experiment to continue until the deck was depleted.[8] Rhine and his associates calculated the average number of correct guesses that could rationally be attributed to chance was 5 in 25, and used this as a base to determine anomalistic guesses that could be evidence of ESP. The average for their entire group of subjects in 1931 was 6.5—an average that they determined only had a 1 in 250,000 chance of being attributed to blind luck.[9] If that is still low enough odds for some to dismiss, let me introduce Hubert Pearce.

Pearce, a Duke Divinity student, first became involved with Rhine and the Parapsychology Labs after attending a lecture and introducing himself afterward. Indicating that both he and his mother had experienced psychic phenomena, Pearce became involved in the Zener card experiments and, during one of his sessions, recorded twenty-five successively correct guesses. Rhine was so stunned by Pearce's display that he wrote, "Pearce's calling 25 cards in a row correctly was the most phenomenal thing that I have ever observed. If there is anyone in the world who can *believe* that it was due to sheer luck, that would be another phenomenon almost equally startling. The odds against his feat having been due to pure and undiluted chance are 1 in 298,023,223,876,953,125."[10]

J. B. Rhine and his colleagues at the Duke Parapsychology Labs continued to perform tests on psi phenomena until it was disbanded in 1965—the year that Rhine retired from Duke and established the Foundation for Research on the Nature of Man.[11] While Rhine's direct involvement in research and experimentation slowed down around 1945, he continued promoting the efforts of psi research through fundraising and advocacy.[12] The Foundation for Research on the Nature of Man was renamed the Rhine Education Center in 1995. Works by Rhine and more information regarding their studies can be found in the "Parapsychology" sections of the annotated bibliographies in later chapters.

Duke isn't the only university connected to the paranormal, of course. Some universities even offer advanced degrees in parapsychology. For example, Saybrook University in California offers a PhD in psychology with a consciousness and spirituality specialization that includes investigations of dream work, shamanism, and spiritual beliefs.[13] Perhaps the most interesting, however, is the Division of Perceptual Studies at the University of Virginia's School of Medicine. Founded in 1967 by noted reincarnation researcher Dr. Ian Stevenson, the Division of Perceptual Studies (DOPS) is "exclusively devoted to the investigation of phenomena that challenge mainstream scientific paradigms regarding the nature of the mind/brain relationship . . . researchers at DOPS are particularly interested in studying phenomena related to consciousness clearly functioning beyond the confines of the physical body, as well as phenomena that are directly suggestive of post-mortem survival of consciousness."[14] The University of California has two labs that engage in psi research: the META Lab (Memory, Emotion, Thought, and Awareness Lab), and the TANC Lab (Theoretical and Applied Neuro-Causality Lab). Both organizations engage in laboratory experiments on topics like precognition and consciousness.[15]

Another university, Atlantic University in Virginia, is an institute of higher education dedicated entirely to the academic pursuit of consciousness with a specific focus on the spirit, mind, and body connection. Founded by famed psychic and philosopher Edgar Cayce in 1930 and accredited by the Distance Education Accrediting Commission, Atlantic University offers online graduate programs and certificates in such programs as regression hypnosis and dream interpretation. Students of the hypnosis program study "the psycho-spiritual experiential technique that makes deliberate use of altered states of consciousness to enable people to access the many dimensions of the unconscious mind."[16] Included among their current faculty are people who hold PhDs in such fields as geophysical sciences, clinical psychology, zoology, human development, and more.[17] While the examples listed here are by no means an exhaustive exploration of the many programs offered and supported by institutes of higher education, it does clearly indicate that academia has a long-standing relationship with the paranormal.

PROFESSIONAL ORGANIZATIONS CONDUCTING PARANORMAL RESEARCH

Universities aren't the only large organizations that have connections to the paranormal. I mentioned the Rhine Education Center above, and while it has direct roots to academia, it is now its own freestanding organization independent of Duke University that promotes the scientific inquiry of psi phenomena. In 2002, a new building was built to house this organization, and today the Rhine Education Center conducts lectures, offers classes, presents workshops, and publishes the *Journal of Parapsychology*.[18] The Rhine Education Center even holds social events at its library, an important point of note since it strives to make its research publicly available to anyone interested. In its own words, the center conducts "careful scientific studies on the parapsychological dimension of consciousness, in order to answer basic questions about consciousness, its reach, its durability, its power, its healing potential, and the extent of its autonomy and independence of physical constraints."[19] Visitors to the center's website can report their own experiences, view citations of research in the *Journal of Parapsychology*, browse current research projects, look at upcoming public events, and even "ask a scientist." This feature allows curious individuals to pose a question that will be addressed and answered by one of the Rhine's current researchers.

Blending in a more intense focus on spirituality, the Academy for Spiritual and Consciousness Studies (ASCSI) is based out of North Carolina and has the explicit goal to "discern, develop and disseminate knowledge of how consciousness studies and paranormal phenomena may relate to and enhance the development of the human spirit."[20] This organization encourages theologians to work alongside scientists and researchers on topics like psi phenomena, consciousness, and even quantum mechanics. Research can be found in their publication, the *Journal for Spiritual and Consciousness Studies*. One of the most intriguing and helpful aspects of this organization, however, is the freely and openly accessible "Spirituality and Consciousness Resource Library" that can be found on the ASCSI website. Here, visitors can not only find a robust bibliography of sources on certain topics but can also browse biographical sketches of key figures as well as read the "evidence files" of notable cases concerning spirit communication, reincarnation, and extrasensory perception.[21]

Another important organization, and one quite different from those discussed above, is the SETI Institute, which I briefly discuss in the sections on ufology but which I expand upon here. SETI is a research organization dedicated to pursuing and advancing the understanding of life in the universe—not just life here on Earth, but the potential for life elsewhere in our universe as well. SETI was founded in 1984 and employs a wide range of scientists whose work is often contracted by NASA and/or the National Science Foundation. The organization itself is actually a combination of three different hubs: the Carl Sagan Center for the Study of Life in the Universe, the Center for Education, and the Center for Outreach.[22] Their research centers around exploring other planets, astrophysics, biogeoscience, and also astrobiology (life beyond Earth). The astrobiology arm is directly inspired by the famous Drake equation, which estimated the possible number of planets in the universe and is driven by researching the potential for life elsewhere in the universe. One such project, for example, undertaken by astrobiologists, was an extensive study of the lakes of Titan, Saturn's largest moon. The first major research project of SETI was scanning radio frequencies in the hope that they revealed proof of intelligent life, while current studies focus on studying exoplanets and "optical SETI," a project that scans the skies for laser emissions of unknown yet intelligent origin.[23]

Even the category of near-death experience has its own dedicated organization. The Near-Death Experience Research Foundation (NDERF) was founded in 1998 by Jeffrey and Jody Long. Readers may recognize Jeffrey Long as one of the authorities I mentioned earlier in the discussion on NDEs and reincarnation. NDERF was established to be a repository of firsthand near-death experiences. It has grown to become the largest website devoted to NDEs and has compiled more than 4,600 NDE encounters in over twenty-three languages.[24] While the website also serves to provide comfort to those who have had an NDE, visitors to the site can also access a wide variety of articles and research about this phenomena. Their research links to articles from a multitude of publications, such as the *Journal of Consciousness Exploration and Research*, *Psychological Science*, *Psychiatry*, and more.

If you wish to research "out-of-body experiences," a phenomenon somewhat similar to certain NDEs, you can visit the website of the Out of Body Experience Research Foundation (OBERF), an organization also created by Jeffrey and Jody Long. On the OBERF website, not only can visitors share their personal out-of-body experiences, but they have access to a long list of resources including books and articles devoted to the study of out-of-body experiences.[25] In addition to NDERF and OBERF, the Longs also maintain the After-Death Communication Research Foundation, which focuses on providing information about those who have reported communication experiences with deceased loved ones. All three of these websites, created and maintained by the Longs, provide resources that can be helpful in researching any of those phenomena.

In addition to psi, ufology, and NDE phenomena, cryptozoology is also represented by organized pursuits. In 1989, our Canadian neighbors founded the British Columbia Scientific Cryptozoology Club (BCSCC), "dedicated to the investigation of various animals as yet unidentified by science."[26] In its own words, members of this organization are "actively engaged year-round in many different aspects of exciting fieldwork."[27] While based in Canada, this organization conducts fieldwork across the globe, with expeditions in Africa, Scotland, the United States, and more. Those interested in becoming members can join, in fact, though only after completing fieldwork training provided by this organization. Additionally, educating the public is a goal of the BCSCC, which regularly conducts lectures at elementary, middle, and high schools as well as universities. Some of its fieldwork is even sponsored by *National Geographic*.

In addition to the BCSCC, Dr. Karl Shuker is a British zoologist and cryptozoologist who created the *Journal of Cryptozoology* after the original publication *Cryptozoology* ceased publication in 1996 when the International Society of Cryptozoology disbanded due to financial reasons. Dr. Shuker attempts to carry on the original mission of that society by creating the *Journal of Cryptozoology* to serve as a publication venue for researchers and scientists interested in advancing the discussion and understanding of cryptozoology.[28] The field of cryptozoology seems to carry the biggest stigma of pseudoscience, but these organizations provide an interesting and worthy contribution to not only advancing our understanding of the ecological unknown, but also in capturing and recording regional and international environmental snapshots.

ASSOCIATIONS AND SOCIETIES INVOLVED IN THE PARANORMAL

The Rhine Education Center I mentioned above isn't the only organization dedicated to the scientific study of psi phenomena. The Parapsychological Association is the "international professional organization of scientists and scholars engaged in the study of 'psi' (or 'psychic') experiences such as telepathy, clairvoyance, remote viewing, psychokinesis, psychic healing, and precognition."[29] J. B. Rhine first proposed the creation of this group, so it makes sense to discuss this organization immediately following the Rhine Education Center. The notable difference between these two organizations is the intense focus of the Parapsychological Association for affiliated researchers and academics to disseminate and conduct their research on psi phenomena. They also provide grants and scholarships to psi researchers around the world to assist in their studies. This association is also a bit older, having been formed in 1957. In 1969, it became an affiliated member of the renowned American Association for the Advancement of Science (AAAS); it is also a contributor to the *Journal of Parapsychology*.[30] The association held its first conference in 1958 and has continued to convene yearly, meeting not only in the United States but in places like Scotland, Germany, Holland, Canada, France, and more.[31]

Another professional organization that studies psi (and other paranormal) phenomena is the Society for Psychical Research (SPR). This society is the largest professional organization dedicated to the scientific pursuit of paranormal phenomena (not just psi events) and is such an integral member of paranormal history that it is the subject of many publications and books. Many of those will be outlined in the bibliographies below, but here I present an abbreviated history of this organization to add to my discussion in chapter 2. We already know that the SPR was founded in 1882 in London. In their own words, the SPR was "the first scientific organisation ever to examine claims of psychic and paranormal phenomena."[32] The SPR's first president was Henry Sidgwick, a philosophy professor at Trinity College. Some of the earliest scientific inquiries of the SPR focused on "telepathy, hypnotism, clairvoyance, physical phenomena of the séance room, apparitions, and hauntings."[33] Just four short years after the SPR was founded, members published a two-volume work that is hailed as "the first landmark in psychical research," titled *Phantasms of the Living*.[34] This publication summarized the investigation of more than seven hundred accounts in which people claimed to have seen apparitions. Interestingly, the majority of these visions were dubbed "crisis apparitions" since the encounters largely centered on visions of people who were experiencing death and/or near-death scenarios. The work in that publication actually spawned a research project dubbed the Census of Hallucinations, which is described as "the largest survey of its kind ever to have been attempted."[35] In addition to the topics listed above, early endeavors of the SPR focused heavily on ferreting out hoaxes while also establishing scientific guidelines and procedures for future studies. Interestingly, toward the 1930s, the crux of study and experimentation shifted from the UK and the SPR's colleagues in London and synced up with the creation of the Duke Parapsychology Labs in 1930. During this period, the SPR focused heavily on collecting and organizing its vast research and publications while American colleagues took up the torch of scientific experimentation.[36]

The Association for the Study of Esotericism is another professional association dedicated to the inquiry of esoteric concepts. According to their website, esotericism "refers to the field of study of alternative or marginalized religious movement or philosophies" including "alchemy, astrology ... Hermeticism, Kabbalah, magic, mysticism," and more.[37] The goal of this association is to foster the study of these topics and promote a culture of learning surrounding these topics. As part of meeting these goals, the association has a book series titled Studies in Esotericism that readers can locate to learn more about esoteric topics, scholarship, and philosophies.

INFORMATION IS EVERYWHERE

Hopefully this chapter reveals the many different organizations, societies, and even universities associated with pursuits of paranormal research. The various organizations listed above are by no means a comprehensive account of all institutes associated with the paranormal, but they do represent a fairly robust sampling. The wonderful thing about many of the organizations in this chapter is their web presence, which is freely accessible and provides links to resources like books, articles, and other studies that have been conducted on a myriad of paranormal topics. Scrolling through the website of any one of the above organizations can send visitors down a paranormal rabbit hole in no time.

In this chapter, I illustrate that credible information can be found in all types of places. You shouldn't pigeonhole yourself to one type of information or one source on information—especially with a topic that is as wide ranging as the paranormal. While one organization above focuses on near-death experiences, universities are doing research on extrasensory perception, while still another society is investigating poltergeists and haunting phenomena. All of these combined paints a better picture of the paranormal than one of them as a stand-alone authority source. The mark of good research is a diverse bibliography.

Another great quality of the institutions listed in this chapter is their emphasis not only on connecting people with information but connecting people with other like-minded curiosity seekers, and even potentially connecting people to others experiencing similar phenomena. All of these organizations help create a paranormal community that can be called upon time and again in your research. I urge readers to consider the organizations listed here as potential sources of information that sit right alongside the books, articles, journals, and more that I discuss below. The next chapter highlights special collections and museums that preserve and display items of paranormal history—in fact, consider the next chapter an exploration of some weird and wonderful primary paranormal sources.

NOTES

1. Rhine Research Center. (2019). What is the Rhine. Retrieved May 14, 2019, from https://www.rhineonline.org/about-us.

2. Rhine, J. B. (1937). *New frontiers of the mind: The story of the Duke experiments*. New York, NY: Farrar & Rinehart, 40.
3. Rhine Research Center, What is the Rhine.
4. Rhine, *New frontiers of the mind*, 8.
5. Ibid., 10–11.
6. Ibid., 40–50.
7. Ibid., 49–51.
8. Ibid., 59–60.
9. Ibid., 63–69.
10. Ibid., 90–95.
11. Duke University Libraries. (2009). Guide to the Parapsychology Laboratory Records, 1893–1984. Retrieved June 10, 2019, from https://library.duke.edu/rubenstein/findingaids/paralab/ .
12. Ibid.
13. Saybrook University. (2019). Ph.D. in psychology: Consciousness, spirituality, and integrative health specialization. Retrieved May 14, 2019, from https://www.saybrook.edu/areas-of-study/humanistic-clinical-psychology/phd-psychology/consciousness-spirituality-and-integrative-health-specialization/
14. University of Virginia Division of Perceptual Studies. (2019). Rector and visitors of the University of Virginia. Retrieved May 14, 2019, from https://med.virginia.edu/perceptual-studies/
15. TANC Lab. (n.d.). Home. Retrieved May 14, 2019, from http://tanclab.org/ ; META Lab. (2019). The META Lab at UCSB. Retrieved May 14, 2019, from https://labs.psych.ucsb.edu/schooler/jonathan/
16. Atlantic University. (2019). *2019 academic catalog*, page 27. Retrieved June 12, 2019, from https://www.atlanticuniv.edu/media/12617/2019-au-catalog.pdf
17. Atlantic University. (2018). Faculty. Retrieved June 12, 2019, from https://www.atlanticuniv.edu/admin-faculty/faculty/?submit=1&program=0&page=2
18. Rhine Research Center. (2019). About the Rhine Research Center today. Retrieved June 10, 2019, from https://www.rhine.org/who-we-are/rhine-today.html?start=1
19. Ibid.
20. Academy for Spiritual and Consciousness Studies (n.d.-a). About ASCSI. Retrieved June 11, 2019, from http://ascsi.org/overview/
21. Ibid.
22. SETI Institute. (2019). Mission. Retrieved June 10, 2019, from https://www.seti.org/about-us/mission
23. SETI Institute. (2019). SETI. Retrieved June 10, 2019, from https://www.seti.org/seti-institute/Search-Extraterrestrial-Intelligence
24. Long, Jeffrey, & Long, Jody. (2019). Near-Death Experience Research Foundation. Retrieved June 10, 2019, from https://www.nderf.org/index.htm
25. Long, Jeffrey, & Long, Jody. (2019). Out of Body Experience Research Foundation. Retrieved June 11, 2019, from https://www.oberf.org/index.html
26. British Columbia Scientific Cryptozoology Club. (2019). About. Retrieved June 11, 2019, from https://www.oberf.org/index.html
27. Ibid.
28. Shuker, Karl. (Ed.). (n.d.). *The Journal of Cryptozoology*. Retrieved June 10, 2019, from http://www.journalofcryptozoology.com/
29. Parapsychological Association. (2019). What is the Parapsychological Association? Retrieved April 22, 2019, from https://www.parapsych.org/articles/1/1/what_is_the_parapsychological.aspx
30. Ibid.
31. Parapsychological Association. (2019). Convention history. Retrieved June 10, 2019, from https://www.parapsych.org/section/23/convention_history.aspx
32. Society for Psychical Research. (2018). About the SPR. Retrieved June 10, 2019, from https://www.spr.ac.uk/about-spr

33. Society for Psychical Research. (2018). Our history. Retrieved June 10, 2019, from https://www.spr.ac.uk/about/our-history
34. Society for Psychical Research, About the SPR.
35. Ibid.
36. Ibid.
37. Association for the Study of Esotericism. (2020). What is esotericism? Retrieved January 9, 2020, from http://www.aseweb.org/?page_id=6

Chapter Six

Primary Sources, Paranormal Museums, and Special Collections across the United States

In this chapter, I present primary sources of paranormal research and highlight special paranormal museums found throughout the United States. Primary sources are a perfect segue to begin our transition to a presentation of annotated entries of paranormal sources. Some readers may very well know what primary sources are, but a refresher is beneficial. Primary sources are those pieces of information that were created at the very moment an event was happening. For example, a photograph of a presidential ceremony, *The Diary of Anne Frank*, and newspaper accounts of natural disasters are all examples of primary sources. Of course, locations and buildings can be primary sources of the paranormal as well, like the ones I highlight in chapter 1. The goal of this chapter is to highlight physical resources that people can access or consult in their research or inquiry, but also to reveal how readers can locate and access primary sources on their own.

TYPES OF PARANORMAL PRIMARY SOURCES

The topic of primary sources in the paranormal is an exciting one, because you can include locations like the famous Waverly Hills Sanatorium or Alcatraz Island in this category. Consider it this way—just like a history buff may visit Gettysburg to gain a deeper understanding of a key event in the Civil War, so too might a paranormal enthusiast visit the very same battlefield to gather new insight surrounding the many paranormal encounters that have been reported there. Of course, this is a very famous example of a haunted location, but for those interested in visiting paranormal hotspots (i.e., primary sources in their own right), there are a myriad of opportunities spread across the United States (and internationally), some of which are very likely in your own backyard. Of course, a location does not have to be famous or even modestly well known to be considered a paranormal primary source; readers very likely know of locations in their own cities and towns that fit this description.

In addition to visiting locations in which people have experienced paranormal phenomena, you can also interact with primary paranormal sources by visiting any number of museums and collections that highlight paranormal events and phenomena. Just like the locations mentioned above, these museums and collections are scattered all around the United States and are quite often devoted to the regional paranormal history of their surrounding areas. Some of these locations may include digital repositories of information or may require a visit, but they are nonetheless sources that contain a wide variety of information.

Primary sources don't have to be historic homes or old battlefields, of course. There are many other objects that can be included in the primary source category of the paranormal. One museum that I highlight below, in fact, is completely dedicated to the display of reportedly haunted objects from across the United States and the world. It is also a mobile museum, meaning that the curators travel with their museum to locations across the country; I discuss it further below. When people think of paranormal objects, they likely conjure an image of a creepy doll or perhaps a ceramic clown, but some notable examples of paranormal objects include the equipment/tools used by Rhine and his associates in their parapsychology experiments; an infamously haunted doll that goes by the name of Robert and lives in Key West, Florida; or the dress Betty Hill was wearing while she experienced her UFO encounter. All of these items are examples of objects that can be considered primary paranormal sources, and I discuss them to illustrate that this category doesn't have to be limited to real estate.

There is yet another category of paranormal primary sources. One huge arena is eyewitness testimony. In other words, your own friends and family could be primary sources in their own right. For example, some readers may know someone who has recounted a paranormal encounter to them, and some readers may well have encountered something paranormal themselves. A book, for example, that someone writes to document their paranormal experience could also be considered a primary source that falls under the eyewitness testimony category. In fact, some of these types of sources can be found later in this book.

Some may wonder how to locate these primary types of information. One of the ways that people can access primary paranormal sources is by using any number of tools that I discuss above in the section on conducting research. A database one uses via a library or even openly accessible on the internet can be used in a specific way to reveal only certain types of information. In other words, if you are researching the paranormal in an online database, you can often tell that database to limit to sources like newspaper articles or photographs—two item types that can often reveal primary sources. Likewise, you can choose a tool before you begin to do any research that you know will reveal primary sources. For example, you can browse a library or museum's collection of physical or digital newspapers, thereby focusing on a category that you know already contains primary sources rather than sifting through a larger database that contains various sources of information.

Let's start our discussion by highlighting some museums found across the United States, after which I will discuss other, special paranormal collections.

MUSEUMS WITH PARANORMAL COLLECTIONS IN THE UNITED STATES

I don't know about you, but when I think of paranormal hotspots around the United States, Salem, Massachusetts, takes the number one spot on my list. Located about a half hour north of Boston, Salem has a number of locations that you can visit to learn more about the paranormal. One such location is the Peabody Essex Museum, located in downtown Salem. The library at the Peabody Essex contains a variety of information on art, of course, but it also contains information relating to the Salem witch trials.[1] Of course, the Salem witch trials themselves are not necessarily paranormal in nature, though they do touch on paranormal topics, and I include it here since some readers may very well be interested in the broader topic of witch history that so often gets lumped in with the paranormal. Documenting a very dark period in New England's history that witnessed the power of accusation and fear, the subject of Salem witch trials nonetheless is in many a paranormal enthusiast's repertoire.

Another location in Salem that highlights the witch trials (and which is said to be haunted as well) is the simply named Witch House located not far from the Peabody Essex Museum. The Witch House, in fact, is the oldest remaining building that has direct ties to the Salem witch trials. Judge Jonathan Corwin purchased the imposing home in 1675, and a few short years later he became one of the very judges involved in the Salem witch trials. It is said that he conducted inquiries in the home, in fact.[2] Today, visitors can tour the home and not only see examples of early New England life and architecture, but also view artifacts and information that are linked to the witch trials. With the history of the home, it is no surprise that it is also the center of such paranormal claims as cold spots and the phantom voices of small children.³

Another museum in the northeastern United States is the International Cryptozoology Museum. Founded in 2003 and located in Portland, Maine, the museum's mission is "to educate, inform, and share cryptozoological evidence, artifacts, replicas, and popular cultural items with the general public, media, students, scholars, and cryptozoologists from around the world."⁴ Based on this mission, noted cryptozoologist Loren Coleman first founded the museum in the basement of a home in Portland, Maine, though today it occupies its own building and holds a 501(c)(3) nonprofit status.⁵ Some of the items in the museum include hair samples from unidentified animals, foot castings of Bigfoot tracks, numerous artist representations, and newspaper clippings, as well as information on cryptids from across the United States, such as the Mothman of West Virginia and the Dover Demon of Massachusetts. In addition to the exhibits on display inside the museum, visitors to the museum's website can view current cryptozoological news and read more about the origins of this field of study.

The Northeast isn't the only portion of the United States with special museums dedicated to topics of paranormal interest. Readers can also find unique museums a bit more south. One such museum is located in Point Pleasant, West Virginia, and is dedicated to the infamous creature known as Mothman. Mothman gained notoriety in November 1966 when residents began reporting sightings of a large, winged, hairy creature with piercing red eyes. Reports of the creature occurred regularly for just over a year until the tragic collapse of the Silver Bridge on December 15, 1967, that killed forty-six people.⁶ The legend surrounding the creature explains its presence in town as a harbinger of doom, and the lingering effect of the thirteen-month period is still felt in Point Pleasant today. Visitors to the museum can view a large and impressive display of newspaper clippings, eyewitness reports, photographs, movie props, and more surrounding the Mothman enigma. A special treat is the large Mothman statue that sits outside the steps of the Mothman Museum, which can be visited yearly. A festival in the Mothman's name is held in Point Pleasant every September and draws ever-increasing crowds.

West Virginia is host to another interesting paranormal museum known as the Archive of the Afterlife. Located in Moundsville, West Virginia, this museum was founded in 2011 and is located in the Sanford Community Center. The goal of the archive "is to offer an entertaining, but also educational experience into the vast and intriguing realm of the paranormal through exhibits of haunted relics, cursed artifacts, oddities, informational literature and historically significant items."⁷ Visitors to the archives can view an assortment of items gathered and collected mainly from locations and/or investigations in West Virginia. Examples of the items one can view

The Mothman Statue in the Town Square of Point Pleasant, West Virginia. *Creative Commons/Photo by Katherine Bowman, licensed under CC-BY-2.0*

is an old embalming table, numerous dolls, funeral masks, and photographs that are all reported to be the cause of various paranormal phenomena.

Located a few hours west of Point Pleasant, West Virginia, resides the headquarters of the Traveling Museum of the Paranormal & Occult. The museum, founded by Greg and Dana Newkirk, is hailed as "the world's only mobile museum of the unexplained,"[8] and since 2013 the Newkirks have been traveling the country with their collection and "[inviting] curious visitors to inspect, investigate, and even handle rare artifacts collected from infamous hauntings, parapsychology breakthroughs, mysterious cryptozoological discoveries, and more."[9] People can visit this mobile museum at any number of events throughout the year and in different parts of the country, making this museum a truly opportune venue for a multitude of people. Through their museum the Newkirks' goals are as follows: "to preserve and protect items of historical and supernatural significance in relation to the study of the unexplained, and to share those artifacts with the world while educating the public on the reality of paranormal research."[10] Some of the items that people can see includes a nail once used in voodoo rituals,[11] a mirror in which people report seeing themselves age or as corpses,[12] and an African idol referred to as the Idol of Nightmares[13] that was donated to the museum after a new homeowner found it wrapped in burlap and buried in their home. The homeowner soon began having graphic and disturbing dreams that he attributed to the idol; visitors of the museum artifact today still report odd or disturbing dreams after interacting with the artifact. Visitors to the museum's website can learn about many more artifacts and learn about the Newkirks' extensive paranormal background, special projects (especially their documentary *Hellier*), podcast and television appearances, and much more.

For those who live closer to the Pacific Northwest, you can visit the North American Bigfoot Center located in Boring, Oregon. Open in 2019, the museum was founded by researcher Cliff Barackman and contains interactive displays, replicas, and even a movie theater aimed at educating and enlightening visitors about all things Bigfoot.[14]

In addition to the North American Bigfoot Center, the Willow Creek–China Flat Museum located in Willow Creek, California, offers visitors the opportunity to learn more about the reports of Bigfoot in the Humboldt and Trinity Counties of Northern California.[15] The museum, while also catering to the broader history of these two counties, contains a research center devoted entirely to Bigfoot phenomena in this area. Yet another cryptozoological museum located in California can be found by traveling a bit south and visiting the Bigfoot Discovery Museum in Felton. Like those institutions mentioned above, this museum features artifacts and information on local Bigfoot phenomena. Visitors to the museum are also treated to a continuous loop of the famous Patterson/Gimlin Bigfoot footage.[16]

Those traveling through the Southeast can stop by Durham, North Carolina, to tour the museum of the Rhine Research Center. The museum features artifacts that have been used in the parapsychological efforts of the center from 1930 onward and even offers tools for visitors to conduct their own paranormal investigations.[17] Readers may remember from above that the Rhine Research Center is built upon the parapsychological research conducted by J. B. Rhine at the Duke Parapsychology Labs. Directly connected with the center, the museum offers visitors a comprehensive historical timeline of parapsychological research conducted by Rhine and his affiliates.

If you stop by Durham to visit the museum at the Rhine Research Center, you may as well stay in North Carolina long enough to tour the Cryptozoology and Paranormal Museum located in Littleton. According to its website, this museum focuses on and displays items concerning "Bigfoot information and artifacts, ghost evidence and ghost investigation tools, local cryptid and ghost stories and evidence," and more.[18] Interestingly, this museum also hosts an annual event called the Crypto Paranormal Festival that features guest speakers on a variety of topics such as cryptozoology (obviously), the paranormal, metaphysics, local legend and lore, and more.

Another paranormal museum in the Southeast can be found by making a stop in Cherry Log, Georgia. Expedition: Bigfoot! The Sasquatch Museum is a building that contains forty-five hundred square feet of displays and exhibits on the most famous North American cryptid, Bigfoot. Visitors to the museum can listen to audio recordings of supposed Bigfoot phenomena, view an extensive display of plaster footprint castings, and attend special lectures from modern-day cryptozoologists.[19]

OTHER SPECIAL COLLECTIONS

The museums listed above are not a comprehensive listing of every brick-and-mortar building that contains paranormal artifacts. Readers may notice, in fact, that there are certain regions that are not represented, and while I'm sure there are museums and collections dedicated to the paranormal in other states, my goal here is not to provide an exhaustive breakdown of locations but rather to highlight a few notable examples. There are many other organizations that house paranormal artifacts and oddities, and I encourage readers to interact with the weird and the wonderful any chance they get. Choosing to highlight only those organizations above is not a judgment against any others that may exist; it is simply an attempt to introduce the notion that paranormal museums and collections exist and can offer a unique way of investigating and understanding the paranormal, and that they are scattered all across the United States.

In addition to museums, however, there are other resources that can reveal paranormal primary sources. These resources, though not affiliated with a paranormal museum, are still wonderful resources to consider, and all of those listed below can be accessed freely and openly without subscriptions or affiliations. Some of the sources listed below are collections of resources on certain topics while others are governmental entities. Taken together, hopefully this chapter highlights that good research is often a result of consulting an assortment of sources and tools.

Expedition: Bigfoot! The Sasquatch Museum. Located in Cherry Log, Georgia. *Author photo*

The National Archives

This may not seem like an obvious resource to consult when conducting paranormal research, but nevertheless the National Archives can be a good source of information on a variety of topics. As many may know, the National Archives and Records Administration maintains the permanent collection of important documents in U.S. history.[20] Some of that history is paranormal in nature—just consider UFOs and the government, for example. Also, quite often paranormal research will highlight particular peoples and places, in addition to events. Sometimes researching information on those peoples and places can help create a more holistic understanding of an issue. Additionally, it is important to consider tools and resources that are not necessarily devoted entirely to a paranormal focus because, quite simply, sometimes a too-narrow focus will cause you to overlook relevant information. For example, a quick search for "UFO" reveals 349 entries within the National Archives. Of these 349, one source takes you to a home page of information entirely devoted to Project Blue Book, a United States Air Force investigation of UFOs from the 1940s to the 1960s.

A good example of how using the National Archives can reveal unique research paths occurs when you type in the search term "spiritualism." Upon typing this word, a list of more than 2,800 items generates. On the first page

The National Archives Building in Washington, DC. *Creative Commons/ "Archives" by rachaelvoorhees is licensed under CC BY-SA 2.0*

of results, there is a link to a page that describes grant money awarded for projects in Virginia between 1977 and 2019. One of these grants was administered to the Rokeby Museum located in Ferrisburgh, Vermont. The grant was awarded specifically to assist the museum in microfilming a special collection of papers that, among other topics, includes information about spiritualism, a movement and belief concerned with communication with the dead, usually via mediums.[21] From here, you could find the website for the Rokeby Museum and attempt to locate the information regarding that topic. It is safe to assume that one may not have stumbled upon the Rokeby Museum if not for consulting the contents of the National Archives.

Library of Congress

Another resource you can use to find primary sources (and more) on the paranormal is the Library of Congress. While some resources can be viewed and accessed online, other information can only be viewed in person, due to usage and access restrictions. Nonetheless, this is a helpful source to consult when researching the paranormal because it can often reveal some pretty unique historical paranormal artifacts. One example includes the diary of Nathan W. Daniels, a Civil War colonel. Daniels's diary consists of three volumes, and while they contain the obvious military and political entries, woven throughout each volume are entries about his involvement with the spiritualist movement. His wife, Cora Hatch, was in fact a noted medium of the day and also coauthored volume 3 of this diary collection.[22] In his diary, Daniels describes the various lectures and events he attends with Cora, and also details some of her visions, thereby offering a unique firsthand look into a few notable people associated with that movement.

The great thing about using the Library of Congress website to search for paranormal topics is that it reveals information in a variety of formats—newspaper articles, photographs, e-books, diaries, audio recordings, blogs, and more. In any given search, you will find a wide array of information. For example, one piece of information that you'll find when searching "paranormal" is a blog post authored by Clare Feikert-Ahalt, a researcher at the Law Library of Congress.[23] In her article, Clare discusses the legality of disclosing reports of paranormal phenomena when house-hunting in England. Full of wonderful links to a whole swatch of historical and paranormal resources, this blog is just one of the many examples of the paranormal entries you can find on the Library of Congress website.

A BRIEF LIST OF NOTABLE PRIMARY PARANORMAL SOURCES

In addition to the museums and websites listed above, the following is a short list of notable primary paranormal sources that represent topics and events throughout paranormal history. When studied, they can reveal new perspectives and deeper understanding of the paranormal. While this isn't an exhaustive list of primary sources, I include these examples to illustrate not only what primary sources are but why they can be so valuable. I hope it exemplifies what researchers should look for when seeking primary documents in the paranormal. Additional primary sources may be found in the following chapters.

Betty and Barney Hill Abduction Experience

Guide to the Betty and Barney Hill Papers, 1961–2006. (2019). University of New Hampshire Library. Retrieved from https://www.library.unh.edu/find/archives/collections/betty-and-barney-hill-papers-1961-2006#series-7

This resource, curated and housed at the University of New Hampshire Library, provides an extensive list of resources available surrounding the UFO abduction experience of Betty and Barney Hill. While most of the items listed in this index must be requested via photocopy or librarian assistance, there are some images that can be viewed immediately, such as artistic renderings of the creatures encountered as described by the Hills. Additionally, a photograph of Betty Hill's dress is included and readily viewable. An extensive bibliography of newspaper publications reporting the event is available as well and can serve as a finding aid to researchers.

A 1605 Publication on the Nature of Spirits

le Loyer, Pierre. (1605). *A Treatise of specters or straunge sights, visions, and apparitions appearing sensibly unto men wherein is delivered the nature of spirites, angels, and divels: Their powers and properties; As also of witches, sorcerers, enchanters, and such like.* London, England: Val S. 145 pages.

In this work, author Pierre le Loyer provides an overview of seventeenth-century thought on the nature of certain paranormal entities like ghosts and spirits as well as paranormal experiences such as prophetic dreams or other psychical events—of course, long before the term "psychical" was used to describe such phenomena. Not only does le Loyer outline the modern thoughts on these phenomena and experiences, but his work also serves as a historical bibliography of experiences as well as people who have written or mused about these subjects. This work is also interesting to consult, as le Loyer provides a detailed hierarchy of spirits, provides a philosophical overview of theories surrounding the soul, discusses tactics employed by sorcerers, and even includes examples of exorcism and religious techniques people have used to rid their homes or persons of spiritual attachments. As it is published in 1605, the spelling and grammar may take a bit getting used to, but it is a worthy entry here as it provides a huge amount of historical primary source information on certain matters of the paranormal—how people viewed these things and responded to them in the seventeenth century, for example.

Spiritualism Periodical Published in 1882

Gallery of Spirit Art: An illustrated quarterly magazine devoted to and illustrative of spirit photography, spirit painting, the photographing of materialized forms and every form of spirit art. (1882, May). New York, NY: C. R. Miller. Retrieved from Adam Matthew Victorian Popular Culture. http://www.victorianpopularculture.amdigital.co.uk/Documents/Details/GalleryofSpiritArt

This periodical, published in 1882, discusses the creative art form of spirit photography—a popular spiritualist technique. This edition talks about the "incoming tide of spiritual illumination" being made possible by such technologies as phones, photography, and electricity. It specifically discusses "spirit art" and the various mediums who engaged in those forms of divination and artistry. It describes the experiences of mediums who, compelled by a phantom urge, drew unfamiliar yet eerily accurate portraits of long-deceased peoples. It also discusses the specific art of spirit photography and the methods employed by mediums to capture photographic spirits. Still further, it includes interviews with mediums and artists and contains case studies of various occurrences of spirit art.

May 2019 Article from the *New York Times* about Navy Investigations of UAPs

Cooper, Helene, Blumenthal, Ralph, & Kean, Leslie. (2019, May 26). Wow, what is that? Navy pilots report unexplained flying objects. *The New York Times*. Retrieved via Historic *New York Times*, December 17, 2019.

In this *New York Times* article, journalists Cooper, Blumenthal, and Kean interview navy officers who experienced encounters with UFOs, or as they are officially designated by the navy, UAPs—unidentified aerial phenomena. Seasoned aircraft officers reported their experiences not only to their superiors but also to the Pentagon and Congress. So many reports and experiences cropped up that the navy released specific guidelines for how to report these experiences. Within this article, there are references to the government program titled Advanced Aerospace Threat Identification Program operated by the Pentagon. Furthermore, this article reveals that a spike in sightings occurred after updates in aircraft technology were employed—updates that hadn't occurred since as far back as the 1980s in some cases. Reports of personal encounters and detailed descriptions with links to video footage are included in this article as well.

New York Times Article Highlighting the ESP Experiments of J. B. Rhine

Telepathy tested by psychologists: Prof. Rhine's report on extra sensory perception starts wave of experiments. (1937, December 5). *The New York Times*, p. 63. Retrieved from ProQuest Historical *New York Times*.

This article, written in 1937 during the heyday of Dr. Rhine's experimentation with extrasensory perception, not only provides readers with photographic evidence of what a typical experiment looked like and how it was conducted, but it also provides a detailed discussion of the statistics surrounding these ESP experiments. Included in this article are criticisms of Rhine's methods; however, it also offers a serious discussion of the work being done at that time by the Duke Parapsychology Labs. This is not the only newspaper article highlighting J. B. Rhine and his pursuits, and interested researchers would find it beneficial to consult newspaper databases for yet more information.

The Heyday of Mesmerism

Esdaile, James. (1852). *Natural and mesmeric clairvoyance, with the practical application of mesmerism in surgery and medicine.* London, England: Hippolyte Bailliere. 272 pages.

In this work, Dr. James Esdaile describes his friendship with Franz Anton Mesmer and the scorn and ridicule that was heaped upon them as a result of touting their belief in mesmerism and its applications to medicine. Having been scorned and rejected from membership in certain organizations and also publications in certain venues, Dr. Esdaile took to publishing his practices and thoughts instead in local newspapers while working in hospitals in Calcutta. In this work, he discusses the theories of mesmerism and the various styles of mesmerism. Furthermore, he also discusses the anomalous experiences that many have when under hypnosis or mesmerism, such as clairvoyant abilities. He then outlines the procedures and practices he used during his time in Calcutta. Offering a detailed inquiry of mesmerism and how divisive this phenomenon was, Dr. Esdaile's work offers readers a comprehensive view of the thoughts, attitudes, and practices during the heyday of mesmerism.

Witch Trial Documents from the University of Virginia

Ray, Benjamin. (2018). Salem Witch Trials: Documentary Archive and Transcription Project. Scholar's Lab: University of Virginia. Retrieved January 6, 2020, from http://salem.lib.virginia.edu/home.html

A great example of a special online collection of primary source artifacts is the Salem Witch Trials: Documentary Archive and Transcription Project managed by the Scholar's Lab at the University of Virginia. This robust and comprehensive website allows visitors to view transcripts of court proceedings and provides links to view original court documents, books written by such key figures as Cotton and Increase Mather, maps of Salem town and village, as well as a biographic entry of those associated with the trials. In this annotated biography, there are even links to resources affiliated with each person, such as their associated court proceedings. For example, searching for "Bridget Bishop" in the biography will reveal a link to her connected court records. Clicking that link will reveal digitized images of the original documents as well as easy-to-read transcribed versions. One such item is the original warrant for her arrest, issued on April 18, 1692. I strongly encourage readers interested in the witch trials of Salem to consult this vast resource of primary documents. Not only is there a seemingly unending supply of links and resources, the documents are also transcribed and presented in readable formats juxtaposed next to their digitized original formats, making for a truly unique journey back into time.

THE VALUE OF HOLISTIC RESEARCH

In the paranormal, as with any field, there are a number of different types of primary sources to research. Specific to our discussion, primary sources in the paranormal include, but are not limited to: haunted locations, individuals with eyewitness testimony, newspaper clippings, photographs, diaries, research equipment, and more. Primary sources are a great way of deepening your understanding of certain topics and also serve to bring your research to life. Knowing how and where to access primary resources can often be the biggest roadblock. In this chapter, therefore, I define and discuss primary sources and offer some avenues for accessing them. I outlined some of the paranormal museums scattered around the United States as well as introduce readers to other tools they can use to locate primary paranormal sources. Some of these may not seem like obvious research avenues, and my hope is that by highlighting some of those not-so-obvious sources, readers will understand the value of thinking outside the box when it comes to paranormal research. The mark of good research is consulting a wide variety of tools and resources to arrive at a well-informed and educated conclusion about any given topic.

NOTES

1. Peabody Essex Museum. (n.d.). The Phillips Library. Retrieved July 14, 2019, from https://www.pem.org/visit/library
2. Witch House. (n.d.). Witch House: History. Retrieved July 14, 2019, from https://www.thewitchhouse.org/
3. Amy's Crypt. (2018, April 16). The story behind Salem's haunted Witch House [Blog post]. Retrieved July 14, 2019, from https://amyscrypt.com/salem-witch-house/
4. International Cryptozoology Museum. (n.d.). Mission & vision. Retrieved July 14, 2019, from http://cryptozoologymuseum.com/mission-vision
5. International Cryptozoology Museum. (n.d.). History of the ICM. Retrieved July 14, 2019, from http://cryptozoologymuseum.com/history-of-the-icm
6. LeRose, Chris (2001, October). The collapse of the Silver Bridge. *West Virginia Historical Society Quarterly, 15*(4). Retrieved July 14, 2019, from http://www.wvculture.org/history/wvhs/wvhs1504.html
7. Archive of the Afterlife. (n.d.). Welcome. Retrieved July 15, 2019, from https://archive-afterlife.weebly.com/
8. Traveling Museum of the Paranormal & Occult. (2018). About the museum. Retrieved July 14, 2019, from http://paramuseum.com/about/
9. Ibid.
10. Ibid.
11. Traveling Museum of the Paranormal & Occult. (2018). Hoodoo coffin nail. Retrieved July 14, 2019, from http://paramuseum.com/pieces/voodoo-coffin-nail/
12. Traveling Museum of the Paranormal & Occult. (2018). The dark mirror. Retrieved July 14, 2019, from http://paramuseum.com/pieces/the-dark-mirror/
13. Traveling Museum of the Paranormal & Occult. (2018). The idol of nightmares [Billy]. Retrieved July 14, 2019, from http://paramuseum.com/pieces/idol-nightmares-billy/
14. North American Bigfoot Center. (2019). The museum. Retrieved July 14, 2019, from https://northamericanbigfootcenter.com/museum
15. Willow Creek–China Flat Museum: Bigfoot Country. (2019). Home. Retrieved July 14, 2019, from http://bigfootcountry.net/
16. Bigfoot Discovery Project. (n.d.). Retrieved July 15, 2019, from https://www.bigfootdiscoveryproject.com/
17. Rhine Research Center. (2019). Museum. Retrieved July 15, 2019, from https://www.rhine.org/what-we-do/rhine-newsletter/86-who-we-are/rhine-today/106-museum.html
18. Cryptozoology and Paranormal Museum. (n.d.). About. Retrieved July 15, 2019, from https://crypto-para.org/about/
19. Expedition: Bigfoot! The Sasquatch Museum. (2016). About us. Retrieved July 15, 2019, from https://www.expeditionbigfoot.com/about
20. U.S. National Archives and Records Administration. (n.d.-b). What is the National Archives and Records Administration? Retrieved July 15, 2019, from https://www.archives.gov/about
21. U.S. National Archives and Records Administration. (n.d.-a). Vermont: Records projects. Retrieved July 15, 2019, from https://www.archives.gov/nhprc/projects/states-territories/vt.html

22. Library of Congress. (n.d.). *Collection: Nathan W. Daniels diary and scrapbook.* Retrieved July 15, 2019, from https://www.loc.gov/collections/nathan-w-daniels-diary-and-scrapbook/about-this-collection/

23. Feikert-Ahalt, Clare. (2012, October 31). Revealing the presence of ghosts. *In Custodia Legis: Law Librarians of Congress.* Retrieved July 15, 2019, from https://blogs.loc.gov/law/2012/10/revealing-the-presence-of-ghosts/

Chapter Seven

Handbooks, Dictionaries, and Encyclopedias

The remainder of this work contains an annotated bibliography of a vast array of sources that readers can consult to learn more about the paranormal. In this chapter, I focus on handbooks, dictionaries, and encyclopedias on various topics of the paranormal. To provide some organization, I have arranged this chapter by presenting all handbooks, dictionaries, and encyclopedias under their respective paranormal headings—that way, readers are able to stick to a certain section of this chapter if they are only interested in reincarnation, for example, without having to switch back and forth among multiple sections. The first headings you see, then, are the paranormal categories followed by this succession of headings: handbooks, dictionaries, encyclopedias. Then, the next paranormal heading is presented, and so on until the last topic is outlined. Hopefully arranging it this way is most efficient.

The resources presented here—handbooks, dictionaries, and encyclopedias—are reference materials that readers may consult time and time again. Anyone who has used an encyclopedia understands that you use these types of resources much differently than you would a novel, which you read from beginning to end. Of course, if one wishes to read a dictionary from beginning to end there's nothing to stop them, but the works in this section are meant to be consumed in pieces—for example, maybe you are researching the Mothman phenomena of West Virginia. When consulting a cryptozoological dictionary for that topic, you browse past the listings for many other topics like Bigfoot and the Loch Ness Monster in order to go straight to your chosen section on Mothman.

While you browse these titles, remember our earlier discussion regarding libraries and how they can help you access titles. Libraries prove invaluable at not only helping you save money, but also in tracking down and accessing rare or out-of-print titles. I attempt to provide a robust bibliography, but this is by no means an exhaustive and complete list. I urge readers to use the resources in this list to lead them to additional titles. A great way to do this is to always consult the references and bibliographies within each of these sources. Readers may note that some of these works are well over fifty years old (or older). Due to the nature of reference materials, which take longer to compile and produce than monographs (single-topic books), it makes sense that this category contains works that are a bit older. However, it also makes sense to include older titles because of the long history of inquiry into the paranormal. Readers who recall our discussion of credibility in chapter 4 will recall that titles that are a bit dated can provide unique historical information on any given topic. Of course, it is always beneficial to gather a balanced mix of modern and historical items, and so I include publications that are also very recent. For these reasons, readers should not be surprised to find titles that are a bit dated.

GHOSTS AND HAUNTINGS

Handbooks

Auerbach, Loyd. (2016). *ESP, hauntings and poltergeists: A parapsychologist's handbook.* Loyd Auerbach: CreateSpace. 348 pages.

This work, an updated edition of its original from 1986, could be relegated to a number of categories in this book, most notably parapsychology. The word is in the title, after all. However, I place it here in the "Ghosts and Hauntings" category because the majority of the content is centered around hauntings, ghosts, and poltergeists and even offers a detailed, lengthy section on how to conduct your own paranormal investigations. This work also includes some highlighted case studies of infamous hauntings, including the Amityville case, and discusses the ways in which ghosts and hauntings have been portrayed in film and literature. Auerbach's work really includes a little bit of everything—it even contains a section on near-death experiences and reincarnation, but the crux of this book rests upon the connections back to the world of ghosts and hauntings. This is a wonderful resource for those new to the topic.

Blackman, W. Haden. (1998). *The field guide to North American hauntings: Everything you need to know about encountering over 100 ghosts, phantoms, and spectral entities.* New York, NY: Three Rivers Press. 208 pages.

This work, though not labeled as a handbook, is a reference-style compendium of notable ghost and haunting cases in North America, hence its inclusion here in the handbook category. After a brief introduction, the author provides a handy exposé of how to use this book—a helpful addition for any reference work, really. In chapter 1, Blackman discusses haunted houses, the most typical entry for most of us, and includes such notable cases as the Amityville case, the LaLaurie Mansion, and the Winchester Mystery House. The second chapter contains information about haunted ships, airplanes, and trains—vessels of transportation, in other words. The third chapter contains a listing of prominent haunted cemeteries and burial grounds, while chapter 4 provides information on hauntings that occur in certain landmarks or public outdoor spaces like gardens or parks. In each of these sections, Blackman provides the address so that readers can potentially visit these places. He also provides an overview of the number of ghosts, their supposed identities, and the nature of the haunting before digging into the more detailed entry for each location. Reminiscent of John Spencer's *The Ghost Handbook*, this book is a great source for those interested in visiting paranormal hotspots in the United States and Canada. In fact, Blackman provides a geographical listing of locations broken down by state and province at the end of this work. The appendixes included in this work set it apart from similar resources. Blackman provides an appendix offering a sample questionnaire to use when interviewing eyewitnesses of paranormal phenomena and includes a second appendix for those conducting their own paranormal investigation.

Miller, Keith. (2019). *Subtle spirits: a handbook of hauntings, spirits and mediumship.* [N.p.]: Turtles & Crows. 172 pages.

Author Keith Miller, a teacher and psychic who obtained his master's degree in transpersonal psychology from Atlantic University, provides a handbook that explores the different types of hauntings but that also explores exercises in mediumship. The first half of Miller's book is an exposé of the various types of spirits and hauntings that occur. For example, he goes far beyond the simple notion of "ghost" and tells readers that we can classify spirits in a number of ways: whether they are wandering spirits or spirits of place, whether they are passive or intelligently interactive, whether they seem to influence the environments around them, and whether they seem to embody some elemental attributes (e.g., fire, water)—distinctions of which he goes into great detail. In the next section, he discusses hauntings and describes some of the most common locations for hauntings and why these locations may appear more prevalent for paranormal activity than others. This section is just as nuanced as the section outlining types of spirits, and it presents a fairly robust exploration that goes above and beyond the old haunted house trope. He follows this with a section on possessions and hauntings of the body, during which he also discusses oracles and haunted objects. He offers a chapter on best practices for paranormal investigating before he delves into the nuances of using meditation for enhancing one's own psychic abilities and follows this with a discussion of specific psychic phenomena such as psychometry, imprinting, clairvoyance, and automatic writing. Following this discussion, he presents an interesting section on divination practices using such things as marbles, pendulums, and candles. At the conclusion is a list of references and further reading.

Randles, Jenny. (1996). *The paranormal sourcebook: The comprehensive guide to strange phenomena worldwide.* London, England: Judy Piatkus. 250 pages.

This work presents twenty-one of the world's strangest phenomena, and while that may not necessarily sound like a lot, the way Randles treats each topic makes this title worthy of inclusion. For each entry, the author includes a detailed definition followed by a historical sketch of the issue at hand. Following the definition and historical overview, she then provides an article from an eyewitness/experiencer point of view. Immediately after this, she includes a more scientific, research-style essay on the topic, offering readers some further explanation for the phenomena. At the very end of each entry Randles includes information on relevant societies or organizations that readers can reach out to, along with certain books and periodicals supporting her entries and for further reading. It's convenient that each chapter contains its own references and further reading, making each entry and the information contained therein extremely accessible.

Rogo, D. Scott. (1978). *The haunted house handbook.* New York, NY: Tempo Books. 172 pages.

D. Scott Rogo, author of this work and others on poltergeists and phantoms, was a paranormal investigator, author, and researcher. He worked with such institutions as the Psychical Research Foundation, as well as the parapsychology department at Maimonides Medical Center. He also served as research director of the Southern California Society for Psychical Research. In this work, Rogo tell us that "I'm not going to bore you with a lot of corny campfire tales about headless spectres . . . instead I'm going to recount many accounts of well-authenticated haunted houses." This work begins by exploring what exactly we mean when we say "haunted house" and provides some notable case studies. Then, Rogo moves on to compare historical hauntings alongside their contemporary counterparts. He then outlines his experience living in a haunted house in Los Angeles for two years before progressing to a discussion about specific types of hauntings and spirits like poltergeists and animal spirits. He concludes by exploring the parapsychological evidence behind what hauntings are and also provides some guidance for those who wish to conduct their own paranormal investigations. Complete with black-and-white photographs of notable hauntings.

Spencer, John. (1994). *Ghostwatching.* London, England: Virgin Books. 278 pages.

John Spencer, a member of the Society for Psychical Research, presents a work geared toward those interested in becoming paranormal researchers themselves. Even though this work is a bit dated (1994), it provides a solid amount of information that is still useful today. Furthermore, Spencer intersperses his chapters with personal experiences during his own paranormal investigations, further adding to the wealth of information about haunted locations in the United Kingdom.

This work begins with a detailed overview about ghostly phenomena, including different types of hauntings such as residual or intelligent hauntings and poltergeist activity. Following this overview, Spencer provides some examples of how technology has been used to both capture paranormal evidence as well as act as a conduit to enhance paranormal activity. Following these sections, Spencer then introduces readers to tactics they can employ to jump-start their paranormal endeavors. He begins by outlining what it means to conduct a paranormal "vigil" and prepares the reader for establishing their own protocols for hosting a vigil. Of course, the word "vigil" has many connotations, but in this sense, Spencer tells us that it requires the controlled usage of teams and equipment to record paranormal activity. Think of it then as the much more commonly used phrase "paranormal investigation."

After outlining how to set up and conduct one's own vigil, Spencer discusses how to conduct interviews with people who have reported paranormal experiences, including throughout this work examples of his own experiences as a paranormal investigator. Included in this section is also a brief overview of the methods that people have employed to "banish" paranormal activity, including the obvious exorcism strategies but also mentioning psychological techniques that some believe can help ease poltergeist activity.

Part 3 of Spencer's work is all about how to set up a paranormal team of one's own and includes tips and information on locating haunted locations as well as advice on presenting oneself professionally. At the back of this work are appendixes that list paranormal organizations of the United Kingdom, sample interview questions for eyewitnesses, further reading, an overview of recommended equipment for paranormal investigators, and even a sample report of a paranormal investigation.

Spencer, John, & Spencer, Anne. (1998). *The ghost handbook.* London, England: Macmillan. 309 pages.

This book is designed specifically for our ghost-loving friends in the UK. The authors' goal is to create a compendium of ghost stories, hauntings, and urban legends in Britain with a special emphasis on highlighting those locations that are open to the public so that readers can actually visit them. This work also contains special sections titled "While You're There," which references other phenomena such as UFO sightings, monster legends, and more, near the locale already being discussed. Keen on creating opportunities for readers to go and get a firsthand look at these locations, the authors also include, in the final chapter, a list of restaurants and hotels so that readers can even create their own paranormal vacations. In the preface to chapter 1, the authors discuss different types of hauntings and the prominent evidence surrounding ghostly phenomena. They additionally discuss their own experience as paranormal investigators and recount the locations they've visited and the evidence they've captured. The first section of this work focuses mainly on haunted castles, churches, palaces, theaters, and residences, and they not only list the places that are reportedly haunted but also discuss the reasons why these hauntings may have arisen in the first place. Each entry in these chapters are, on average, a page in length, which sounds sparse at first, but when you consider the first section is nearly one hundred pages in length, readers soon see that there is a wealth of information contained there.

The second category in this book refers to paranormal phenomena that are directly linked to untimely deaths, such as murders or wartime casualties. The third category is unique in that it focuses on paranormal phenomena that have been reported outside and therefore unattached to physical buildings. Included in this category are reports of "phantom hitch-hikers" as well as ghostly phenomena attached to transportation such as phantom cars or phantom trains. Following this section is a fun section titled "Ghostly Extras" in which the authors discuss things like "time-slips" or visions of the future, psychokinesis, and poltergeist activity. Yet another unique section follows this and is titled "Anniversary Ghosts," in which readers can browse for a listing of ghostly activity that is only reported during certain months of the year. The last section, titled "Ghosts on the Menu," is a wonderful conclusion to this work, listing the haunted hotels and restaurants in the UK and even providing each with its own ghostly five-star rating. At the end of this book the authors include references and recommended reading. This work is a unique edition for anyone interested in spirits of the UK and, in particular, those who are interested in paranormal tourism of the UK. John Spencer is also the author of another handbook titled *Ghosthunting: The Ghosthunter's Handbook*, which readers are encouraged to browse.

Dictionaries

McGovern, Una. (Ed.). (2007). *Chambers dictionary of the unexplained: A guide to the mysterious, the paranormal and the supernatural.* Edinburgh, Scotland: Chambers Harrap. 760 pages.

A work that contains more than thirteen hundred entries, the *Chambers Dictionary of the Unexplained* is, as explained in the introduction, a collection of information "relating to a wide range of subjects that sit on the edge of, or even wholly outside, the widely accepted beliefs about the nature of the world in which we live." Beautifully arranged and with an assortment of images, the dictionary contains information not only on paranormal phenomena, but also on prominent figures, associations, and organizations affiliated with the paranormal. Following the preface, this work contains a list of "subjects of particular interest" as well as "cases of particular interest" that are a great way for those new to the topic to begin browsing this work. Compiled with the assistance of Bob Rickard, founder of the *Fortean Times*, a British publication released monthly that focuses on reports of paranormal events, this dictionary is a useful resource for any reference collection on the paranormal, for those just beginning to engage their interest in this topic, and even for more seasoned researchers who want to learn something new.

Underwood, Peter. (1978). *Dictionary of the supernatural.* London, England: Harrap. 389 pages.

Peter Underwood was president of the Ghost Club, an organization said to be the oldest established paranormal research organization, having been founded some twenty years prior to the Society for Psychical Research.[1] Underwood, a noted parapsychologist, was also a member of the SPR, and along with other publications published this dictionary of supernatural terminology. The foreword of this publication, written by Paul Adams, describes this dictionary as a "concise and far ranging examination of the world of what [Underwood] calls the 'supernatural,' [belonging] firmly to the 1970s, a decade that saw the seeds of the occult revolution of the 1960s begin to grow and thrive." As Underwood tells us in the introduction, his goal was to cover as comprehensively as possible, all cults/organizations, phenomena, and the research associated with the occult *and* the supernatural. The entries themselves are detailed, contain citations at the end of entries for further reading, and contain the occasional image. The back cover of this work proclaims that it is a compendium of hauntings, witchcraft, possession and demonology, and while it does contain entries on those topics, it also contains much more. For example, it contains a detailed entry for acupuncture. Some entries contain outdated terms (see the entry on "acenesthesia" for an example), but it is still a worthy addition to the dictionaries of the paranormal and provides, if anything, a snapshot of paranormal thought from the 1970s.

Encyclopedias

Belanger, Jeff. (Ed.). (2009). *Encyclopedia of haunted places: Ghostly locales from around the world.* Franklin Lakes, NJ: Career Press. 360 pages.

In this work editor Jeff Belanger, historian and paranormal investigator, compiles information on haunted locations around the world. What sets this title apart from other encyclopedias, however, is that other paranormal investigators contribute to the entries themselves, including their own personal experiences as well as notes from firsthand investigations of the locations included therein. This work is also set apart by the fact that it is international in scope and is a true worldwide compendium of some of the most famous haunted locations across the globe.

Beginning with haunted locations in Canada, Belanger even separates the hauntings by regions within each country when necessary. Canada, for example, is broken down into "Western," "Central," and "Eastern" categories. The United States, too, is broken down by geographic region including "New England," "Mid-Atlantic," "Alaska/Hawaii," "Great Lakes," and more. This organization makes for quick browsing for readers interested in navigating to their preferred regions. Additional countries that include fewer entries are not broken down by geographic area. While it begins with Canada and the United States, the work is a true international compendium and includes entries on locations in Mexico, the Caribbean, Cambodia, Singapore, Japan, Australia, Iceland, England, Italy, and many more.

Belanger begins his work with an introductory chapter outlining how the entries included are handpicked from the most memorable experiences of the paranormal investigators who contributed each entry. The entries themselves often contain an image of the location under focus along with an address, telephone number, and website if applicable. An overview and history of the location follows, along with the personal experience of the entry's author. Each entry is, on average, about a page in length, which, at 360 pages, makes this work a robust compendium of haunted locales around the world.

Included at the end of the work is a brief biographical chapter on well-known paranormal researcher Hans Holzer, followed by two appendixes. Appendix A is written as a guide for those who are experiencing paranormal phenomena and are looking for someone to help them learn more about their situation. It provides information on what to expect from a paranormal investigator and how to confidently seek out these people. Appendix B is like a telephone book of paranormal investigators and includes contact information for those investigators who contributed entries to the work. The directory is organized by geographic region.

Campbell, Joseph. (Ed.). (1954). *Spirit and nature: Papers from the Eranos Yearbooks.* Bollingen Series 30, Vol. 1. New York, NY: Pantheon Books. 492 pages.

This volume is just one of many published in the Eranos Yearbooks series, making it similar to an encyclopedia, hence its inclusion here. Eranos is a yearly gathering of international scholars who meet in Switzerland to discuss a wide range of topics, including the soul, the meeting of Eastern and Western philosophies, fairy tales, legends, symbols, and much more. Founded by Dutch scholar and spiritualist Olga Frobe-Kapteyn in the late 1920s, the goal was to "create a free space for the spirit [and] where the relation between the individual, the spirit and the peculiar images of the soul [could be] unceasingly re-imagined."[2] In this volume, titled *Spirit and Nature*, a number of essays are included that discuss various aspects of the spirit world, such as the mystical/religious perspective, the historical attitude and thoughts on spirits, as well as an exposé on spirits in fairy tales. This edition, published in 1954, provides a unique historical perspective on the notion of spirit and can help researchers not only understand historical underpinnings of this topic, but trace its trajectory from earlier times to today.

Cardin, Matt. (Ed.). (2015). *Ghosts, spirits, and psychics: The paranormal from alchemy to zombies.* Santa Barbara, CA: ABC-CLIO. 409 pages.

This work is edited by Matt Cardin, scholar of the ways in which religion, horror, and psychology intersect, and editor of other volumes. Contributors to this work include Fiona Bowie, founder of the Afterlife Research Center; Callum E. Cooper, a PhD student at the Centre for the Study of Anomalous Psychological Processes; Brenda J. Dunne, president of the International Consciousness Research Laboratories; and John G. Kruth, executive director of the Rhine Research Center. Along with many other contributors whose credentials are simply too lengthy to list here, this work contains more than 120 entries and is "a sweeping compendium of information about the paranormal—including information about the very history and meaning of 'paranormal' itself as a word and concept." Moreover, the introduction to this work is an absolute must-read in terms of a starting point to this work as it presents a very skilled discussion of the ways in which the paranormal has influenced and is manifested through not only pop culture, intellectual culture, religion, and anthropology, but much more. It argues for a more nuanced understanding of the paranormal through a more comprehensive and multidisciplinary lens that recognizes that the Western worldview is only one small way of looking at this topic. A wonderfully intellectual and thought-provoking essay in its own right, it sets the stage for a chronology of the paranormal that follows. This chronology begins at 3000 BC and moves forward to the present day, providing a robust overview of how the paranormal has been embedded in the human experience throughout history. The chronology is so comprehensive and detailed that readers could spend a significant amount of time mining the references contained in just this one section of the encyclopedia. The encyclopedia entries themselves are thorough and may contain their own brief chronology as well as references and suggestions for further reading.

Cheung, Theresa. (2010). *Element encyclopedia of ghosts and hauntings.* London, England: Harper Element. 576 pages.

A few editions of this work have been published, so readers looking for this work may find one of two subtitles: *The Ultimate A–Z for the Entire Magical World* or *The Ultimate A–Z of Spirits, Mysteries & the Paranormal.* In this work, Cheung compiles entries not only on ghosts and hauntings, but affiliated theories, evidence, prominent figures, and more. There is a brief historical overview that focuses primarily on noted psychical researchers and the role of psychics throughout history, followed by another brief overview of the debate regarding proof of ghostly phenomena. Entries are not limited to just North America, however; this work contains references to worldwide phenomena and folklore. For example, there are entries about the Akashic records, haunted castles in England, Scottish folklore, Native American spirit beliefs, and more. Additionally, these entries often contain references to prominent researchers, figures, events, or additional resources. Readers may also wish to consult Theresa Cheung's similar encyclopedic work titled *Element Encyclopedia of the Psychic World*, first published by Harper Element in 2006.

Guiley, Rosemary Ellen, & Taylor, Troy. (2007). *The encyclopedia of ghosts and spirits* (3rd ed.) New York, NY: Facts on File. 564 pages.

Rosemary Ellen Guiley, noted paranormal author and researcher, and Troy Taylor provide here an updated encyclopedia of events, cases, people, terms, and more affiliated with ghosts and spirits. Updated to include new phenomena as well as modern researchers, this work contains a wide variety of information, such as entries on a notable eighteenth-century haunting in Nova Scotia; a discussion of animism, folklore, and urban legends of Britain; and a whole host of other topics. International in scope, each entry contains resources for further reading. For an older edition, readers can also seek out Guiley's *The Guinness Encyclopedia of Ghosts and Spirits*, which was published in 1994 and, though shorter than the work listed here, contains similar information.

Illes, Judika. (2009). *Encyclopedia of spirits: The ultimate guide to the magic of saints, angels, fairies, demons, and ghosts.* New York, NY: HarperCollins. 1,072 pages.

Author Judika Illes is an independent researcher of the paranormal as well as the author of *Encyclopedia of Witchcraft* and *Encyclopedia of 5,000 Spells.* In this *Encyclopedia of Spirits*, a tome at more than one thousand pages, Illes prefaces her work with a discussion of how pervasive spirits are in our everyday lives—for example, she reminds us that saying, "Oh frigg" is actually an oft-forgotten reference to the Norse goddess Frigg (Fricka). Illes goes far beyond just common phrases, though, to show how deeply embedded the world of spirits is in cultures the world over. In fact, this work contains a very detailed introduction to the world of spirits of all types, including discussions on their place in the historical record, in folklore, and in traditions that continue today, as well as how to communicate with spirits and where potentially to find them. The entries themselves contain definitions and descriptions, including place of origin and any icons associated with them, and sometimes even include the ways in which each spirit is said to manifest. This book is so much more than an "encyclopedia" and is a great resource to consult to begin your journey of understanding spirits on a cultural level.

PARAPSYCHOLOGY

Handbooks

Ashby, Robert H. (1987). *The guidebook for the study of psychical research.* New York, NY: Samuel Weiser. 190 pages.

This work is a unique addition to the handbook category as it includes lists of resources for both the beginning researcher as well as for the more seasoned researcher. Ashby, who investigates psychical phenomena himself, begins this work with an introduction to psi phenomena and the research that has been done to date. Chapter 2 provides a bibliography of resources for those who are new to this topic, and within this chapter Ashby breaks resources down not only by topic, but also by research type. For example, Ashby includes a list of general surveys as well as quantitative studies, and further includes a list of philosophical and theoretical resources for these topics. At the end of the chapter, he includes a nonannotated list of resources that is akin to "further reading." Chapter 3 contains resources, organized in a similar way, on more advanced sources for those already familiar with these topics. Chapter 4 is a short chapter, but a very interesting one as it outlines the ways to contact mediums and how to interact with them. As Ashby writes, "Every serious student of psi will wish to experience paranormal phenomena personally, and the most readily available possibility is a series of 'sittings' with mediums." Chapter 5 provides a list of research organizations, libraries, special collections, and bookshops in both the U.S. and the UK. Rounding out the work is a concluding chapter of brief biographies of prominent psi researchers. A glossary of terms is also included and helps readers navigate terminology previously unfamiliar.

Cardeña, Etzel, Palmer, John, & Marcusson-Clavertz, David. (Eds.). (2015). *Parapsychology: A handbook for the 21st century.* Jefferson, NC: McFarland. 413 pages.

This edited work can be considered a modern complement to the 1977 *Handbook of Parapsychology*, which will be more suitable to situating a historical understanding of psychical research. This 2015 work is a compilation of articles written by current researchers, such as Carlos S. Alvarado, a research fellow of the Parapsychology Foundation and editorial board member for publications such as the *Journal of Near-Death Studies* and *Journal of the Society for Psychical Research*.[3] This work is divided into nine distinct sections that begins with an overview and introduction of concepts in parapsychology followed by a section on research methods and statistics. Following this, there are three sections that combine parapsychology with specific fields: biology, psychology, and physics, followed by sections highlighting specific cases studies of anomalous phenomena. Wrapping up the work is a section that highlights the prevalence (or day-to-day happenings) of psychical phenomena and how it impacts our lives. Each article in this edited work contains references that readers can consult to find even more information about the topics discussed therein.

Corliss, William R. (1982). *The unfathomed mind: A handbook of unusual mental phenomena.* Glen Arm, MD: Sourcebook Project. 754 pages.

Although the author of this work, William Corliss, professes to be a bit conservative in his treatment of psychical phenomena, this work nonetheless is a wonderful addition to any researcher's list of works on parapsychology. Corliss tells us that the sources in his handbook are "almost exclusively publications in general science, psychology, and psychiatry," with a few sources thrown in from the Society for Psychical Research. He emphasizes, however, a strong desire to steer away from parapsychological resources and instead to compile the many strange reports that can be found in more conservatively scientific publications. The author himself was a physicist and author of more than thirty titles, many of which were published through the Sourcebook Project, a publishing house on anomalous phenomena. Concerning the contents, this work is broken down into seven sections of phenomena, including topics such as "multiple personality," "automatic communication," "altered states of consciousness," "possession," and even "anomalous dream behavior." The selections themselves are often copied segments of the works themselves, so that readers view original portions of the works that Corliss compiles in each category. In that sense, this handbook can be viewed not as a compendium of annotated bibliographies but of citations and their abstracts. I found this to be wholly engrossing as the handbook reads more like a collection of stories than as an annotated compendium in one cohesive voice.

Irwin, Harvey J. (2009). *The psychology of paranormal belief: A researcher's handbook.* Hertfordshire, England: University of Hertfordshire Press. 213 pages.

Written by Harvey Irwin, a psychical researcher and research fellow at the Manchester Metropolitan University in England,[4] this work explores the psychological origins of belief in the paranormal. As Dr. Caroline Watt and Richard Wiseman tell us in their foreword to this work, the notion of the "paranormal" is an extremely nuanced one and includes with it a myriad amount of beliefs. The introduction to this book shows just how nuanced Irwin is in his treatment of this issue—for example, he spends a great deal of time discussing the particular problems of defining the paranormal (as it is used to pertain to an extremely large amount of differing topics), and lays out his solution to categorizing the paranormal. His classification scheme is quite robust and includes such topics as "cryptozoological creatures, extraterrestrial aliens, Judeo-Christian religious beliefs, spiritism," and "esoteric systems of magic," to name just a few. In organizing the paranormal this way, he creates the ability to gain a very niche understanding of the beliefs of certain subsets of the paranormal and, as a result, offers readers a more nuanced discussion about paranormal belief that goes deeper than superficial discussions that don't adequately define "paranormal." Irwin's work contains much discussion about dominant psychological theories of why people believe in the paranormal but also discusses the limitations and consequences of research and theories born with the assumption that paranormal phenomena cannot possibly exist. In chapter 2, Irwin discusses the role that sociocultural learning has on the development of paranormal beliefs, and in chapter 3 he discusses the ways in which researchers have attempted to study and classify paranormal belief, giving readers a history lesson of paranormal psychological research along the way. In chapters 4–7, he critically evaluates the dominant psychological theories on paranormal belief and concludes his work by integrating portions of those aforementioned theories and highlights issues for future research. This is for those especially interested in how the world around us shapes our beliefs in the paranormal.

Wolman, Benjamin B. (Ed.). (1977). *Handbook of parapsychology*. New York, NY: Litton Educational. 967 pages.

This work, at nearly one thousand pages long, compiles "the history, achievements, scope, and problems as well as the implications and issues of an emerging science." In this case, the emerging science is parapsychology and this edited handbook includes articles on the history, research, and theories of the field. Written almost exclusively by MD- or PhD-holding authors, some of the authors include J. B. Rhine and Ian Stevenson, which readers may remember from my discussion on both parapsychology and reincarnation. The handbook begins by including approximately fifty pages of historical background of the field, followed by specific research methods used by parapsychologists. The work then goes on to focus on some specific subsets of parapsychology, including psychokinesis, paranormal photography, and reincarnation. After some exploration of unique research, the handbook provides articles that join parapsychology with other scientific fields such as anthropology, physics, religion, and even literature. Following this, there is a section devoted to parapsychological theories of the time, and the book ends with a bibliography of further reading. Interestingly, this work includes a brief section of research conducted in Russia—since at the time of this work's publication, psi research had gained a substantial popularity in that country.

Dictionaries

Pleasants, Helene. (Ed.). (1964). *Biographical dictionary of parapsychology*. New York, NY: Helix Press. 371 pages.

The publisher's note in this work clearly lays out the impetus for the publication of this work, and that is the fact that (at least in the 1960s) it was hard to locate which researchers were involved in psychical inquiry. At the time, the term "parapsychologist" was often eschewed in favor of other disciplines. For example, psi researcher Charles Richet was simply known as a physiologist and William Crookes as a chemist. Furthermore, this work attempts to solve the issue of scarce biographical information on those who *are* defined primarily by their psi research. The result is a biographical compendium of more than 350 pages of sketches of psi researchers that details not only their research but their lives as well. International in scope and chronicling the lives of both men and women, the entries also include their associations with various psi organizations. Noted psi experiencers are also included—mediums, for example. It truly cannot be overstated how massive of a biographical compendium this is—a work whose creation was funded by the Parapsychology Foundation of New York. Readers can use this work to find biographical information on researchers they encounter in other works and/or as a starting place of its own to learn more about prominent researchers. The fact that it was published in 1964 shouldn't be a deterrent, as the field of parapsychology dates back much further and this work can be used as a way of locating historical and foundational resources on this topic. A glossary at the end of the work helps readers interpret technical psi terminology.

Encyclopedias

Berger, Arthur S., & Berger, Joyce. (1991). *The encyclopedia of parapsychology and psychical research.* New York, NY: Paragon House. 554 pages.

The most unique aspect of this encyclopedia is the intentional focus on international parapsychological research. Specifically, this work contains information on the research from eighteen different countries, including Argentina, Italy, South Africa, and Spain. The authors explicitly state that they were motivated by the pervasive curiosity people have surrounding parapsychological phenomena, and as such wanted to create as comprehensive a work as possible that could be used by laypersons but also scientists and educators. The authors themselves are experienced paranormal researchers; Arthur Berger, specifically, was president of the Survival Research Foundation at the time of publication. The authors also include a section of "noted witness" stories from people who have experienced psi phenomena. A wonderful aspect of this work is that the authors specifically note that they did not exclude a topic due to its pseudoscientific reputation. As they put it, "Our position is that both parapsychology and psychical research should take cognizance of *all* paranormal phenomena that lie outside the pale of orthodox science." This attitude is, of course, a beneficial one to take when compiling international resources, and the authors attempt to remain as unbiased as possible. The entries themselves contain citations, but the authors also include a bibliography of further reading. In appendix A of this work, the authors include a list of articles that briefly highlight the history of parapsychological research in other countries, thereby compiling some of the entries found earlier in the book. What is most helpful and unique, though, is that in this section the authors also list prominent publications, universities, organizations, associations, and research centers that engage in parapsychology. This work is a true gem for international psi research.

Cheung, Theresa. (2010). *The Element encyclopedia of the psychic world.* London, England: Harper Element. 864 pages.

In this work, which contains more than eight hundred entries on psychical phenomena but also general phenomena on ghosts and hauntings, Cheung, in much the same format as her work on ghosts and hauntings mentioned above, includes a brief overview of distinguished psychics throughout history, followed by a discussion of the points that both skeptics and believers bring to the table when discussing psychic events. She follows this with a brief discussion of activities that could help readers enhance their psychic abilities, before moving on to the entries, which cover not only prominent people but studies, research, events, places, and more pertaining to "the psychic world." References included for further reading.

Fodor, Nandor. (1966). *Encyclopedia of psychic science.* New Hyde Park, NY: University Books. 416 pages.

In this work, "here are hundreds of articles and biographies dealing with [psi] phenomena and the people involved, the famous mediums and the wonder-workers who did these things and the reporters and scientists who investigated them." The time period covered by this book includes early 1800s to 1966. The foreword includes suggestions to readers on which entries to start with, especially if they are new to the topic of psychical research. Complete beginners, for example, should start with "spiritualism" and "psychical research," the foreword tells us. It gives further suggestions from here, pointing out key entries even after delving into the introductory topics.

Melton, J. Gordon. (Ed.). (2001). *Encyclopedia of occultism and parapsychology* (5th ed.). 2 vols. Detroit, MI: Gale. 1,939 pages.

This two-volume reference work covers nearly two thousand pages' worth of topics in occultism and parapsychology, including phenomena, notable researchers and persons, famous cases, organizations, and more. With certain topics that are considered controversial, information both for and against is provided. This work begins with an introduction outlining the historical timeline of occultism and parapsychology, and in which Melton explains the juxtaposition of the parapsychological with the broader occult. He covers not only the historical timeline of these topics but also outlines why a new edition is needed and how it differs from those of the past. Following this is an overview of how the entries are organized and arranged before delving into the encyclopedic entries themselves.

The entries themselves provide information on the entire gamut of topics subsumed by the occult and parapsychological. The entries are international in scope and concern prominent people, phenomena, locations, organizations/groups/cults, objects, research, philosophies, and more concerning these topics. Modern and ancient topics are included. Most entries contain references for further reading. The second volume concludes with an appendix of internet links to organizations that deal with many aspects of the occult, the paranormal as well as New Age, theosophy, and more. Some of these links and organizations may no longer be in use since this fifth edition was published in 2001, though the sheer amount of entries within this work is what makes it a worthy addition to this list.

CRYPTOZOOLOGY

Handbooks

Parsons, Brian D. (2015). *Handbook for the amateur cryptozoologist.* Twinsburg, OH: BP Guy Productions. 192 pages.

Brian Parsons is a paranormal researcher and author who, in addition to broader paranormal subjects, has investigated claims of a cryptozoological nature. In this work, noted cryptozoologist and researcher Loren Coleman provides the introduction, outlines the research done by cryptozoologists, and muses on the field's struggle with entry into mainstream science. Coleman notes that Parson's handbook serves as a guide for those who are interested in pursuing cryptozoology beyond an amateur level. Parsons, in the preface to this work, reinforces this notion by informing us that this book is akin to a field guide for conducting cryptozoological research. He pulls from folklore as well as scientific investigations to paint a broad but comprehensive understanding of this topic before diving into a discussion of how to establish an investigative team, interview witnesses, and make case reports, as well as how to track, and more. The last section of this book is titled "Resources" and provides a sampling of witness interviews from a variety of different cryptozoological settings. This title is beneficial for anyone interested in how cryptozoological research is conducted and who wants an introductory lesson on the topic.

Dictionaries

Coghlan, Ronan. (2004). *Dictionary of cryptozoology.* Bangor, Northern Ireland: Xiphos Books. 274 pages.

Author Ronan Coghlan presents here a dictionary of cryptids from around the world. In his brief introduction he reminds readers that a handful of accepted and well-known animals today were once considered "legends" and nothing more than mere campfire fodder. Here, in this work, he presents an alphabetical, international listing of cryptids and provides references for source materials on each entry, allowing readers to consult those works for further information. In the beginning of this work, Coghlan includes a brief glossary of animal terminology as well as a listing of animal adjectives such as "bovine," "equine," and "simian," to aid the reader as they browse the dictionary. The entries themselves are very short; each page averages about ten entries. At just under three hundred pages, this work may not seem like a robust tome, but it nevertheless contains a large amount of references. At the end of each entry is an entry that matches up to sources in the bibliography so that Coghlan not only cites where these cryptids were prominently mentioned, but so readers can uncover further information as well. International in scope, this cryptozoological dictionary is a must-have for any researcher interested in this topic.

Encyclopedias

Coleman, Loren, & Clark, Jerome. (1999). *Cryptozoology A to Z: The encyclopedia of Loch Monsters, Sasquatch, Chupacabras, and other authentic mysteries of nature.* New York, NY: Fireside. 270 pages.

This work highlights a wide range of topics associated with cryptozoology—from legendary creatures to scientists who study them, to geographic locations rife with cryptozoological sightings. This dictionary is international in scope, and readers can find information on cryptids of New Zealand, the United States, Africa, the Himalayas, Sweden, and more. Author Loren Coleman is a noted and experienced cryptozoologist, having written seventeen books and hundreds of journal articles on this topic. His own cryptozoological fieldwork, in fact, began in 1960.[5] Coleman and Clark take their inquiry into this topic seriously but also note that "for the sake of argument, we take the best available evidence—even if, by the more demanding standards of scientific proof, it may not be satisfactory in one fashion or another—and scrutinize it through the lens of what zoology does know about conventionally recognized animals, living and (allegedly) dead, and early protohumans." Each entry is quite detailed and often contains images. At the end of this work, readers can find a list of periodicals and websites to consult for additional cryptozoological information. This work is an extremely comprehensive list of creatures, persons, and locations regarding cryptozoology and is a great resource for not only seasoned researchers of this topic but for those interested in beginning their understanding of this field.

Eberhart, George M. (2002). *Mysterious creatures: A guide to cryptozoology.* 2 vols. Santa Barbara, CA: ABC-CLIO. 723 pages.

Henry Bauer, emeritus faculty member of chemistry and science studies at Virginia Polytechnic Institute, provides a wonderful introduction to this work on cryptozoology. In the introduction, Bauer discusses how this topic contributes to both natural and social sciences; from the discovery of giant squid, often regarded as the creature that spawned kraken legends, to the ways in which monsters and creatures have embedded pop culture and our imagination, the field of cryptozoology has much to bring to the table. This introduction alone makes this title a worthy addition to the cryptozoological literature.

Following the introduction is an overview of cryptozoology—both a definition of the field and the work of cryptozoologists is discussed. Following this is a detailed outline to the reader of how this work is organized. The first portion of the work contains nearly eleven hundred entries of unknown animals presented in a way that a cryptozoologist might make a field report. In other words, the name of the creature is listed, followed by its etymology, scientific name, other names, physical description, behavior, tracks, habitat, notable sightings, and more. Eberhart organizes this massive list into forty distinct types of cryptids, including (but not nearly limited to) amphibians, bears, dogs, freshwater monsters, primates, wildmen, and more.

The second part of this book is titled "Animals Discovered since 1900" in which Eberhart lists 431 creatures that have been discovered since 1900 in an attempt to showcase that creatures are continuously being discovered to dispel the claims from skeptics that all animals that could have been found by now would have been found. The third portion of the book is a listing of all the 884 bodies of water that are rumored to contain freshwater monsters. Given these numbers, readers can certainly understand the immense amount of information that is contained in these two volumes.

In this work, Eberhart addresses the concept of analyzing sources for credibility—a truly refreshing reminder in works of a paranormal nature. He also includes a lengthy discussion on the value of eyewitness testimony in cryptozoology and furthermore discusses the need for continued research and biological inquiry of the world around us, as he cautions readers that no new discoveries can be made if nobody is willing to look. Each entry in the encyclopedia contains source information, and the presence of two indexes (based on geographic region and creature) helps readers navigate to those sections that they're most interested in.

Newton, Michael. (2005). *Encyclopedia of cryptozoology*. Jefferson, NC: McFarland. 584 pages.

Author Michael Newton presents this five-hundred-plus-page encyclopedia that compiles cryptozoological entries from around the world, and for which he relies upon his extensive experience as a field researcher. He had visited Loch Ness, for instance, a total of seven times upon the publication of this work. Newton makes a point at the beginning of this compendium to alert readers that they will not find mythical or supernatural creatures in this book and that he has instead chosen to focus on ethnoknown creatures and/or those once believed to be extinct. Newton begins by providing a brief overview of the field of cryptozoology and includes a chronological history as well as key figures. He also discusses some instances of creatures once believed fable turning out to be real, and he briefly touches on the procedures that cryptozoologists take in their research before delving into his encyclopedic entries. At the end of each entry, Newton provides a citation, which proves an invaluable resource for readers to dig deeper into their study.

Ruickbie, Leo. (2016). *The impossible zoo: An encyclopedia of fabulous beasts and mythical monsters.* London, England: Robinson. 272 pages.

The author of this work, Dr. Leo Ruickbie, is a noted author of many paranormal publications, has a PhD from King's College in London, and is a scholar on the topics of witchcraft and magic. In this work, Ruickbie delves into the historical mythological record to conjure up the myths and legends from which our modern-day fascination with cryptids emerges. He tells us quite openly in the introduction that this work concerns "parazoology," which he defines as "the biology of the supernatural." Included in this work are the "impossible" monsters that still haunt our collective imagination. As such, this book could easily be relegated to folklore and organized below in the general "Other" category, but since so many modern cryptozoological creatures have their roots in mythologies of the past, I include it here. This work does, however, include many firsthand accounts of brushes with strange creatures and reported sightings of unknown animals. Not all the entries in this work date back to ancient times—there is an entry, for example, about "alien big cats" of the Scottish Highlands that occurred as recently as 1980. As such, I consider the firsthand accounts and legends of strange creatures to be worthy of entry in the cryptozoology category. Rife with illustrations and source materials, Ruickbie's work lies somewhere between the realms of mythology and modern-day creature sightings and is a wonderful addition to understanding humanity's both fascination and long history with strange creatures.

UFOLOGY

Handbooks

Glenday, Craig. (1999). *The UFO investigator's handbook: The practical guide to researching, identifying, and documenting unexplained sightings.* London, England: Running Press. [no page numbers].

In the foreword to this work, noted ufologist Stanton Friedman calls this title a "unique" addition to UFO handbooks and states that he would comfortably recommend this title as a primer to anyone interested in learning more about ufology. The work itself is broken down into four major sections. The first portion of this book provides a historical overview of unidentified flying objects throughout history and remarks about the unifying characteristics of eyewitness testimonies. Glenday goes into great detail outlining the various types of UFO phenomena, from simply the mysterious and unexplainable presence of light in the sky all the way to the more stereotyped instances of strange crafts in the air.

The second portion of this work discusses how to collect and assess evidence, while the third section offers advice and tips on how to locate the research that has currently been done on UFOs. The last section includes a listing of UFO hotspots that have been the location of many reported UFO sightings through the years. This section is international in scope. Following this is an index of organizations and societies that compile UFO research and is again international in scope. Resources and recommended reading are included. This work contains a large amount of images and is a great addition to understanding more about UFOs, especially if you are interested in potentially having an experience yourself.

Haines, Richard F. (1980). *Observing UFOs: An investigative handbook.* Chicago, IL: Nelson-Hall. 300 pages.

Author Richard F. Haines is a former research scientist at NASA and associate fellow with the Aerospace Medical Association, a nonprofit organization still in existence today. In the prologue to this work, the author stresses the impetus behind this book, stating, "There is almost nothing available in print for use by the UFO field investigator or others involved in the analysis of sighting 'data.'" This work, in fact, is written for those who are interested in researching eyewitness testimony or perhaps conducting their own interviews. In that regard, Haines's work is more so a testimony to and discussion of how humans perceive visual phenomena and how that data can be collected and studied to reveal information about UFO phenomena. He openly tells us in his prologue that this work isn't where you'll find extensive breakdowns and prominent UFO case studies or information on government conspiracies and involvement. This work is primarily a discussion of the ways in which people currently perceive phenomena and how to use your current physical abilities to learn more about the world around you.

In the introduction, Haines outlines the various types of perceptual obstacles that can obscure eyewitness testimony of UFO experiences, such as memory problems, before briefly outlining what constitutes UFO phenomena in chapter 2. Beginning in chapter 3, however, Haines begins to provide detailed steps and methods for how to detail your eyewitness experiences—he even offers sample flowcharts and categories to include in your notes. Chapter 5 provides even further detailed discussions of how to obtain and evaluate eyewitness testimonies and includes sample charts and diagrams to use when either gathering your own data or analyzing others'. Haines includes diagrams to help elicit information about how the UFO was shaped and what other details it may have included. Further in this chapter, he shows how to take a written eyewitness testimony and break down the components to code it for certain characteristics or themes, creating by doing so a type of UFO research code book. Chapter 6 deals with natural phenomena that may account for the sudden disappearance of an object, as this is a major feature of UFO sightings.

He presents the information not necessarily in the hopes that the UFO sighting can be outright debunked and dismissed but to help ensure that it is tested and evaluated as scientifically as possible. Likewise, chapter 7 outlines (in great detail) the physical limitations of the human eye. Chapters 8–11 all discuss scientific and technical terminology that is used to describe visual experiences; chapter 12 discusses the specific changes that occur to sight in darkness and/or in darkness where a sudden light source is revealed. The remaining chapters discuss natural explanations for things that otherwise appear quite unnatural and include photo examples of these things like reflection and illumination. It concludes with a glossary and bibliography.

While it may seem like this work is presented by Haines in an attempt to debunk and discredit past experiences of UFO phenomena, it is anything but. Haines applies the rigors of the scientific method through the lens of UFO experiences to show how eyewitnesses and those researching the phenomena can analyze information through a more critical and scientific exploration. The sheer amount of charts, graphs, sample investigative reports, and more make this book a unique and worthy addition to the topic of UFOs.

Hendry, Allan. (1979). *The UFO handbook: A guide to investigating, evaluating, and reporting UFO sightings.* Garden City, NY: Doubleday. 297 pages.

Allan Hendry is a ufologist and astronomer who, after becoming discouraged by the lack of any scientific and rigorous outlining of UFO experiences, decided to come up with one on his own. When evaluating cases of UFO sightings, Hendry realized that many UFO sightings became IFOs (identified flying objects) after certain natural or biological factors were taken into consideration. However, Hendry was still left with a small number of cases that were simply unexplainable; these were the cases that motivated him to create a scientific method of case reporting to help eliminate the overwhelming amount of UFO reports that can be dismissed or explained. In other words, he wanted to create a system that would help bring those unexplainable instances to the top, so they didn't get lost in the copious amount of sightings people report.

As a result, Hendry spent two years poring through thirteen hundred UFO reports to come up with his method for scientifically reporting UFO experiences. In the first one hundred pages of this work, Hendry provides examples of natural explanations for UFO sightings ranging from reflections, to oddly shaped clouds, to weather balloons, and more. He provides photographic examples to illustrate how easy it is for the mind's eye to transform these IFOs into UFOs. Beginning in chapter 9, Hendry discusses the 113 cases out of the total 1,300 that were deemed UFO experience, and which could not be explained. A detailed discussion of the various types of encounters is presented here, enabling readers to understand that not all UFO experiences are created equal.

The second portion of his book, however, deals with specific tools that ufologists and eyewitnesses can use when researching reports or experiencing events themselves. These range from making special usage of photography, hypnosis, lie detectors, radar, and fellow eyewitnesses to create a recounting of the event that is as thoroughly documented and analyzed as possible. His appendix offers procedures and suggestions for documenting and researching events, and the work concludes with a bibliography for further reading. This is a work that attempts to present an unbiased discussion of a very paranormal topic but also attempts to provide readers the tools to scientifically document their anomalous experiences.

Encyclopedias

Birnes, William J. (Ed.) (2004). *The* UFO Magazine *UFO Encyclopedia.* New York, NY: Pocket Books. 384 pages.

UFO Magazine ran from 1986 until 2012 and featured articles from prominent ufologists and researchers as well as a variety of UFO-related information and news. It also claimed to be the breaking news source for a whole host of UFO cases such as the Phoenix Lights and John Keel's experience with cryptids in West Virginia. Running monthly at first and then sporadically until its eventual decline in 2012, the magazine also spawned the publication of the encyclopedia work here. Pulling not only from its immense archives but from other sources as well, the *UFO Encyclopedia* is a compendium of UFO-related phenomena in the United States. Included in this work are many images depicting various prominent cases or people associated with UFO activity; an index at the back of the work helps readers navigate to desired sections. While not as robust as other works on this topic, it is a unique addition to the UFO literature and still contains a large amount of information at nearly four hundred pages in length. Editor William J. Birnes reminds us that this work focuses primarily on United States UFO history, though there are references to international influence as well.

Clark, Jerome. (2000). *Extraordinary encounters: An encyclopedia of extraterrestrials and otherworldly beings.* Santa Barbara, CA: ABC-CLIO. 290 pages.

In the introduction to this encyclopedic work, author Jerome Clark discusses his personal experiences with a friend who claimed to receive extraterrestrial messages after his own UFO sighting and reported abduction experience. Regardless of Clark's own skepticism regarding the validity of his friend's experience, he nonetheless concludes that the otherworldly happens all around us, though we may not yet be able to fully understand what these experiences are or where they come from. As a result, Clark compiles here a robust amount of information on personal experiences with extraterrestrials from the past two centuries. As such, this is an entirely unique addition to the UFO literature—one that focuses exclusively on eyewitness testimony of contact with otherworldly beings. Each entry contains a source for reference and further reading.

Clark, Jerome. (1998). *The UFO book: Encyclopedia of the extraterrestrial.* Detroit, MI: Visible Ink. 705 pages.

A second entry from author Jerome Clark, an internationally respected ufologist and editor of the *International UFO Reporter*, this work is an abridged version of Clark's lengthier encyclopedic work *The UFO Encyclopedia*, discussed just following this entry. Clark actually authors all but four of the entries included in this work—entries that cover the span of UFO history from noted figures to key events and ufological terminology. Many of the entries in this book are more akin to essays or book chapters due to the amount of information contained in them. They all contain detailed references at their conclusion and many include charts, tables, and a whole assortment of various images. There are no entries for "Y" or "Z," unlike other works, but it does include contact information for UFO research organizations as well as a list of UFO-related films and documentaries. A worthy addition even if it is an abridged version of a lengthier work.

Clark, Jerome. (1998). *The UFO encyclopedia: The phenomenon from the beginning* (2nd ed.). Detroit, MI: Omnigraphics. 1,178 pages.

Updated to contain additional information not found in the first edition of this work, this encyclopedia covers the entire range of UFO-related phenomena as reported or experienced up to the time of its publication in 1998. Clark begins by including an introduction that provides a historical overview of UFOs and UFO experiences and then includes a list of commonly used acronyms and abbreviations for the reader. He then provides a list of UFO websites before the entries begin.

The entries themselves are comprehensive as well as international in scope, and many of them could even be referred to as essays. They each contain a detailed bibliography at their conclusion, making finding additional resources on that topic easy for the reader. Many of the entries contain photographs and other images to supplement the text. Key concepts or figures in each entry are highlighted in bold, alerting the reader to additional entries and further reading, which is a nice feature. The entries themselves not only discuss prominent figured and famous UFO events but also include notable phrases and quotes regarding UFO lore and experiences. The encyclopedia contains a particularly lengthy section about crashes and retrievals of supposed UFO craft broken down by the nineteenth and twentieth centuries. This is notable not only due to its length but also due to the fact that (at least in the United States) many people assume that the UFO craze started in the 1940s, when in fact it has much deeper roots than this. A notable entry for its comprehensive treatment of subjects and its international scope.

Lewis, James R. (2000). *UFOs and popular culture: An encyclopedia of contemporary myth.* Santa Barbara, CA: ABC-CLIO. 392 pages.

A foreword by Thomas E. Bullard and author James Lewis's own introduction are worthy enough on their own to include this work in the list of UFO-related literature. In these two sections, Bullard and Lewis muse about the folkloric nature of UFOs and how this phenomenon doesn't settle nicely into either fact or fiction since it has become so embedded in the history of human experience. Both authors provide a rich exploration of the phenomenon, especially Lewis as he provides a detailed exposé of the UFO timeline throughout human history. Of particular emphasis in this work is information relating to the abduction experience. Like Clark's work above, author James Lewis believes that this area of ufology is often overlooked or outright dismissed in previous reference works on this topic. Lewis covers everything from ancient astronauts to Roswell to New Age theories in his introduction, and that's all before even getting to the encyclopedic entries themselves.

Assisted by a large group of scholars, Lewis and others compile a detailed and exhaustive list of terms, figures, prominent cases, and phenomena associated with UFOs. Each entry is detailed and contains source information and titles for further reading. The references in each entry are robust—more so than seemingly any other reference work on this topic—and this is just one of the many reasons this work is an invaluable addition to the field of ufology.

Story, Ronald D., & Greenwell, J. Richard. (Eds.) (1980). *The encyclopedia of UFOs*. Garden City, NY: Doubleday. 440 pages.

It is worth pointing out that in the editors' preface to this work, they note that at the time this book was published in 1980 it was the only encyclopedia dedicated entirely to the topic of UFOs. Included in this encyclopedia are more than three hundred articles on a variety of topics and as written by more than one hundred unique authors. The entries themselves fall into one of three categories: entries about people, features of UFOs including evidence and theories, and prominent case studies of UFO phenomena. The entries are international in scope and seek to represent the most prominent incidents, peoples, and dominant thoughts on the UFO topic.

Organized alphabetically, the entries include images and are quite comprehensive. Many of them contain scores of references to further reading and/or additional entries in this compendium. Topics that one wouldn't normally think are included are discussed, such as "astronomers and UFOs," "Earth-based UFOs," and "biblical UFO sightings." Appendix A offers a chronology of some of the noteworthy UFO-related events throughout history, while appendix B offers an international listing of UFO-related journals that readers can research. A bibliography is included at the end; no references or further reading are included at the end of individual encyclopedia entries.

REINCARNATION AND NEAR-DEATH EXPERIENCES

Handbooks

Heath, Pamela Rae, & Klimo, Jon. (2010). *Handbook to the afterlife*. Berkeley, CA: North Atlantic Books. 272 pages.

Drs. Heath and Klimo, two authors who have an extensive research dossier and with ties to professional psychical organizations, present in this work an exploration of life after death. They begin with an analysis of what major world religions believe in terms of the afterlife, followed by a chapter titled "Sources and Means for This Book," in which they explain that their sources are reports from mediums as well as from their own interviews, from their own experiences with seances, or in the written record of the past two hundred years. Part 1 of their book, which includes a religious overview as well as a timeline of historical research and methods at divining information about the afterlife, is a wonderful historical resource for afterlife studies. Part 2 includes information from those who they consider "eyewitnesses," or as they point out specifically, psychics, visionaries, or people who have endured a near-death or out-of-body experience. They use these eyewitness testimonies to outline the stages of the afterlife, which begins at the moment of death and loops around to the point of reincarnation. Interspersed in this work is information about the authors' own extraordinary experiences.

Robak, Mindy, Stevenson, Ian, & Head, Joseph. (1979). *A handbook on reincarnation.* New York, NY: Death Education Books. [no page numbers].

This work is one that will likely only be found in a library collection or requested via your local library through interlibrary loan. Composed of loose pages bound together in a file-folder type of binding, this work is actually a combination of two books. The first book contains an interview with famed reincarnation researcher Ian Stevenson in which he is interviewed by Eugene Kinkead, a writer for the *New Yorker.* Originally published in June 1978, this fairly lengthy interview also contains some titles for further reading. Following the interview are four papers that were shared at "The Child and Death" symposium held at the College of Physicians and Surgeons of Columbia University in January 1979, and one paper that was presented at a "Thanatologic Aspects and Aging" conference held at the same university one year prior. The presenters include S. L Cranston, editor of *Reincarnation: The Phoenix Fire Mystery,* as well as other researchers and scholars. The final section of book 1 contains lectures given by Cranston at a reincarnation conference held in 1978. Book 2 is a truly unique addition, as it compiles a list of frequently asked questions regarding reincarnation and points readers to specific pages in Cranston's aforementioned text for answers. In addition, it provides an immense amount of reference for further reading through mentioning other works and researchers.

Encyclopedias

Taylor, Richard P. (2000). *Death and the afterlife: A cultural encyclopedia.* Santa Barbara, CA: ABC-CLIO. 438 pages.

In this work, author Richard Taylor provides a compendium of information on the funerary and afterlife beliefs of cultures across the world. While this work doesn't necessarily focus on the scientific endeavors to investigate the presence of life after death, it is a worthy addition to the reincarnation literature since it provides multiple entries about those cultures that hold deep-seated beliefs in reincarnation and are likely referenced in other resources on the topic of reincarnation. This work will provide a useful resource for better understanding those cultures that hold seemingly paranormal beliefs at their cores.

Chapter 7
ASTROLOGY, DIVINATION, AND MYSTICISM

Handbooks

Albertsson, Alaric. (2017). *A handbook of Saxon sorcery & magic: Wyrdworking, rune craft, divination & wortcunning.* Woodbury, MN: Llewellyn. 360 pages.

In this work, author Alaric Albertsson draws upon his many years of practicing magic to present a compendium of how to incorporate magical practices in your own life. Less a historical overview and more of a practical how-to, this work is a worthy addition to this topic as it provides a firsthand account of the ways in which people apply magical practices in their lives. Supplement this work with a historical overview of the topic and you'll have a decent start to understanding magic and certain occult traditions. His first chapter is spent defining the use of the word "magic" and providing a clear picture of this topic to readers. Following this are chapters that outline a sampling of tools necessary to perform certain magical rituals; after this Albertsson focuses on some specific magical applications such as using runes to receive messages, or how to use herbs and flowers to create potions and ointments and how to use them. This book is much more of a "guide to using magic" than some other sources listed here, but it is useful for that very reason as it gives a glimpse into a practitioner's life. The information contained in this work can assist readers with understanding what magic ritual looks like, how to begin incorporating it themselves, or to simply add to their general understanding of divination and magical practices.

Arrien, Angeles. (1997). *The tarot handbook: Practical applications of ancient visual symbols.* New York, NY: Jeremy P. Tarcher/Putnam. 320 pages.

Author Angeles Arrien, a cultural anthropologist, presents this work as a way of discussing how the tarot can be used as a universal language through its use of symbols to relay message and meaning. Arrien specifically set out to write this work when she was discouraged by the lack of discussion surrounding the mythological, psychological, and cultural meanings behind the tarot. Influenced by Jung and his discussion on the psychological impact of symbols, Arrien decided to interpret the Thoth tarot deck of Aleister Crowley (a very common and well-known deck illustrated by artist Frieda Harris). Specifically choosing this deck for its inclusion of cross-cultural symbolism, Arrien provides a general history of the tarot before she discusses the symbolism found in all the arcana of that tarot deck. Arrien also includes her own methods for reading tarot decks and applying symbology to your own readings—a method she developed after testing nearly six thousand readings. Included at the end of her work is a glossary of symbols as well as a summary of each tarot card. Beautifully illustrated and with a wealth of information on the cultural and psychological underpinnings of tarot, this work is a great addition to anyone's list for furthering their understanding of this topic.

Baker, Jim. (2013). *The cunning man's handbook: The practice of English folk magic 1550–1900*. London, England: Avalonia. 556 pages.

In the preface to this work, author Jim Baker tells us that this book is a "survey of the documented magical resources of the English-speaking Cunning Folk." The term "cunning folk" is used to refer to those who practiced folk magic in England and the Americas in the years between 1550 and 1900, and Baker takes particular pains in his introduction to remind us that cunning folk are identified as such because they were not influenced by spiritualism or cabalism, nor did they even make use of magical tools like tarot cards. The first portion of this work is devoted to detailing the culture of England as well as the cunning folk in this time period. After an exhaustive treatment on that topic, Baker dives into what it means to be considering "cunning" and what characteristics really set this population apart. Following this, he presents a detailed discussion of the divination practices of cunning folk before diving into a discussion of geomancy, a topic set out separate from other divination practices. He furthermore goes on to discuss the ways in which cunning folk used dreams and charms and astrology in their practices; the result is a work that presents, exhaustively, an anthropological look at this specific population of magical peoples. This work delivers such a unique historical inquiry on this topic that it must be included for readers wishing to get a detailed look inside a culture centered around magic. Appendix A outlines the various laws enacted throughout history aimed at persecuting magical acts and is a wonderful source of information for readers curious about the judicial timeline of magic. A detailed bibliography and endnotes provide ample "further reading" for researchers. Other works can be found that discuss this topic, but Baker's handbook is a truly unique addition.

Dean, Liz. (2019). *The divination handbook: the modern seer's guide to using tarot, crystals, palmistry and more.* London, England: Fair Winds Press. 176 pages.

Author Liz Dean is a tarot reader from the UK who is not only the author of several additional works on this topic, but who also has more than twenty years' experience using divination methods. In this book she outlines various methods of divination using different tools such as crystals, tarot cards, palms, and more. Full of colorful images to assist the overall discussion, Dean also provides step-by-step methods for performing these divination rituals yourself. This work is not only extremely current but is a good resource for those who want a clear picture of how divination rituals are performed.

Dombrowski, Kiki. (2018). *A curious future: A handbook of unusual divination and unique oracular techniques.* Nashville, TN: Phoebe. 136 pages.

Dombrowski, an author, tarot reader, and life coach in Nashville, Tennessee, introduces readers to "fascinating and curious forms of divination," such as using wine or dice in divination methods. Dombrowski chooses not to focus on those topics that are prevalent in the literature already, such as palmistry and astrology. Each chapter concludes with a bibliography; in addition, there are multiple sources of recommended reading at the conclusion. The author, a practitioner of the methods described in this book, offers readers a unique and authoritative perspective on modern divination practices.

Esmann, Jan. (2017). *The ultimate handbook of psychological astrology.* Copenhagen, Denmark: Blue Pearl. 818 pages.

At more than eight hundred pages, it is safe to say that this work is more than merely a handbook and can reside firmly in the realm of reference material on the topic of astrology, with a unique focus on using it for psychological interpretations of subjects. Beginning with a "crash course" on astrology, this work is an extremely detailed exploration of astrology and how it is used to interpret certain traits associated with people. Esmann doesn't even touch the topic of the planets until nearly one hundred pages into this work, which reveals not only how complex the issue of astrology is, but also how richly detailed this work is. Readers may even think that once Esmann discusses the planets that there wouldn't be more to discuss, but that couldn't be further from the truth as there remains nearly six hundred pages' worth of information once Esmann has finished introducing readers to the planets and their affiliated symbolism. She goes on to discuss astrological houses, aspects, and synastry, which is astrologic compatibility or astrological matchmaking. Readers new to the topic of astrology may find this work overwhelming or need to read the "crash course" entry multiple times as the author herself suggests. Nevertheless, a wonderful addition to this topic for its detailed treatment of astrology.

Greer, John Michael. (2010). *The geomancer's handbook: Divination and magic.* Iowa City, IA: Renaissance Astrology. 122 pages.

Author John Michael Greer, an author and divination practitioner, compiles here a compendium of information on a lesser known method of divination, geomancy, which uses sixteen patterns composed of dots to discern messages. Referred to by Greer as the forgotten oracle, he discusses not only the historical, ancient roots of this method of divination but also the many different ways to use this method and how to interpret its meanings. Composed of seven chapters with an index and a bibliography for further reading, Greer's work is a detailed account not only of what geomancy is but how to conduct it. A worthy addition to anyone's research on divination as it presents an often overlooked ancient divination method.

Gutierrez, Cathy. (Ed.). (2015). *Handbook of spiritualism and channeling.* Leiden, Netherlands: Koninklijke Brill. 511 pages.

In this work, editor Cathy Gutierrez compiles articles from scholars versed in the era of spiritualism and the divining method of channeling. International in scope, what makes this book unique from others is the particular focus on the ways in which both of these have been used politically and socially—especially as concerns the role of (and effects on) women and minorities. The articles in this work examine how these two topics contain a "progressive spirit," and how it has been used to highlight the experiences of marginalized peoples. The first section of this edited work contains a historical and sociological investigation of spiritualism and channeling, followed by a section that juxtaposes them alongside "various other religious and cultural movements." The third section traces the path of spiritualism as it traveled to Latin America and the East, where it was influenced by new notions, particularly reincarnation, which allowed a new resurgence of interest in these topics. Chapter 4 focuses on modern channeling and its place within the New Age movement, and the concluding chapter discusses additional modern topics such as remote viewing, pop culture, and the role of channeling and spiritualism in the future.

Magee, Glenn Alexander. (Ed.). (2016). *The Cambridge handbook of Western mysticism and esotericism.* New York, NY: Cambridge University Press. 474 pages.

In this work, editor Glenn Alexander Magee compiles articles on the topics of Western mysticism and esotericism, or, as he puts it, "the hidden intellectual history of the West." The articles are compiled from the leading experts on these topics and include Wouter J. Hanegraaff, Anne L. Clark, Cathy Gutierrez, and more. The book is divided into five major portions, the first four of which tackle a different time period in the world's history. Part 1, for example, discusses mysticism and esotericism from antiquity, including chapters on Plato, hermetism, Jewish mysticism, and the ancient mysteries. Part 2 focuses on the Middle Ages and includes topics such as medieval Christian mysticism, kabbalah, and women's mysticism. Part 3 focuses on the Renaissance and early modern era and includes such topics as Freemasonry, mesmerism, Christian kabbalah, and more. Part 4 discusses the nineteenth century and afterward, with such topics as spiritualism, the Golden Dawn, C. G. Jung, paganism, and New Age. The final portion, part 5, is titled "Common Threads" and discusses mystical and esoteric concepts such as alchemy, astrology, magic, and more.

Meyer, Michael R. (2000). *A handbook for the humanistic astrologer: The complete guide to understanding your birth chart.* San Jose, CA: ToExcel. 328 pages.

This work was originally published in 1974 with a new edition released in 2000 and an e-book version released in 2011. Written during a time when astrology was hugely popular (as I'd argue it still is today), this work presented for the first time a number of methods, theories, and techniques that were relatively new to the astrological scene. The introduction tells us, in fact, that this book attempted to focus astrological methods from a human-centered and holistic approach versus the traditional emphasis of astrology as relating to major events. In other words, this book sought to shift the astrological narrative; because of that alone it is a unique work to consider in astrological research. The first portion of this work discusses the philosophy of astrology including a historical overview and the reasons why astrology is used as a divination method. The second portion of the book focuses on the major components of astrology and provides definitions and discussions of these major components such as zodiac, planets, aspects, midpoints, and more. The third portion of the book discusses techniques for interpreting these astrological components and how to apply their messages toward self-reflection. It provides a lengthy list of case studies using prominent figures such as Bob Dylan, Sigmund Freud, Lewis Carroll, and more. This work contains an overwhelming amount of information, but for that reason and more it is worth including in this section.

Tompkins, Sue. (2006). *The contemporary astrologer's handbook: An in-depth guide to interpreting your horoscope.* London, England: Flare. 362 pages.

In this work, Sue Tompkins, lecturer and cofounder of the London School of Astrology, offers an extremely detailed investigation of astrology. Going far beyond the simple horoscopes that most readers may be familiar with, Tompkins begins by exploring the philosophical questions that the practice of astrology raises, including an intriguing section on how astrology can be viewed in a macrocosmic and microcosmic perspective. In this section, though, she also presents many historical references and precedents of this practice, discussing the role of alchemy and the hermetic tradition. After the introductory session in which she makes a case for astrology as an important historical practice, the next section is an exploration of the elements and the "modes" of astrology—this section lays out the core tenets of astrology, in other words, and sets the stage for her next section outlining the zodiac signs. Following this section, she outlines the role that planetary bodies play in astrology (such as the sun, the moon, Jupiter, etc.). "Outlines," though, is an insufficient word, because each section is meticulously detailed—she even includes an essay on the mythology of each planetary body. Her next sections include deep astrological explorations of "aspects," "houses," and "non-essential bodies." She concludes her work with case studies, if you will, on certain figures and cases throughout history as pertains to the use of astrology. This work is truly a reference-style handbook on astrology.

Dictionaries

The Steinerbooks dictionary of the psychic, mystic, occult. (1973). Blauvelt, NY: Rudolf Steiner. 254 pages.

In the introduction to this work, William Bacheman claims that this work is the first "comprehensive dictionary devoted to the field of the supernatural sciences." Whether or not this is the case, it is certainly an early addition to occult dictionaries and is a useful addition to our list. The entries in this dictionary include not only prominent figures and phenomena of the occult, but also information on an international level as well. While seemingly user friendly for any level of preexisting understanding with the occult, this dictionary is best used after one has a basic exposure to and understanding of occult philosophy, as this work uses some arcane terminology to refer to certain topics. Although this could be a symptom of when this work was published, it is nonetheless a source that will likely be most useful to those with a small amount of exposure to the topic already. Of course, its use of more arcane terminology means that terms and definitions will be found here that will not be found elsewhere, yet again making it a worthy addition to our list.

Encyclopedias

Campbell, Joseph. (Ed.). (1960). *Spiritual disciplines.* Bollingen Series 30, Vol. 4. New York, NY: Pantheon Books. 505 pages.

This volume is part of the same publication as *The Mystic Vision*, discussed just two entries above. Edited by Joseph Campbell, noted scholar of mythology and comparative religion, the articles in this volume discuss a wide range of spiritual and mystical topics, hence its inclusion here in the "Mysticism" category. One such article written by Friedrich Heiler, "Contemplation in

Christian Mysticism," discusses the roots of Christian mystical visions and the influence of Roman mysticism. This volume, however, branches beyond the traditional Western religions, as evidenced by Erwin Rousselle's article "Spiritual Guidance in Contemporary Taoism." In this article Rousselle discusses the "metaphysical need to fathom and know the unknowable" and discusses the role that meditation plays in connecting the conscious with the unconscious in Taoist practice. In yet another chapter, John Layard offers an overview of the ritual "Journey of the Dead" practiced by the Malekulan culture, a people in the Pacific region of New Hebrides.

Campbell, Joseph. (Ed.). (1968). *The mystic vision.* Bollingen Series 30, Vol. 6. Princeton, NJ: Princeton University Press. 487 pages.

This work, a sister volume to *Spirit and Nature* listed in the above encyclopedic annotations for "Ghosts and Hauntings," is one volume of a yearly publication that comprises the Eranos Yearbooks, making it much like an encyclopedia and hence its inclusion here. In this volume, titled *The Mystic Vision*, eleven articles discuss various aspects of religious world mysteries. Wilhelm Koppers's article discusses the connection between ancient mysteries and its connection to anthropology and provides readers with some examples of different cultures and the esoteric traditions they practice. The final article by Erich Neumann is titled "Mystical Man" and is an intriguing exploration of the inherent mystical qualities of humanity. Each essay contains footnotes for further reading and also contains, at the end, an appendix listing the contents of the previously published volumes in this set.

Ferguson, John. (1977). *An illustrated encyclopedia of mysticism and the mystery religions.* London, England: Thames and Hudson. 228 pages.

Though author John Ferguson provides no introduction to this work, his brief foreword tells us that this work is an attempt to compile information on the great mystics and mystical traditions around the world. Included in this encyclopedia are entries not only on prominent figures and traditions, but also on key concepts and phrases found throughout the world's mystical traditions. As the title suggests, there is a fair number of images found throughout the work, be they drawings of key figures or sketches of astrological concepts, and/or modern photographs of people. Each page contains an average of five to six entries, so even though this work is not as lengthy as some others, it still contains a wealth of information. What is most useful and unique about this work is its focus on key figures of mystical traditions—readers interested in learning about significant mystical figures will find this book useful, while those looking for detailed information about the philosophies of each tradition may wish to find a more detailed source.

Godwin, David. (1994). *Godwin's cabalistic encyclopedia: A complete guide to cabalistic magick* (3rd ed.) Woodbury, MN: Llewellyn. 832 pages.

David Godwin, author, expert, and researcher of esoteric traditions, presents a compendium of terms, figures, beliefs, and practices associated with the Jewish mystical system known as kabbalah—spelled here as "cabala"—to refer to ceremonial magic and rituals. Godwin begins by providing a detailed overview of the core cabalistic tenets such as the Tree of Life as well as elements of the Hebrew alphabet that are strongly present in cabalistic traditions. He then delves into examples of cabalistic magic, examples of using cabalistic techniques to interpret dreams, and how to use gematria (the interpretation of messages and meaning through numbers) to interpret messages about any number of situations—kind of like using tarot, in a sense. The amount of detailed information included in this work is overwhelming, and this is a true encyclopedic reference work in that sense. Those interested in a detailed understanding of the Tree of Life, the cabalistic paths, and gematria will want to add this to their must-read list.

Guiley, Rosemary Ellen. (1991). *Harper's encyclopedia of mystical and paranormal experience.* New York, NY: HarperCollins. 666 pages.

Included in the "Other Paranormal" category due to its broad focus, this work was compiled by prominent paranormal researcher and author Rosemary Ellen Guiley, who unfortunately passed away in 2019. In her own words, "this encyclopedia is intended for the layperson who is curious about a good many topics that fall under the 'alternate realities' umbrella." What distinguishes this work from others is not only its broad inclusion but also an intentional focus on paranormal experience and phenomena versus a compendium of biographical entries. To be sure, there are some biographical sketches one can find in this work, but the author intentionally limited these in favor of phenomena. This was specifically done to provide resources "to those readers who are trying to understand and come to terms with unusual experiences they have had themselves." This encyclopedia is an immense reference tool for both new and seasoned paranormal researchers, and it is international in scope. The entries themselves are detailed and include citations for further reading. Researchers who are curious about paranormal phenomena in general should begin their research with this work.

Lewis, James R. (1994). *The astrology encyclopedia.* Detroit, MI: Visible Ink Press. 603 pages.

Readers looking to enhance their understanding of astrology should look no further than Dr. James Lewis's *Astrology Encyclopedia*. This work, at 603 pages long, is a comprehensive listing of all things astrology. In this work, readers can find 780 individual entries on topics such as Chinese astrology, Hindu astrology, the historical timeline of astrology in the United States, and much more. A wonderful aspect of this work is the author's introduction in which he guides readers through the best way to "read" this work. For example, he suggests that new initiates of astrology begin by reading all entries associated with the zodiac—Cancer, Virgo, and so forth. He then suggests an order of categories to follow to help ensure a more fluid understanding of this topic. Dr. Lewis then goes on to provide a brief discussion of astrology through history, its relation to Christianity, as well as modern metaphysical aspects of astrology. Dr. Lewis also includes charts of astrological symbols (glyphs) and common abbreviations for terms. In the appendixes, Dr. Lewis shares with readers information on how to create their own astrological chart and provides a list of astrological organizations and publications where readers can obtain further information.

Roob, Alexander. (2016). *The hermetic museum: Alchemy & mysticism.* Cologne, Germany: Taschen. 573 pages.

This work is included here in the encyclopedia section for its treatment of the topics of alchemy and mysticism. Though it isn't arranged like a typical encyclopedia with entries following each other alphabetically, it is nevertheless an encyclopedia treatment of these two topics. Author Alexander Roob begins by providing a lengthy introduction that gives readers a history lesson on the timeline and major characteristics of alchemy and mysticism—two topics that are intimately linked with one another. On that note, Roob does a wonderful job showing just how these two topics are intertwined.

What sets this work apart is its particular focus on the images and artwork associated with these movements. This is an encyclopedia of artwork, images, drawings, and symbols, and it centers around four major categories depicted by these artforms: the macrocosm, the opus magnum, the microcosm, and rotation. In each of these categories a large amount of artwork is shown; Roob provides not only a citation for each image but also a brief discussion of what each image depicts and represents. Though there is no alphabetical organization within each of these four sections, an index helps readers interested in navigating to a particular topic, artist, or prominent figure. A wonderful resource for those interested in the topic of alchemy and how it is intimately connected to mysticism and the ways in which mankind has illustrated its connection to both of those through art.

OCCULT AND OTHER PARANORMAL

Dictionaries

Durrant, Jonathan, & Bailey, Michael D. (2012). *Historical dictionary of witchcraft* (2nd ed.). Lanham, MD: Scarecrow Press. 271 pages.

In this work, the authors (both scholars and professors at institutes of higher education in the U.S. and the UK, respectively) present a historical timeline of witches and witchcraft with a focus on North American and European history. They also discuss modern-day witchcraft, often referred to as Wicca, and include a discussion on the prevalence of modern beliefs in witches that persist to this day. Their book includes entries not only on seminal figures of the infamous witch hunts that occurred in both North America and Europe, but also the various symbols, tools, beliefs, literature, music, and more associated with witchcraft. As such, and at nearly three hundred pages, this dictionary provides an intensive listing of witchcraft terminology. The authors begin by including a detailed chronology of witch history followed by a robust historical introduction to the topic before beginning their alphabetized entries.

Franklyn, Julian. (Ed.). (1973). *A dictionary of the occult.* New York, NY: Causeway Books. 301 pages.

Offering an analysis of occultism-related topics up to the 1930s, this dictionary provides readers a historical lens to the occult. The introduction tells readers that entries span the fields of alchemy to astrology to black magic, fairies, ghosts, witchcraft, and more. Occult experts from a variety of backgrounds contributed to the entries in this work, and what is most helpful and unique about this title is its breakdown of "Principal Contents" just after the introduction. Here, each subcategory of the occult is listed and readers are informed which pages to consult if they're most interested in alchemy or ghosts or devil worship or any number of other subtopics. "White Magic," for example, can be found on pages 283–289 while "History of Occult Ideas" can be found on pages 112–143. Each section, then, reads less like a dictionary and more like a loosely connected series of essays about the occult. Prefacing each section is an alphabetized listing of key concepts mentioned in those categories and the paragraph in which they can be found.

Opie, Iona, & Tatem, Moira. (Eds.). (1989). *A dictionary of superstitions.* Oxford, England: Oxford University Press. 494 pages.

This work is a compilation of superstitions originating from Great Britain and Ireland. The editors, in their preface, write, "The vast subject of 'superstitions,' taken by us to include divinations, spells, cures, charms, signs and omens, rituals, and taboos, has never before been systematically organized." Some readers may wonder why a book of superstitions is included here. I include it because a great number of sources for these included superstitions are rooted in topics of a paranormal nature. For example, one of the entries included comes from a 1643 record of a witchcraft trial in Orkney, Scotland. Other entries include tactics on what to use to divine information on a number of topics—think of the game children play where they twist an apple stem while reciting the alphabet to determine the first letter of their future lover's name. This work is a comprehensive exposé of the local, cultural superstitions found throughout the English and Irish countryside.

Wedeck, Harry E. (1956). *Dictionary of the occult*. New York, NY: Philosophical Library. [no page numbers listed].

This work contains no introduction or preface and instead immediately jumps into alphabetical listings of occult subjects beginning with "Aaron's Rod," a magic wand engraved with the image of a snake. It is, however, a worthy addition to this list as upon review, it contains many entries that are not found in other occult dictionaries. The entries are international in scope and include reference to peoples, spells/divinations, and magic objects, as well as a seeming focus on demons and demonology. Each entry is only about a sentence or two long, so it is best used to find references that can then be researched in other works a bit more comprehensively. Due to its brief nature, however, this work can be helpful for the beginning researcher to just become familiar with occult terminology.

Encyclopedias

Greer, John Michael. (2003). *The new encyclopedia of the occult*. St. Paul, MN: Llewellyn. 576 pages.

Author John Michael Greer has practiced "mystery traditions" for more than forty years and is also the author of additional resources on the occult. This work presents more than fifteen hundred entries on topics related to the occult such as prominent figures, rituals, alchemy, tarot, notable organizations, and even philosophical systems such as theosophy. This work contains a large amount of information relating to cabalistic magic and practices and key figures, so those interested specifically in learning more about that tradition will want to consult this book. The entries themselves vary in length—some, which are just definitions of important concepts, are relatively short while the entries for key figures are much lengthier. The sources for each entry are listed collectively at the end of the work in one comprehensive bibliography, and while it would be nice for sources to be connected with their individual entries, it is a tool nonetheless for readers to use to ferret more information on these topics.

Guiley, Rosemary Ellen. (1999). *The encyclopedia of witches and witchcraft* (2nd ed.). New York, NY: Checkmark Books. 417 pages.

Written by renowned paranormal researcher Rosemary Ellen Guiley, this encyclopedia focuses primarily on Western witchcraft and magical and ritual practices. Being the second edition, it contains an additional focus on modern witchcraft and Wicca. Similar to her other works, Guiley prefers to focus on the experiences and traditions of witchcraft instead of focusing too heavily on biographical entries of key figures. This is a pleasant reference work to consult, as it is not only comprehensive in covering historical and modern witchcraft, but it also contains a wide range of photos and an extensive bibliography at the end.

Joshi, S. T. (Ed.). (2007). *Icons of horror and the supernatural: An encyclopedia of our worst nightmares.* 2 vols. Westport, CT: Greenwood Press. 798 pages.

In this work, scholars contribute essays that discuss twenty-four categories of supernatural topics found in fiction and literature such as "the alien," "the devil," "the psychic," "the witch," and more. While this isn't a compendium of clinical paranormal researching trying to prove or disprove the existence of ESP or the like, it is nevertheless a worthy addition for anyone wishing to better understand the ways in which the paranormal interacts with society and culture. These essays—book chapter length, I should add—discuss the fiction, yes, but they also delve into the icons' historic and folkloric roots, and often investigate the topic through an anthropologic lens. The article on UFOs even mentions the UFO craze that blossomed in the United States around 1947 and the fact that many people worldwide have reported experiences of seeing unidentified flying objects. There is a treasure trove of information to be had within these essays, and what I find most appealing about this source is that it takes the horrific and supernatural and discusses the ways in which it's interwoven itself into our collective psyche and pop culture. This source gives a unique perspective to the topic of the paranormal and provides an interesting lens through which readers can understand how pervasive the paranormal is.

Lewis, James R. (1999). *Witchcraft today: An encyclopedia of Wiccan and neopagan traditions.* Santa Barbara, CA: ABC-CLIO. 377 pages.

In this work, Dr. James Lewis focuses on the modern neo-pagan movement. He includes information not only on the beliefs and organization of this group, but also on the rituals and "spirit beings" associated with the movement. As such, the work contains information on the magical practices this group engages in. The introduction of this work is particularly useful as it outlines the rise and fall of occult practices and highlights prominent historical figures that engaged in magic and ritual. In the introduction, the author also spends a good deal of time outlining multiple spiritual groups including Norse paganism, Unitarian Universalist pagans, and Egyptian neo-pagans. The work highlights some of the more obscure groups and ritual practices that novice researchers have likely never heard of. The author also includes a chronology of occult movements in the Western world as well as documents detailing ritual practices.

Robbins, Russell Hope. (1960). *The encyclopedia of witchcraft and demonology.* New York, NY: Crown. 571 pages.

Robbins's encyclopedia is a unique entry to the topic of witchcraft as it specifically focuses only on the time period between 1450 and 1750 and further focuses on the accusations and trials suffered by those accused of witchcraft. It is a work entirely dedicated to the atrocities committed by those who accused others of being witches. The author writes a robust introduction in which he provides a historical overview for readers, but he also provides a discussion of other prominent collections of work on witchcraft should readers be interested in learning more.

Spence, Lewis. (1960). *An encyclopaedia of occultism: A compendium of information on the occult sciences, occult personalities, psychic science, magic, demonology, spiritism, mysticism, and metaphysics.* New Hyde Park, NY: University Books. 440 pages.

This work was originally published in 1920 and, according to the publisher's preface, remained the premier reference compendium on occultism for the next forty years, at which point it was reprinted due to the original edition being out of print and difficult to find. Famed parapsychologist J. B. Rhine even wrote the publisher pleading for an updated edition to be written that would span the era between 1920 and 1960, but the cost of a new edition proved too problematic and a mere reprinting was issued. This isn't necessarily a weakness, though, especially nowadays when there are other reference works that cover the time period that Rhine suggested.

The current work by Lewis Spence is a collection of twenty-five hundred entries that discuss all matters related to occultism such as prominent figures, ritual items, divination methods, select terminology, and much more. International in scope, this work begins with a publisher's preface and an author's introduction that alone make this work a worthwhile read for any inquiry into occultism. After the introduction there is an index—unique as it is placed at the beginning of the work. Immediately following the index is a bibliography of sources broken down by topics such as "alchemy," "magic," "mysticism," and "spiritualism." The items in this bibliography were chosen, the author tells us, because they represented general overviews of the major branches of occultism. Of special note is the twenty pages' worth of images and artwork affiliated with occultism that appears at the very beginning of this work, even before the title page and publication information is presented. These pages depict drawings, paintings, and other illustrations of prominent occultist themes such as magic rituals, astrological charts, Babylonian demons, kabbalah, spiritualism, and more. The entries themselves are detailed, and some of them span multiple pages, while other simply occupy a few paragraphs. Since this work was originally published in 1920, there are many entries that do not appear in more modern texts, perhaps because they have been a victim of obscurity and time, making this work even more valuable for occultist research. Of course, there are some terms used in this work that are not recognized as acceptable to use today, so readers will want to keep the historical context in mind as they browse this work. While there is no comprehensive bibliography listed to highlight all the sources used to create this work, the author does include bibliographies on select articles that represent major themes or topics.

White, Kim Kennedy, & McCormick, Charlie T. (Eds.) (2011). *Folklore: An encyclopedia of beliefs, customs, tales, music, and art.* 3 vols. Santa Barbara, CA: ABC-CLIO. 1,260 pages.

Some readers may wonder what folklore is doing in a compilation about paranormal research. I've included some folklore resources here because folklore can often shed light on the attitudes, traditions, and beliefs within communities. It can be a bridge between the paranormal and the ways in which people interpret and make sense of these events. Folk traditions create a wide array of products—not just stories and urban legends but also rituals, behaviors, and traditions that can sometimes have very mystical roots. Let me put it another way: folklore is intimately connected with the paranormal, and having a core understanding of folk traditions can also enhance one's understanding of how humans interpret paranormal events.

This work, a three-volume set, is nearly thirteen hundred pages in length and contains information on topics relevant to our paranormal discussion such as "cryptozoology," "exorcism," "UFO," and more. Compiled under the guidance of two editors and with more than eighty individual contributors, the result is a massive reference source on all things folklore. The work begins with a basic introduction of how the work was compiled along with a list of some commonly used abbreviations in folklore before digging into the encyclopedic entries themselves. The entries themselves are fairly robust—

some of them being six or more pages long—and each entry contains source information for further reading. The references at the end of each entry are actually worth looking at not just for further reading but because they often represent an international sampling of an issue. The references for "Exorcism," for example, contain sources that discuss Japanese, Slavic, and African beliefs and practices. Overall a great source to use for researching folklore.

Throughout this chapter, I provided an annotated listing of the various handbooks, dictionaries, and encyclopedias that discuss the paranormal. Some readers may wonder why, in a book that claims to highlight credible resources available on the paranormal, I include books on astrology, geomancy, UFOs, and cryptids. I suspect that many readers may wonder this at any number of points in this book, in fact, and I would point them to the chapter on credibility above. The authors listed here are authorities on the various topics above; simply because these topics deal with the paranormal does not mean that there are *no* credible resources that can help you understand these phenomena better. The paranormal has many intersections in our daily lives, and it is a field that shows the importance of questioning the status quo—especially the Westernized notions of materialism and accepted science. I urge readers to constantly evaluate their own biases regarding the paranormal; the works presented here will actually help readers engage in *exactly* that activity.

Additionally, the works in this chapter represent not only a sampling of paranormal subtopics but also a sampling of various eras that represent a whole range of paranormal inquiry and thought. Some readers may wonder why I included titles that are well over thirty (or more) years old, and my answer to those readers is that you cannot equate modernity with comprehensiveness. Older titles can reveal trends over time such as shifts in the way the paranormal was treated or viewed as well as shifts in major paranormal theories or the overall reception of the paranormal within society. Additionally, older titles often contain more archaic information that may simply not appear in newer, more modern titles. For all these reasons, it is important to have a healthy mix of recent titles alongside their older predecessors to help ensure that you have a holistic outlook of the issue at hand. Let's use an example to help illustrate. Without the work of parapsychologists, for example, in the thirties, forties, and fifties, where would our understanding of psychical phenomena rest today? Current understandings rest upon the shoulders of those who investigated these topics before us, and it is important to include them here.

If you find a title of interest in this chapter and would like to access it yourself, remember our discussion of using libraries and interlibrary loaning services to obtain any one of the resources listed here. This is a useful tactic not only to save you from going broke but also because some of these titles are simply not available for purchase online and/or may be out of print and difficult to find in bookstores. Consult with a librarian at your nearby public or academic library if you aren't sure how to begin locating these resources. Additionally, using WorldCat online can help you locate the nearest library that may have a copy of the titles listed here. WorldCat is a freely available web resource that allows you to search titles and authors and which displays library holdings based on your zip code. In other words, you can type in the title "The UFO Encyclopedia" to see if any nearby libraries have a copy for you to enjoy.

The titles listed above are, of course, not a comprehensive list of *all* handbooks, dictionaries, and encyclopedias that exist under the vast umbrella of the paranormal. The titles listed here simply represent a good sampling of resources to begin your research and will provide a core understanding of each paranormal subtopic. When conducting your own research, remember not to stifle yourself by only referencing the works listed here. There are new reference materials listed every year, and any omission is not a statement of the work's worthiness of this list but moreover just a symptom of my own human oversight. The following chapter presents a list of monographs (books) on these topics that can be used simultaneously with any of the above resources.

NOTES

1. Ghost Club. (2012). The Ghost Club. Retrieved August 19, 2019, from http://www.ghostclub.org.uk/
2. Eranos Foundation. (n.d.). Who we are: History and meaning of ERANOS. Retrieved August 20, 2019, from http://www.eranosfoundation.org/history.htm
3. Parapsychological Association. (2019). Carlos Alvarado. Retrieved August 19, 2019, from https://www.parapsych.org/users/carlos/profile.aspx .
4. Parapsychological Association. (2019). Harvey Irwin. Retrieved August 19, 2019, from https://www.parapsych.org/users/hirwin/profile.aspx
5. The Cryptozoologist: Loren Coleman. (2012). Who is Loren Coleman? Retrieved July 25, 2019, from http://lorencoleman.com/who-is-loren-coleman/

Chapter Eight

Monographs

In this chapter, readers can find a list of monographs (books) associated with the paranormal. Like the previous chapter, I organize these resources according to their paranormal subcategory so that readers can navigate to the section they are most interested in. These monographs include titles that discuss the phenomena, offer biographical sketches about prominent figures associated with those topics, and more. Like the previous chapter, the publication dates of these monographs vary—some are very recent and some were published a hundred years ago. There is much to be learned from older texts, and I think most readers understand the value that these older titles bring to this subject. The books listed here are by no means a comprehensive and exhaustive listing of books published on the various paranormal subcategories below, and any omission of a relevant title is simply due to my own human error and not a judgment call on its worthiness of inclusion. It simply wouldn't be possible to list all scholarly and credible monographs related to the paranormal, and that's actually an amazing thing to realize. This chapter hopefully represents a core collection that readers can build upon. In addition, new titles are continuously written and published on these topics. Readers should use the titles presented below as a jumping-off point to the paranormal. Let me stress again that any omission of a title here is not an indication of its value to the overall topic.

    A note regarding categories—the problem with attempting to categorize the paranormal is that it so often defies categorization. I merely provide categories in this book to help connect readers with the topics they wish to begin with or are most curious about. There are some titles below that can very easily fit within multiple topics. To help readers locate what they may be looking for, I have included titles on spiritualism within the "Ghosts and Haunting" category. The previous chapter included a category labeled "Occult and Other Paranormal," but in this chapter, however, due to the immense number of monographs on the paranormal, I have rearranged some categories. "Occult" is now "Occult and Magical Practices," since the two are so intimately linked. Additionally, I created the new category of "General Paranormal and Paranormal Philosophy." In this new section, you'll find books that discuss general paranormal philosophies and/or works that combine many different topics and are thus hard to classify. The "Astrology, Divination, and Mysticism" category remains the same even though magical practices can so often fit in here. The topic of the occult and magical practices, however, does appear immediately after astrology, divination, and mysticism, so I encourage readers to consult both categories if they are interested in any of these topics.

Some may disagree with a title's location in the lists below, and that's actually quite fine as the titles all tend to ebb and flow into different categories at different times in their narratives. The labels presented below are by no means an attempt at pigeonholing a certain work and are instead merely intended to assist the reader in locating those topics they may be most interested in. Due to the fluid nature of the paranormal, though, I do urge all readers to browse the topics below for additional desired materials.

Remember that you can find the titles below through your local public and academic libraries. Using Amazon to get your hands on a copy of these books may seem like a knee-jerk response in the immediate-gratification technology-driven world that we live in, but it will only take a few minutes to either blow your budget or quickly discover that the internet doesn't provide magical access to every resource. Don't forget about the power of your local libraries. As you browse this list, please also remember that these books simply represent a sample of the titles available on these topics and were chosen based on their ability to provide a core understanding of each paranormal topic presented below.

GHOSTS AND HAUNTINGS

Buckland, Raymond. (2018). *Buckland's book of spirit communications* (2nd ed.). Woodbury, MN: Llewellyn. 263 pages.

Author Raymond Buckland is a renowned scholar of the occult who has both lectured and taught at universities across the country. In this work, Buckland presents a comprehensive overview of spirit communication. To do this, he incorporates both a history of spirit communication as well as detailed descriptions of tactics along with exercises for readers to practice their own spirit communications. He begins with a discussion of mediumship followed by a discussion of the types of encounters people experience during spirit communications. After this, he presents a couple of chapters outlining the history of the spiritualism movement before diving into specific techniques such as automatic writing, spirit boards, trance, channeling, and more. Each chapter includes a "profile" of some person or event that illustrates the topic of the chapter, such as the profile on Abraham Lincoln's prophetic dream of his own assassination. There is an appendix of information on prominent cases of spirit fraud as well as another appendix listing answers to the exercise questions provided at the end of each chapter.

Clarke, Roger. (2012). *Ghosts, a natural history: 500 years of searching for proof.* New York, NY: St. Martin's Griffin. 359 pages.

Author Roger Clarke was motivated to write this book after developing a fascination with ghosts—perhaps this was due to the haunted houses he grew up in. This interest also led him to become a member of the Society for Psychical Research, and in this work, he presents a highly readable discussion of our fascination with all things ghostly. After an introductory chapter in which he outlines some of his own personal experiences, chapter 2 offers a taxonomy of ghosts. For example, he notes that ghosts often take many different forms—there's the poltergeist, the imprint, visions of recently or tragically departed ghosts, and then there's instances where they aren't even people at all—haunted objects, for example. He follows this with a discussion on the history of ghost hunting, told mainly through the case study of noted ghost hunter Harry Price, whose work is mentioned later in this section. A vast portion of this book details some prominent cases and encounters with ghosts during which Clarke also discusses the reasons for society's fascination with and attraction to ghosts and hauntings. Offering solid background information and reference for further reading, this novel also touches on the cultural role ghosts and hauntings play and is a wholly enjoyable read to boot.

Davies, Owen. (2007). *The haunted: A social history of ghosts.* Hampshire, England: Palgrave Macmillan. 299 pages.

Researcher Owen Davies presents a sociological history of ghosts in England—a country still considered to be a "ghost-ridden nation." He notes, however, that many scholars focus on the era of spiritualism and beyond when it comes to understanding the role of ghosts and hauntings in England, and that few focus on the modern era—being the period roughly from the 1500s to the 1800s. This is the era that Davies focuses on in this work. As such, it is a unique entry to this list and essential for a more holistic understanding of the paranormal culture of a nation. In the first part of this book, Davies discusses the ways in which people experienced and made sense of the paranormal. This discussion ranges from type of paranormal experience to the spaces in which people encountered them. He also discusses the political reaction to people who dabbled in the paranormal or in rituals associated with magical acts, reminding us that the history of the paranormal has always been intimately connected with politics and religion.

In the second portion of his work, he discusses the dominant theories that people had in the modern era regarding ghostly phenomena—many theories that were once again intimately connected to religious thought. In the third and final portion, Davies discusses present-day paranormal belief in the UK and entertains reasons why these beliefs have lingered and morphed over time—media representation and secularization being two main reasons, Davies posits. This work is not only engaging and entertaining, but it also offers a unique focus on the reality of paranormal thought and experience in the modern era.

Houran, James, & Lange, Rense. (Eds.). (2001). *Hauntings and poltergeists: Multidisciplinary perspectives.* Jefferson, NC: McFarland. 330 pages.

This work is a compilation of fourteen selected journal articles as curated by editors (and well-known researchers) James Houran and Rense Lange. Each of these articles represents a unique perspective into the world of hauntings and poltergeists and are broken down into the following three categories: a sociocultural lens, a physical/physiological lens, and a psychological lens. As such, this work represents not only a wide spectrum of theories and topics relating to haunting phenomena, but it also offers a wide variety of research methods and experimentation into the paranormal. For example, an article titled "Seeking Spirits in the Laboratory" by Dean Radin provides an overview of many experiments that have been done in regard to apparitions, and even includes detailed diagrams and charts of data in relation to these experiments.

An article by David J. Hufford that resides in the sociocultural perspective provides a detailed discussion of paranormal beliefs and the importance of understanding how people experience the paranormal in their lives. Furthermore, an article by Fátima Regina Machado discusses poltergeists and hauntings from a psychological lens and interprets these phenomena via semiotics, or the signs that we ascribe to these paranormal experiences.

Taken as a whole, this work presents not only different perspectives of the paranormal but offers readers a robust scientific starting point to understand the many different nuances of critically understanding the paranormal. It alerts readers to the fact that the paranormal can be understood in a variety of different ways—socioculturally, psychologically, and physiologically. This book will point readers to a wide range of additional resources, as this work contains a lengthy bibliography.

Kontou, Tatiana, & Willburn, Sarah. (Eds.). (2016). *The Ashgate research companion to nineteenth-century spiritualism and the occult.* London, England: Routledge. 454 pages.

This work focuses on spiritualism and its role during the Victorian era, and since a main component of spiritualism was to make contact with the dead, hence its inclusion here with the topics of ghosts/hauntings. The contributors to this edited work include researchers from Canada, England, Scotland, and the United States. The authors in this work, however, don't just relegate themselves to discussing the techniques employed by the mediums and practitioners of spiritualism. In addition, they take a comprehensive dive into the cultural and social roles that spiritualism bred. The first portion of this work investigates the intersection of spiritualism and science. Here, authors present works that highlight modern thought and research on this topic as well as works that discuss the strengths and weaknesses of Victorian scientific thought and how that impacted spiritualist practices and views. One article in particular discusses the rise of "spirit poetry" and how it impacted notions of both plagiarism and authority in the Victorian era. The next section of this work presents chapters that discuss spiritualism's effect on sex and politics in this era, while the third and final section focuses on the theatrics and methods used by spiritualists. Offering a deeper, sociological and cultural perspective on the ways in which spiritualism influenced and shaped the Victorian era, the discussions in this book help craft a deeper understanding of this movement.

McCorristine, Shane. (2010). *Spectres of the self: Thinking about ghosts and ghost-seeing in England, 1750–1920.* Cambridge, England: Cambridge University Press. 288 pages.

Dr. Shane McCorristine is a professor of British history at Newcastle University who, in his own words, examines the "social attitudes towards death, dreams, ghosts, hallucinations, and the 'more than rational.'"[1] In this work, he takes readers on a symbolic journey of the spectral, focusing on the years 1750–1920 during which ghosts, the psychological, and sociology intertwined dramatically. It is an inquiry, he tells us, that helps reveal societal notions of death and superstition as experienced via "ghost-seeing." He focuses specifically on the ways that this played out in the bourgeois of England, and even though he is concerned with the symbolism and social implications of ghostly phenomena, he does offer a chapter on the Society for Psychical Research and its efforts at scientifically investigating these phenomena. The discussion of the SPR, though, is still steeped in symbolic meaning—in other words, what did it mean that such an organization was formed and was willing to entertain the notion of entire worlds beyond our understanding? Readers looking for a social commentary that focuses on the symbolic nature of ghosts in pre-1920 England will want to add this to their must-read list.

Price, Harry. (1940). *The most haunted house in England: Ten years' investigation of Borley Rectory.* London, England: Longmans, Green. 255 pages.

Harry Price was a psychical researcher who, due to his penchant for showmanship and publicity, often caused rifts among his colleagues. He was briefly connected with the Society for Psychical Research before leaving this organization due to the aforementioned conflict and creating his own organization, the National Laboratory of Psychical Research, under the auspices of the London Spiritualist Alliance.[2] In this work, Price describes his ten-year investigation into and experiences at the Borley Rectory, considered perhaps the most haunted house in England due to its intense activity and Price's lengthy accounts of activity. Price begins with an overview of the rectory's history along with the rumored origins of its haunted happenings. He includes eyewitness reports and statements as well. After hearing the tales of Borley Rectory, Price decided to rent the entire property for the sole purpose of paranormal investigation. In the course of this, he even placed ads in local newspapers for people willing to come stay and spend time investigating alongside him. To help facilitate this, Price created the Borley Rectory "Blue Book," a booklet of instructions for fellow investigators. The remainder of the book is a discussion of their investigations. At the end of the work, Price includes six appendixes that include the Blue Book, a summary of investigator reports, and a list of everyone involved, as well as a timeline of the paranormal happenings at the rectory.

Ramsland, Katherine. (2001). *Ghost: Investigating the other side.* New York, NY: St. Martin's Press. 322 pages.

Dr. Katherine Ramsland, who once taught philosophy at Rutgers University, draws upon her journalist experience and presents here a memoir of participant observation in the world of ghost hunters. Dr. Ramsland grew up fascinated by ghostly lore and decided to set out on a journey in the hopes of having a paranormal experience herself. Her travels took her across the country—from haunted hotels in Savannah, Georgia, to Princeton Battlefield State Park in New Jersey, to the New Age community of Sedona, Arizona. In this wholly readable and fascinating firsthand account of someone who begins to have strange and unexplainable encounters along this journey, Dr. Ramsland admits that while she may not know exactly what is out there, she's convinced that something is. This is quite a departure from the works listed so far, but through the use of memoir and participant observation, readers get a very close-up look at the world of paranormal investigators.

Schmitt, Jean-Claude. (1998). *Ghosts in the Middle Ages: The living and the dead in medieval society.* Chicago, IL: University of Chicago Press. 290 pages.

Author Jean-Claude Schmitt offers a work on how medieval society and culture shaped a belief in ghosts. Putting it best in the introduction, Schmitt writes, "It is by considering this reality that we will understand how the Christian culture of the Middle Ages enlarged the notion of ghosts and created other opportunities for the dead to appear." Schmitt focuses on the fifth through fifteenth centuries and the role in which Christianity and shifting social dynamics greatly influenced the ways in which ghosts were not only represented, but how intimately notions of ghosts related to the resurrection of the dead. A religious and sociological inquiry of the ways in which ghosts were made manifest in the Middle Ages, thereby offering a unique focus on a particular time period and its relationship to the paranormal.

Stuart, Nancy Rubin. (2005). *The reluctant spiritualist: The life of Maggie Fox.* Orlando, FL: Harcourt. 393 pages.

You may recall from earlier chapters a discussion about the infamous Fox sisters of New England, who in the mid-1800s became famous for their spirit knockings and communications with the dead. In this book, author Nancy Stuart presents a biographical look at Maggie Fox—the sister who claimed, forty years after the fact, that the methods of her and her sisters were all a hoax. Causing what can only be described as an uproar within the general public and especially the spiritualist movement, Maggie again recanted *that* confession one year later, muddying the water even more. Clearly dealing with a complicated case, Stuart draws upon primary source documents to tell the story of Maggie and her sisters in an eye-opening way. The Fox sisters are an integral part of the spiritualism movement, and any understanding of this movement requires an understanding of the Fox sisters. Stuart's book will help with that.

PARAPSYCHOLOGY

Broughton, Richard S. (1991). *Parapsychology: The controversial science.* New York, NY: Ballantine Books. 408 pages.

At the time of writing this work, Dr. Richard S. Broughton was the director of research at the Institute for Parapsychology in North Carolina. A noted parapsychologist, Dr. Broughton at one point served as president of the International Parapsychological Association. In this work, he seeks to present an easy-to-understand account of the long history of parapsychology, the evidence for various phenomena, the many researchers and scientists who have contributed to advancing this field, and much more. Described as the first attempt at presenting the psychical literature to the general public, Dr. Broughton's book takes a detailed look at the science and methodology behind psychical research.

This work is divided into three main parts: In the first part, Dr. Broughton introduces parapsychology and presents an overview of the field. For example, he outlines and describes what types of experiences are considered psychical—he even provides detailed examples from case studies of psychical researchers. Following this, he moves into a discussion of how psychical researchers classify and organize these phenomena. In this section, he includes a discussion on what isn't considered parapsychology, such as astrology, ufology, and cryptozoology. Perhaps the most important aspect of this section is his detailed descriptions of the methodologies that parapsychologists use to study this phenomenon. This is extremely useful not only for evaluating the merits of psychical research but also for assisting readers with their own research and experiments. He concludes this portion by discussing psychical pioneers and the reasons why this field is still so controversial.

In part 2 of this work, Dr. Broughton focuses on notable contemporary psychical research and provides detailed discussions of recent experiments and research, much of which focuses on extrasensory perception and psychokinesis. In chapter 7 he focuses specifically on those psychical researchers who investigate ghost and haunting phenomena, recognizing that this is not only a popular topic with which to engage and "hook" people, but also noting that these phenomena represent a very real portion of the human experience and, as such, are no less worthy of scientific inquiry than other psychical phenomena such as ESP. Following this chapter, he introduces research that focuses on near-death experiences and the idea of life after death before concluding his work by musing on the future of psychical research. This work, even though it is vast and comprehensive, is a great starting point for anyone wishing to begin their understanding of psi phenomena and parapsychological research.

Brown, Courtney. (2006). *Remote viewing: The science and theory of nonphysical perception*. Atlanta, GA: Farsight Press. 313 pages.

Dr. Courtney Brown is a researcher who founded the Farsight Institute in 1995—a nonprofit educational organization that studies remote viewing phenomena. In this book, Dr. Brown sets out to describe how remote viewing works and to present case studies of remote viewing experiments. He informs readers from the beginning that this work isn't a how-to manual of remote viewing and is instead a work that discusses the science and theory of remote viewing. The preface to this work is not to be missed, as Dr. Brown crafts a wonderful discussion about the seeming inability of science and researchers to calmly inquire into that which is extraordinary. He puts it best when he writes, "The reality is that extraordinary claims really require only calm consideration of evident facts, and the call for 'extraordinary evidence' is typically used only to refuse to consider these evident facts." I fear that sometimes prefaces and introductions in nonfiction works get overlooked in the excitement to jump to meatier sections, and I point this out to remind readers of the many valuable discussions often included in these introductory portions.

After this wonderful discussion, Dr. Brown begins this work with a definition of remote viewing and its main characteristics and includes a brief overview of the scientific procedures of remote viewing experiences. He then discusses some history of remote viewing, including his own personal experiences with the phenomena before diving into, in chapter 2, a detailed and heavily scientific outline of the theories surrounding remote viewing. This chapter will undoubtedly be a challenge for those who are relatively new to the concept of remote viewing but can also be challenging for anyone who doesn't have core knowledge of physics and space-related concepts. This isn't to say that Dr. Brown's writing is jargon filled or confusing. The book is easy to follow in this manner; it's simply that readers will likely have to pause to look up concepts unknown or hazy to them. There's certainly nothing wrong with that, though. In this sense, Dr. Brown's book challenges readers to enhance their understanding of this phenomenon. He then discusses some of the remote viewing methodologies conducted at the Farsight Institute as well as notable experiments conducted by other researchers.

Following these discussions, Dr. Brown mentions the nuances of data collection and analysis when it comes to remote viewing before offering detailed case studies of certain remote viewing experiments. In these experiments, Dr. Brown and colleagues hosted a public demonstration of remote viewing in which people around the world were chosen at random to participate. One researcher selected certain targets that they hoped the remote viewers would pick up on during their sessions. Some of these targets included things like the Washington Monument or the eruption of Mount Vesuvius, and the results from the remote viewers, who described and often sketched their sessions, were oftentimes uncanny and downright accurate. This work, while undoubtedly a challenge to many readers, offers a unique scientific perspective in remote viewing and is valuable for anyone wishing to understand the physics and space/time implications demonstrated by remote viewing.

Gurney, Edmund, Myers, Frederic W. H., & Podmore, Frank. (1886). *Phantasms of the living.* 2 vols. London, England: Trubner. 573 pages.

Early psychical researchers Gurney, Myers, and Podmore present this two-volume work that is a staple of paranormal research. In the first volume, they begin with some philosophical discussions on the merits of psychical research before introducing and defining the concept of thought transference, as well as presenting some notable examples of this phenomenon. From here, they discuss differences between experimental and spontaneous telepathy and the research implications for both. They spend some time addressing the criticisms of such phenomena before presenting a thorough discussion on the different types of telepathic experiences, again presenting notable cases to the reader. Finally, they go into greater detail discussing research on dream telepathy, hypnagogic (what they call borderland) experiences, and external impressions or ghostly visions (what they call hallucinations).

In the second volume, the researchers begin with a discussion of how they investigate or control for instances of chance or coincidence in telepathy cases. Following this, they present an outline of visual telepathic experiences versus auditory experiences, and even discuss cases where telepathy occurs simultaneously between two or more people. After these chapters, they conclude with a summary of their research and findings, noting the weaknesses of their present studies and calling for future research into the matter. Nevertheless, this work is an important key resource that highlights early psychical thought and experiment.

Haynes, Renée. (1982). *The Society for Psychical Research, 1882–1982: A history.* London, England: Macdonald. 240 pages.

This work presents a detailed historical account of the most prominent psychical research organization—the Society for Psychical Research. Beginning with the events that led to its formation in 1882, Haynes presents a wealth of information on this organization that still exists today. This work provides an account of the philosophical underpinnings of the society in terms of using scientific methods to better understand the paranormal, while also presenting discussions of major works and prominent figures in the society. Haynes outlines the particular issues the society faced with the popularity of spiritualism and the rise of mediums. As such, this work presents a sociocultural overview alongside the historical timeline of this organization. Haynes does not hesitate to discuss controversial studies and claims and provides detailed information on the various experiments and studies undertaken by many scientists affiliated with this organization. The result is an unbiased, complete portrait of the first one hundred years of the SPR, making it an invaluable resource for those wishing to learn more about the scientific pursuit of psychical phenomena. References are included in footnote entries, and a who's who of past SPR presidents appears at the conclusion of this work.

Irwin, H. J. (1989). *An introduction to parapsychology.* Jefferson, NC: McFarland. 321 pages.

This work, author H. J. Irwin tells us in the acknowledgments, is a culmination of research from teaching ten years' worth of parapsychology at the University of New England. This work begins with an introduction and discussion of the early days of psychical research in which Irwin includes common definitions of various psychical phenomena alongside prominent research scientists. These sections read like a textbook, in that Irwin includes key terms and study questions at the end of each chapter. This format is helpful even to those who aren't students, though, as it helps beginning researchers grasp key concepts and research in a way that other texts may not facilitate as much. In chapter 3, Irwin focuses on extrasensory perceptions and outlines the various experiences captured in case studies and reports done by psychical researchers. Following this, Irwin presents a chapter outlining experiments and methods of testing ESP. He then goes on to discuss psychokinesis, poltergeists, near-death and out-of-body experiences, ghost phenomena, and even reincarnation. Each chapter ends with key terms and study questions, offering a way for readers to review and synthesize the information they've read. A perfect choice for anyone new to parapsychology. This work also appears in later editions—the fifth addition, in fact, written in 2007, was coauthored by well-known psychical researcher Dr. Caroline Watt.

Mavromatis, Andreas. (1987). *Hypnagogia: The unique state of consciousness between wakefulness and sleep.* London, England: Routledge. 360 pages.

Author Andreas Mavromatis, who studied both philosophy and psychology, presents here a compendium of information on hypnagogic experiences. These are experiences that happen in the liminal space between sleep and wakefulness. Often referred to as hypnagogic hallucinations, this phenomenon has been well documented since ancient times, though this work is touted as the first English-language source to compile a comprehensive overview of the phenomenon. These experiences that happen between being asleep and coming awake can be auditory, visual, or even psychosomatic in nature. They are unique manifestations of the strange inner workings of the human mind and are not entirely understood by scientists. In other words, we know that these things happen, but we can't map exactly how. In this work, Mavromatis outlines the various types of hypnagogic experiences and its relation to dreams, meditation, and even psychical phenomena. For example, some claim that hypnagogia is a precursor to more advanced experiences of ESP, and others even posit that it's connected to out-of-body experiences.

This work is extremely academic in both nature and scope and provides an exhaustively detailed treatment of hypnagogia, a truly unique and mystifying experience manifested by the human mind.

McConnell, R. A. (1983). *An introduction to parapsychology in the context of science.* Pittsburgh, PA: University of Pittsburgh. 337 pages.

In 1973, author R. A. McConnell taught a course on parapsychology at the University of Pittsburgh, and a majority of this book is the content of the lectures he had prepared for that class. As you might guess, then, this book is a comprehensive treatment of parapsychology, and at twenty-six chapters there is ample room to discuss all of its nuances. McConnell begins his work by discussing some psychosocial factors of parapsychology, including both the zeitgeist of trance mediumship alongside societal notions of consciousness and its various states. He then discusses some factors that may influence psychical phenomena before providing an overview of parapsychology both in the UK and the United States.

Following the history of parapsychology, McConnell devotes the next seven chapters to discussing various methods and experiments involving psi phenomena, especially psychokinesis. His last section, part 3, discusses some of the major theories found in parapsychology alongside the growth the field has made throughout the years. He even includes a chapter in this section that introduces some cases of fraudulent activity and research involving parapsychology—disheartening yes, but beneficial nonetheless. The work concludes with eight distinct appendixes. One of these appendixes is an annotated list of core reading for parapsychology, whereas another is a biographical listing of prominent psychical figures. McConnell even includes an appendix listing the professional centers and organizations dedicated to psychical research.

Rhine, J. B. (Ed.). (1971). *Progress in parapsychology.* Durham, NC: Parapsychology Press. 313 pages.

This book was written in memory of William McDougall, a renowned psychologist and member of the Society for Psychical Research. Editor J. B. Rhine notes that even though McDougall didn't consider himself a parapsychologist, he nevertheless helped pave the road for the future of parapsychology due to his open-minded investigations of psychical questions, especially in his seminal work *Body and Mind*. In this current edited work, Rhine puts together a sampling of the most innovative psychical research with the goal of not only highlighting the progress of parapsychological research, but also in the hopes of connecting a general readership with research they otherwise wouldn't have encountered.

The first portion of this book presents articles that discuss novel approaches to testing psychical phenomena. One of these articles, for example, investigates the psychical behavior of mice, while another article discusses an experiment of ESP using roulette wheels. Part 2 of this work focuses on psychokinesis, and part 3 focuses on specific issues regarding methodology in psychical research. Part 4 is especially interesting as it focuses on psychical researchers whose work has shown steady progress in the field, including Dr. James Carpenter's work on how mood is correlated to instances of precognition. The final portion of this work presents articles that ponder both the progress to date and the future of parapsychology.

Rhine, J. B. (1937). *New frontiers of the mind: The story of the Duke experiments*. New York, NY: Farrar & Rinehart. 275 pages.

This book is an absolute must for anyone wishing to obtain a historical foundation of parapsychology and in particular its ties to science, research, and academia. Written by the father of parapsychology himself, J. B. Rhine, this work outlines the pursuits that he and his colleagues undertook at the Duke Parapsychology Labs, which existed from 1930 until 1965. In this work, Rhine outlines the beginnings of the work done under the auspices of Duke University with precognition, extrasensory perception, and other psychical research. The first chapters of this work offer a philosophical discussion regarding the importance of scientific endeavors that are outside the box and outlines some of Rhine's own experiences and/or experiences recounted to him. Beginning with chapter 4, Rhine provides a detailed overview of the research and findings done at the parapsychology labs while also addressing the critics of the day. He further goes into great detail discussing components of precognition and extrasensory perception and the detailed experimental settings that he and his colleagues considered and tested. The last portion of the book outlines the frequently asked questions Rhine and his colleagues received and muses on the future of psychical research and its possible implications.

Rhine, Louisa E. (1961). *Hidden channels of the mind.* New York, NY: William Slone Associates. 291 pages.

Louisa Rhine, psychical researcher and wife to colleague J. B. Rhine, presents here a compendium of psychical research designed for the masses—designed specifically, as noted in the foreword, for those laypeople who have experienced psychical phenomena and not had an opportunity to feel seen or to understand what has happened to them. Additionally, author Louisa Rhine hoped that this work, through its specific target at the general public, would help dispel the skepticism surrounding these phenomena. She begins this work by outlining the various types of psychical phenomena before diving into a discussion of the ways in which these experiences manifest. For example, some of these experiences come through the form of dreams, whereas others come via intuition; some of them are extremely detailed and picturesque, while others are a bit hazier and may or may not involve people or places familiar to the experiencer. Rhine then discusses how easy it is for people to overlook that they've had a psychical event: there is no clear way of identifying the phenomena as such, since they take so many forms and varieties. This section in particular offers a wonderful discussion on the assumptions we harbor about the world around us and our willingness to disregard that which is exceptional.

Following these chapters, Rhine discusses the ways in which time and space are experienced through psychical events and then provides an overview of the various subject matter experienced by people. This offers a segue to her next section, in which she outlines the differences in psychical experiences between men, women, and children. Furthermore, she spends an entire chapter outlining how psychical phenomena are not a symptom of mental illness, and that these two things don't automatically go hand in hand. In the next chapter, she describes catastrophic visions and dreams experienced by people and the various ways in which they have responded to them—sometimes the result being an avoidance of the prophesized danger itself! This book not only highlights the work and contribution of Louisa Rhine but also attempts to bridge the gap between a skeptical public and the laboratory researcher. In a way, this book helped pave the road for the continued discussions and attempts at breaking the stigma of paranormal research.

Richet, Charles. (1923). *Thirty years of psychical research: Being a treatise on metaphysics.* New York, NY: Macmillan. 646 pages.

Dr. Charles Richet was a noted French physiologist credited with discovering anaphylaxis. In addition, he was greatly intrigued by metaphysics and the psychical, and due to this interest, he published this work in 1923 presenting an overview of the past thirty years of psychical research and information. Even though this work is written from a staunchly materialistic perspective, Richet writes in his preface that "I do, however, claim that science, strict and inflexible science, ought to admit these three strange phenomena that it has up to the present refused to recognize." The three phenomena that he references and which are the main focus of his book are cryptesthesia, telekinesis, and ectoplasm. Divided into three portions, this work presents a vast amount of extremely valuable information. For example, in part 1 Richet presents a historical timeline of metaphysics and accepted thoughts on psychical phenomena. Part 2 focuses primarily in cryptesthesia, what we now refer to as extrasensory perception. He discusses experiments that have been done to test this phenomenon using a variety of methodologies and test subjects. This portion, at nearly 350 pages long, is an entire book unto itself and offers an exhaustive treatment of extrasensory perception research up to 1923. His final section, part 3, discusses telekinesis (what we now refer to as psychokinesis) and the various experiments conducted to test this phenomenon. Included in this section is also a discussion of ectoplasm and haunting phenomena. Full of immense historical details that paint a vivid picture about the zeitgeist of paranormal thoughts and inquiry, this historical work is a necessary inclusion on anyone's research list.

Schoch, Robert M., & Yonavjak, Logan. (2008). *The parapsychology revolution: A concise anthology of paranormal and psychical research.* New York, NY: Jeremy P. Tarcher/Penguin. 419 pages.

In this work, authors Schoch and Yonavjak do essentially the very same thing I attempt to do in my work: present an annotated bibliography of resources. In their case, however, they specifically focus on parapsychology and present to us reprinted portions of select resources alongside the authors' commentaries. Separated into four parts, the book's first portion is dedicated to resources that discuss spontaneous paranormal instances. Within this section, for example, are sources on telepathy, mediumship, poltergeists, and psychokinesis. The publication dates from these resources range from 1886 to 2003, offering a comprehensive time span on this topic. In part 2, the authors present sources that outline laboratory experiments on psi phenomena such as the ESP work of J. B. Rhine; the articles here span 1934–1996. In part 3, the authors present sources that apply data found during psi experiments. For example, one article discusses the possibility of distance healing using known psi phenomenon, and another article discusses how remote viewing has been used by the government. The final portion discusses the future of psychical research and muses on the theories behind the phenomena. Through including select reprinted portions of these resources alongside the authors' commentary, the authors give readers a more nuanced understanding of the resources contained herein.

Targ, Russell, & Harary, Keith. (1984). *The mind race: Understanding and using psychic abilities.* New York, NY: Villard Books. 294 pages.

In the foreword to this book, William Harman, a social scientist and former president of the Institute for Noetic Sciences, writes that authors Targ and Harary "have written the first comprehensive and popular book" on the subject of remote viewing and particularly of its usage by United States and Soviet governments. Author Russell Targ is a physicist who worked with the Stanford Research Institute—an organization that contracted with the United States government to research psychical phenomena.[3] Coauthor Keith Harary is a noted parapsychologist whose main body of work focuses on out-of-body experiences.

The first five chapters of this book present an overview of United States and Soviet research using psychical phenomena such as remote viewing and precognition abilities. In these chapters, they illustrate the fact that many people involved in these experiments don't necessarily have preexisting psychical abilities, but rather develop them with the assistance of psychical researchers. This is a huge statement to make—that essentially large swaths of people can develop the ability to preconceive information via remote viewing tactics. In the following three chapters, they discuss reasons why this isn't such common knowledge or why people don't engage in these activities more often. Here, they discuss things like media representation of extrasensory abilities and try to break down some of the myths and stereotypes that lead people to be skeptical or even fearful of such phenomena.

The final portion of their work is perhaps the most intriguing. In this section, they provide guidance on developing your own psychical abilities—an activity they refer to as doing "psychic sit-ups." They begin by discussing how psychical abilities can be a practical benefit in your life, and then they provide detailed discussions on how to practice developing these abilities. This work is full of case studies, sketches, and photographs outlining the history and usage of remote viewing and offers a practical guideline for anyone wishing to personally experiment with the phenomena.

Watt, Caroline. (2016). *Parapsychology: A beginner's guide.* London, England: Oneworld. 240 pages.

Dr. Caroline Watt, a well-known parapsychologist, presents this overview of parapsychology that is targeted at beginners or those unfamiliar with the field. Presenting both a historical overview and modern progress of parapsychological research, Dr. Watt presents the information in an easy-to-follow way. She begins with a list of common terms, defining them for the reader. Following this, the first portion of the book presents the historical overview and early experiments with psi phenomena, while the second portion outlines specific phenomena like out-of-body experiences, hauntings, and more. The third and final portion goes into more detail on scientific methods used to test psi phenomena before she closes with a discussion on the value of parapsychological research.

CRYPTOZOOLOGY

Arment, Chad. (2004). *Cryptozoology: Science & speculation.* Landisville, PA: Coachwhip. 393 pages.

Chad Arment is an author and researcher who compiles in this work a treatise for the scientific treatment of the field of cryptozoology. In other words, he outlines the reasons why cryptozoology is a serious field while acknowledging the factors that create a haze of pseudoscience in the larger academic community. He spends the first 139 pages of this book making the case for cryptozoology. Specifically in this first half, for example, he breaks down definitions of this field and explains to the reader what is and isn't considered cryptozoology, thereby making definite boundaries between this field and others. He follows this by outlining the many merits of adhering to strict methodologies, giving the reader quite a lesson on the nuances of research, I might add. Chapter 4, "An Ethnozoological Foundation for an Investigative Methodology," begins with a discussion on the utility of folklore as concerns cryptozoology before diving into a discussion on the role of ethnobiologists and how they study the ways in which people name and classify species of plants and animals and how an understanding of this can aid the cryptozoological researcher.

In chapter 5, Arment goes straight to the heart of why cryptozoology is a valid scientific pursuit. Within this chapter he not only outlines a history of biological discoveries, but he also discusses how and why animals remain hidden and undiscovered to this day. He ends this chapter with an intriguing conversation about the important role that amateur cryptozoologists can play, as professional and academic zoologists rarely get funding for such pursuits. The next chapter is all about methodology and what to include in your own investigations, followed by some chapters discussing the feasibility and credibility of cryptozoology. In those chapters, Arment not only discusses the geographic landscape of cryptozoology and the practicalities of research, but he also outlines the weaknesses in the field that have led to challenges of its credibility. However, he also references many researchers whose work has only helped to advance the cause of this field.

The second half of this work consists of the speculative side of cryptozoology—in other words, Arment provides cases of cryptid sightings around the world such as strange cats, sea creatures, and mysterious snakes. Arment points out that the speculative side of cryptozoology—the eyewitness reports and sightings—serve to assist researchers with the science side of the field, hence the subtitle to this work. This title both presents a wonderful philosophical and historical overview of cryptozoology and also outlines the scientific pursuits and advances, while also offering mysterious tales of the biological world.

Coleman, Loren. (2003). *Bigfoot! The true story of apes in America.* New York, NY: Paraview Pocket Books. 288 pages.

Loren Coleman is a distinguished cryptozoologist and curator of the International Cryptozoology Museum in Portland, Maine. Here, Coleman provides a historical overview of the Bigfoot phenomena in North America and draws upon forty years' worth of research and interviews to craft this work that presents a comprehensive inquiry into the possibility and evidence of undiscovered bipedal creatures. He begins this work by providing an overview of some prominent Bigfoot cases that include Native American legends and also more modern encounters such as the Patterson-Gimlin film. He then reflects on the intersection of high strangeness and the Bigfoot phenomena while also discussing the future of the phenomena. Two appendixes are included: one that outlines some Bigfoot-sighting hotspots and another that presents a compendium of footprint castings.

Conway, D. J. (2018). *Magickal mystical creatures: Invite their powers into your life* (3rd ed.). Woodbury, MN: Llewellyn. 259 pages.

Author D. J. Conway is an occult researcher who has written more than twenty books related to the paranormal and its subfields. This work, a third edition of the initial title published in 1996, is extremely folkloric in nature and is a marked difference from Arment's work above. In fact, this work could very easily be placed in the later section on astrology, divination, and mysticism, but I include it here due to its specific focus on creatures. In this book, Conway does not discuss the ways to scientifically investigate the presence of undiscovered species, but what she does provide is a wealth of folklore surrounding mysterious creatures. As we know, folklore is intimately connected to cryptozoology, whether that fact irritates some researchers or not. Conway provides an overview of magical creatures and discusses the ways in which these creatures are connected with magic thought, practice, and ritual. In the entries of these folkloric creatures from around the world, Conroy discusses the symbolism of each creature along with its associated culture and time period. While some readers may question the value of folklore to a broader scientific understanding of cryptozoology, it is necessary to understand the very powerful ways in which strange and mythical creatures have woven themselves into the tapestry of human history. Anything that helps you have a holistic understanding of some topic can only be beneficial, even if this works seems tangential to the topic of cryptozoology—it is relevant, however. Understanding folkloric creatures, for example, can help to further understand the ways in which people might report or describe encounters with strange, unknown creatures today.

Godfrey, Linda S. (2014). *American monsters: A history of monster lore, legends, and sightings in America.* New York, NY: Jeremy P. Tarcher/Penguin. 384 pages.

The entries in this section are overwhelmingly dominated by Sasquatch, or as it is sometimes referred—Bigfoot. In this work, Godfrey does not limit her discussion to these large bipedal enigmas, instead presenting a compilation of monster legends and sightings from across the United States. She organizes this work by grouping cryptids into the categories of air, sea, and land. As such, we get a much more diverse set of curious creatures that have cropped up from time to time in the American landscape. The sightings and reports in this work span centuries ago, like the sea serpent spotted in New England in 1817, to more recent sightings, like a strange and giant bird seen in Minnesota in 2005. Godfrey includes eyewitness sketches and photographs as well as a chapter outlining her own personal experiences, giving a unique conclusion to this compendium of creature sightings. While some readers may dismiss this work as merely a collection of stories, the entries are all rooted in some form of eyewitness encounter, and as other researchers have reminded us, these encounters can often assist the eventual discovery of some heretofore unknown creatures. Regardless, it illustrates the depth and breadth of strange sightings across the country.

Halpin, Marjorie M., & Ames, Michael. (Eds.) (1980). *Manlike monsters on trial: Early records and modern evidence.* Vancouver, Canada: University of British Columbia Press. 336 pages.

This work is a compilation of articles presented at the May 1978 conference titled "Sasquatch and Similar Phenomena" held at the University of British Columbia. This conference, the editors note, was necessary and probed the divide between myth and science since more and more countries were beginning to seriously investigate sightings and reports of Bigfoot-like creatures. They also recognize the tenuous nature of this topic and the fact that there is no abundance of experts to turn to when discussing this matter. This conference included a variety of intellectuals engaged in this topic—from physical field researchers to anthropologists, to historians, folklore experts, and even one psychoanalyst. The result is a multidisciplinary look at the topic of manlike creatures.

The articles within this work are extremely varied, making it a strong contender for inclusion in cryptozoological research, in my opinion. For example, one conference attendee discusses the reports of Bigfoot-like creatures in Newfoundland, while another researcher discusses the cultural roles that such creatures play in Canada. A handful of speakers address North American monster myths, and still others discuss Bigfoot-esque visages in art throughout the world. Following these sections, this work includes entries from modern scientists, including one article that analyzes the pitch and tone of alleged Bigfoot vocalizations. A truly multidisciplinary look into this topic and a resource that will help ferret out the nuances of this topic.

Heuvelmans, Bernard. (1995). *On the track of unknown animals* (3rd ed.) (Richard Garnett, Trans.). London, England: Kegan Paul International. 677 pages.

Bernard Heuvelmans is known as the father of cryptozoology and was a French Belgian researcher who penned other works related to this field. This title, however, is often hailed as the forerunner of cryptozoological research and was originally published in French in 1955. This third edition, published in 1995 and translated into English, is an indispensable resource for anyone wishing to gain a more scientific understanding of this field. At nearly seven hundred pages, it is a massive tome full of seemingly endless references, international case studies, and discussions of scientific pursuits and discoveries.

Heuvelmans begins this work with a discussion on the "great days of zoology" in which his first chapter is titled "There Are Lost Worlds Everywhere." As you might guess, he advances the idea that many scientists, for varied reasons, are very dismissive of the notion of undiscovered species due to a belief that they simply would have been discovered by now due to the number of explorations and expeditions. And even though he never lived to hear the catchphrase "fake news," he nevertheless discusses the impact of news fallacies, particularly on the public attitude and perception of cryptozoology. He even dives into geographic discussions of certain regions of the world, outlining how vast they are and how much space there is, giving further credence to the notion that there is a great possibility of undiscovered animals roaming these places.

Furthermore, the first one hundred pages of this work contain innumerable references to species and animals that were discovered alongside the academic zeitgeist of having discovered all there was to discover. And these are discoveries that have happened within the last fifty years! Starting with chapter 4, however, Heuvelmans moves on to a discussion of ethnoknown or rumored species and discusses in great detail the nuances of their reports. Still within these chapters, you can find references to instances of zoological discovery once thought impossible, including sketches and photographs throughout to aid in discussion, some taken by Heuvelmans himself.

His final chapter is particularly interesting, as it depicts a detailed case study of the perils of zoological closed-mindedness when it comes to advancing our understanding of the natural world. In this chapter, Heuvelmans writes, "While they [skeptical scientists] remain obstinately deaf to rumours about unknown or supposedly fossil animals, these animals die out, some are already extinct, and we have lost the opportunity of studying them except as wretched remains." He references the case of Admiral Étienne de Flacourt who, upon traveling to Madagascar, wrote about and detailed his encounters with certain species of birds in this part of the world. However, his reports were dismissed as nothing more than exaggerated traveler's tales, and it wasn't until centuries later that scientists were able to confirm that his reports were based on flesh-and-blood creatures that were left undiscovered due to blatant dismissal. A cautionary tale, to be sure, but also steeped in references, making it an absolute must-read for anyone interested in cryptozoology and the very long history of scientific pursuit of unknown creatures.

Keel, John A. (1991). *The Mothman prophecies.* New York, NY: Tom Doherty Associates. 300 pages.

This book is yet another that could easily be classified in a number of subtopics in this work. However, as the entire impetus for this book was the investigation of sightings of a large, red-eyed bird tormenting the residents of a small West Virginia town, I have chosen to include it here with inquiries of other strange creatures. The case of the Mothman, perhaps known to some through the 2002 film starring Richard Gere and Laura Dern, originated in November 1966 in the town of Point Pleasant, West Virginia. A group of young couples were driving along a road one night when they spotted a creature they described as having large red eyes and a huge wingspan. The creature actually followed them, keeping pace with their car even as they accelerated to escape the creature. These eyewitnesses were so shaken by their experience that they reported their encounter to local police. Over the next year, residents of this region reported strange sightings of this creature as well as mysterious men and even UFO sightings.

Author John Keel, an investigative reporter, was already very familiar with West Virginian anomalies by the time of the Mothman sightings. He was, in fact, good friends with local Point Pleasant resident Mary Hyre prior to these events, and when he heard what was happening, he traveled to the town to interview eyewitnesses and research the case for himself. The result is this work, originally published in 1975 and which could easily be placed in the "Ufology" section. I place it here simply because many people likely aren't aware of how much overlap this case had with ufology and likely will find it due to their interest in the creature known as Mothman. An indispensable addition to anyone researching UFOs or strange creatures and especially for those who are curious about the ways in which these various phenomena intersect.

Krantz, Grover S. (1992). *Big footprints: A scientific inquiry into the reality of Sasquatch.* Boulder, CO: Johnson Printing. 300 pages.

Grover Krantz was an anthropologist and cryptozoologist who had postings at the University of Minnesota; the University of California, Berkeley; and the University of Utah. He is credited as one of the first academic researchers to tackle expeditions and studies on the specific cryptid known as Bigfoot. In this work, he outlines the evidence that exists to date (or at least in 1992) regarding Bigfoot, or as it is sometimes referred, Sasquatch. In his introduction, Krantz discusses some of the more prevalent criticism for such a creature's existence as well as references the work of many other researchers who have studied this topic.

In chapter 1, he outlines what he defines as the most prominent evidence we have for the existence of Bigfoot: the footprints. Krantz provides scores of photographs along with descriptions about what these footprints tell us about the biological makeup of these creatures, even down to what it reveals about the way they walk, and further expands upon what it reveals about anatomy in chapter 2. He then spends time discussing the nuances of the famed Patterson-Gimlin film and its implications for Bigfoot research before engaging in a discussion about other evidence that has been collected such as hair or skin. After these topics of evidence are laid out, Krantz dives into a discussion on what all of this evidence seems to point to and at this point brings the fossil record into the discussion to illustrate trends in biological evolution. Following this he includes a section on other bipedal creatures found around the world and then transitions into a discussion about the emergence of amateur "Bigfoot hunters" and the implications of their methods and motivations—a worthy entry to this topic and one readers shouldn't miss out on. In a segue from that perspective, though, Krantz also includes a discussion on the implications of this research for academia, especially regarding anthropology, and he discusses both the resistance and the open-mindedness he has encountered. He ends this work with a discussion on the future of this research.

Meldrum, Jeff. (2006). *Sasquatch: Legend meets science.* New York, NY: Tom Doherty Associates. 320 pages.

Dr. Jeff Meldrum is an anthropology professor at Idaho State University who also happens to investigate cryptozoology. In this work, dedicated to his fellow cryptozoological researcher Grover S. Krantz, Dr. Meldrum presents a companion book to the documentary of the same title. The documentary was created after a nature film producer spotted a rather curious seventeen-inch footprint while on location filming trout in Canada. This event sparked what would eventually become a documentary on the Bigfoot phenomenon and, subsequently, this companion monograph.

In this work, Dr. Meldrum not only provides great background on the documentary but also presents a discussion of the evidence for Bigfoot along with notable legends, eyewitness reports, case studies, and more. He even includes an entire chapter on vocalizations of alleged Bigfoot along with some common reasons for Bigfoot misidentifications. Dr. Meldrum's work is essential to anyone researching cryptozoology and especially Bigfoot. In his lab at Idaho State University, for example, Dr. Meldrum has more than three hundred footprint casts of alleged Bigfoot creatures, and his fieldwork takes him across the globe.[4]

Napier, John. (1973). *Bigfoot: The Yeti and Sasquatch in myth and reality.* New York, NY: E. P. Dutton. 240 pages.

At the time of writing this book, author John Napier was working at the University of London as a professor of primate biology. Through a focused discussion on the Yeti and Sasquatch—a discussion that spans from the Himalayas to North America—Napier seeks to disentangle myths from reality. He begins by reminding readers that popular and widespread fascination with tales of the Yeti is only about sixty-five years old. In fact, it was only due to the publication of a legendary photo taken by Eric Shipton during his expeditions in the Himalayas. Cultures of the East undoubtedly knew these tales, but the rest of the world remained mostly unaware until this noted photograph.

In his first chapter, Napier examines Bigfoot's connection to folklore and mythology; he also discusses the scientists and researchers who have investigated these reports and muses on the difference between other monster myths (such as cyclops) and that of strange, bipedal hominids. In chapter 2 he discusses Yeti reports and sightings from the Himalayan region, including many references of reports and fellow investigators. Then in chapter 3, he discusses the North American Bigfoot, a chapter once again full of references for further reading. His next chapter is devoted to the curious case of the Minnesota Iceman, a creature that Napier himself concluded was a cast made of latex—in other words, a potential hoax. This chapter is an interesting and worthy discussion of the intersection of commercialism, fascination, and cryptozoology, and any researcher should be aware of those controversial cases within their chosen field of study. After this discussion, Napier moves on to less controversial topics—such as that of footprints, and animals that cause misidentification, and then provides us with an overview of the fossil record before concluding his work. A comprehensive and scientific inquiry into the Bigfoot phenomena from a noted anthropologist that will enhance anyone's research into this topic.

Sanderson, Ivan. (1961). *Abominable Snowmen: Legend come to life.* Philadelphia, PA: Chilton Company. [no page numbers].

Scottish zoologist Ivan Sanderson is attributed with coining the word "cryptozoology," and any discussion of the topic would be remiss without mentioning his work on the bipedal creatures sighted in Tibet and the Himalayas, which is compiled here in this work. *Abominable Snowmen* is not only an overview of his experiences in the East, but it also provides a historical overview of sightings of these creatures from around the world. This work contains a large number of photographs compiled by Sanderson—many of which include snowy, bipedal footprints as well as alleged skeletal remains and even some animals that have been mistaken for strange bipeds. An updated 2008 edition of this work with an introduction by Loren Coleman is easily found as well.

Sprague, Roderick, & Krantz, Grover S. (Eds.). (1979). *The scientist looks at the Sasquatch II.* Moscow: University Press of Idaho. 195 pages.

This work is a compendium of research articles that were published in the *Northwest Anthropological Research Notes*—articles that were actually triggered by an editorial to that journal that lamented the lack of anthropology-related research into the Sasquatch phenomenon. As a result, this work includes articles that address Sasquatch from a variety of viewpoints. One article, for example, discusses the linguistic variations used to describe these creatures around the world. Yet another article discusses the cultural role that Sasquatch played to North American Indian tribes. Another article investigates the anatomy of anomalous bipedal footprints, while yet another article outlines historical reports of sightings of these creatures. One of the editors is an author whose work is included above, as some readers may note. Even though this work is more than thirty years old, it still provides a wonderful amount of useful and relevant information that readers can build their research upon.

UFOLOGY

Al-Khalili, Jim. (Ed.). (2016). *Aliens: The world's leading scientists on the search for extraterrestrial life.* New York, NY: Picador. 232 pages.

The editor of this work, Dr. Jim Al-Khalili, is a quantum physicist at the University of Surrey in England. In this work, he compiles essays from scientists around the world regarding aspects of life beyond Earth. These scientists come from a wide variety of backgrounds—some are astrophysicists, some work for NASA, and some are even geneticists. The articles in this work discuss the topic of aliens and life beyond our planet from a variety of different angles. For example, author Chris French discusses the psychology of UFO/alien experiences, while contributor Chris McKay discusses just what it takes for a planet to sustain life. Yet another contributor explores the reasons why we may be the only intelligent life form in the galaxy—there is relevance in dissenting perspectives, after all. A compilation of diverse topics from a variety of researchers and scientists, Dr. Al-Khalili's work is a great starting point for anyone interested in diving into some hot topics of UFO and ufology.

Boss, Alan. (2009). *The crowded universe: The race to find life beyond Earth.* New York, NY: Basic Books. 227 pages.

This book, written by author and astrophysicist Alan Boss, isn't necessarily about UFOs, but it does present a discussion about the scientific search for life on other planets—a related concept and one that may be helpful for those interested in learning more about ufology. In this work, Boss puts forward his theory that space exploration missions will soon succeed in finding life on other planets. Organized via a chain of chronological markers of recent space exploration news, Boss also presents a historical overview on space and planetary exploration. This book offers a perspective on recent space advances and also presents various reasons for the likely notion that similar planets to Earth exist in our galaxy.

Bryan, C. D. B. (1995). *Close encounters of the fourth kind: Alien abduction, UFOs, and the conference at M.I.T.* New York, NY: Knopf. 476 pages.

This work is a unique addition to the UFO literature because it centers around an "Abduction Study Conference" held at the Massachusetts Institute of Technology (M.I.T.) that focused specifically on abduction experiences. The conference, organized by M.I.T. physicist David Pritchard and his psychiatrist colleague at Harvard, John Mack, sought to examine the commonalities among abduction experiencers, as well as to simply dig deeper into the experiences of these people. As organizers Pritchard and Mack mused, this topic is important to study because clearly something is happening if millions of people report having endured similar experiences. And while Dave Pritchard at first set out to write a book researching this topic, he decided instead to spearhead a conference of credible and reliable authorities to sift through the nuances of this topic. The conference contained researchers as well as abduction experiencers themselves, sometimes these two categories intermingling. This five-day conference was held in June of 1992 in which author C. D. B. Bryan attended. In this book, he outlines each day of the Abduction Study Conference and provides hundreds of pages of postconference interviews with abduction experiencers.

Devereux, Paul, & Brookesmith, Peter. (1997). *UFOs and ufology: The first 50 years.* London, England: Blandford. 192 pages.

Authors Devereux and Brookesmith present a detailed compendium of the years between 1947 and 1997, which they dub the first fifty years of ufology. As we know, UFO experiences seemed to take off beginning in the 1940s, and in this work, the authors outline the various prominent cases but also discuss the theories and dominant thoughts regarding UFOs and aliens. Furthermore, they discuss how the field of ufology was born. They begin with an overview of ufology as a movement before diving into a discussion of the various experiences with UFOs and alien encounters. They then discuss the rise of UFOs in popular culture before presenting a chapter outlining the research attempts as classifying, organizing, and identifying patterns of UFO experiences. They further discuss ancient encounters with aliens and strange craft while also discussing dominant conspiracy theories surrounding this topic. They conclude with a chapter on abduction experiences. Full of photographs, sketches, newspaper clippings, books, and more, this work offers a wonderful overview of ufology and the UFO experience, making it a solid choice both for anyone new to this topic as well as those already familiar.

Eberhart, George M. (1986). *UFOs and the extraterrestrial contact movement: A bibliography.* 2 vols. Metuchen, NJ: Scarecrow Press. 1,298 pages.

In this two-volume work, author George M. Eberhart presents an exhaustive bibliography of information on UFOs and its related components. You can use this work to track down the sources that Eberhart lists, in other words, making it a bit different than other titles listed here. Not merely a bibliography of select works on the general topic of UFOs and ufology, though, Eberhart's work is minutely detailed. The first volume of this work covers the topic of unidentified flying objects while the second volume discusses the extraterrestrial contact movement. Within his volumes Eberhart does begin with a general set of bibliographic entries but divides them into categories such as "UFO Monographs by Proponents" and "UFO Monographs by Skeptics," which is something you don't see very often. It does, however, add immense research value to the topic of ufology, as it is always beneficial to understand both viewpoints of a particular issue. Furthermore, in this initial section he also includes a section labeled "UFO Material in Non-UFO Books," highlighting the fact that researchers shouldn't only limit themselves to the most obvious works when researching. After presenting an initial bibliography, which on its own is more than a hundred pages, Eberhart presents a bibliography of resources on select "case studies" such as "UFOs on Radar," "Identified Flying Objects and Hoaxes," "Abduction Cases," and more. He further goes on to provide bibliographic entries for topics such as "Historical UFOs," "UFOs and Sociology," and "Foreign Language UFO Monographs." Volume 2, which covers the extraterrestrial contact movement, is perhaps slightly less detailed in organization and length, but no less comprehensive than the first volume and offers information on prominent ufological researchers, popular theories, scientific advancements, and more.

With a foreword written by famed ufologist and scientist J. Allen Hynek, this volume is an absolute must-have on any UFO researcher's list.

Friedman, Stanton T. (2008). *Flying saucers and science: A scientist investigates the mysteries of UFOs; Interstellar travel, crashes, and government cover-ups.* Pompton Plains, NJ: New Page Books. 320 pages.

Any bibliography of ufology would be incomplete without at least one work by Stanton Friedman. Friedman, considered the father of modern ufology, was a nuclear physicist and ufologist and is perhaps most well known for his research into the Roswell incident. In this work, Friedman pulls from forty years of personal research and experience to explain, in friendly terms, the physics and science of space travel. In the foreword to this book, Dr. Bruce Maccabee writes, "This book should help you break through the tradition barrier," and I think this is a perfect description for Friedman's monograph because it challenges readers to reject the standard and traditional understandings that mainstream science presents to us and presents information that challenges those understandings. In this work, he discusses the origins of the UFO phenomenon as well as the physics showing how space travel is possible in its various forms, while also offering a critique of SETI and postulating on the public opinion and cover-ups regarding UFOs. In discussing all of this, Friedman delivers not only a scientific book understandable for the general public but also a challenge to think more critically about the UFO phenomenon.

Stanton Friedman is also the author of an additional work titled *Captured! The Betty and Barney Hill UFO Experience: The True Story of the World's First Documented Alien Abduction* that readers should seek out as well. Detailing the case of the Hills, a couple who experienced an abduction encounter in New Hampshire in 1961, this book investigates their experience and was cowritten with Kathleen Marden, the Hills' niece.

Hynek, J. Allen. (1977). *The Hynek UFO report.* New York, NY: Dell. 304 pages.

In this work, famed ufologist J. Allen Hynek, who was contracted by the government to investigate and debunk UFO cases and sightings, presents here a work discussing Project Blue Book, an air force program that investigated claims of UFO sightings and experiences. Project Blue Book was kept under wraps for many years; even though, as the author tells us, the project was never officially labeled classified, the information was not readily available to the public. Author Hynek was, in fact, a consultant for Project Blue Book from its inception, when it was known as Project Sign. Here he summarizes and compiles the findings from Project Blue Book along with his personal experiences as well, making this work essentially a public report of the entire project. Readers should also seek out Hynek's other works such as *The UFO Experience* and *The Edge of Reality*. A new edition of this work, *The Hynek UFO Report*, was released January 2020.

Hynek, J. Allen. (1972). *The UFO experience: A scientific inquiry*. Chicago, IL: Henry Regnery. 276 pages.

Noted ufologist J. Allen Hynek set out to write this book after his nearly twenty years' worth of experience investigating UFOs at the bequest of the government. He specifically discusses the UFO case report—that is, what a UFO report is, what anomalies are reported, and what commonalities exist among them. In this work, he first provides a discussion of UFOs, citing the contempt that many scholars have for this topic while also highlighting various UFO experiences. He follows this with a more detailed discussion of UFO phenomena and experiences while also outlining his system of "close encounters." He concludes with a discussion of what we've learned from Project Blue Book and the implications for ufological research of the future.

Jacobs, David M. (1992). *Secret life: Firsthand, documented accounts of UFO abductions*. New York, NY: Fireside. 336 pages.

At the time of publication, Dr. David Jacobs was a history professor at Temple University. In this work, he presents a comprehensive report on the abduction experience. In an effort to identify patterns among the many reports of abduction experiences, Dr. Jacobs provides a detailed look at the common traits of abduction encounters through the use of hypnosis. This work identifies three main areas of the abduction experience—the primary, secondary, and ancillary—and discusses the traits of each. He provides transcripts of his interviews with twenty of the sixty people he studied as well as outlines his methods in detail. He begins by introducing the reader to the phenomenon of abduction experiences before diving into the detailed traits and characteristics that he identified in his research. Interested readers may wish to consult Dr. Jacobs's other work, *The UFO Controversy in America*.

Keel, John. (2013). *Operation Trojan Horse: The classic breakthrough study of UFOs*. San Antonio, TX: Anomalist Books. 356 pages.

Author John Keel was a well-known ufologist and journalist who is perhaps most popularly known for his work *The Mothman Prophecies*. In this present work, though, Keel presents four years' worth of intense study and research into UFO phenomena. This work was originally published in 1970 under the title *UFOs: Operation Trojan Horse*, so readers may stumble upon different editions. The edition here from Anomalist Books simply represents the latest printing and edition. In this work he presents interviews with UFO experiencers and consults a huge variety of sources that investigate these phenomena—from primary sources to books to newspapers to journal articles and more. Keel even provides a select bibliography for readers, though he notes that the original bibliography tallied some two thousand books alone. Full of immense detail and a seemingly endless number of items for further reading, Keel's work advances the notion that our understanding of UFOs and ufology will only be advanced once we embrace the idea that a multidisciplinary perspective is necessary for this topic.

O'Connell, Mark. (2017). *The Close Encounters man: How one man made the world believe in UFOs.* New York, NY: HarperCollins. 403 pages.

This work is a biography of J. Allen Hynek, the man hired by the air force to investigate (and debunk) reports of UFO sightings. Hynek, a noted astronomer whose professional employment includes Johns Hopkins University, was at first a staunch skeptic who became, after decades of research and inquiry into ufology, a fervent believer. Author Mark O'Connell tells us specifically that his goal is to provide a "first telling of Hynek's significant accomplishments as an astronomer who pioneered the science of celestial imaging and as a researcher who was on the scene at many of the most amazing UFO encounters in history, and made serious discussions of the UFO phenomenon scientifically—and socially—acceptable." O'Connell succeeds at this goal, presenting here a wonderful biographical account of a man central to our modern understanding of ufology. Full of detail and with an immense number of resources for further reading, this account of Hynek's life is a must-read for anyone interested in ufology.

Pasulka, D. W. (2019). *American cosmic: UFOs, religion, technology.* New York, NY: Oxford University Press. 288 pages.

Author D. W. Pasulka is chair of the philosophy and religion department at the University of North Carolina, Wilmington, where she teaches religious studies. In this present work, she presents six years' worth of ethnographic research in which she interviewed scientists and tech entrepreneurs who believe in extraterrestrial life. In doing so, she highlights that this belief is not just some stereotypical belief relegated to one type of person, but is instead a very nuanced matter that people of all different strata believe in. Bringing in a religious and philosophical view to this issue, she discusses how this belief actually rivals and mimics religious beliefs. In her own words, Pasulka tells us, "This is a book about UFOs and technology, but also about a group of people who believe anomalous technology functions as creative inspiration. I found these people." Offering a unique commentary on the modern reality of belief in UFOs and extraterrestrial life, this work provides a philosophical though wholly readable discussion.

Strieber, Whitley. (1998). *Confirmation: The hard evidence of aliens among us.* New York, NY: St. Martin's Press. 290 pages.

Author Whitley Strieber is perhaps best known for his 1987 memoir *Communion*, outlining his personal encounter two years prior in an abduction experience. In this book, and as part of a response to the critics of *Communion*, he presents here a work that attempts to bridge the scientific divide between evidence and his personal experience. Strieber discusses the ways in which we can potentially understand more about UFO phenomena, such as delving deeper into psychology or atmospheric science, or even through an intense look at propulsion technologies. He brings to light those scientists and leaders who have expressed an open-mindedness about the possibility of life beyond Earth and who discuss just exactly what it will take to find evidence of that. Along the way, Strieber presents current items that serve as potential evidence—including photos and videos of UFO encounters, testimonies from experiencers, and physical objects removed from those who have had abduction experiences. Strieber's case and his writings, though they may be divisive to some, are something every researcher of ufology should at least be familiar with, and they are unique in that they are written from a personal experiencer's point of view—something valuable to this discussion as well.

Vallée, Jacques. (2014). *Passport to Magonia: From folklore to flying saucers.* Brisbane, Australia: Daily Grail. 374 pages.

This work was originally published in 1969. The edition mentioned here is the 2014 edition that contains a new foreword written by the author himself. Jacques Vallée is a Silicon Valley–based investor who holds an astrophysics master's degree and a computer science PhD. He has worked at the Paris Observatory and within the University of Texas Astronomy Department.[5] He is considered to be a seminal scientific figure within ufology. In *Passport to Magonia*, considered now a classic ufological work, he discusses the similarities among worldwide cultures regarding the existence of intelligent creatures and crafts from space. Having worked with J. Allen Hynek, Vallée was motivated to create a database of UFO case studies compiled from the Project Blue Book data as well as his own data generated from Europe. In doing so, he began to notice cross-cultural similarities, and this further motivated him to evaluate the ufology folklore from around the world. Vallée himself calls this work a philosophical treatment of ufology and folklore and the intersection of the two, but that is precisely what makes it valuable reading for anyone interested in ufology. Not only does it highlight how UFOs are intimately woven into folklore, it presents a worldwide narrative of this phenomenon—one that shows, in fact, that UFO legends and encounters didn't originate with the 1940s flap in the United States and are instead phenomena that date much further back than that. Readers would also benefit from Vallée's additional work *Wonders in the Sky* (2010).

REINCARNATION AND NEAR-DEATH EXPERIENCES

Atwater, P. M. H. (2007). *The big book of near-death experiences: The ultimate guide to what happens when we die.* Charlottesville, VA: Hampton Roads. 473 pages.

Author P. M. H. Atwater has nearly forty years' experience in researching near-death experiences. The author of multiple books and articles, she presents a comprehensive overview of the phenomenon in this present work. At the time of publication, Atwater had investigated nearly 3,300 cases of near-death experiences—277 of those being from children. Atwater herself is not merely a researcher of the phenomenon; she has had three NDEs herself, stemming from health complications in 1977. Her first book, in fact, details her own experiences. In this book the goal is to present a comprehensive and detailed picture of NDEs, and Atwater divides this book into five major portions. The first part, labeled "The Experience/The Experiencer," discusses not only the historical underpinnings of NDEs and NDE research but also presents the major types of NDEs and how they are experienced by different groups of people, such as adults and children. Part 2 focuses on the aftereffects of the NDE experience, while part 3 dives into some philosophical questions and "frequently asked question" type of thoughts that many readers likely have regarding NDEs. Part 4 discusses some more aftereffects, but those that are decidedly more paranormal or supernatural in nature. Part 5 covers more NDE research as well as the implications of what this phenomenon tells us about human consciousness. There are also multiple appendixes including a dictionary of commonly used words, a list of websites for further study, and items for further reading, as well as information about the International Association for Near-Death Studies.

Hagan, John C. (Ed.). (2017). *The science of near-death experiences.* Columbia: University of Missouri Press. 208 pages.

Author John C. Hagan is an ophthalmologist and editor of the *Missouri Medicine* journal. In this work, he presents a compilation of chapters each written by a leading scholar on the topic of NDEs. Contributors include Dr. Pim van Lommel, Dr. Dean Radin, Dr. Jeffrey Long, and more. With a foreword by noted researcher Dr. Raymond Moody, this work combines personal experiences alongside scientific discussions behind the phenomenon, the experience of children, what neuroscience tells us about this event, and more. A wonderful overview of the phenomenon written by a handful of the prominent NDE researchers, this work offers a comprehensive introduction to the topic.

Head, Joseph, & Cranston, S. L. (Eds.). (1977). *Reincarnation, the phoenix fire mystery: An East-West dialogue on death and rebirth from the worlds of religion, science, psychology, philosophy, art, and literature, and from great thinkers of the past and present.* New York, NY: Julian Press. 620 pages.

In this work, editors Joseph Head and S. L. Cranston compile essays that discuss the historical and philosophical notions of reincarnation and life after death. These essays span philosophies from around the world and include religious perspectives as well as perspectives of a more scientific nature. For example, part 6 of this work features essays that discuss "New Horizons in Science, Psychology, and Philosophy" and which highlight prominent researchers and philosophers about reincarnation. In terms of the religious perspective, belief systems of many different cultures are presented in this section. The editors even provide a section that outlines the timeline of Western thoughts on death and reincarnation. Offering an immense number of essays in which can be found a treasure trove of further reading, this compilation offers not only scientifically oriented essays but philosophical and religious perspectives as well, making a researcher's understanding of this topic a bit more nuanced.

Kelly, Emily Williams. (Ed.). (2013). *Science, the self, and survival after death: Selected writings of Ian Stevenson.* Lanham, MD: Rowman & Littlefield. 424 pages.

This work presents the research and papers of Dr. Ian Stevenson, a prominent figure in the world of reincarnation, near-death experiences, and consciousness. Dr. Stevenson received his medical degree in Scotland and then went on to work at such institutions as Cornell University, Tulane University, the Louisiana State University School of Medicine, and finally the University of Virginia. It is there that he founded the Department of Parapsychology, now called the Division of Perceptual Studies. In 1960, he wrote an article detailing the medical cases he had come across of children who harbored memories foreign to them—memories from other people. Following this initial inquiry, Dr. Stevenson went on to investigate hundreds of cases of reincarnation from around the world. Not only relegating himself to reincarnation, though, Dr. Stevenson also internationally investigated cases of ghosts, hauntings, psychical events, and more. Because of this, his publication history is immense, as he has published nearly two hundred articles on these topics. In this book, then, editor Emily Williams Kelly presents snippets of Dr. Stevenson's books as well as snippets or entire publications of articles relating to his research. At more than four hundred pages in length, this is an extremely comprehensive introduction to the work of Dr. Stevenson. As such, it also serves as a wonderful bibliographic resource where readers can find additional sources, as the works of Dr. Stevenson alone are too many to list.

van Lommel, Pim. (2010). *Consciousness beyond life: The science of the near-death experience.* New York, NY: HarperCollins. 442 pages.

Author Pim van Lommel is a cardiologist and researcher into the phenomenon of near-death experiences. Since his seminal article on NDEs appeared in the *Lancet* in 2001, he has continued to amass research experience on this phenomenon; in this present work, he outlines his research and theories behind the origin and implications of NDEs. He begins by discussing the profound ways that NDEs change people's lives. Starting with this discussion differs from other works on this topic that tend to introduce this notion later. Following this, he then presents an overview of NDEs, giving common terms and definitions before digging into certain types of NDEs, such as the variations between adult and children experiencers. Prominent research and studies are introduced in the next section before discussing the physiological changes that happen to a person's body during an NDE. After this discussion, van Lommel spends a number of chapters discussing NDEs in relation to consciousness and what it implies about consciousness beyond death. An appendix at the end offers practical guidelines for health care practitioners to help patients deal with the aftereffects of NDEs. Van Lommel's work is a must-read for those interested in the academic pursuit of NDEs.

Long, Jeffrey, & Perry, Paul. (2010). *Evidence of the afterlife: The science of near-death experiences.* New York, NY: HarperCollins. 215 pages.

Author Jeffrey Long is an oncologist and cofounder of the Near-Death Experience Research Foundation (NDERF) along with his wife, Jody. NDERF captures and compiles the experiences of those who have endured an NDE; after years of gathering research through his organization, Dr. Long and his coauthor present here an overview of the research as well as the basic components that make up an NDE. Unlike in other texts on this topic, each major component of an NDE is given its own chapter and investigated in detail. For example, in chapter 3, the authors discuss the factor "lucid death," followed by a chapter discussing the "out of body" experience, followed further by a discussion on "blind sight"—all factors that are common to the NDE. These chapters provide in-depth detail and discussion about the core components of this phenomenon. The authors also provide information that highlights the worldwide pervasiveness of this experience and furthermore discuss the ways in which NDE experiencers are affected in the aftermath of the event.

Moody, Raymond. (2015). *Life after life: The bestselling original investigation that revealed "near-death experiences."* New York, NY: HarperCollins. 211 pages.

This work, a special-anniversary edition of the 1975 original, presents the work of Dr. Raymond Moody. Dr. Moody is a physician credited with coining the phrase "near-death experience." This work presents a study of one hundred near-death experiencers and the common aspects and unique components of their experiences. He begins by outlining what commonly happens to the body physiologically during death and then progresses into a detailed discussion of the major components of the near-death experience, calling this section "The Experience of Dying." Following this is a section labeled "Parallels" in which Dr. Moody introduces similarities of near-death experiences found in different religious texts such as the Bible or the Tibetan Book of the Dead. He even discusses the mystic Emanuel Swedenborg and his discussions of the afterlife. A wonderful section on frequently asked questions follows this before he dives into a handful of chapters offering explanations for the NDE, both from a religious and scientific perspective. Considered a classic within the NDE literature, this title is essential to anyone's bibliography on NDEs.

Morse, Melvin, & Perry, Paul. (1990). *Closer to the light: Learning from children's near-death experiences.* New York, NY: Villard Books. 206 pages.

Authors Morse and Perry bring a notable and respected amount of information with them in this present work. Dr. Morse is a pediatrician who graduated from the George Washington University School of Medicine and has in-depth experience researching NDEs of children; co-author Paul Perry has written works with Dr. Raymond Moody and was also editor of *American Health Magazine.* Dr. Moody, in fact, writes the foreword for this book in which he tells us that Dr. Morse is responsible for discovering that a person has to be very close to death in order to have an NDE, a discovery that helped dispel many critics of the phenomenon who claimed it was nothing more than hallucination or fever. Additionally, Dr. Morse and colleagues claim to have located the area of the brain in which the NDE occurs, which brings a whole host of implications for matters of consciousness and the soul. Drawing on interviews conducted with children who had an NDE, this work offers compelling evidence of the possibility of life after death.

Ring, Kenneth, & Valarino, Evelyn Elsaesser. (2006). *Lessons from the light: What we can learn from the near-death experience.* Needham, MA: Moment Point Press. 368 pages.

Dr. Kenneth Ring is the cofounder of the International Association for Near-Death Studies where he also served as past president. Additionally, he is a psychology professor at the University of Connecticut and is considered by many to be an eminent researcher on near-death experiences. Here, with his coauthor Evelyn Elsaesser Valarino, readers receive a compilation of years of research into NDEs. Dr. Ring tells readers point-blank that he was inspired by the work of Raymond Moody and set out to highlight the very real phenomena of NDEs to the general public and his fellow researchers. In this work, the authors discuss the NDEs of special populations such as blind people and children. They also discuss the seemingly paranormal abilities that many NDErs have after their experience, such as an inexplicable ability to heal certain ailments. The authors discuss new theories and research along with the implications of what NDEs tell us about our world. An appendix of further reading is provided in addition to the references for the book in general.

Tucker, Jim B. (2005). *Life before life: A scientific investigation of children's memories of previous lives.* New York, NY: St. Martin's Press. 256 pages.

In this work, Dr. Jim B. Tucker tells us that at the University of Virginia, there are more than twenty-five hundred case reports from doctors who have investigated children who exhibit memories not seemingly their own. In other words, potential cases of reincarnation or altered consciousness. This work details those cases and presents readers with a wide swath of examples of possible reincarnation from around the world. Dr. Tucker, a psychiatrist who works with children himself, presents a summary of those twenty-five hundred case reports, making this work a wonderful introduction to not only the work of Dr. Ian Stevenson, but the continued work of reincarnation and consciousness.

Weiss, Brian L. (1988). *Many lives, many masters: The true story of a prominent psychiatrist, his young patient, and the past-life therapy that changed both their lives.* New York, NY: Fireside. 219 pages.

Author Brian L. Weiss is a graduate of Yale Medical School and current chairman emeritus of psychiatry at Mount Sinai Medical Center. A prominent psychotherapist who was well into his professional career when he met a remarkable patient in 1980, Dr. Weiss outlines how his entire outlook was shifted when he began using hypnosis as a treatment method. His patient began recalling past-life memories and personally significant details relating to Dr. Weiss that could not be ignored. This story is the tale of that experience and how it forever transformed a doctor once skeptical that such a thing could ever occur. Considered a classic of reincarnation literature, this readable and provocative work provides a compelling case study.

ASTROLOGY, DIVINATION, AND MYSTICISM

Cooper, David A. (1997). *God is a verb: Kabbalah and the practice of mystical Judaism.* New York, NY: Riverhead Books. 333 pages.

Rabbi David A. Cooper has studied Jewish mysticism for years and is also the author of a handful of other works. In this work, he presents an overview of the mystical Jewish tradition of kabbalah, which was, prior to the mid- to late 1900s, not widely discussed in Jewish intellectual circles. Rabbi Cooper tells us that these teachings were kept mostly inaccessible—so much so that when he began discussing this topic openly, he was met with resistance. In his own words, Rabbi Cooper reminds people that "Jewish mysticism is a profoundly sensual, nature-connected spiritual practice that openly discusses angels and demons, souls' journeys after death, reincarnation, resurrection, and the goal of achieving messianic consciousness." The purpose then, of this book, is to highlight the history of Western mysticism in such a way that a person of any faith system will be able to easily follow along. He begins with an introduction where he lays out some definitions of terms associated with both Judaism and Western mysticism before diving into a historical overview of mysticism. Following this, he presents a section on the mysticism of today. Part 3 discusses the paths, or specific philosophies, found with kabbalah while part 4 discusses kabbalah's views on the afterlife.

Curry, Patrick. (Ed.). (2010). *Divination: Perspectives for a new millennium.* Surrey, England: Ashgate. 289 pages.

In this work, editor Patrick Curry compiles essays presented at a 2007 conference on divination at the University of Kent. The topics discussed represent the span of human culture and history, with discussions ranging from ancient Greece to the modern world. Essays include discussions of dream oracles, shamanism in both Central Asia and Northern Europe, astrology, hermeticism, and more. The authors of the essays not only outline certain divinatory practices, but also represent a fusion of different disciplines. In addition, the authors come from different academic and philosophical backgrounds; as a result, their work represents a different academic lens through which to interpret divination practices, making for a richer and more critical discussion of how divination affects societies, cultures, and individuals. This work is a useful starting point for anyone interested in divination practices from around the world.

Dean, Liz. (2018). *The ultimate guide to divination: The beginner's guide to using cards, crystals, runes, palmistry, and more for insight and predicting the future.* Beverly, MA: Fair Winds Press. 224 pages.

Author Liz Dean is a practicing tarot diviner in London. In this work, she presents a beginner-friendly overview of some of the most common types of modern divination practices. She begins with an introduction that discusses the basics of divination practices. She then moves on to a discussion of the oracles used in the ancient world, outlining their methods and tools. Following this, she discusses divination practices with tea, coffee, and salt. Chapter 4 outlines the practice of palmistry while chapter 5 presents an overview of tarot and its use in fortune-telling. Chapter 6 is all about numerology while the final chapter discusses the act of scrying with crystals, water, and mirrors. Full of pictures and wonderfully arranged, this work offers a solid introduction to divination practices, both historical and modern.

Decker, Ronald, & Dummett, Michael. (2002). *A history of the occult tarot: 1870–1970.* London, England: Gerald Duckworth. 320 pages.

Authors Decker and Dummett present a historical overview of the tarot. They trace its path around the globe, from its beginnings in northern Italy in the early 1500s, to the modern ways we still engage with this divination practice. They explore the different iterations the tarot has taken, such as how its modern usage differs from the original formation. They include a discussion of the role of hermeticism and the Golden Dawn, as well as the popularization by Arthur Waite and the Rider-Waite tarot deck. They discuss its appearance in countries around the world as well as the different ways in which it is used and consulted for divination purposes. Offering an overview of the tarot, this work is beneficial for anyone wishing to learn more about this specific practice.

Dudley, Underwood. (1997). *Numerology; or, What Pythagoras wrought.* Washington, DC: MAA Service Center. 316 pages.

In this book, author and mathematician Underwood Dudley tells us that the history of numerology can be traced directly back to Pythagoras, who introduced the concept of number mysticism, or, the belief that numbers indicate messages about events in the world around us. He begins his discussion with Pythagoras and the birth of this theory, as well as the general way in which the Greeks philosophized about numbers. He further includes a chapter on gematria, or the practice of turning letters into numbers. He then goes on to discuss popular and infamous numbers, and their backgrounds, such as the numbers 666, 7, and 13. Even though Dudley is critical and dubious of any real impact that numerology has in terms of delivering messages about events, he nonetheless acknowledges that this belief is fascinating and worth investigating for knowledge's sake. There are several criticisms woven throughout this work, but it succeeds in offering a comprehensive history of our fascination with numbers and the ways that numbers are used as a divinatory tool.

Peek, Philip M. (Ed.). (1991). *African divination systems*. Bloomington: Indiana University Press. 230 pages.

This edited work is a compilation of essays that discuss the divinatory practices of cultures throughout Africa. Offering a unique insight into the ways in which divination practices play out beyond the United States and the United Kingdom, this work presents an overview of how divination is often very central to a culture's identity. Part 1 of this work discusses the ways in which people become diviners in the Zulu culture. Part 2 offers a discussion of how divination plays a key role in the decision-making process of communities, and part 3 discusses how divination in Africa is often a central component of maintaining cultural identity and order. Part 4 discusses how divinatory messages are construed and interpreted. This work is relevant for any researcher wishing to obtain an international and ethnographic understanding of the role of divination.

Robbins, F. E. (Ed.). (1940). *Ptolemy: Tetrabiblos.* Cambridge, MA: Harvard University Press. 467 pages.

This text, consisting of four books, is considered the foremost ancient authority on astrology and served as the dominant idea of the heavens until later scientists such as Galileo entered the scene. It offers a firsthand look into the ancient thought of the sun, moon, and the planets and the influence they exert in everyday lives. Each book goes into great detail concerning various aspects of the planets such as implications for travel and for relationships, as well as using it for divination.

Smith, Richard Furnald. (1975). *Prelude and science: An exploration of magic and divination.* New York, NY: Charles Scribner's Sons. 129 pages.

In the preface to this work, author Richard Furnald Smith tells us, "Magic and divination certainly flourished before science, but they are still with us. They have refused to be swept away by modern science in all its majesty. So if they constitute a prelude, it is a Wagnerian one, introducing themes that recur and evolve throughout the scientific opera that has followed." In this work, then, Smith discusses ancient magical practices such as tarot, astrology, and oracles. These discussions are all framed within their contribution to our modern scientific understandings of the world around us and how, perhaps, they should not be viewed as something less than scientific inquiries but merely as a prelude to better understanding our world.

Snodgrass, Mary Ellen. (1997). *Signs of the zodiac: A reference guide to historical, mythological, and cultural associations.* Westport, CT: Greenwood Press. 243 pages.

Noted scholar and author Mary Ellen Snodgrass presents a historical overview of astrology and dissects the astrological beliefs of cultures around the world from antiquity. Snodgrass points out in her preface that this work is designed to provide readers with a broad understanding not only of each zodiac sign and its inherent symbolism but also to provide readers with an understanding of how astrological beliefs play out in different cultures. Her research includes astrological beliefs from antiquity through to modern times. In her first chapter, she provides a broad overview and definition of "zodiac," breaking down the characteristics not only of each planet but each zodiac sign. She briefly describes how horoscopes are cast and concludes by mentioning the influence of astrological "houses."

The next chapter in this work focuses on the historical foundations of astrology and goes into great detail beginning with ancient civilizations. It is here that Snodgrass tells us the first recorded evidence of "symbolic analysis of stars dates to 2750 B.C." She goes on to discuss the ties of astrology to religious figures as well as the differences in astrological theories among cultures, such as the Mayan, Chinese, Egyptian, and Hebrew philosophies and structures. Snodgrass additionally examines the specific ways cultures used the zodiac both personally and politically as well as how the zodiac features into society in other ways, from architecture to film and even psychology.

The remaining chapters dive into a detailed analysis of each zodiac sign before presenting further information in appendixes such as a chronology of the ways people have studied the zodiac, the planetary counterparts to zodiac signs, and astronomical characteristics of stars and constellations. This is a good resource for readers wishing to gain a deeper historical understanding of astrology's influence.

Trobridge, George. (1945). *Swedenborg: Life and teaching* (4th ed.). London, England: Swedenborg Society. 343 pages.

This work, a fourth edition of an original biography published in 1907, presents a thorough portrait of the life of Emanuel Swedenborg, a Swiss mystic and scientist born in 1688. Among his many scientific pursuits and achievements was a fascination with life after death; he even claimed to be able to converse with spirits, angels, and possess the ability to see "into the other world." Many may simply relegate Swedenborg to the realm of theologians and perhaps outside the scope of this work, but his fascination with and experiences of the afterlife make him an undoubtably worthy entry here. This work contains an overwhelming amount of detailed biographical information, such as quotes from a four-year-old Swedenborg concerning his fascination with spiritual thought. This work presents a unique, historical overview of a significant figure in early mystical thought.

OCCULT AND MAGICAL PRACTICES

Agrippa, Heinrich Cornelius. (2009). *Three books of occult philosophy.* Donald Tyson (Ed.). Woodbury, MN: Llewellyn. 1,024 pages.

The *Three Books of Occult Philosophy* are a trio of works written by Heinrich Cornelius Agrippa in 1531 and which serve as the backbone for modern occultist philosophy. Agrippa, who studied the occult as well as theology, lays out over the course of three books a history of pagan and Neoplatonic magic that he synthesized from countless readings of the occult philosophers who came before him. This work is full of symbols, diagrams, sigils, rituals, and more; in the introduction, editor Donald Tyson calls it a "magical encyclopedia of the Renaissance." This translated edition by Tyson contains a section on Agrippa's life, notes about the text and its history, and a biography of key figures mentioned throughout the text. There are a total of eight appendixes that discuss geomancy, magic squares, kabbalah, and more. Readers interested in the occult or magic must not overlook Agrippa's contribution.

Atwood, M. A. (1850). *A suggestive inquiry into hermetic mystery.* Glastonbury, England: Lost Library. 597 pages.

Author Mary Anne Atwood and her father, Thomas South, were avid readers of and philosophers about the hermetic tradition—which is a philosophical and esoteric system based upon the mythology of Hermes Trismegistus. After many years of reading and researching this tradition, the father-daughter duo set out to publish their own essays and prose about the subject. After time composing their works, sending them to the printing press, and beginning delivery to libraries and stores, Thomas South had a seemingly intense change of heart due to the nature of the work (perhaps fueled by his intensely religious beliefs or a fear of what his writing may imply), and gathered the copies that had not yet been delivered to their locations and burned them on his front lawn. His contribution to the literature perished that day, but copies of Mary's book were still found out in the world. Though scarce, the edition survived, and readers can still locate it today.

In this work, Mary provides a historical overview of the hermetic tradition, which she sometimes refers to as alchemy. The first portion of her work spells out the prominent writers of this movement as well as lays out the mythology of Hermes Trismegistus. The second portion discusses specific theories of hermeticism in more detail, while the third portion outlines the methodologies of hermeticism as well as traits that are often beneficial to have in order to conduct certain practices. The fourth portion explores hermetic practice and ritual in detail. A primary source and a unique entry on this topic, this resource will prove relevant to readers' studies of hermeticism.

Aveni, Anthony. (2002). *Behind the crystal ball: Magic, science, and the occult from antiquity through the New Age.* Boulder: University Press of Colorado. 361 pages.

In this work, author Anthony Aveni outlines a history of occult practices. More specifically and in the author's own words, "There was a time when science and the occult happily coexisted under the same roof, one scarcely discernible from the other in method and practice. How they parted company and why one was relegated to the darker side of history while the other came to bask in the limelight of mainstream belief is our subject matter." Aveni begins with a discussion of magic from antiquity, such as the practices found in Egypt and Mesopotamia. Following this, he discusses the trajectory of magical practices from the Dark Ages through the Enlightenment. After this discussion, he introduces readers to the practices of the 1800s and occultism and spiritualism. The last two parts are a discussion of modern magical practices and beliefs. This work is full of magical beliefs and practices from around the world; anyone who is interested in a general (yet very detailed) history of magical practices since antiquity will find it helpful.

Carr-Gomm, Philip, & Heygate, Richard. (2012). *The book of English magic.* New York, NY: Overlook Press. 562 pages.

Authors Philip Carr-Gomm and Richard Heygate present here a comprehensive discussion of the magical history of England. They discuss the different eras of magic while outlining key figures along the way. Chapter 1 discusses the ancient roots of English magic, while chapter 2 outlines the magical history of the Druids. Chapter 3 discusses the role of sorcerers, which provides a perfect segue for chapter 4, which discusses Merlin and the wizardry literature attributed in his name, such as Geoffrey of Monmouth's work *The Prophecies of Merlin*. Chapter 5 introduces a discussion of witches and warlocks, and chapter 6 introduces readers to the world of alchemy. Chapter 7 gives readers an overview of English astrology; cunning folk and fairy lore are discussed in chapter 8. Chapter 9 brings with it Freemasonry and numerology, and the remaining three chapters discuss additional magical practices including the resurgence of magical practice in the twenty-first century. Anyone interested in learning about the magical history of England will want to be sure to consult this work.

Carroll, Peter J. (1992). *Liber Kaos.* York Beach, ME: Samuel Weiser. 218 pages.

Author Peter Carroll is an occultist who offers here a discussion of chaos magic theory. This work is also a very technical book on the workings of chaos magic in general. In the first portion of this book, Carroll reviews various theories of chaos magic, such as nods to quantum physics and the theory of relativity. In the second portion, he details specific practices and rituals of chaos magic, including a discussion of the eight paths of magic popular in this practice. Carroll is recognized as a leading figure on chaos theory; any researcher wishing to know more about this practice will wish to seek out his work.

Conway, David. (2016). *Magic: An occult primer.* Newport, RI: Witches Almanac. 374 pages.

The title of this work offers a perfect illustration of how the topics of "magic" and the "occult" are intimately linked. This work is divided into two major sections: a discussion about magical theory followed by a discussion of magical practice. Originally published in 1972, this work begins with an introduction to the current edition that reminds us the premise of magic is much different than what we may have perceived via media and television. The magic that this book discusses is the magic of the unconscious mind, which also taps into the connection between the universe and humankind. What author David Conway does in this work, though, is connect magic theory and practice to modern scientific thought and theory whenever he can, offering a way to lodge the importance and relevance of magic to anyone, especially the skeptic who so often dismisses these conversations from the start.

The first portion of this work discusses magical theory and is broken into five chapters that discuss magic and its relation to natural law, a history of magical theory, and the importance of training and ritual. The second portion of this book dives into the specifics of occult ritual and practice, discussing how to prepare for your rituals and the objects used, as well as some prominent rituals and the role of talismans and charms; it also touches upon astral projection and prophecy. Appendixes include information on magical "recipes," a list of prominent occultists, and an overview of magical alphabets.

Cunningham, Scott. (2017). *Earth, air, fire & water: More techniques of natural magic.* Woodbury, MN: Llewellyn. 220 pages.

Scott Cunningham was a renowned magical practitioner who had more than twenty years' experience and had written more than fifty books by the time of his death. This work, originally written in 1991, is a companion to his earlier title *Earth Power* (1983) and presents a discussion of magical folk practices. He begins by discussing the basics of magical practice, such as the tools and basic techniques used. He follows this with a discussion of magic associated with the elements—that is, earth, air, fire, and water. In this chapter, he offers simple rituals associated with each element. Following this is a chapter on natural magical practices, such as those using stones, candles, mirrors, or other such objects. The final chapter reviews some guidelines for how to craft your own rituals and create your own sense of magical practice. He includes an appendix of magical symbols.

Davies, Owen. (2003). *Cunning-folk: Popular magic in English history.* London, England: Hambledon and London. 246 pages.

Author and researcher Owen Davies teaches at the University of Hertfordshire, where his research focus is that of contemporary English magic. In this book he discusses those people known as cunning folk, or folk magicians of the United Kingdom. Upon discovering a general lack of information and study regarding this population of magic practitioners, Davies set out to fill the gap. He provides a comprehensive case study of the cunning folk, including how English society viewed and responded to them throughout the years. He discusses the demographics of cunning folk and outlines some of their traditional practices and reasons why people would seek their services. After this discussion, he concludes with a chapter on the present-day cunning folk of the United Kingdom. Those interested in folk magic of the United Kingdom must ensure that Owen Davies's work is on their to-read lists.

Davies, Owen. (1999). *Witchcraft, magic, and culture: 1736–1951.* Manchester, England: Manchester University Press. 337 pages.

Author Owen Davies is a researcher and writer of several additional works on the topic of magic and the paranormal. Referenced frequently in chapter 10 of this book, "The UK's Intimate History with the Paranormal," Davies's work here focuses on the role and reality of witchcraft and magic in both England and Wales in the aftermath of the witch trials craze. He begins this work with a glossary of additional resources for the reader. The first portion of this book discusses the attitudes and popular beliefs concerning both witchcraft and magic, tackling this topic from all angles including legal, psychological, and religious. The second portion of this work examines the particulars of witchcraft and justice, where he discusses the decline of witch persecution and the rise of witch mobbing. In the third section, we see magic alongside both witchcraft and popular literature. The following section is a discussion of the folk practices and archetypes of the witch, while the last chapter offers a discussion of occult practitioners such as astrologers, fortune-tellers, and cunning folk. This work is a great addition for anyone wishing to learn more about this often overlooked era of English magic and witchcraft.

Godwin, John. (1972). *Occult America.* Garden City, NY: Doubleday. 314 pages.

In this book, author John Godwin presents an inner look at the workings of the occult movements and personalities in the United States. In Godwin's own words, "The one thing I was looking for—a dispassionate inquiry into the motivations and workings of America's occultism—seemed not to exist at all. If I wanted one I would have to write it myself." This work presents a comprehensive discussion of the ways in which people interact with various occult phenomena. He discusses topics such as astrology, divination, telepathy, and UFOs, all while tracing the history of spiritualism and occultism throughout the United States. A cultural exposé of how occult topics played out in American life, this book offers a wonderful sociological representation of various paranormal phenomena. Godwin uses the term "occult" not necessarily to indicate ritualistic magic, but instead to signify any one of various activities. This work will help researchers who are interested in learning more about the intersection of popular culture and the paranormal.

Hine, Phil. (1995). *Condensed chaos: An introduction to chaos magic.* Tempe, AZ: Original Falcon Press. 192 pages.

Phil Hine is a magic practitioner who not only leads workshops on magic practices but has also written a number of books and articles on this topic. In *Condensed Chaos*, Hine offers an overview and practical guidance of chaos magic, a movement that he tells us sprung up in 1970s England and which offers a contemporary set of magical practices. He begins with a discussion of the core components of chaos magic as well as an outline of its basic tenets. He also offers a detailed discussion of chaos magic practices and how to engage with this practice. Readers interested in modern magical practices or who wish to learn more about the specifics of chaos magic will find Hine's work to be a good introduction.

Luck, Georg. (2006). *Arcana mundi: Magic and the occult in the Greek and Roman Worlds; A collection of ancient texts* (2nd ed.). Baltimore, MD: Johns Hopkins University Press. 544 pages.

In this work, author Georg Luck discusses the role of magic in the Greek and Roman worlds. Organized via a discussion of magic, miracles, demonology, divination, astrology, and alchemy, Luck discusses the ways in which these topics were explored and practiced in Greek and Roman culture. He explores the thoughts and attitudes of magical practices, especially any tensions existing in the legal or religious spheres, while also discussing key figures and practices. For researchers who wish to understand more about the magic of antiquity.

Owen, Alex. (2004). *The place of enchantment: British occultism and the culture of the modern.* Chicago, IL: University of Chicago Press. 355 pages.

Author Alex Owen focuses on the role of occultism in the United Kingdom prior to World War I. She discusses the curious reality of how occultism became firmly entrenched within the highest intellectual circles. She posits that amid changing social realities, occultism offered a kind of escape from the realities of a changing world, which explains the embrace of these philosophies with certain prominent social groups. Combining occultism with a sociological inquiry, this work offers a unique perspective on the topic of the occult in the UK.

Regardie, Israel. (2018). *The Golden Dawn: The original account of the teaching, rites, and ceremonies of the Hermetic Order* (7th ed.). Rev. and corrected by John Michael Greer. Woodbury, MN: Llewellyn. 918 pages.

When it comes to a discussion of the occult, no overview would be complete without mentioning hermeticism and the rituals associated with the Hermetic Order, also referred to as the Hermetic Order of the Golden Dawn, a secret society in the late 1800s and early 1900s that tasked itself with the intense study of occult phenomena and paranormal events, through which developed a new mystical belief system. This work, compiled by occultist Israel Regardie (a seminal figure in occultism who worked to make magical practices known and available to all), explores the Golden Dawn's ritual practices. Divided into nine "books," it is an exhaustive compendium of mystical, ritual, and ceremonial magic. Book 1 offers "lectures and instructional papers" and lays out the different stages of initiation into the Golden Dawn—think of this as the skills and knowledge needed in order to "level up." Books 2 and 3 discuss the rituals of the outer and inner orders, respectively. Book 4 is titled "Primary Techniques of Magical Practice," and goes into great detail about specific rituals and the items used in them, along with the associated symbolism and meaning. Book 5 discusses more teachings of the "inner order," while book 6 is dedicated to ceremonial magic. Book 7 discusses clairvoyance and the use of talismans and sigils in occult ritual. Book 8 is all about divination and divinatory practices, while the final book, book 9, discusses magic done while invoking spirits or angels. At nearly one thousand pages, this work on ritual practice naturally includes a multitude of figures and diagrams and is an intense focus on occultism. This work is essential for any researcher interested in occult ritual and practice.

Ryan, W. F. (1999). *The bathhouse at midnight: Magic in Russia.* University Park: Pennsylvania State University Press. 504 pages.

At the time of this book, author W. F. Ryan was the chief librarian at the Warburg Institute at the University of London as well as author of several additional works on the topic of Russian magic. In *The Bathhouse at Midnight*, Ryan gives an exhaustive treatment to the topic of magic throughout Russia's history. He begins with an outline of the history of magical practice in Russia, in which he tells us that the majority of Russian magic has its roots in Byzantine, Western Europe, and Jewish influence. He follows this with a discussion of popular magic, such as protection spells, magical places, and the belief in evil spirits. Following this is a discussion of witches and wizards, and then a chapter on divinatory practices. Subsequent chapters cover such topics as alchemy, dream divination, spell work, numerology, astrology, geomancy, and more. At just over five hundred pages, this work offers a comprehensive look at the history and influence of Russian magic and is especially useful for anyone interested in comparative magical practices or who wishes to understand magic on an international scale.

Shumaker, Wayne. (1972). *The occult sciences in the Renaissance: A study in intellectual patterns.* Berkeley: University of California Press. 284 pages.

Author Wayne Shumaker makes it very clear to readers in his preface that he is not a believer in any of the phenomena that he discusses in this book. This might seem to be a curious thing, since he's taken the pains to write an entire book on the subject, but he tells us he became intrigued when he kept encountering occult literature in the historical record of his own research interests. Having encountered it so often, he decided to research more about that topic. The result is a sometimes critical but historical and factual overview of many occult topics including astrology, witchcraft, alchemy, and hermeticism. And to be fair, it is a good tactic to seek out literature that presents criticism of your chosen research topic in order to obtain a holistic understanding of all sides of an issue.

Just because Shumaker is a die-hard skeptic doesn't mean that this book doesn't contain relevant information. Quite opposite, in fact; Shumaker presents historical overviews and even includes a "pro" and "con" section in the portion about astrology. The many topics presented in this work are set against the backdrop of the Renaissance and offer readers an in-depth and critical exploration of the ways in which occult topics influenced the philosophy and life in that era.

St. Clair, David. (1976). *Pagans, priests, and prophets: A personal investigation into the living traditions of occult Mexico.* Englewood Cliffs, NJ: Prentice-Hall. 218 pages.

Author David St. Clair, a researcher of the mystical and metaphysical, presents here a study of the occult practices in Mexico. This work discusses ancient mystical beliefs and practices held by such cultures as the Aztec while also highlighting the modern practices still found in Mexico today. Told through a wholly readable narrative, St. Clair includes discussions of witchcraft, divination, herbalism, and shamans as found through Mexican culture and history. Offering a specific look on how mystical beliefs and practices influence Mexican culture, this work is relevant for anyone interested in the occult and mystical traditions of Mexico or for anyone interested in obtaining an international perspective on this topic.

Waite, Arthur Edward. (2011). *The book of ceremonial magic: Including the rites and mysteries of goetic theurgy, sorcery, and infernal necromancy.* Eastford, CT: Martino Fine Books. 374 pages.

This work by Arthur Edward Waite was originally published in 1898 as a limited publication and was more widely produced just a few short years later in the early 1900s. Waite was a mystic and avid researcher of occult practices and philosophy. He is part of the duo who created perhaps the most well-known tarot deck, the Rider-Waite tarot. In this book, Waite outlines the history, literature, and practices of ceremonial magic. A detailed overview of the background, prominent texts, and detailed rituals of magical practices, this work of Waite is not to be missed.

Yates, Frances A. (1979). *The occult philosophy in the Elizabethan age.* London, England: Routledge & Kegan Paul. 217 pages.

In this work author Frances A. Yates discusses the "occult philosophy" of the Elizabethan era. Yates points out that the occult philosophy of the time was really a mixture of hermeticism and the Jewish mystical system kabbalah and that most historical treatments of this topic (at least up till 1979) tended to only focus on the aspects of hermeticism. Yates begins her discussion with a section on the occult during the Renaissance and Reformation, including case studies of Pico della Mirandola, Johannes Reuchlin, and Henry Cornelius Agrippa, prominent figures in the history of occult philosophy and, in Agrippa's case, of ritualistic magic. Yates follows this section with a discussion of the occult during the Elizabethan age in which she introduces Christian cabala and even Shakespeare's contribution to the occult philosophy of the times. Included in both of these sections are chapters about the reactions, both positive and negative, to certain philosophies and practices. The last section discusses Rosicrucianism and Puritanism, and how they were ideologies influenced by the occult philosophies of years prior. Researchers looking for a deep historical overview on the origins of occult philosophies will benefit from this work.

GENERAL PARANORMAL AND PARANORMAL PHILOSOPHY

Aizpúrua, Jon. (2013). *Fundamentals of spiritism: The soul, the afterlife, psychic abilities, mediumship, and reincarnation and how these influence our lives*. Jon Aizpúrua: CreateSpace. 330 pages.

This work is an English translation of the original Spanish work by author Jon Aizpúrua in 2000. The author, a psychology professor who has worked in clinical psychiatry and also as an economist, presents here a comprehensive work discussing a multitude of paranormal topics and how they relate to the philosophy of spiritism. Spiritism, broadly popular in Latin American countries, is simply a belief that our world is populated by both the physical and the spiritual—in other words, spirits are all around us. Born out of the scientific endeavors of French researchers in the 1800s to better understand the nature of spirits and the paranormal, spiritism nonetheless promotes knowledge gained through experimentation, study, and research. After outlining the basic tenets of spiritism as well as the historical foundations of this philosophy, Aizpúrua takes a deep dive into a number of paranormal topics such as mediumship, reincarnation, and parapsychological phenomena. In each of these sections, he offers a brief historical overview before presenting prominent examples or cases as well as notable researchers. It is important to understand the ways in which the paranormal is interpreted and studied internationally, and those interested in such a perspective may especially enjoy Aizpúrua's work.

Braden, Gregg. (2007). *The Divine Matrix: Bridging time, space, miracles, and belief.* Carlsbad, CA: Hay House. 224 pages.

Author and researcher Gregg Braden presents a work that pulls from the theories and principles of quantum theory to discuss how supernatural our world really is. Through the concept of the Divine Matrix, which Braden tells us is a "field of energy that connects all of creation," he goes into the ways that harnessing this knowledge can be beneficial. He discusses the science, theories, and researchers behind the Divine Matrix and also explores the link between imagination and reality. Naturally, this raises conversations on the role of consciousness with manifestation, all of which is discussed in this work. Offering a unique analysis that connects quantum physics with consciousness, Braden's work is a valuable entry to the general paranormal.

Carlton, Eric. (2000). *The paranormal: Research and the quest for meaning.* Aldershot, England: Ashgate. 194 pages.

At the time of this work, author Eric Carlton worked within the sociology department at the University of Durham. The author of several additional books, Carlton provides in this work a timeline of paranormal thought before diving into essays that discuss the roles the paranormal plays culturally and personally. Carlton begins with a review of paranormal research through the ages before analyzing the paranormal through specific lenses. Each chapter tackles the paranormal, in a critical way, by focusing on various meanings the paranormal may play and/or via certain explanations people have ascribed to the paranormal—religion, mass hysteria, a hope for life beyond death, and of course, the genuine scientific pursuit. At the end of each of these chapters, Carlton provides a section marked "Excursus," which is a case study exemplifying and further elucidating the points in the chapter. Carlton's work offers insight into the criticisms of the paranormal while also highlighting the scientific pursuits of those who accept the paranormal as a genuine phenomenon to learn from and provides insight into the many ways the paranormal plays a role in our society.

Combs, Alan, & Holland, Mark. (1990). *Synchronicity: Science, myth and the trickster.* New York, NY: Paragon House. 176 pages.

Famed psychiatrist Carl Jung coined the term "synchronicity" to describe those seemingly random coincidences that occur in life. After experiencing and hearing about these random encounters, he began to think that perhaps there was more to this phenomenon than random happenstance and enlisted the help of his contemporary, Wolfgang Pauli, a quantum physicist. Working together to develop a working scientific hypothesis on synchronicity, authors Alan Combs and Mark Holland present the work of Jung and Pauli in this work. Discussing both the science behind and the mythology of synchronicity, they begin by tracing how synchronistic events have been viewed throughout the course of human history—a discussion that naturally involves the role of religion, myth, and science. Following this introduction, they explore synchronicity through the lens of science, discussing the historical timeline of study into synchronicity as well as the work of Wolfgang Pauli and the connection of synchronicity with quantum physics. They then discuss psychology and its relation to synchronicity, discussing the role of archetypes here as well, before moving into a more detailed discussion of Carl

Jung and his work with synchronicity. Appendixes included discuss omens, divination practices, and the statistical probability of synchronistic events.

Eberhart, George M. (1980). *A geo-bibliography of anomalies.* Westport, CT: Greenwood Press. 1,114 pages.

At the time of this work, author George M. Eberhart was the reader services librarian at the Kansas Law Library. In other words, he knows how to locate information, and in this work he presents a veritable tome of resources on various anomalous phenomena such as UFOs, ghosts, extrasensory perception, divination, and more. In his own words, this work is "a comprehensive list of mysterious events, discoveries, people, and places in North America" and contains "over 22,100 separate events . . . grouped under 10,500 geographic place-names." He provides a list of the journals he used to gather these events and even offers an outline of the anomalies to provide a brief definition to the reader, followed by a glossary for further assistance. Following this, the rest of the book is a geographical listing of anomalous events. He arranges this work by regions such as "Pacific," "Southwest," and "Great Plains," breaking down the categories into specific states and further breaking events down by city. Each listing contains a word or phrase that indicates the basic type of anomalous event followed by the date and the source of information. The result is an immense and indispensable bibliography of anomalous events from the United States and northern Canada.

Fort, Charles, & Knight, Damon. (1974). *The complete books of Charles Fort.* New York, NY: Dover. 1,152 pages.

This book is a compilation of works of Charles Fort that includes *The Book of the Damned, New Lands, Lo!,* and *Wild Talents.* Charles Fort was an American researcher and writer who compiled reports of strange phenomena and who pushed back against the scientific mainstream in terms of what it means for something to be acceptable science. These works discuss a range of paranormal phenomena that Fort discovered in newspapers, in archives, and through his interviews with people. While many of the phenomena in this book relate to UFO and UFO-related events, Fort also muses on scientific understanding and advancement of paranormal research. A seminal figure in the popularization of paranormal phenomena and a researcher whose impact still echoes through science fiction today, Charles Fort's works are good additions to a paranormal researcher's toolkit.

Hanegraaff, Wouter J. (2012). *Esotericism and the academy: Rejected knowledge in Western culture.* Cambridge, England: Cambridge University Press. 468 pages.

Author Wouter J. Hanegraaff teaches at the University of Amsterdam where he conducts courses in the history of hermetic philosophy. In this book, he addresses how academia (that which he calls the academy) has a long history of overlooking the intellectual contributions and history of traditions that are referred to simply as "Other." Beginning in the Renaissance and moving his way forward, he discusses the ways in which academics have handled that which is considered occult, esoteric, or even magical. Using a multitude of primary sources throughout, this work not only presents a historical overview of academic reaction to occult philosophies but also lays out a discussion that is still needed today. He makes very clear that this work isn't a historical treatment of the topic of esotericism itself but rather is a historical inquiry of how that very topic has been treated by the academy since the Renaissance.

In the first portion of this book, Hanegraaff discusses the discoveries of the wisdom of past cultures and the natural effect it had on challenging dominant worldviews. The next section is spent exclusively discussing paganism and how it was misinterpreted or represented via the academy before he moves on to a similar discussion involving the occult. After that, he reviews modern academic treatments of these topics, with discussions of Mesmer and Jung, for example. At nearly five hundred pages, this work is full of detailed references to scholars, topics, and resources on any number of paranormal entreaties. Moreover, it is a comprehensive treatment of the tension that has always existed between these topics and academia, making it both a unique and indispensable resource.

Hansen, George P. (2001). *The trickster and the paranormal.* George P. Hansen: Xlibris. 564 pages.

Using the archetype of the trickster, author George P. Hansen presents a work that discusses many aspects of the paranormal and the paranormal's inherent characteristic of being connected with change, disruption, chaos, and dissent. He explores the many ways in which paranormal inquiry has been, and largely remains, a tenuous pursuit in society. In doing so, the perspective he provides is a unique entry to this work. At nearly six hundred pages, his thesis that the paranormal is intimately connected with chaos and disruption is not ephemerally treated; he goes into great detail discussing the various reasons for this and the many scholars who have noted these similarities and whose research further contributes to this philosophical argument. A major question in his work is ferreting out the reasons why paranormal research remains so firmly on the fringe of science despite a robust research history. From sociology to anthropology to shamans and mystics and UFOs, and even further into the realm of imagination, archetypes, and culture, Hansen discusses it all, and presents in this work a truly uncategorizable but absolutely necessary thesis on the paranormal.

Jenzen, Olu, & Munt, Sally R. (Eds.). (2013). *The Ashgate research companion to paranormal cultures.* London, England: Routledge. 471 pages.

Offering an international exploration of belief in the paranormal, this work features a variety of scholars who discuss the nuances of paranormal belief. Divided into three major sections, this work begins by offering an assortment of essays on "paranormal epistemologies," that is, an overview of dominant paranormal beliefs. Articles in this section include intersections of technology and the paranormal, UFO experiences, discussions of paranormal research endeavors and methods, and the afterlife. Section 2 discusses "the paranormal and social change," and examines the political, literary, and film influences of the paranormal and the ways in which it is represented and manifested through those mediums. The third section, titled "Paranormal Phenomenologies," addresses subjects like the culture of ghost hunting, music and art influenced by the paranormal, performance and divination/conjuring, and strange creatures. Discussing paranormal belief on an international scale and examined through essays and case studies of specific events, this work offers a comprehensive look at the ways in which the paranormal influences not only our beliefs but our practices as well. And since it's on an international scale, readers get a keen sense of how the paranormal is a truly worldwide agent.

Jung, C. G. (1960). *Synchronicity: An acausal connecting principle.* Princeton, NJ: Princeton University Press. 135 pages.

Respected psychiatrist Carl Jung coined the term "synchronicity" to describe coincidences that appeared to be meaningful and not just the result of some random occurrence. As a result of his own experiences as well as those relayed to him via his patients, he began to investigate these coincidences a bit deeper. He worked alongside his friend and contemporary Wolfgang Pauli, who developed a principle of synchronicity explained by quantum physics. In *Synchronicity*, Jung outlines his theory about these coincidental, meaningful moments and uses it as a basis for acknowledging the presence of the paranormal in our world. While undoubtedly a more intense resource relating to the paranormal, any discussion would be remiss without mentioning Jung's contribution to this topic. It may be helpful to consult a review of synchronicity before diving into this work, as the jargon and concepts may be unfamiliar at first.

Knight, Damon. (1970). *Charles Fort: Prophet of the unexplained.* Garden City, NY: Doubleday. 224 pages.

Author Damon Knight presents here a biographical exploration of Charles Fort, the journalist and researcher we pay homage to when we use the phrase "Fortean phenomena." Mr. Fort collected stories of people who experienced strange phenomena and compiled them into books detailing these anomalies. His work is still in print today and has particularly influenced science fiction writers, even though the contents of Fort's works aren't based in fiction. In this work, Knight presents a biography of the man who captured the cultural role of the paranormal and whose influence still resonates today.

Kripal, Jeffrey J. (2019). *The flip: Epiphanies of mind and the future of knowledge.* New York, NY: Bellevue Literary Press. 239 pages.

Author Jeffrey J. Kripal is a professor at Rice University where he is also chair in philosophy and religious thought. He is also the author of many additional works that explore the nuances and intersections of the paranormal, religious, mystical, and philosophical. In this work, Dr. Kripal advocates for a synthesis of science and the humanities in order to obtain a deeper and more critical understanding of the mysteries of the world, that is, that which may be dubbed the paranormal. In his own words, Dr. Kripal tells us that this book is an "essay about a tipping point, about the future—be it near or far—of a new worldview, *a new real* that is presently forming around the epiphany of mind as an irreducible dimension or substrate of the natural world."

Radin, Dean. (2018). *Real magic: Ancient wisdom, modern science, and a guide to the secret power of the universe.* New York, NY: Harmony Books. 258 pages.

Dr. Dean Radin teaches transpersonal psychology at California Institute of Integral Studies. In addition, he is a researcher with the Institute of Noetic Sciences, and he received his psychology PhD from the University of Illinois, Urbana-Champaign. In this work, Dr. Radin provides a history of magical practices as well as notable scientific research in the field of consciousness and psychical studies. He follows these with a conversation on how magic is something we can all tap into and provides a discussion for what magic implies about the state and future of human consciousness. He spends time addressing why magic and magical practices have been feared and the ways in which it has been stifled or silenced, especially in relation to the church during its heyday of imperialism. Furthermore, he explores the shifting views on magic throughout the ages, from ancient to modern times. These discussions all center around Dr. Radin's thesis, which is that magic is real and has great implications for human consciousness if we would only recognize its long history and the great timeline of scientific inquiry.

Strieber, Whitley, & Kripal, Jeffrey J. (2016). *The super natural: A new vision of the unexplained.* New York, NY: Jeremy P. Tarcher. 365 pages.

Whitley Strieber is perhaps best known for his memoir *Communion*, annotated above in the "Ufology" section and detailing his abduction experience. A prominent figure of the ufology literature, Strieber teams up with coauthor Jeffrey J. Kripal, a professor at Rice University and author of several additional works on mysticism and the paranormal. In this work, their thesis is simple, and that is that the natural world is really the "super natural" world and that the paranormal, magical, and mystical is around us at all times. In other words, our world is infinitely stranger than we acknowledge or realize, and a simple shift in perspective is all that is needed to recognize this. In their discussion, Strieber and Kripal address the major materialist concerns that are so often at the heart of paranormal criticism, and they provide a wide range of philosophical and practical arguments advocating for the reality that the paranormal is not beyond normal at all, but has been a part of our world all along. Readers interested in philosophical discussions of the paranormal and its connection to both science and religion will undoubtedly enjoy this book.

In the next chapter, you will find information on how to use databases and journals to locate relevant paranormal research. At the end of the chapter there is also a sampling of journal articles on various paranormal topics to illustrate just how much diversity you can find within journals and databases.

NOTES

1. McCorristine, Shane. (n.d.). About me. Retrieved December 20, 2019, from https://www.shanemccorristine.net/
2. Harry Price. (n.d.). In *Psi encyclopedia.* Society for Psychical Research. Retrieved December 20, 2019, from https://psi-encyclopedia.spr.ac.uk/articles/harry-price
3. Russell Targ. (n.d.). In *Psi encyclopedia.* Society for Psychical Research. Retrieved December 19, 2019, from https://psi-encyclopedia.spr.ac.uk/articles/russell-targ
4. Idaho State University. (2019). Faculty. Retrieved December 18, 2019, from https://www.isu.edu/biology/people/faculty---professors/jeffrey-meldrum/
5. Jacquesvallee.net. (2019). Jacques Vallée. Retrieved December 29, 2019, from https://www.jacquesvallee.net/

Chapter Nine

Journals and Databases for Finding Paranormal Resources, with a Selection of Relevant Journal Articles

Handbooks, dictionaries, encyclopedias, and monographs are not (by any means) the only sources to consider when researching the paranormal. Journals and databases are overflowing with information on various paranormal subtopics. In fact, there are entire journals dedicated to the paranormal in which scholars regularly publish their theories and findings regarding paranormal experimentation. Even if a journal is not, in its entirety, dedicated to the paranormal, researchers can find paranormal articles in journals subsumed under the disciplines of religion, anthropology, sociology, psychology, and more. This should bring even more awareness to the fact that the paranormal has been (and continues to be) investigated from a wide variety of perspectives and lenses. In this chapter, I highlight a handful of relevant databases and journals to consult when gathering paranormal research. Additionally, I include a select handful of relevant articles to provide an example of what journals publish and how an article can be helpful. Just as with monographs, it is not possible to list all journals and articles here, so readers should use this chapter as a jumping-off point to more information.

The reason why databases and journals are so important to include in any discussion of gathering paranormal research is not just that there is a robust amount of information to be found. Journals publish articles multiple times a year and, as such, are quicker to publish than entire books on a topic. Additionally, journal articles are smaller and therefore quicker to read and digest. They often provide an overview of some type of theory or experiment/research that the authors have done on a particular topic. Many of them are peer reviewed, as well, a factor that I discuss later in this chapter.

Another great aspect of databases is that, because they are accessible online, you can choose any number of filters to display your search results. For example, many databases will allow you to choose a date range that you are most interested in. This can be very helpful if you are looking for the most updated and current information about a topic, for example, or if you want more historical information. Using these filters are often times referred to as using "limiters" and can simply be a great way to help you find the most relevant information as quickly as possible. Another filter that you may wish to use is filtering by source type—magazine, newspaper, journal article, and so forth. Yet another wonderful filter is limiting to those results that are published in a particular journal or which cover a particular subject. The number of filters and limiters that you can apply to your database searches is nearly endless. As you become more and more familiar with searching in databases, using these filters will become easier and more intuitive.

Those not currently a university student or employee, however, may not realize that there is an entire world of databases and journal articles about paranormal topics. In fact, I think that databases and journals are easily forgotten as potential avenues for research by members of the general public. That's understandable, of course, given the fact that databases and journals are not necessarily as easy to access by the general public. In other words, you can't just go to Amazon or your local bookstore to find these things. The subscription fees are often quite high, and therefore access is usually only available via some institution that pays a subscription fee and provides access to its users. Most often, these are university libraries, but some larger public libraries may provide access as well.

Perhaps another reason that databases and journals are overlooked or forgotten is that most people assume they must be a university student or employee to access these databases. That's not often the case, especially in public universities. For example, members of the general public are welcomed and able to obtain library cards at my university library, and once they have a card, they are able to access the same library databases that students can. Oftentimes people express to me how they had no idea they could use the university library, and I would hazard a guess that it's likely a common misconception among people.

The noticeable difference between a nonstudent or nonemployee is that by and large access to these databases and journals is usually only available inside the physical library itself. In other words, students and employees have off-campus digital access, but that is often not a feature available to community members who are unaffiliated with the university. For that reason, there is somewhat of a barrier for nonstudents and nonemployees to access this information, but the payoff is immense because of the abundance of paranormal research contained in the databases and journals I discuss in this chapter.

To provide some clarification before simply plunging into a review of these sources, it is beneficial to break down the components of databases, journals, and articles and discuss some of their unique characteristics. To put it simply, a database is a container of information—it can be a collection of multiple journals that are accessible and compiled together in one database, or it can be a collection of other resources such as books, pamphlets, newspaper articles, transcripts, and so forth that have been compiled around a common theme. Take for instance, the database titled Victorian Popular Culture. This database contains all types of information about the Victorian era such as the cinema, circuses and sideshows, music and theater, and (important for our purposes here) a collection of resources on spiritualism. On its website, this database tells visitors that the main source of information on its spiritualism topic comes from special collections at both the University of London and the University of Texas, Austin.[1] Furthermore, this page tells visitors that the collection on spiritualism is a combination of books, periodicals (journals), photographs, posters, and more.

Other databases are simply a combined access point to a variety of journals that focus on a certain topic or discipline like religion or philosophy or psychology. These databases enable you, as the researcher, to search among all the journals contained therein simultaneously. In other words, a database serves as a collective access point that hopefully assists researchers in finding information a little easier. Instead of having to find each separate journal on a particular topic, for example, you can search a database that will mine each journal's contents in one session.

That doesn't mean, of course, that you can't locate specific journals and scour their contents for relevant research. This is a tactic I recommend to researchers, actually. If, for instance, you know of a specific journal that publishes research on a topic you are interested in, it makes perfect research sense to go straight to the source. Quite often, though, people aren't familiar with specific journals and begin their research within databases. As you locate articles within databases, you may begin to see the same journal titles mentioned over and over, and at that point you may wish to locate the collections of that specific journal.

There is no wrong way to begin your research. If you wish to locate one journal and begin your search there, that is just as valid a tactic as locating a database and diving in there. Still just as valid is browsing library catalogs and websites for books, encyclopedias, and other reference works on your topic. What's most important as a researcher is understanding that you can only have a broad understanding of your topic by intentionally incorporating diverse materials. What you shouldn't do, for example, is limit yourself to only one type of resource, because by doing so you are eliminating an entire world of additional information and will, as a result, only have a limited understanding of your topic.

The topic of database and journal researching is not complete without a discussion of what a journal article is, what it means for something to be primary or secondary research, and in particular what it means for something to be peer reviewed. Journal articles are shorter works that are published at certain intervals within a journal. They can be scholarly (peer reviewed) or popular in nature. A journal article that is scholarly simply means that it has undergone the peer-review process. This process occurs when a researcher submits their article to be considered for publication within a scholarly journal. It's not an automatic acceptance, though. The editors of the journal, if they choose to pursue the submitted article, will send it to a group of peer reviewers—these reviewers are other scholars and researchers who have experience in the topic at hand. For example, if I am a Bigfoot researcher and I want to publish my article on the tracks of Bigfoot found in the Midwest to a scholarly journal, my article will be sent to other Bigfoot researchers who will evaluate it for things like accuracy or comprehensiveness, and who will offer suggestions for enhancing the article or for pointing out those portions that didn't make sense or weren't as well formed. The peer reviewers send their suggestions and critiques back to the original author, who will make the suggested changes and resubmit the article, which will either be accepted for publication, be rejected, or have to undergo another round of proposed changes. The peer-review process is often touted as the pinnacle of credible research since it has been analyzed by a group of scholars with experience in that particular topic.

This doesn't mean that articles that are not peer reviewed are not worthy of inclusion in a scholarly discussion; it just means that they have not undergone a peer review and as such, the burden of double-checking, so to speak, rests on you as the information consumer. Some examples of popular journals are *National Geographic*, *Nature*, *Popular Science*, and *Psychology Today*. Of course, this isn't to say that you should blindly trust that all peer-reviewed sources are automatically credible and relevant. Every research has its weaknesses, and one article can only present so much perspective on a certain topic. Again, what is important is to gather diverse and multiple resources that will help you obtain a robust and holistic understanding of a topic.

Journal articles often contain primary or secondary research, and it's important to understand the basic difference between the two. Primary research is research that has been conducted by the authors themselves—in other words, it means that the authors have used some research method to test a certain hypothesis. Quite often these articles contain charts of data and a detailed discussion of how they set up their experiment. Secondary research, on the other hand, is simply an overview of research that has been done on a particular topic. This entire book is secondary research since I am presenting a compilation of resources that you can use to find information about the paranormal. This doesn't mean that one is inherently better than the other, it just means that they are a different type. Secondary research is quite valuable in assisting researchers with providing a summary or overview of a particular topic, or perhaps adding a new perspective to a certain argument or theory. Additionally, they are wonderful resources to use as finding aids. Browsing their references and bibliography, for example, will yield additional resources on your topic. Primary research is fascinating as it presents real-world experiments and data gathering. Taken together, primary and secondary research help present different sides of a topic and both should be consulted when doing any research.

The resources I present here are by no means comprehensive, but they will give readers a good start for researching paranormal topics. Remember to consult your local public and academic libraries to see if they provide access to these databases. Also, remember that when looking for information inside databases and journals, it is important to search using the keyword strategy I reviewed earlier. Stay away from typing entire questions like you're used to doing in Google. Break your research question down into "key" components and consider doing a word cloud to help organize your ideas and simply get them down on paper.

In this chapter, I first present an overview of helpful databases, followed by a description of useful journals. Following that, I present a small sampling of journal articles on each paranormal subtopic so that readers understand that journal articles provide an endless and myriad opportunity for locating relevant information. Savvy readers will pick up on the fact that the databases I begin with don't appear to have anything to do with the paranormal at first glance. However, once you dig into these databases, you will discover that they have a wide array of articles and information on the paranormal. I make this point to stress that you can't assume that there won't be any paranormal-related information in a database with a name like "America: History and Life." The paranormal is embedded into the fabric of pretty much every arena of life; for that reason, it's important to understand that you will find research in seemingly unlikely places. One database, for example, may provide a psychological lens to the paranormal, whereas another may discuss cultural significance of paranormal events, while still another database may discuss the philosophical underpinnings of paranormal belief. Disregarding something on title alone will result in disregarding entire troves of research into the paranormal, so keep this in mind as you move forward with your research.

Chapter 9

DATABASES

Academic Search Premier

I always tell students that if they don't know where to start, Academic Search Premier is the place to go. This database is a broad, multidisciplinary database where you can find information on a broad range of subjects and topics. You can also find information about the paranormal in this database. The great thing about this database is that you can find scholarly, peer-reviewed articles alongside magazines and newspapers. Academic Search Premier does, however, only go back to about 1975, so if you are looking for older, more historical information about the paranormal, you may wish to start elsewhere. The coverage of this database is simply something to be aware of; it isn't necessarily a reason not to use it to find information. This database is one of many that are owned by the EBSCO company, and it provides access to more than seventeen thousand journals and magazine—more than fifteen thousand of which are peer reviewed.[2] Not all of these journals and magazines provide the full text of their contents, though, which is something that as a researcher you will encounter. What this means is that many databases include citations to articles that are not necessarily available in full, complete format in that specific database. However, it is helpful having a citation and knowing that something exists that you can check via another database or with a librarian.

Of course, you shouldn't worry too much about the whole citation-versus-full-text issue in Academic Search Premier because it includes more than forty-six thousand journals and magazines that include full-text access. To illustrate the types of things you can find in this database, let's work through a couple of examples. A simple keyword search for "psychical research" yields 1,948 results. The vast majority of these are academic journals articles—1,248 of them to be exact. Some of the article titles include "Fragments of a Life in Psychical Research: The Case of Charles Richet," and "Telepathy, Mediumship, and Psychology: Psychical Research at the International Congresses of Psychology, 1889–1905." I could continue, but you get the point.

Another search for something a bit more specific like "near death experience and paranormal" yields seventy-four results, a much smaller number than our first inquiry. Of course, the more nuanced and specific your keyword searches are, the lower your search results will be. If, for example, we simply type "near death experience" into this database, we retrieve more than sixty-seven thousand results. Clearly this database, the title of which isn't necessarily one that implies paranormal inquiry, is a valid resource to consult when you are looking for paranormal-related information.

America: History and Life

This database is another that doesn't necessarily seem obvious in terms of finding paranormal information; however, it does contain a certain number of paranormal-related resources. This database is another that is owned by EBSCO, and it contains information from more than seventeen hundred journals from prehistory to the present. This database covers historical information on the United States and Canada.[3] In this database, you can find information on different cultures throughout history in both of these countries, including cultural articles on paranormal topics.

While it doesn't yield as many results as Academic Search Premier does, it is still a valuable database to consider using when compiling paranormal research. For example, using the keyword strategy "paranormal or occult" yields 246 results, which may not sound like much if you just got done reading about Academic Search Premier, but there are titles that are still relevant, such as articles from the *Journal of Popular Culture* on the social aspects of occultism and more. The great thing about this database is you can find information on how cultures experience paranormal events and/or how paranormal beliefs play out in society. There are, for example, many articles on both reincarnation and near-death experiences, and even information on UFOs. As you might imagine, there are an overwhelming number of articles on the subject of folklore, all of which can help add to a general understanding of any number of topics in the paranormal community.

BASE

This database is an acronym for Bielefeld Academic Search Engine and is owned and operated by the Bielefeld University Library in Germany. Inside this database exist more than 150 million articles that originate from more than seven thousand different resources. Sixty percent of the sources inside this database are immediately available as full-text documents.[4] What this means is that the remaining 40 percent will simply need to be requested via interlibrary loan from your local libraries and/or double-checked to see if full-text access exists in some other database. Librarians can help you do that.

Within the BASE database, you can locate information on various topics of the paranormal, and the great thing is that these resources are international in scope. For example, when you search the keyword "cryptozoology," you receive ninety results. This may seem like a small number, but the first three results originate from the Smithsonian, the Australian National University, and the Portland Public Library, highlighting the diversity of material immediately. Let's say you're interested in ESP. Searching the keyword "extrasensory perception" yields you 371 results. Some of the articles contained inside this database are journal articles, but others still are book chapters or news articles, and the like.

Gale Primary Sources

Primary sources are items such as diaries, photographs, newspaper articles, and objects that are associated with a particular event. For example, photographs of presidential inaugurations are primary sources because they were captured at the exact moment that something was occurring. Gale Primary Sources is a database that can help researchers find, as you may guess, primary sources. It contains information from the seventeenth century through to modern times.

Primary sources are fascinating because they capture such unique and powerful nuances of any given event. It's quite different, I think most would agree, to read someone's review of *The Diary of Anne Frank* than it is to read her diary itself. The information and impact from primary sources are the very quality that makes them invaluable for understanding certain topics, and the paranormal can be studied this way as well. Researching how people react to and experience the paranormal through the years is particularly fascinating as it is so often a polarizing topic.

One example of something unique is a file of documents including newspaper articles and memos outlining a legal case in 1978 between NBC and a group called the Committee for the Scientific Investigation of Claims of the Paranormal alleging the social dangers of broadcasting paranormal-related television. This file, which you can access in this database, reveals that, in the seventies, simply broadcasting shows with a paranormal theme moved some to seek legal counsel.[5] This also presents an opportunity to watch an issue as it unfolded in time, which is a benefit that secondary sources don't provide. Primary sources, then, allow for researchers to come to their own conclusion about a particular event as it helps present an unbiased presentation of an issue or event.

Historical *New York Times*

This database, as you may guess from the title, provides access to the contents of the *New York Times*. The word "historical" in the title may, however, be a bit misleading as the contents of this database include articles written between 1851 and 2015. Newspaper databases are wonderful resources where you will find primary sources. Primary sources, as mentioned above, are those items such as diaries, photographs, newspaper and magazine articles, and more that were published at the specific time of some event or topic or phenomena. A newspaper article reporting on a natural disaster as it is happening in the world is one example of a primary source. Newspaper articles can be great places to find primary sources on the paranormal as well; you can find articles that report eyewitness testimony of reports of strange creatures, encounters with poltergeists, and more. If you come across a certain event in another source, you can use that event as a keyword in this database to discover what was being reported about that event in the days and weeks that it was occurring. One event that comes to my mind is the Roswell UFO incident. To find primary source material on this event, use keywords like "Roswell and UFO" and combine this with telling the database to only search for articles written in the days and weeks immediately following when this event happened. Use Google if you need to look up a date or even another entry in a work that you've perhaps already uncovered. Newspaper articles often contain images as well, allowing you to find valuable and nuanced information that you may not be able to find in another database.

MLA International Bibliography

This database is produced by the Modern Language Association, and it is international in its scope of providing information on literature, language, folklore, and more. Like all the databases listed here, it isn't one that would necessarily indicate to the novice researcher that paranormal research was included in its contents, but it nevertheless does. A quick search for "psychical research," for example, yields forty-six results, many of which are connected to literature, such as one article that combines Sherlock Holmes and the Society for Psychical Research.[6] Not all articles are relegated to juxtapositions of literature and the paranormal, however. When searching "ghosts and folklore," you retrieve 386 results, and because this database is international in scope, you retrieve many articles that discuss paranormal beliefs on ghosts and hauntings in other countries.

The MLA International Bibliography provides a look at how the paranormal intersects mainly with culture through literature and art, although it's not exclusive to those categories. Offering a perspective that some may overlook, the intersection of the paranormal and culture can provide insights about the ways in which the paranormal acts as an undercurrent to even that which we read and see.

Philosopher's Index

The Philosopher's Index is an international database that provides information not only on philosophy, but on metaphysics, religion, anthropology, and more. The scope of this database ranges from 1940 to the present. I include this database because it is important to understand the philosophical underpinnings of the paranormal, especially on an international scale. One fascinating search to do in this database is "metaphysics and paranormal." This search provides a small number of results—twenty-seven to be exact—but the topics and discussions range from dissecting materialism to comparing compassion to clairvoyance, even to musing on how normal brain functions can be viewed as very paranormal.

Of course, many of the articles in this database are also religious in nature. Searching "reincarnation" in this database, for example, brings up many articles that discuss the religious worldviews of cultures around the world. Even though many view religions as getting outside the realm of understanding something clinically and scientifically, I argue that it is extremely important to understand how cultures place value on paranormal phenomena and how that impacts their daily lives. That is something that can be scientifically evaluated and researched. This database is beneficial for anyone wishing to dive into a philosophical discussion of paranormal topics.

ProQuest Dissertations and Theses

The ProQuest company operates a database completely devoted to indexing and providing access to more than a million dissertations and theses written by students around the world that are immediately available for download and reading. According to its website, it is the "database of record for graduate research" and it adds more than seventy thousand new dissertations and theses each year.[7] This database contains information from a wide variety of topics, as you may guess. As such, it is a database that can be used to locate paranormal research. The unique thing about dissertations and theses is that they are often the culmination of years of research, which results in most of them being more than one hundred pages in length. In other words, the resources located in this database are more akin to books than they are articles even though they aren't labeled as monographs. What this means is that dissertations and theses are often wonderful resources in which to locate comprehensive discussions of a particular issue. One resource I list below, in fact, discusses UFO phenomena and subculture and is more than four hundred pages in length.

To highlight the vast potential of this database, when you search the keyword "parapsychology," you receive 2,876 publications written between 1927 and today. If you search the keyword "ufology," you receive 143 results. Searching the organization "Society for Psychical Research" yields you 1,411 results. From here you see the publications of students from universities around the world. When viewing these publications, a good tactic is to review the abstract and the table of contents to get a better idea of what their publication is really all about. And especially since the publications in this database are quite lengthy, using the table of contents can help you navigate to those sections in which you are most interested or which are most relevant to your research.

PsycARTICLES

Spanning coverage from 1894 to present day, the PsycARTICLES database contains the publications of the American Psychological Association as well as the Canadian Psychological Association and a handful of others.[8] Since a huge segment of the paranormal involves psychical phenomena as studied by parapsychologists, it should come as no surprise to readers that psychology databases are found here. A search, in fact, for "parapsychology" in this database reveals 172 articles. Tackling the issue of the paranormal from a psychological lens, this database will help researchers understand the more current work being done by parapsychologists such as James Houran, Rense Lange, and more.

This is also a great database to encounter the critics of paranormal phenomena, but in order to have a holistic understanding of an issue, it is important to also (and intentionally) seek out those sources that point out the weaknesses of certain theories or beliefs. This is an important point to keep in mind so that you don't become blind to the issues and criticisms surrounding the topics you research. Those interested in understanding more about the psychological perspective of paranormal topics should make sure this database is on their research list.

SocINDEX

With more than 2.6 million records contained in this database, SocINDEX is the premier database to find sociological research. It provides access to more than eighteen hundred journals and dates back to 1895 in its scope.[9] A valuable quality of this database is that many of its articles contain ethnographic research. Ethnographic research is a method in which scholars may observe and/or interact with their study subjects in their everyday environments. To provide an example, one article found in this database is "Haunted Objects: English Paranormal Investigation and the Material Mediation of Doubt" by author Michele Hanks.[10] In this article, Hanks uses ethnographic research to embed herself in the culture of paranormal investigators to look specifically at the ways in which material objects both add to and reduce their paranormal doubts.

In this database you can find articles that contain information on how groups interact with the paranormal, be it through paranormal beliefs, experiences, or any number of other phenomena. In particular, there are many articles that discuss how the paranormal is often intimately connected with spiritual identities and other articles that discuss prevalent paranormal beliefs. Because it is international in scope, researchers will also find articles discussing other countries as well as certain historical periods.

Victorian Popular Culture

This database, owned by the Adam Matthew company, compiles information on four key areas of Victorian popular culture, which primarily focuses on the span between 1779 and 1930, specifically in the United States, Britain, and Europe. The four key areas are spiritualism and magic; circuses and sideshows; music and theater; followed by the cinema. Of course, for purposes of paranormal research, the section on spiritualism will be of most relevance. Most of this database contains primary sources, which are sources such as diaries, posters, newspaper articles, objects, photographs, and more.[11] Primary sources are, in other words, those items that were created during a specific time in question. For example, the set of Zener cards used by J. B. Rhine in his labs at Duke University are considered primary sources.

Some examples of what you can find in this database include posters advertising seances; an 1851 book titled *The Celestial Telegraph; or, The Secrets of Life to Come, Revealed through Magnetism*; a periodical titled *Professor Anderson's Psychomantic Reporter*, which documents mediumship and seances; and reports outlining fraudulent activities of mediums. This database offers a unique perspective into the heyday of spiritualism and will help supplement an understanding and deeper nuance of this topic when aligned with other resources.

These are just some databases that will be helpful in locating paranormal-related research. This is not an exhaustive list, but it does offer, I believe, a core group of databases to begin your paranormal research. Hopefully this discussion illustrates the potential of thinking outside the box when it comes to locating paranormal research.

In addition to databases, there are specific journals that contain paranormal research. Some of these journals, in fact, are dedicated entirely to paranormal topics. Even though some of these journals are not entirely dedicated to the paranormal, they are resources in which you can find paranormal information. Beyond that, however, these resources are also where you can find information that can help you better understand the nuances of how the paranormal impacts our lives. For example, a psychology journal can help you understand how our brains process information, which could be useful knowledge when reading personal accounts of paranormal experience. Likewise, an anthropology journal could help you realize the ways in which ritual, symbolism, and performance play into the paranormal cultures of different societies. I raise this point not to imply that broader knowledge should only be used to discredit and debunk (certainly it sometimes can, though), but to show that sometimes in order to understand paranormal phenomena, you need to look at it from a different perspective, perhaps even one that isn't paranormal in nature at all.

I begin with an outline of peer-reviewed journals followed by their popular counterparts. Keep in mind, of course, that this is not a discussion of which journals are better than others; rather, it is all in how you combine multiple resources to gather a clear picture of some topic. As above, the journals listed here are not an exhaustive listing of all journals that contain paranormal information; this is simply a core group of journals with which to begin.

SCHOLARLY AND PEER-REVIEWED JOURNALS

British Journal of Psychology

The *British Journal of Psychology* is just one of the many scholarly journals published by the British Psychological Society. It is listed as a journal specializing in psychology, of course, but it also contains a large amount of interdisciplinary information. This journal, even though the title may seem to indicate otherwise, is international in scope and openly welcomes contributions from around the world.[12] Even though this journal isn't specifically dedicated to topics of the paranormal, it does contain a large amount of information on parapsychology and related phenomena. For example, a search inside this journal using simply "parapsychology" as a keyword yields forty-eight articles that discuss not only belief in psychical phenomena but also experimental methods and discoveries within this topic. Still other articles can be accessed with additional keywords such as "paranormal" or "Ganzfeld" and can offer a unique perspective into paranormal phenomena. Additionally, this is a wonderful journal to consult to help boost your own understanding of how our minds work and the psychological processes that impact belief and experience.

Journal for Spiritual and Consciousness Studies

This journal has undergone a number of iterations throughout the years, beginning in 1990 and having once been referred to as the *Journal of Religion and Psychical Research* as well as the *Journal of Spirituality and Paranormal Studies*, to its current iteration, which began in 2012 when its governing association changed its name to the Academy for Spiritual and Consciousness Studies.[13] Articles in this journal investigate topics such as electronic voice phenomena, strange dreams, near-death experiences, and reincarnation, among others. As you may guess from the title, many of the articles contained herein discuss issues surrounding consciousness and its connection to the paranormal. One such article discusses the juxtaposition of labeling introvertive visual experiences as hallucinations versus spiritual visions, and thereby illustrates how different perspectives yield entirely different contexts on personal experiences.[14] Other articles in this journal include essays describing personal paranormal experiences, which offers a nice mixture of personal accounts alongside academic and theoretical discussions of the paranormal.

Journal of Abnormal Psychology

This journal is a peer-reviewed journal published by the American Psychological Association beginning in 1906, and even though "abnormal" may strike an offensive chord in some, abnormal psychology is simply a branch of psychology that focuses on abnormal behaviors and beliefs that are analyzed in a clinical setting. It shouldn't be confused with meaning that the paranormal is "abnormal." This journal isn't interested in presenting treatments or diagnoses; it merely focuses on that which falls outside the norm.[15] It is simply another journal that can be used to find paranormal-related information. Up to 1964, this journal was listed as the *Journal of Abnormal and Social Psychology*. Within this journal readers can find articles on extrasensory perception experiments, links between telepathy and emotion, biographical entries of psychical researchers, discussions of UFO eyewitness experiences, and more. This journal is a good choice for those specifically interested in parapsychology, as it doesn't contain much information on the other topics listed in this book.

Journal of American Folklore

This journal is published by the American Folklore Society and began in 1888. Currently it is published four times a year and is an indispensable resource for those interested in researching the paranormal via a folkloric lens.[16] Within this journal, researchers can find an abundance of information on any one of the paranormal topics discussed in this book, making it a great resource in which to find a little bit of everything. To give an example of what you may find in this journal, a search for "UFOs" reveals a list of twenty-eight articles. This may not seem like much, but the articles themselves are fascinating discussions of how that topic plays out culturally. One of these UFO articles, for instance, is titled "The 'Men in Black' Experience and Tradition: Analogues with the Traditional Devil Hypothesis" by Peter M. Rojcewicz.[17] This article discusses how the modern phenomena of "men in black" mirrors older folkloric traditions and beliefs in the devil. As you can see, this journal provides an immense amount of cultural information and experience ranging from modern to historical times and sometimes makes links between ancient thoughtforms and how they still manifest today.

This journal offers a great reminder about the power of keyword searching and the importance of always questioning how your keywords can be worded differently. For example, when you type the keyword "cryptozoology" into this journal, you receive a page that tells you there are no results. If you stopped here and just assumed that the journal didn't contain any information on this topic, you would be extremely remiss. Simply considering another way to describe what you are looking for yields results. For example, using the keyword "monster" instead of cryptozoology yields 395 results. Many of these results, in fact, are international in scope and discuss cultures that are no longer in existence. The amount of useful information that can be gathered from these is immense and would have been completely overlooked if it weren't for a critical and creative contemplation of keywords.

Journal of the American Society for Psychical Research

This journal, published by the American Society for Psychical Research (ASPR), is the U.S. branch of the preeminent UK research organization, the Society for Psychical Research. The ASPR was founded just a few short years after its parent organization. While the journal of the ASPR is somewhat difficult to access—many of their issues are out of print and can only be accessed by requesting a copy from the ASPR itself—there is nonetheless a point of entry to this journal. The issues that you can access are older issues that exist in the public domain. However, these older issues not only contain a wealth of information but can help you trace the historical roots of the scientific inquiry into psychical phenomena. This historical information, coupled with the more modern information you can access from the other databases and journals listed here, will more than make up for any inability to access certain issues of this singular journal.

One way that researchers can access the contents of this journal is via HathiTrust, a digital library consisting of members from various research organizations and libraries around the world who work together to digitally preserve (and make accessible) information that has entered the public domain.[18] As a result, the contents within HathiTrust are older materials by nature, but it is within this database that researchers can find issues of the *Journal of the American Society for Psychical Research* ranging from 1907 to 1927. Digital copies of these issues are made available from the collections of both Harvard University and the University of Michigan. In volume 1 of the 1907 issue, for example, you will find articles on automatic writing, telepathy, mediumship, and a whole host of other commentaries, theories, and editorials on various psychical topics. Using BASE, one of the databases listed above, can also yield information on the journal's proceedings and contents.

Journal of Near-Death Studies

On its website, the editors of this journal describe it as "the only peer-reviewed scholarly journal dedicated exclusively to the field of near-death studies" but highlight that it is multidisciplinary as well.[19] First issued in 1981, this journal is currently published three times a year and, as you might have guessed, contains articles about NDEs and afterlife phenomena. The great thing about this journal is that it openly provides access free of charge to any article older than three years. This is still very current information, and honestly, there are many journals that, even after a hefty subscription, you can still only access articles that are five years old or later. If you wish to access articles from this journal that have been published in the last three years, you can order them for a fee. But you can also check with your local libraries to see if they can retrieve these articles on your behalf.

Dating back almost forty years, this journal is a great resource for those specifically interested in learning more about near-death experiences and afterlife phenomena. This journal is supported by the International Association for Near-Death Studies, and as such, the information contained in this database spans the globe. Its coverage contains not only information on near-death experiences but also on the spiritual and transcendent experiences that people have during (and as a result of) NDEs. Included in some of its volumes are articles discussing specific phenomena like tunnel vision or the specific experiences in certain regions like the Pacific Northwest and still even more articles that discuss the potential of NDEs as proof of consciousness succeeding bodily death.

Journal of Parapsychology

This journal, published by the Rhine Research Center, is a compendium of research articles, theoretical discussions, and reviews. It even contains transcripts of presentations given at the annual Parapsychological Association's conference. First published in 1937, this journal contains scholarly inquiry of various aspects of parapsychology including ESP, haunting experiences, paranormal beliefs, out-of-body experiences, psychokinesis, poltergeist phenomena, and much more. The editor in chief of this journal, Etzel Cardeña, is a psychology professor at Lund University in Sweden where he also serves as director of the Center for Research on Consciousness and Anomalous Psychology. The editorial board is composed of scholars from around the world and from such institutions as the University of London, Duke University, Harvard University, Manchester Metropolitan University, and more.

Inside this journal, you will find an almost overwhelming amount of research on not only various paranormal phenomena, but also the many methods and theories that abound in the field. One such method is interpretive phenomenological analysis, which is a technique that aims to evaluate how people interpret, or make sense of, certain experiences—in this case, paranormal encounters. To illustrate, in 2013 three researchers began to wonder why so much research on subjective paranormal experiences took a quantitative approach—that is, an approach that categorizes data numerically.[20] While these researchers acknowledge the wonderful data that quantitative research has yielded in terms of paranormal experiences, they began to wonder what a more human-centered qualitative approach would yield and therefore set out to study personal paranormal experiences through the lens of interpretive phenomenological analysis, a method that yields much different data than its quantitative research counterparts. They discovered, among other things, that paranormal experiences often resulted in a sense of disembodiment. This is just one example of the type of research and methods that can be found in this journal.

Aside from the *Journal of the Society for Psychical Research*, this is perhaps the most premier scholarly journal on the topic of the paranormal, as it is entirely dedicated to the field of parapsychology. Even a brief overview of the contents of one issue reveal how robust and varied the research and procedures in this journal are. Other journals, of course, also relegate themselves uniquely to issues of the paranormal, but for researchers wishing to dive headfirst into the scholarly literature of the paranormal, I would recommend beginning with this journal, as it contains eighty years' worth of psychical research and information, making it not only a key resource for contemporary scholarship but also helpful when investigating the historical timeline of this research.

Journal of Scientific Exploration

The *Journal of Scientific Exploration* is the scholarly, peer-reviewed publication of the Society for Scientific Exploration, an organization founded in 1982 with the goal of exploring unconventional topics overlooked by the mainstream. The journal is open access as well, meaning that anyone who visits its website can get immediate access to 120 issues' worth of articles. Within this journal you can find information on several paranormal topics, such as electromagnetic fields and their connection to anomalous phenomena, ufology, reincarnation, paranormal philosophy, psychical phenomena, and much, much more. Each issue contains original research articles alongside commentaries, which discuss paranormal philosophies or theories, as well as book reviews, making it a great place to find your next greatest scientific paranormal read. Issues also contain a section titled "Historical Perspectives," in which a paranormal topic or case from the past is presented. The fact that this journal is so widely inclusive to strange and anomalous phenomena while also focusing on the relationships of the paranormal to other disciplines and the fact that you can access it freely and openly make it a truly indispensable resource for paranormal research.

Journal of the Society for Psychical Research

The SPR is mentioned a multitude of times in this book, so it shouldn't be a surprise that its journal counterpart is listed here. First published in 1884, this is the official scholarly publication of the Society for Psychical Research. In its own words, the journal "includes reports of current laboratory and fieldwork research, along with theoretical, methodological, and historical papers" on a variety of psychical phenomena.[21] Paranormal researchers from around the world submit their articles to this journal. Inside its pages you can find research on Icelandic mediums, UK poltergeists, haunted houses, consciousness, possession, out-of-body experiences, psychical research in France, medieval concepts of the afterlife, modern concepts of the afterlife, and much, much more.

The editorial board of this journal consists of scholars from the University of Northampton, the Natural History Museum of the UK, the University of Edinburgh, the University of Gothenburg in Sweden, and more, including a small number of scholars from the United States. The main contents of this journal fall into one of three main types of articles: empirical research, research notes, and letters to the editor. Within these articles, you will find primary research, theoretical discussions, case studies, editorials, and more.

While this journal is one of the must-haves on anyone's paranormal research list, it is nonetheless a bit difficult to access if you are not a member of the SPR itself. Nonetheless, the digital library known as HathiTrust makes certain editions of the journal freely accessible. The impetus behind HathiTrust, though, is to make available items that are in the public domain, which indicates that materials are dated. However, you can view the full-text contents of this journal in HathiTrust from 1884 to 1922. Even though it may initially seem discouraging, the fact that these more historical issues are freely and openly available is quite amazing, since a large amount of seminal work was done in those years, setting a perfect stage for understanding how the field of psychical research was born and progressed. An index of the contents of the more modern issues can be found, and you can request articles via interlibrary loan from your local public and university libraries. Of course, not every interlibrary loan request can be granted, but this is one technique to use to get your hands on the more modern research in this journal.

Paranthropology: Journal of Anthropological Approaches to the Paranormal

Paranthropology is a freely accessible academic journal that focuses on "the promotion of social-scientific approaches to the study of paranormal experiences, beliefs and phenomena in all of their varied guises."[22] Its board of reviewers includes scholars from across the world from such places as the University of Bristol in England, California State University, the Rhine Research Center, the University of Oxford, Arizona State University, and more. The goal of this journal, as stated very clearly on its website, is to engage in an interdisciplinary discussion about the paranormal that moves beyond the simple dichotomy of skeptic or believer in which so many get caught. Some of the articles in each issue are peer reviewed and are combined with other non-peer-reviewed yet academic articles to create a diverse issue of perspectives and insights. I think it's actually good form to intentionally pursue different types of information including scholarly and popular materials.

Examples of topics that can be found in this journal include possession experiences during Korean shamanic rituals, spiritual interpretations of certain medical symptoms, belief systems of vampire subcultures, remote viewing, and UFOs. What you will find in this journal is a multitude of perspectives that are applied to these topics and more. For example, an anthropologist may study religious practices of certain cultures and how they're related to supernatural beliefs, while parapsychologists may conduct studies on remote viewing, while other psychologists examine if there is a correlation between gender and anomalous beliefs. This journal is particularly relevant to those researchers wishing for a multidisciplinary approach to the paranormal that investigates the phenomena from an anthropological foundation.

Sociology of Religion

It is so often difficult to have a discussion of the paranormal without also having a discussion of how the paranormal plays out from a religious perspective and vice versa. As such, this journal, the official publication of the Association for the Sociology of Religion,[23] provides a unique lens through which to view the paranormal. To give an example, one article found in this journal muses how certain aspects of the paranormal are inherently found inside religion while certain other paranormal characteristics are outright vilified, denounced, and demonized, no pun intended. The researchers in this article discuss how certain religious practitioners uphold only those paranormal beliefs that fall distinctly within their dogmatic framework while simultaneously rejecting anything paranormal that falls outside the scope of their religious beliefs. They also investigate, however, the prevalence of people, such as Christians, to hold both religious paranormal convictions and general paranormal convictions and investigate the many nuances of how these two topics intersect.[24]

Yet another article within this journal discusses how engaging in paranormal investigation serves as a spiritual practice for some people, and specifically investigates how people are diversifying their spirituality by openly incorporating aspects of the supernatural into their spiritual worldviews.[25] For researchers who are interested in the unique juxtaposition of religion and the paranormal, this journal is a key resource.

Supernatural Studies

This journal, a peer-reviewed publication of the Supernatural Studies Association, is dedicated to analyzing and discussing the ways in which the supernatural is expressed via artifacts. These artifacts could be books and literature, movies and film, or any number of other cultural artifacts.[26] Some readers may wonder why this is included since it doesn't necessarily investigate supernatural phenomena itself. I include this journal because it is important to understand how far reaching the paranormal and supernatural interacts with the world around us. Understanding that we, as a collective society, have an intense fascination with the paranormal can help us better understand the phenomena from a holistic angle. In other words, the supernatural can be "felt" in any number of ways and through any number of mediums. Some of the journals listed above will help you to better understand the paranormal in a clinical way, whereas this journal can help you understand the ways in which the paranormal influences our culture and the ways in which we interpret artifacts and books and movies and plays, and so forth.

One article, for instance, explores instrumental transcommunication and how it represents views of the afterlife. This article, which discusses the instruments and tools that have been used to communicate with the afterlife, mentions experiments done by Nikolas Tesla and Thomas Edison and actually offers a nice historical overview of the methods that people have employed to communicate with the dead.[27] This journal is a perfect example of how important it is to not limit your research to any one type of journal or publication. The paranormal influences so much of our lives that good research that posits interesting theories and asks meaningful questions can be found in almost any discipline.

POPULAR JOURNALS

The journals I discuss above are all examples of scholarly or peer-reviewed publications. These types of publications, though they are often touted as the pinnacle of scholarly research, are not the only credible and valuable resources out there. Popular journals (or magazines) can also provide worthy information. Some examples of popular magazines are *Discover*, *Popular Science*, and *Science* magazine. What differentiates popular journals from scholarly publications is that their articles are not peer reviewed and aren't necessarily written by an expert in the field being discussed. They are usually, for example, written by staff reporters who, even though they are not scholars in that field, are nonetheless professionals at writing and delivering a report on some news or phenomena. Articles in these publications are often written to inform the general public about a certain event or story; as a result, they are not often full of technical jargon. This makes them easier to read for a larger number of people. Articles in these publications may not include a bibliography or works cited, meaning that you can't trace their information back to its original source material.

This doesn't mean that the information contained in popular journals is automatically untrustworthy; it just means that you may want to find additional sources to verify what you've read in that article. Often, popular journal articles are the entryway that motivates someone to undertake a more rigorous investigation of some phenomena. They provide an overview, if you will, allowing researchers to capture a snapshot of some event that they can then choose to research further. Personally, I find popular journal articles to be great at providing me a basic understanding of something I don't know much about. They're a great place to start, in other words, and they can be perfectly acceptable resources in which to find paranormal information. The resources I list here are a small sampling of relevant popular journals/magazines.

Discover

According to its website, the mission of *Discover* magazine is to "enable readers to lead richer lives by explaining and expanding their universe" via articles that discuss "various topics ranging from technology and space to the living world we live in."[28] It's a journal where you can find a wide variety of information, but which also sometimes includes information of a paranormal nature. Take, for example, an article written in March 2012. The article, written by staff writer Yudhijit Bhattacharjee, discusses the life of Daryl Bem, a respected psychologist who became fascinated with psychical research after a colleague urged him to read some of the psychical literature. Bem, completely unaware of the serious and methodical endeavors of psychical researchers, undertook his own experiment on precognition and went on to publish his results in the *Journal of Personality and Social Psychology*. Bem's article was both praised and reviled, and the rest of this story outlines the continuation of Bem's work from this point.[29] This article mentions many additional researchers and journals and topics that can be further researched, and as such, it provides a great entry point into the topic of precognition, for example.

The great thing about popular journals is that they provide interesting and relevant information in a storytelling fashion. In other words, it's simply enjoyable to read the articles in these publications because one of the goals, in addition to informing you about some topic, is to entertain you and weave a story. That's not to say that "story" is synonymous with "fiction"; it simply means that the manner in which the information is presented is much different than the way it is presented in scholarly, peer-reviewed journals and it's an entirely different experience. Popular journal articles have a way of hooking you into a story, because the staff writers are experts at doing that. As such, popular journals are a great place to start if you aren't sure where to begin or you don't know much about a topic, because you will find information presented in a novice-friendly way—information that you can continue to build upon.

Popular Science

This publication, issued quarterly each year, contains a lot of similar information that you might find in *Discover*. Its readership is aimed at the general public and its articles are written at a level easy enough for the public to understand. In this journal, for example, you can find articles written by Daryl Bem, the psychologist who became fascinated with psychical research and began conducting his own experiments. You can also find articles on ufology and essays written by researchers affiliated with SETI. One article written in September 2019 actually debunks the popular notion that more UFO sightings are seen along the thirty-seventh parallel than any other location across the country. Staff writer Matthew Phelan uses information from the National UFO Reporting Center (NUFORC) and the Mutual UFO Network (MUFON) to write the article.[30]

Articles from popular journals, like the one written here by Matthew Phelan, are great places to begin gathering additional keywords, key figures, events, and more that you can research further. These resources are not going to provide a comprehensive treatment of some issue; rather, they provide an introduction or overview or vignette of some topic. What makes them so valuable, though, is how user friendly and chock-full of additional resources they are.

Science

This journal was first issued in 1880, using start-up money provided by Thomas Edison. It is an official publication of the American Association for the Advancement of Science (AAAS) and has been a front-runner to report on many scientific breakthroughs and discoveries.[31] As you might imagine, there is a wealth of information in this journal relating to all types of scientific endeavors that seek to better understand paranormal phenomena. A quick search using the word "paranormal" alone yields more than one hundred results. That may seem like a relatively low number to some, though, so let's try another word. Using the key word "psychical," for example, yields 690 results, proving yet again the importance of keyword searching and using different words to find what you might be searching for. "UFO" yields you 102 results, while "reincarnation" yields a modest seventy-six. Even typing the word "Bigfoot" yields results—thirty to be exact.

In terms of the type of information you can find when you type these (and more) keywords into this journal are news articles, blog entries, commentaries/editorials, research and reviews, and a category known as "Scientific Community." As you can see, then, there is a wide range of different types of resources you can find via this journal—some of them are extremely scientific and methodical while others are less so, like commentaries and blog entries. The commentaries themselves, however, are often penned by fellow scientists and researchers, so you shouldn't brush them off as mere editorializing. The research articles themselves, moreover, undergo a peer-review process, which places this publication squarely between the two realms of scholarly and popular resources. I find it quite refreshing, actually, that this journal is a combination of all types of different resources and places the scholarly conversation alongside the popular one. Listed last here simply as a result of its alphabetical place in line, *Science* magazine is a wonderful resource that should be in every paranormal researcher's toolkit.

The three popular journals I discuss here are by no means an exhaustive representation of the popular journals in which you can find paranormal information. There are plenty of others, to be sure, and I encourage you to seek out additional resources. At this point you should have all the resources you need to critically evaluate whether a resource is credible. Keep in mind also that it's all about balance when conducting research—solely consulting popular journals will only ever reveal a small percentage of an issue. You must be able to locate a variety of resources to be able to construct a comprehensive understanding of any issue, paranormal or not.

SAMPLE JOURNAL ARTICLES ON PARANORMAL TOPICS

In this next section, I provide a sample bibliography of journal articles on each paranormal topic in this book. By doing so, I hope to not only shine a light on the credible and scholarly work being done on the paranormal, but to provide a jumping-off point for you in your own research. You know where to go to find the articles, but now highlighting them will give some idea of what you will find when you begin your own research. Additionally, this section highlights a variety of different researchers, methods, theories, and topics that illustrate just how pervasive and varied paranormal research has been and continues to be.

Ghosts and Hauntings

Dubaj, Vladimir, & Mowbray, Tony. (2019, Fall). Magnetospheric and lunar interactions with reported sensory hallucinations: An exploratory study. *Journal of Parapsychology, 83*(2), 193–208. doi:10.30891/jopar.2019.02.06

These researchers set out to test the hypothesis that geomagnetic fields and the lunar cycles foster an increase in hallucinations among people. Employing content analysis, the researchers obtained access to 723 eyewitness reports of paranormal activity that were reported over the course of twenty-six years. They begin by outlining previous research that has asked the same questions and use this research to help inform their study. The biggest difference, however, in the current study is the massive sample size of reports and the length of time covered that the authors were able to obtain. Specifically, the researchers gathered reports from the Port Arthur Historic Site Management Authority in Australia—this organization oversees the once functioning Port Arthur penal settlement, which existed between 1830 and 1877. The management authority began collecting paranormal accounts beginning in 1989 and through to 2014. Using those reports that contained date and time information allowed the researchers to track moon phases as well as geomagnetic fluctuations in the specific area mentioned in the report. The ages and genders of individuals, times of day, and types of paranormal encounter all varied in scope. They combined these reports with available sunspot and moon phases as provided on government websites.

They discovered that there were more reports of paranormal experiences in those months that had collectively higher averages of geomagnetic activity even though there didn't necessarily appear to be more reports from year to year. They also discovered a higher reporting of events during the full and new moon phases, and they speculate as to some of the reasons for these results before suggesting avenues for further research.

Houran, James, Lange, Rense, Laythe, Brian, Dagnall, Neil, Drinkwater, Kenneth, & O'Keeffe, Ciarán. (2019, Fall). Quantifying the phenomenology of ghostly episodes: Part II—A Rasch model of spontaneous accounts. *Journal of Parapsychology, 83*(2), 168–192. doi:10.30891/jopar.2019.02.05

The researchers in this article set out to determine if characteristics of paranormal experiences could be quantified in such a way that sets them on a more even keel with events in the biomedical and social sciences. They determined that paranormal experiences can indeed by quantified in such a way and point out that doing so allows paranormal experiences to be more amenable to statistical inquiry. Additionally, they discovered that paranormal experiences can be tracked via their frequency and their variety (type of encounter, etc.), but that it was also possible to track paranormal encounters via their intensity as well. In order to test this, the researchers presented a survey to respondents in both the United States and Great Britain, using authentic reports as well as fabricated reports of paranormal experience and administered to each person a thirty-two-item checklist of characteristics to agree or disagree upon in a true-or-false answer style. Offering a unique perspective in how paranormal experiences are labeled and classified, this study also, as a result, presents to us a way of quantifying paranormal phenomena that can hopefully facilitate identifying patterns and/or anomalies in much the same way other nonparanormal subjects are analyzed, which will in turn help situate the paranormal more firmly within the scientific record.

Laythe, Brian R., & Owen, Kay. (2013, Fall). A critical test of the EMF-paranormal phenomena theory: Evidence from a haunted site without electricity-generating fields. *Journal of Parapsychology, 77*(2), 212–236.

The authors begin this work by reminding readers that while previous research has also tested the effect of EMF (electromagnetic fields) and geomagnetic fields (GMF) on paranormal experiences, they have mainly been relegated to the realm of hallucinations. With this study, the authors attempt to determine whether EMF fields affect "non-hallucinatory paranormal phenomena." They specifically aim to study the subjective versus objective paranormal experience alongside EMF and geomagnetic fields. The researchers begin by outlining the previous EMF/GMF literature done by other researchers, thus offering a trove of additional reading for those interested in obtaining more information on this topic. They note, however, a lack of research on objective phenomena and EMF/GMF.

Using members of two local paranormal investigative groups, the researchers conducted their experiment at a location called Black Moon Manor in east-central Indiana. The authors provide a brief historical overview of this home built in 1862 that was once reported to house smallpox patients. Using electrical meters and observation, the researchers concluded that there were no active forms of electricity apparent at the location. During the investigation, a milk crate mysteriously vanished from the researchers' video recorders and seven-foot-tall shadows were captured passing from one side of a room to another. Additionally, children's voices were captured on audio devices even though, as you may assume, no children were present during the investigation. Moreover, there did appear to be significant increases in both EMF and GMF activity at the moments in which these activities were captured. As such, the authors contend that their research helps rule out the assumption that paranormal phenomena are entirely neurological and rooted in hallucination. They conclude by pointing out some of the limitations of their study while providing recommendations for future research. A worthy article for anyone interested in obtaining a deeper dive into the realm of EMF and paranormal phenomena.

Wiseman, Richard, Watt, Caroline, & Greening, Emma. (2002, December). An investigation into the alleged haunting of Hampton Court Palace: Psychological variables and magnetic fields. *Journal of Parapsychology, 66*(4), 387–408.

Hampton Court is a palace in England that has gained a reputation for being one of the country's most haunted buildings. The researchers in this article set out to study whether eyewitness reports were influenced by suggestions, a personal belief in ghosts, and/or magnetic fields. The authors introduce the previous literature that has been done to determine correlations between paranormal belief and likelihood of interpreting events as paranormal. In this study, they used the notion of suggestion to tell participants certain areas of the castle had been a focus of paranormal activity; however, they varied the locations that they told certain participants to further test the suggestion theory. By testing magnetic fields, they sought to study whether geomagnetics could physiologically affect someone. Perhaps not surprisingly, they discovered that belief in the paranormal resulted in a higher probability of reporting something as a paranormal experience. In other words, those who labeled themselves believers reported feeling more paranormal activity than those who labeled themselves as nonbelievers. There was also a modest correlation between paranormal activity and magnetic fields, adding to the hypothesis that geomagnetic fields can alter someone physiologically. Suggestion, however, did not seem to be a significant factor in whether someone reported paranormal activity in this study. They conclude their study by calling for similar experiments in buildings with less robust reputations for being haunted. This article is one of many that juxtapose paranormal experience with belief in the paranormal and is an essential type of study for any researcher's paranormal toolkit.

Ufology

Bender, Bryan. (2019, April 23). U.S. Navy drafting new guidelines for reporting UFOs. *Politico*. Retrieved November 27, 2019, from https://www.politico.com/story/2019/04/23/us-navy-guidelines-reporting-ufos-1375290

In this recent newspaper article, staff reporter Bryan Bender outlines how the U.S. Navy is creating new guidelines for military personnel to document and report their encounters with unidentified aerial phenomena—now the preferred government term when referring to UFOs. The navy's impetus in doing so is due to an immense amount of personal experience but also as an attempt to help destigmatize these encounters and the subsequent reporting of them. These new guidelines help make the statement that the U.S. Navy acknowledges that its officers are highly trained, highly educated people who aren't likely to be making their eyewitness reports up *or* confusing them for known phenomena. It also helps set the stage for exploring these encounters rather than relegating them to some forgotten corner of those things we just don't talk about. This isn't, of course, the first time that the government has openly given support to inquiries of a more paranormal nature, but it is nevertheless worthy information for anyone researching the history of UFO reporting in the United States, especially as pertains to government response and involvement. This article also provides key terms, programs, and figures that can be researched for further information.

Cross, Anne Boyle. (2000). A confederacy of faith and fact: UFO research and the search for other worlds (Doctoral dissertation). Yale University. Retrieved from ProQuest Dissertation and Theses. (Document No. 304641753)

A dissertation from a doctor of philosophy student at Yale University, this work discusses UFO phenomena and its subsequent research. At 237 pages, this source is more akin to a book than a journal article. Cross discusses in this work how UFO research pushes against the intellectual status quo due to its unique combination of science and belief-based understandings. In her acknowledgments, Cross thanks UFO researcher Stanton Friedman and experiencer Betty Hill for their help with her work, along with members of MUFON and other UFO organizations. Clearly Cross has consulted some authority figures on this matter.

Beginning with her experience at a UFO conference in Roswell and building from her near immersion into the UFO community, Cross outlines here a worthy overview of UFO phenomena and its affiliated research and key figures. She not only discusses the sociological characteristics and qualities of ufology as a group of people and a movement, but she also outlines the research conducted in this field and presents it to the reader in an unbiased manner. Chapters 2 and 3 are entirely devoted to outlining the eyewitness reports, scholarly journals, research, theories, and scientists who have all played pivotal roles in ufology. What is particularly interesting about Cross's work is her inclusion of religion within her discussion, seen mainly through ufology's inclusion of mystical experiences and ideas of beings from beyond. This dissertation is full of personal interviews and reading more like a novel than a clinical exposé of some topic, and I highly recommend it to anyone wishing to learn more about ufology.

Dewan, William J. (2011, February 8). Occam's beard: Belief, disbelief, and contested meanings in American ufology (Doctoral dissertation). American Studies Electronic Theses & Dissertations. University of New Mexico Digital Repository. Retrieved November 27, 2019, from https://digitalrepository.unm.edu/amst_etds/10

This dissertation, at more than four hundred pages in length, represents approximately ten years' worth of investigation into this matter from author William Dewan. Similar to Cross's analysis of the UFO community above, Dewan dives deep into the New Mexico UFO community to research the ways in which this phenomenon has shaped, and continues to shape, a community. Above and beyond that, though, Dewan engages in a larger historical conversation about the rise of ufology in the United States and the many overlapping factors that contribute to our fascination with this subject. He discusses the Cold War paranoia that helped give rise to this fascination as well as the subsequent folklore of UFOs that permeates through to today. He also mentions scientific pursuits at understanding this phenomenon by organizations like SETI and more. A valuable resource for anyone specifically interested in New Mexico UFO history as well as anyone looking for a comprehensive discussion on UFOs in our broader cultural and social record.

Hynek, J. Allen. (1966). UFOs merit scientific study. *Science, 154*(3747), 329.

In the letters section of this 1966 publication of the journal *Science*, noted scientist J. Allen Hynek openly calls for more physical and social inquiry into UFOs. He acknowledges that a large quantity of UFO reports can be traced back to weather balloons, visual distortions, and so forth but points out that there still exists a number of UFO cases that cannot be traced back to any known source. And it is these cases that he draws upon as rationale for urging the scientific community to devote serious intellectual pursuits to this matter. He then breaks down some popular UFO myths, like the fact that, contrary to assumption, the majority of reports are made by those with no real or preexisting fascination with UFOs and that these people are not unstable or unreliable witnesses. He ends by telling readers, "I have begun to feel that there is a tendency in 20th-century science to forget that there will be a 21st-century science, and indeed, a 30th-century science, from which vantage points our knowledge of the universe may appear quite different. We suffer, perhaps, from temporal provincialism, a form of arrogance that has always irritated posterity." Any research of UFO phenomena would be remiss without the letters and works of J. Allen Hynek.

Poher, Claude, & Vallée, Jacques. (1975, January). Basic patterns in UFO observations. Paper presented at the AIAA 13th Aerosciences Meeting, Pasadena, CA.

Noted scholars and astrophysicists Dr. Claude Poher and Dr. Jacques Vallée presented this paper at the thirteenth meeting of the American Institute of Aeronautics and Astronautics. In this paper, they call for an organized scientific research process for investigating UFO reports. They begin by reviewing those things that can cause misidentification and then move on to discussing the curious reports of prolonged eyewitness encounters with objects at a very close range and the common characteristics surrounding those reports. They then discuss some demographics of the eyewitnesses before exploring all possible reasons that might explain known reasons for these encounters. They conclude by saying their analysis can be expanded to broader collections of eyewitness reports to help generate any patterns or further overlapping characteristics of UFO phenomena such as the ones they discuss here.

Ramet, Sabrina P. (1998). UFOs over Russia and Eastern Europe. *Journal of Popular Culture, 32*, 81–99. doi:10.1111/j.0022-3840.1998.3203_81.x

In this article, author Sabrina Ramet discusses the cases of UFO sightings in Russia and Eastern Europe from the 1940s and especially the number of reports that skyrocketed in 1989. Interestingly, she also discusses how Communism viewed UFO reports and how it was actually incorporated into political propaganda directed at capitalist countries—a unique entry, no doubt, to the UFO literature. She provides detailed case studies of prominent UFO reports, weaving the political history of this region of the world alongside throughout. She also discusses the surge of UFO enthusiast groups that cropped up, especially around 1989 when reports were coming in at an accelerated rate. She concludes by addressing possible explanations that have been brought forth as well as the many shows and publications that these sightings spawned in Soviet pop culture.

Swords, Michael D. (2006). Ufology: What have we learned? *Journal of Scientific Exploration, 20*(4), 545–589.

Michael D. Swords is an emeritus professor of environmental studies at Western Michigan University and penned this article to highlight the need for continued, serious inquiry into UFO phenomena while also reminding us that the field will not benefit from rigid conservative techniques but from open-minded, outside-the-box thinking. He begins by providing an overview of early scientific inquiry into UFOs, mentioning such key figures as Dr. J.

Allen Hynek and Dr. Jacques Vallée. He also comments on some prominent cases that arose in the 1950s and '60s before openly discussing his own personal UFO experience and the events that led him to become a personal believer in the phenomena—events that include government projects into UFO research. One section I particularly enjoy is the section where he attempts to break down what it means for someone to be an expert or authority on some topic—reminding us that nobody is, at any given time, privy to the knowledge of all phenomena and for that reason alone we shouldn't fall prey to intellectual hubris or assumption, especially regarding fringe topics that are so often easy to dismiss. Furthermore, he brings up how UFO phenomena can so easily meld into other arenas of the paranormal and openly discusses Bigfoot, Mothman, hallucinations, and other psychical phenomena, which brings an important point about not pigeonholing oneself within your research. This is a wonderful article to keep on hand not only for its overview of the UFO phenomena and research on this topic but also to consult as a trove of further reading. Any single page of this article would yield, even as a modest estimate, another twenty sources of information for the reader to consult.

Parapsychology

Alvarado, Carlos. (2014, Spring). Mediumship, psychical research, dissociation, and the powers of the subconscious mind. *Journal of Parapsychology, 78*(1), 98–114.

In this article, parapsychologist Carlos Alvarado presents a discussion of mediums and how some prominent psychical researchers believed them to possess supernormal abilities that allowed them to display psychical powers. Alvarado reminds us that any understanding of mediums should not overlook this theory espoused by researchers, many of whom were noted members of the Society for Psychical Research themselves, and whose theories and research helped promote the idea that the subconscious mind could enable people to display phenomenal abilities. Alvarado begins with a historical overview of psychical research, particularly the efforts of the SPR in its studies of mediums. He then discusses the individual efforts and research of select psychical researchers including Frederic W. H. Myers and Eduard von Hartmann before highlighting some special cases of mediums themselves, like Eusapia Palladino. A robust and detailed overview of the historical inquiry into mediumship, this article provides an almost endless supply of source materials, key figures, and further reading while providing a good entry point for anyone wishing to get their feet wet with mediumship and psychical research.

Avramidis, Stathis. (2013). Paranormal experience in a medico-swimming rescue: A case study. *Journal of Religion and Health, 52*(2), 408–417. doi:10.1007/s10943-011-9488-2

This article reviews the case of a young man who suffered a traumatic head injury while swimming. Before the accident, the young man had visited a monk who intuited that he might encounter some event and who anointed his head in the exact places where he became injured days later. Specifically this article investigates the impact that this paranormal event, a precognition of the monk, had on the recovery of the young man. The author, who has affiliations with the Hellenic Centre for Disease Control and Prevention in Greece, wished to study this as there appears to be a lack in the literature regarding how paranormal events may impact a person's recovery process. While this article does contain very religious themes and discussions, it remains a worthy addition to this list because it recognizes a gap in the literature and isn't afraid to tackle the question of how the paranormal might be tied into our physiological recovery processes.

Breen, Rosemary. (2019). The nature, incidence, impact and integration of spontaneous parapsychological experiences: An exploratory mixed methods research study (Master's thesis). Retrieved from Figshare. doi:10.26180/5c5d010e7528b.

This article, accessible via the BASE database discussed above, is a thesis written by a master of education candidate at Monash University in Australia. In this thesis, Breen discusses the overwhelming number of personal paranormal experiences that are reported—specifically reports of spontaneous parapsychological events such as déjà vu, telepathy, seeing an apparition, NDEs, psychokinesis, and more. However, given this abundance of eyewitness reports, she noted a lack of discussion in the scholarly literature about trends and patterns in spontaneous parapsychological events. Using a survey instrument, Breen collected more than three thousand reports from a total of fifty-nine different countries. In this survey, she collected data on the frequency of the experience and type of experience, as well as other data like the earliest age of onset with experience. Respondents not only filled out this questionnaire, but they were also given the opportunity to provide reflections on how these experiences affected them and/or their thoughts on potential reasons why they encountered these phenomena.

Of the things Breen discovered is that 80 percent of first encounters with a parapsychological event occurred in the respondent's childhood, thereby indicating that paranormal experience is not relegated to the realm of adulthood. Breen also discovered that people often experienced these phenomena more than once and that females tended to report experiences more often. Of the many different types of paranormal events quantified, the top three were déjà vu, premonitions, and apparitions. Her thesis also discusses recommendations for further research in addition to many other findings you can read in her report. Additionally, she spends a great deal of time discussing the juxtaposition of two dominant viewpoints of the paranormal: paranormal as entertainment (popular) and paranormal as research (scholarly). In the midst of this juxtaposition, Breen writes, is the unsure middle group—those who neither take a strong stance for or against the paranormal and who are the intended audience of her research. Within this thesis, Breen provides an immense amount of information not only on popular research (such as eyewitness accounts that abound online), but scholarly literature as well.

Kripal, Jeffrey. (2014, April). Visions of the impossible: How "fantastic" stories unlock the nature of consciousness. *Chronicle of Higher Education, 60*(29), 6–11.

A section on parapsychology would not be complete without at least one reference by distinguished researcher Jeffrey Kripal. Kripal, a professor at Rice University in Houston, Texas, researches many things including the intersection of consciousness, culture, and religion. In this essay, he discusses the importance of challenging a materialistic worldview while acknowledging the professional fear that many have of engaging in just that type of challenge. Kripal writes, for instance, of the many thousands of accounts of people seeing their departed loved ones and how these types of experiences are outright dismissed because they do not fall within a materialist worldview—a worldview that posits that the only "real" things matter. Kripal calls for academics and researchers to put these "extreme narratives" and "impossible stories" into the center of our focus once more—as perhaps we once did in the time of Plato and Aristotle. He argues that doing so will help reveal more about what we currently understand about human consciousness. He further argues that a reticence of investigating consciousness studies exists because we are perhaps afraid of what we might uncover, afraid of the implications our discoveries will have on our current materialist understandings of ourselves and our relation to the world. Explaining this essay is inherently a challenge; no summary can ever be as effective as Kripal's own style, but suffice it to say this essay is a necessary inclusion to the topic of consciousness studies and parapsychology.

May, Edwin. (2014, Spring). Star Gate: The U.S. government's psychic spying program. *Journal of Parapsychology, 78*(1), 5–18.

This article is an overview of the years that author Edwin May spent investigating and researching the various organizations with the U.S. government that spent money and time investigating psychical phenomena. In 1975, May himself was recruited, at the bequest of the U.S. government, to participate in the Stanford Research Institute and gather information on remote viewing for the agencies. May tells us that from 1972 to 1979 the aim of the Stanford Research Institute was to use extrasensory perception (such as remote viewing) to obtain information about the Soviet Union, the Eastern Bloc, and China. They also investigated psychical researching coming from the Soviet Union as well as conducted experiments themselves on the mechanics of ESP. In addition, the people in the program conducted remote viewing to aid in the gathering of such critical information as locating a kidnapped army general. Once the general was found, he reviewed the sketches of his whereabouts that the remote viewer had drawn and remarked that government officials should train their officers to think and project when they found themselves in dire circumstances to aid the potential remote viewers who might be working to rescue them. May also details some of the methods used by remote viewers and how those methods assisted government offices, and he spends a good deal of time outlining the various committees and offices that reviewed their procedures and performance. Full of diagrams, departmental memos, and detailed overviews of the specific ways in which ESP was sanctioned and used by the U.S. government, this article (and as such the larger topic discussed) is pertinent to any research on parapsychology.

Roll, William G., & Joines, William T. (2013). RSPK and consciousness. *Journal of Parapsychology, 77*(2), 192–211.

In this article, researchers William Roll and William Joines outline three cases of RSPK, or recurrent spontaneous psychokinesis. This phenomenon occurs when some object is moved without any apparent physical exertion from a human. In other words, no seeming explanation other than some undetected energetic force. The three cases discussed in this article focus on the poltergeist explanation for RSPK; in each of these cases, RSPK activity spiked in the presence of certain individuals. In one case, for example, one of the authors himself witnessed a kitchen table levitate and rotate about forty-five degrees before crashing down to the floor. One such theory proposed by the authors is that of zero-point energy, which is energy that remains when other energies are removed. In these cases, the authors noted that the effect of RSPK weakened the further the suspected individual moved from certain buildings and/or rooms, making them believe that somehow those persons affected electromagnetic fields by transferring that energy into kinetic energy. Furthermore, they noted that the activity usually abated when the suspected person was asleep, making them think that some sort of psychical phenomenon was also taking place. They also noticed that each person appeared to affect certain types of objects more than others—such as bottles or kitchen tables versus other items in the house or room. In their study, however, they found that each RSPK "agent" did not seem to emit curious amounts of electromagnetic energies, nor did there appear to be any geomagnetic upheavals to explain the movement of large objects. They conclude their study by postulating on psychometry, which is the practice of seeing past images or sensations based on the viewing or touching of an object. They also posit that further research on the emotional states of those experiencing RSPK is needed, as in all three cases, the RSPK "agents" were greatly disturbed by the phenomena.

Taylor, Jon. (2014, Spring). The nature of precognition. *Journal of Parapsychology, 78*(1), 19–38.

In this article, author Jon Taylor discusses one theory of precognition that uses the block universe model of understanding. This model proposes that all past and future events exist currently in the world via the space-time continuum. Also using David Bohm's theory of implicate order, Taylor proposes that precognition is a result of some quality already existing in brain functions and neural processes. In other words, he posits that precognition could be a result of someone tapping into a neural experience of their future self. The article discusses physicists and other scientists who support the block universe model and spends a great deal of time explaining the nuances of this model, especially in terms of enabling precognition. Taylor further dives into a discussion of quantum mechanics and introduces a further discussion of David Bohm's theory of implicate order and how it relates to past and future cognition before offering an overview of experiments that have been done to test these models and theories. This article will undoubtedly be one that readers may wish to read a few times over to fully comprehend or even consult other works that offer overviews of some of the theories and concepts discussed within; it is a truly fascinating overview and representative of a major school of thought regarding the nature of precognition, making it valuable for anyone wishing to more fully investigate precognition and psychical phenomena.

Watt, Caroline. (2014, Spring). Precognitive dreaming: Investigating anomalous cognition and psychological factors. *Journal of Parapsychology, 78*(1), 115–125.

Parapsychologist and researcher Dr. Caroline Watt takes a targeted look at the role that dreams play in precognition experiences. Reminding us that a majority of spontaneous precognition experiences involve dreams or those in-between stages of wake and slumber, Dr. Watt also realized that there was little research into the role that dreams play with precognition and developed a study to help fill this gap. Recognizing that people undoubtedly feel more comfortable sleeping in their own homes, Dr. Watt relied on the internet to conduct this study and had participants keep a dream diary and fill out questionnaires regarding their dreams and experiences. They were told to focus on a video that would later be sent to them and record their dreams leading up to the video. Their dream summaries and the video clips themselves were also rated for similarity by judges in a blind-review process. While there did appear to be a small correlation between dreams and precognition of video clips, Dr. Watt discusses factors of the study that may have complicated matters, which always sets the stage for further recommendations for research on this topic. This article, through its specific focus on dreams and its role in psychical phenomena, offers a unique perspective for researchers.

Zingrone, Nancy L., & Alvarado, Carlos S. (2019, Fall). On women in parapsychology. *Journal of Parapsychology, 83*(2), 286–289. doi:10.30891/jopar.2019.02.15

In this editorial to the *Journal of Parapsychology*, authors Zingrone and Alvarado remind readers of the long history, involvement, and contribution to psychical research by scores of female researchers. These female researchers, however, often get overlooked in the study of parapsychology, and this editorial attempts to rectify this lapse of awareness. Providing an immense amount of material and figures for further reading, this article is beneficial for any researcher of the paranormal because it sheds light on those populations that often get left out of the historical conversation—or, if they are included, who get shuffled to the side in favor of those in the dominant group. Unfortunately, I likely don't have to explain to readers that certain populations of people are often overlooked in the scholarly literature—especially the historical record, and this article will help anyone find those researchers who made great contributions even though they are a bit harder to find. In doing so, this article will help you become a more informed researcher; more importantly, it will help you become a more ethical, responsible researcher as well.

Reincarnation and Near-Death Experiences

Greyson, Bruce. (2014). Congruence between near-death and mystical experience. *International Journal for the Psychology of Religion, 24*(4), 298–310. doi:10.1080/10508619.2013.845005

Dr. Bruce Greyson is the former director of the University of Virginia's Division of Perceptual Studies, and in this article, he discusses the intersection of mystical experience and NDEs. Dr. Greyson begins his article by reminding readers that although mysticism is a union with divine reality, that doesn't necessarily mean God. It could mean a union with nature or the universe or even what some people coin "ultimate reality." He goes on to discuss some of the nine defining characteristics of a mystical experience as outlined by researchers in the 1970s, and how certain aspects of the NDE are similar to the mystical experience scale. Items on the mysticism scale, created by R. W. Hood in 1975, include such things as a feeling of cosmic unity, a sense of timelessness or lost time, overwhelming joy, and a profound feeling of sacredness.

Dr. Greyson set out to determine if, in fact, people who experience an NDE are more likely to also have mystical experiences. Using the mysticism scale, he administered a survey to NDE experiencers. he discovered that 66 percent of those with an NDE also showed scores within a range of experiencing a mystical encounter. Those people who were near death but did not report a specific NDE were also included in this study as a comparison group. Interestingly, zero respondents who were near death but did not have an NDE reported having any overlap on the mysticism scale. Moreover, gender, ethnicity, and religious affiliation did not appear to be significant factors in someone's mysticism scale. Dr. Greyson's study not only shows that there is a unique and intimate relationship between NDE and mystical experience, but it also calls for more inquiry into the transformative experience of NDEs that often cause people to become entirely different versions of themselves after the fact. This article highlights the fact that oftentimes certain paranormal phenomena can benefit from an intentionally mystical and spiritual inquiry.

Lake, James. (2016). The near-death experience: A testable neural model. *Psychology of Consciousness: Theory, Research, and Practice, 4*(1), 115–134.

Dr. James Lake, a psychiatrist at the University of Arizona College of Medicine, researched the NDE phenomenon and proposed a longitudinal study that specifically employs the use of EEGs and brain mapping. Dr. Lake begins by outlining the fact that there is not necessarily one agreed-upon definition of brain death, which automatically muddies the issue of medically capturing brain activity during NDEs. He continues by reviewing the definitions of a near-death experience as well as providing an overview of some NDE studies. Furthermore, he discusses that some events are labeled as NDEs when they technically shouldn't be and how certain functions like "syncretic cognition" could be what is occurring in a patient instead of a genuine NDE. Dr. Lake provides an overview of his models of NDE events through something known as connectomics—a concept that understands brain imaging and activity via complex systems theory. In other words, Dr. Lake posits that all types of sociocultural, biological, and psychological or physiological factors impact, at any given time, the ways in which our brains filter experiences and can result in all types of "phenomenal content" in moments of near death, fear of death, or even during dreaming. All of this raises the issue of NDE as something that can only happen in extreme, life-threatening experiences. Dr. Lake stresses that the brain must somehow be the culprit with NDEs since these events are not reported as frequently in those who suffer traumatic head injuries, and he calls for advanced research using brain imaging to help elucidate what we currently understand about NDEs. This article challenges the standard definition of an NDE, and it is important to intentionally seek out those articles that highlight alternate perspectives of theories. In other words, ensure that your research doesn't all fall into the same repeated theories—look for the novel or even the controversial intentionally.

van Lommel, Pim. (2013). Non-local consciousness: A concept based on scientific research on near-death experiences during cardiac arrest. *Journal of Consciousness Studies, 20*(1–2), 7–48.

Author Pim van Lommel is a doctor in the cardiology department of Rijnstate Hospital in the Netherlands. He states, at the very beginning of the article, that due to the long history of personal experiences, he comes to his research automatically acknowledging that NDEs are very real phenomena occurring in people. He further acknowledges that those who experience NDEs are permanently changed and different than the person they were prior to the event and that a materialist theory cannot provide adequate understanding into this phenomenon.

Dr. van Lommel is, in fact, one of the researchers who designed and carried out a seminal Dutch study on NDEs of cardiac arrest patients. In that study, they found that there appeared to be no medical reason why certain cardiac arrest patients near death experienced profound NDEs while others did not. In other words, it was not due to length of cardiac arrest, medication administered, presence or absence of intubation, or even a previous knowledge of the NDE phenomenon itself. They did discover, however, that cardiac arrest patients who experienced an NDE appeared, eight years later, to have pronounced positive attitudes on the afterlife and enhanced spirituality in general. This would seem to make sense, of course, for someone who almost died, but what van Lommel and colleagues also discovered is that these people had enhanced intuitive abilities that they often labeled directly as paranormal. These abilities included knowing when someone had taken ill or was about to die or sensing the emotions of those around them.

In addition to outlining the results of their longitudinal study, Dr. van Lommel also discusses NDE research from scholars around the world before diving into a discussion of some prominent theories surrounding the NDE phenomenon. In this section, however, he outlines how these dominant theories don't suffice—such as in the case of anoxia or a lack of oxygen. This is one prevailing theory behind NDEs, but it still doesn't hold up, Dr. van Lommel points out, in explaining why NDE experiencers report hyperawareness and consciousness.

Following these predominant theories, Dr. van Lommel goes into a very detailed outline of the different types of processes that occur in the brain during cardiac arrest. He does so, I believe, in an attempt to illustrate the conundrum of consciousness occurring in NDEs of cardiac arrest patients when the brain activity should not be allowing such activity to occur. He proceeds to engage in a discussion of how activities like mindfulness actually change the structure of our brains, giving further proof that our activities and emotions alter our physical brains and to highlight his point that consciousness increasingly appears to be independent from the brain. This article is a truly massive source of information; I highly recommend it to anyone wishing to have a more scientific and medical understanding of the nuances of NDEs, consciousness, and the brain.

Morse, Donald R. (2004). Near-death experiences: Modern examination, definition, historical precedents, personal, types, usual stages, cases, research, possible explanations. In Proceedings of Annual Conference, the Academy of Religion and Psychical Research, 113–132.

This article, presented at the annual conference of the Academy of Religion and Psychical Research, provides a wealth of information on the history of NDEs as well as case studies, research, and possible explanations. Dr. Morse begins by presenting a brief outline of the standard characteristics of a near-death experience before delving into a historical discussion of the phenomenon that begins in the fourth century BC with an account of a soldier who came back after death and who reported seeing souls traveling from Earth and into the heavens. What is notable about this article is that Dr. Morse includes international cases of NDEs, such as deloks or "death visionaries" of Tibet as well as additional detailed encounters from England, from France, and from the Native American culture as well. Following these international examples, he provides a personal report from someone who discovered that they were nowhere near death when they experienced their NDE. This gives further emphasis to Dr. Lake's article above that points out NDEs can occur in non-life-threatening events as well.

Following this unique case study, Dr. Morse provides a discussion of the major types of NDEs, as researched by noted scholar Dr. P. M. H. Atwater, and further follows this with the typical stages of an NDE. After outlining the typical stages of an NDE, he provides further cases of a more peculiar and unique nature, such as the NDE of a blind woman who was able to detail the clothing of people in the next room as she was clinically dead. Upon outlining these particularly notable cases, Dr. Morse provides an overview of research on NDEs, including some of the researchers already listed above. An interesting component of this article is the "theory" and "rebuttal" section that follows next in which Dr. Morse deconstructs some of the dominant theories of NDEs and the weaknesses of those theories. Though this article is not as lengthy as some of the others in this section, it nonetheless provides an overwhelming amount of information and is especially helpful for the beginning researcher interested in establishing a foundational understanding of NDEs.

Cryptozoology

Dendle, Peter. (2006, August). Cryptozoology in the medieval and modern worlds. *Folklore, 117*(2), 190–206. doi:10.1080/00155870600707888

In this article, scholar Peter Dendle includes a vast number of references to cryptozoological encounters across the globe, and he investigates the social and cultural constructs surrounding the importance of cryptozoology in our lives. He argues that belief in undiscovered creatures is one of the oldest rituals that humans engage in and through which they create cultural boundaries and define safe spaces. Above and beyond a mere philosophical argument, however, Dendle reminds us that the field of cryptozoology is more than just symbolism through which cultures define spaces. He writes, "There are, of course, new species that remain to be discovered, and early reports of them will naturally appear folkloric before a specimen is secured and the scientific community can verify it."

Following his introduction in which he briefly outlines the long history of cryptozoological belief and encounters, Dendle provides a more detailed exposé of cryptozoological inquiry in the medieval world, specifically focusing on how cryptid folklore was often interpreted as moral symbolism. He then moves onto a discussion of cryptozoology in the modern world—a time marked not only by vast exploration and expansion that brought an assumption of knowledge of all species but one that also eventually bore a guilt over decimation of species and habitats. Specifically, Dendle argues that modern cryptozoology serves to alleviate some of the guilt we feel as modern humans who have caused the extinction of many species. It also, however, serves to reignite that frontier spirit that seems so distant and foreign to modern humans. Furthermore, it offers a venue to push back against the status quo—in this case, the academic and scientific status quo, which so often dominates what are and are not acceptable beliefs and pursuits.

This article is beneficial because not only does it include a robust number of references to cryptozoological encounters, works, and notable figures, but it also helps philosophically outline the reasons why cryptozoology attracts certain researchers. Dendle ends his article by saying that cryptozoology is an important topic because it "represents a quest for magic and wonder in a world many perceive as having lost its mystique." This article will help you understand some of the foundational motivations for cryptozoological research; it also highlights the very real divide that exists between these researchers and those elsewhere in the academic community. Being aware of the tensions and conflicts that exist in this field is extremely important.

Hillary, Edmund. (1960, January 24). Abominable—and improbable? *The New York Times*. ProQuest Historical Newspapers.

This newspaper article is a primary source document that outlines the experiences of members of Sir Edmund Hillary's expedition team when traversing through the Himalayan Mountains. Hillary outlines the time that his team member encountered a strange tuft of hair only to have it snatched out of his hand and thrown off the side of the mountain by a superstitious Sherpa. Additionally, he discusses the time that other team members encountered strange footprints in the snow in a region where later hikers encountered additional strange footprints. This is a unique newspaper article detailing the experience of a firsthand mountain climber in the Himalayas and the strange experiences encountered therein. Newspaper articles such as this one are often rife with personal experiences and can be a great place to uncover additional primary source material that often gives nuanced details and vignettes of experiences that secondary research just doesn't capture.

Meldrum, Jeff. (2016). Sasquatch & other wildmen: The search for relict hominoids. *Journal of Scientific Exploration, 30*(3), 355–373.

This article is a transcript of a presentation given at the 2016 Meeting of the Society for Scientific Exploration. Dr. Jeff Meldrum, an anthropology professor at Idaho State University, begins his speech by discussing the problematic connotations brought forth by the word "Bigfoot," which is so often reminiscent of tabloids, and arguing for the need for researchers to shift their language to help separate their research from being lumped in with urban legends, stories, and tabloid fodder. He specifically focuses on the use of the word "relict" in relation to the phrase "relict hominoid" and then provides an overview of how dominant scientific theories of the 1950s and '60s prevented a serious inquiry into the work of cryptozoologists like Ivan Sanderson, who researched unknown human species, and furthermore discusses how it wasn't until the 1970s that this dominant scientific worldview was shaken. Dr. Meldrum tells us that now we recognize more than twenty-five species of hominin and that the scientific community continues to expect more discovery and revelation on this matter. At one point Dr. Meldrum tells us that "these discoveries confirm that we shared the landscape with other hominin species until only a few thousand years ago—or perhaps even into the present." He goes on to point out how the recent discovery of *Homo flore-*

siensis jolted the anthropological community and how the premier journal *Nature* quoted paleoanthropologists who mused that this discovery shifts the tabloidesque nature of Bigfoot mythology from something entertaining to something with a very high scientific probability.

Dr. Meldrum continues his essay by discussing how, even amid such discoveries and prominent journal publications, there still exists an intense academic skepticism on this matter. The remainder of his essay discusses what is, to him, the largest body of evidence for further relict hominoids: footprints. He goes into great detail outlining those that he has studied and discovered before concluding his speech by urging researchers to continue their explorations. This article not only contains a large amount of further reading and events and people to research further, but it also provides a good historical background of the scientific pursuits of cryptozoology.

Opit, Gary. (2017). Citizen science and cryptozoology: Data received from listeners during 18 years of wildlife talkback on ABC north coast New South Wales local radio. *Australian Zoologist, 38*(3), 430–456. doi:10.7882/az.2016.008

In 1997, a local radio station in New South Wales, Australia, began a citizen scientist endeavor to try to determine public interest in local wildlife. What began as an inquiry to determine the level at which local citizens were active in and interested about Australian wildlife turned into an effort that spanned eighteen years. In those eighteen years, callers discussed 342 unique species of wildlife that indicated there was indeed a large amount of interest in the wildlife of the area. Something else that occurred, though, is that callers also reported encounters with unknown or extinct species of wildlife. Some of these were emails instead of phone calls, but contained information on the location and time of the sighting, as well as a description of the animal and any observations about its behavior, making for a quick and easy way to map these odd sightings. In total, 117 reports came in of animals that could not be identified by either the callers or the wildlife experts, including twenty specific reports of an animal similar to a gorilla. The article even contains photos and eyewitness drawings submitted by those calling or emailing with these encounters. Interestingly, this very effort resulted in the discovery of a larvae beetle thought to have been extinct. This article contains a vast amount of information not only on the specific 117 cases of unknown animals reported to this radio station, but also in the field of Australian cryptozoology in general. It also provides an example of how dismissing eyewitness reports could have resulted in the continued ignorance of a once believed extinct species and is a great entry point for anyone wishing to learn more about cryptozoology, especially those interested in Australia.

Regal, Brian. (2008). Amateur versus professional: The search for Bigfoot. *Endeavor, 32*(2), 53–57. doi:10.1016/j.endeavour.2008.04.005

This article, much like the above article from Peter Dendle, helps readers understand the tension that exists (both historically and still today) between some academics regarding the field of cryptozoology. More importantly, however, author Brian Regal provides an overview of the early cryptozoologists like Bernard Heuvelmans, Grover Krantz, and Ivan Sanderson. He discusses those researchers who literally took to the fields and mountains looking for evidence of creatures reported in the many eyewitness encounters. Regal also discusses the early role of amateur researchers and naturalists who, due to a lack of professional organization, training, and simply as a result of their time, became the well-respected scientists of their day. When scientific organizations and academic institutions, however, blossomed onto the scene, these naturalists were scorned and dismissed due to their lack of professional training and education, thus setting the stage, Regal argues, for the tension that exists between more mainstream academics and those researchers who kept the cryptozoological torch flaming. Regal discusses how these researchers attempted to work alongside and get the attention of their more mainstream colleagues but were often met with scorn and skepticism and outright dismissal, albeit in light of a few exceptions. Regal goes on to discuss the specific case of Grover Krantz, who was a professor of anthropology at Washington State University, and who began gathering and collecting cryptozoological specimens in a hunt to link these creatures with the evolutionary history of mankind. Regal ends by commenting on the still-present divide that exists within this field today, but his article nonetheless provides a multitude of resources for further reading as well as an overview of the divisive history of this field.

Regal, Brian. (2009, January). Entering dubious realms: Grover Krantz, science, and Sasquatch. *Annals of Science, 66*(1), 83–102. doi:10.1080/00033790802202421

Another entry from Brian Regal, a professor of history at Kean University in New Jersey. In this article, Regal provides an in-depth overview of the work of noted cryptozoologist Grover Krantz. His specific goal, however, is to highlight Krantz's work through an anthropological lens. Regan begins by informing us that even through Krantz sought to research the existence of creatures like Bigfoot, he was snubbed by amateur researchers as well as those in the academic community and relates that this could perhaps be due to his own criticism of those aforementioned amateurs. Regal even mentions some of these tense encounters between Krantz and his Bigfoot-enthusiast colleagues. Regal then moves on to a discussion of the birth of naturalism and the subsequent focus on cryptozoology in the 1950s and '60s onwards before delving specifically into Krantz's work. He provides an overview of the evidence that Krantz gathered along with his predominant thoughts and theories on Sasquatch specifically. Regal additionally reviews some of the criticism to Krantz's work and the methods that Krantz employed to promote his research, since he was largely rejected by the academic community. Some of these tactics included presenting at nonacademic conferences and appearing on television shows. Offering an abundance of additional reading, this article provides an interesting biographic vignette of one of cryptozoology's noted researchers.

Schembri, Elise. (2011, Fall). Cryptozoology as a pseudoscience: Beasts in transition. *Studies by Undergraduate Researchers at Guelph,* 5(1), 5–10.

In this article, author Elise Schembri explores how the field of cryptozoology resides in a gray area between mainstream, accepted research and pseudoscience. She outlines some of the reasons why the field has not penetrated the mainstream science market—like the fact that many people just assume that all cryptozoologists do is search for the two most infamous cryptids, Bigfoot and Nessie, and that there can't possibly be anything beyond this fact. She also discusses the importance for it to be separated from simply dumping it into the field of folklore. In addition, she provides an overview of key figures in cryptozoological research as well as prominent works and research. She further goes on to discuss certain discoveries that would lend a more openminded reception to cryptozoology, such as the discovery in 2003 of nearly a thousand unknown islands near Indonesia or the estimates from marine scientists that there are thousands, if not millions, of undiscovered species in the world's oceans. She spends a bit of time talking about the public's awareness and perception of cryptozoology as well as how it sometimes gets confused with paracryptozoology—the search for mythical creatures like unicorns and dragons. This article sheds light on the struggles that the field of cryptozoology faces and the inherent biases that many have toward it.

Astrology, Divination, and Magic

Bruckerl, Frank. (2013, Autumn). The Quaker cunning folk: The astrology, magic, and divination of Philip Roman and sons in colonial Chester County, Pennsylvania. *Pennsylvania History: A Journal of Mid-Atlantic Studies,* 80(4), 479–500.

Author Frank Bruckerl begins this article by reminding us that while much attention is given to Salem, Massachusetts, as the witch capital of the United States, many lose sight that there also existed early magic practitioners in Pennsylvania known as cunning folk—people who engaged in mystical practices and who also drew the scorn of judges, magistrates, and their communities. He goes on to discuss the specific case of Philip Roman and his two sons, Robert and Philip Jr. In November 1695, Robert was investigated on claims of engaging in astrology, geomancy, necromancy, and chiromancy (palmistry). His father became the target of inquiry and suspicion as well, and Bruckerl outlines all of this in great detail in this article. Offering a unique case study that investigates the esoteric practices of one prominent family of Chester County, Pennsylvania, this article provides a wonderful vignette regarding early American attitudes and perceptions toward esoteric practices and provides many references for further reading.

Buck, Stephanie. (2018). Hiding in plain sight: Jung, astrology, and the psychology of the unconscious. *Journal of Analytical Psychology, 63*(2), 207–227.

This article delves into Jung's fascination with the occult and in particular with astrology. Jung believed that astrology proved effective via its usage of symbolism, a belief bolstered by his own personal experiences with the occult. Author Stephanie Buck posits that certain occult practices, specifically astrology, played a large role in helping Jung develop his theories of the unconscious mind. Buck discusses, in particular, how Jung used astrological natal charts alongside his own clinical practices to help develop his notions on synchronicity, though Buck goes on to mention that Jung did not publicly discuss this method as much due to a fear of ridicule, a concern that can be ferreted out in his letters and correspondence to friends. Even though Jung eventually began to openly discuss the ways in which occult sciences and practices can help inform modern understandings of fields like psychology, his initial reticence represents an attitude that still exists today when it comes to discussing so-called fringe ideas or concepts. Buck points out that there still seems to be a hesitancy to openly discuss Jung's involvement with the occult, and specifically with astrology—something she finds puzzling given what we know about the dynamic symbolism that exists within astrology. This article does a good job not only outlining the ways in which Jung embraced occult concepts but also in highlighting the tension that still exists today when fringe topics make their way into the intellectual arena.

Crockford, Susannah. (2018). A Mercury retrograde kind of day: Exploring astrology in contemporary New Age spirituality and American social life. *Correspondences, 6*(1), 47–75.

Author Susannah Crockford spent two years engaging in participant observation in Arizona to study astrology as a divinatory art, and how in certain communities it actually adds to social capital. Crockford begins by outlining the general reception of astrology in American culture while also highlighting some prominent works by other researchers, especially those who have investigated it from a social perspective. Crockford herself aims to combine esoteric theories alongside anthropological ones to reveal a more nuanced understanding of the role of astrology within the Sedona, Arizona, community. She discovered that within this community, astrology was widely accepted as having its own truths, complete with its own set of worldviews, not necessarily unlike what you might find in religious systems. In other words, it has its own knowledge and "truths" that are widely accepted by its proponents. She also discusses the role that rejected knowledge plays in fostering this community—how astrology as a divinatory practice pushes back against that which is accepted by elites and openly embraces that which is "Other" or which is outright rejected. The article serves as a tool for people to enhance or foster their own spiritual journeys, and she concludes by stressing the importance of analyzing this topic from an ethnographic perspective to continue to highlight the very real impact and social capital that astrology has in certain communities.

Karl, Alexis Palmer. (2019, July). Frankincense: Scent of the spirit realm. *Perfumer & Flavorist, 44*(7), 1–6.

This article provides a historical overview of the ways in which frankincense has been used (and continues to be used) in ritual, magical practices. Karl's discussion spans millennia around the globe and also includes a discussion on how and where it is harvested. Also included in this resource are references to books that outline frankincense's use in ritual as well as references for further reading. A short article, but a worthy entry for anyone wishing to have a specific look inside components of ritual. I also include this article to remind readers that relevant information on paranormal aspects can even be found in a publication like *Perfumer & Flavorist*.

A perfect complement to this article is another entry by Karl titled "Grimoires and the Magic of Scent," which can be found in the October 2018 issue of this same journal. In this article, Karl explores how certain fragrances play a role in occult rituals, and outlines specific rituals to show the ways in which fragrances were used and for what purposes.

Larson, Paul. (2019). Psychological assessment and divination: Some parallels of process. *Humanistic Psychologist, 47*(1), 76–91. doi:10.1037/hum0000109

Author Paul Larson, of the Chicago School of Professional Psychology, outlines here some parallels between divination practices and more clinical avenues of psychological assessment. Pointing out that divination practices often involve assisting someone with decision-making processes and/or personal guidance, Larson juxtaposes this with the practices in psychological assessment, specifically in the "complex process of interpreting the signs that convey meaning about relevant factors," and the "nature of a healing relationship" between giver and receiver. Larson dives into an exploration of divination practices and their parallels to psychological methods. Offering great insight into the similarities between mainstream psychology and esoteric practices, this article helps shine a light on the positive psychological impacts that divination practices have on people.

Olbert, Charles Mason. (2018). Divination practices: An empirical psychological investigation (Doctoral dissertation). Retrieved from ProQuest Dissertations and Theses, 1–517.

At more than five hundred pages, Olbert provides an exhaustive discussion of the psychology at play in engaging in tarot as a divinatory practice. Olbert begins his work with a discussion on the importance of analyzing topics, no matter how far they exist on the fringe, from a psychological perspective because "knowing what people do and why they do it helps us understand, however incrementally, what it means to be, to know, and experience the world and oneself as a human being." Olbert further reminds us that virtually every society has engaged in divinatory practices and so, among other reasons, it should not be so flippantly dismissed as worthy of academic pursuit and as a powerful mechanism through which people derive great meaning and significance. He provides a great overview of the history of tarot cards, including how these cards have been used throughout the centuries by various people in regard to divination and magical practices.

Olbert's study specifically looks at the link between tarot and psychotherapy and looks not only at those who practice tarot but also those who seek it out. Using ethnographic methods such as in-depth interviews and participant observation, Olbert provides us with detailed case studies of the ways in which tarot impacts both providers and recipients. A deep dive into the psychological processes at play during tarot practices, this work is a great addition to anyone's research list on divination, especially those interested in tarot.

Young, Francis. (2019). The dissolution of the monasteries and the democratisation of magic in post-Reformation England. *Religions, 10*(4), 1–10. doi:10.3390/rel10040241

In this article, author Francis Young discusses how the dissolution of monasteries in sixteenth-century England resulted in occult and arcane knowledge shifting from the once sole proprietary of clergy and monasteries to the possession of the general public. This was a result of monastic libraries being disbanded as well, and the subsequent dispersal of the works included in these libraries. This also resulted in the emergence of what are referred to as cunning men and women—lay practitioners, in other words, who began to study these occult texts and practice magic themselves. It transformed magical practice from a secret or illicit activity into one that people made genuine livings from. Young provides an overview of some monastic libraries as well as some examples of how clergy engaged with magic and to what ends—one story, for example, discusses a Yorkshire abbot who engaged with magical practices in the hopes of locating the body of his brother who had been presumed dead by way of drowning. Young also mentions how alchemy and astrology were magical practices consulted and engaged in by monks across England and references additional key studies that have analyzed these topics. Young's article is ensconced in the greater discussion of how these things all worked together to facilitate the "democratisation" of magic throughout England. A relevant article for anyone wishing to learn more about English magical history, and especially the ways in which monasteries played a role.

Occult and Other Paranormal

Brooks, Alison Wood, Schroeder, Juliana, Risen, Jane L., Gino, Francesca, Galinsky, Adam D., Norton, Michael I., & Schweitzer, Maurice E. (2016, November). Don't stop believing: Rituals improve performance by decreasing anxiety. *Organizational Behavior and Human Decision Processes, 137*, 71–85. doi:10.1016/j.obhdp.2016.07.004

Since much occult practice is steeped in ritual, it is beneficial to seek out what experts may have discovered about the physiological role that ritual plays in our lives. In this article, the researchers discover that engaging routinely in ritual helps to decrease anxiety, and in fact, they state that engaging in a ritual practice is more effective than other strategies at calming oneself. They note a seeming lack of research into this topic and set out to fill the gap in this literature. Along the way, they posit that ritual engagement also facilitates an enhanced level of performance through reducing anxiety—in other words, if you are nervous about delivering a speech or playing in a football match, ritual can actually help you perform better, not just simply calm you down. For the purposes of their study, ritual was an activity that involved a set routine of steps and which was performed habitually. Using a sample size of four hundred study participants, they asked half to engage in particular rituals before completing the task of singing "Don't Stop Believing" in front of a group of strangers. They discovered that those who participated in ritual performed better and reported less anxiety.

I include this article for a number of reasons. First, it illustrates that even information that isn't necessarily paranormal in nature (in fact, the words "paranormal" or "occult" don't show up anywhere in this article) can still be relevant to your paranormal research. It is a weakness to think that all information has to be paranormal for it to be relevant to some paranormal topic of inquiry. Second, it highlights how engaging in magical practices, via ritual, impacts a person physiologically; engaging in magic ritual has very real and tangible outcomes. This isn't to say, of course, that these are the only outcomes that matter because they are tangible; it simply goes to show that nonparanormal literature and research are relevant to paranormal inquiry.

Ellis, Eugenia Victoria. (2007, April). Ancient mathematical origins of modern day occult practices. Paper presented at the Popular Culture Association Conference, Boston, MA. Retrieved November 27, 2019, from https://idea.library.drexel.edu/islandora/object/idea:1855

In this article, Ellis discusses the magical roots in the iconology of certain concepts and games that exist today such as Sudoku and feng shui. Sudoku, she tells us, is rooted in the ancient concept of the magic square, a Chinese belief that originated more than two thousand years ago. She further reminds us that the magic square also shows up in other cultures and that in its ancient Hebrew iteration the magic square was completed with letters of the alphabet, each of which correspond to a certain number (so that each row could be added to the same desired number) but through which would also create the spelling of a magical name. Ellis goes on to discuss the ways in which these magic squares were used to communicate with the divine and also used as talismans and protective charms. She tells us that beginning in the sixteenth century, we see a breakdown of the magical qualities of these squares due to the burgeoning influence of Western rationalism that results in the magic square being relegated to nothing more than entertaining mathematical endeavors. Further information is included on ancient magical texts and other ways in which mathematical processes are rooted in magical practices, offering a unique insight into activities we likely give very little thought to today.

Geoghegan, Bernard Dionysius. (2015, September). Occult communications: On instrumentation, esotericism, and epistemology. *Communication+1, 4*(1), 1–12.

This article, quite different from those before it, is an annotated bibliography of resources on the cultural context of occult practices and experience. Similar to what I'm doing here, author Geoghegan presents a list of articles along with a summary of their topics and main points. Specifically, Geoghegan has identified a core group of articles that he believes represent a good starting point to understand the cultural context and histories of occult beliefs, practices, and experiences. Some of these sources appear quite critical of occultism, but that is yet another point to consider when doing ethical research—it is often a good idea to intentionally seek out that which provides the opposite argument for something because the "truth" (if truth can ever really be identified in any field, let alone the paranormal) often lies somewhere in the middle. Of course, you always want to analyze any potential biases to ensure that your articles are not being unduly and unfairly influenced, but my point remains that it is a good idea to learn what the critics are saying as well. Some of the articles Geoghegan outlines here talk about women's rights in relation to the spiritualism movement of the nineteenth century, trance and mediumship, occult philosophies dominant in the Elizabethan era, and more. These resources are a combination of articles as well as books. You may find other resources that are annotated bibliographies just like this one; these resources help to essentially connect you with relevant resources so that you don't have to do the digging yourself. As such, these types of resources help save you time and energy, though you shouldn't use them as a comprehensive accounting of your topic, much the same way that I caution you here in assuming that my work is a comprehensive treatment. Nonetheless, these annotated bibliographies are great tools for connecting you with relevant sources quickly.

Morrisson, Mark S. (2008, Winter). The periodical culture of the occult revival: Esoteric wisdom, modernity and counter-public spheres. *Journal of Modern Literature, 31*(2), 1–22.

Author Mark S. Morrisson of Pennsylvania State University discusses occult periodicals that cropped up in the early 1900s during a period known as the occult revival. This was a time that saw a large, renewed interest in hermeticism, magical practices, and ritual. Morrisson also points out that occultists of this time period valued being viewed as modern—less secretive, perhaps, and this time period created the perfect storm of a previous secretive mentality that was shifting to one that wished to engage openly in public conversation and discourse, partly due perhaps to advances in print culture's mass production. As a result, occultists established periodicals to help disseminate their ideas and philosophies. Other reasons for the creation of these new print periodicals, Morrisson states, was to help raise awareness of emerging occult organizations as well as to help "legitimize occult knowledge in the dominant public sphere." Of course, scholars point out that these periodicals often engaged in sanitizing occult knowledge to help place them in line with the dominant scientific narratives and publications. This tactic makes sense if these publications were attempting to find their seat at the table and appeal to the masses. Morrisson provides an immense amount of information on these occult periodicals—all references that can be used to locate additional information, which is indeed the dominant reason I highlight this article. Furthermore, the historical overview on the history of occult periodicals helps promote an understanding of the plight of researchers engaging in occult studies—a plight that perhaps helped set the stage for locating occult research today.

Winslade, J. Lawton. (2000, Summer). Techno-kabbalah: The performative language of magick and the production of occult knowledge. *Drama Review, 44*(2), 84–100.

In this article, author J. Lawton Winslade begins by discussing the notion of a "media golem," or a situation in which occult language and knowledge are played out to unsuspecting audiences via media avenues. He begins by using examples from the popular television show *The X-Files*, using this as a jumping-off point to discuss the ways in which technology helps promote and distribute occult philosophies. Part of the process is also the ways in which audiences interpret these performances laced with occult references, and in this vein, he argues how this gives rise to a new form of technomagic. Specifically, Winslade discusses how technology and media intentionally present half-truths and partial pictures of occult information as a way to lure people into learning more. He further examines the pervasive reality of accessing and interacting with occult information—for example, the internet is the go-to place now to locate, find, and interact with all types of occult information. It's certainly not the only place to locate information and shouldn't ever be treated as such, but it has nevertheless created vast opportunities for occult information to be as accessible as possible to as many people as possible, thus beginning to blur the lines between technology as medium and technology as magical tool. This theory of technomancy is a useful one to at least be aware of in your own occult research.

The articles listed here are by no means exhaustive. They simply represent a core sampling of what you will be able to find in the databases and journals listed at the beginning of this chapter. I attempt to represent seminal researchers and/or studies as well, to help provide you with core citations to track down and jump-start your research from. Remember that the databases and journals I list here are not an exhaustive review of the available sources you can consult to find information on any number of paranormal topics. Don't be afraid to branch out to databases and journals not listed in this work. Your research will benefit from an intentional combination of different types of articles—newspaper articles, scholarly articles, blog posts, magazine articles, and so forth. The important part of research is how you are able to coalesce all that you have learned from a variety of sources—not that you've only consulted the most premier, academic sources.

Also keep in mind that libraries can help you locate those articles that aren't immediately available in a database. Quite often databases include citations to articles but not the full text of the article itself. This can seem frustrating, but your local libraries can help track these down for you. Wouldn't you rather know that your librarians can obtain these items for you rather than not knowing they ever existed in the first place? Don't make it harder for yourself to find relevant material from the start—uncheck those "full-text only" options when you're searching in databases!

NOTES

1. Victorian Popular Culture. (n.d.). Nature and scope—Spiritualism, sensation, and magic. Retrieved October 21, 2019, from http://www.victorianpopularculture.amdigital.co.uk/Introduction/NatureAndScope/Spiritualism

2. EBSCO. (n.d.-a). Academic Search Premier: Magazines and journals. Retrieved October 25, 2019, from https://www.ebscohost.com/titleLists/aph-journals.htm

3. EBSCO. (n.d.-b). America: History and life. Retrieved October 25, 2019, from https://www.ebsco.com/products/research-databases/america-history-and-life

4. Bielefeld University Library. (2019). What is BASE? Retrieved November 27, 2019, from https://www.base-search.net/about/en/index.php

5. Miscellaneous: Committee for the Scientific Investigation of Claims of the Paranormal. 1977–1978. TS Box 797, Folder 15, Item 1219, Years of expansion, 1950–1990: Series 3: Subject files: Freedom of belief, expression, and association, 1939–1988. Mudd Library, Princeton University. *American Civil Liberties Union Papers, 1912–1990*. Retrieved October 25, 2019, from Gale Primary Sources.

6. McPherson, Joyce. (2016, April). Reconciling Doyle's paradox: Sherlock Holmes and the work of the Society for Psychical Research. *VIJ: Victorians Institute Journal*, 1–9.

7. ProQuest. (2019). About ProQuest Dissertations and Theses Global. Retrieved November 27, 2019, from https://search.proquest.com/pqdtglobal/productfulldescdetail?accountid=11654

8. ProQuest. (n.d.). PsycARTICLES. Retrieved October 25, 2019, from https://www.proquest.com/products-services/psycarticles-set-c.html

9. EBSCO. (n.d.-c). SocINDEX. Retrieved October 25, 2019, from https://www.ebsco.com/products/research-databases/socindex

10. Hanks, Michele. (2019). Haunted objects: English paranormal investigation and the material mediation of doubt. *Nova Religio: The Journal of Alternative & Emergent Religion, 22*(4), 60–74.

11. Victorian Popular Culture. (2019). Introduction to Victorian popular culture. Retrieved October 25, 2019, from http://www.victorianpopularculture.amdigital.co.uk/

12. John Wiley & Sons. (2019). Overview. Retrieved October 29, 2019, from https://onlinelibrary.wiley.com/page/journal/20448295/homepage/productinformation.html

13. Academy for Spiritual and Consciousness Studies. (n.d.-b). The Journal of ASCSI. Retrieved November 7, 2019, from https://ascsi.org/the-journal-of-ascsi/

14. Pandarakalam, James Paul. (2017). Understanding introvertive visions and extrovertive apparitions. *Journal for Spiritual and Consciousness Studies, 40*(2), 127.

15. American Psychological Association. (2019). Journal of Abnormal Psychology. Retrieved October 29, 2019, from https://www.apa.org/pubs/journals/abn/

16. ITHAKA. (2019). The Journal of American Folklore. Retrieved October 29, 2019, from https://www.jstor.org/journal/jamerfolk

17. Rojcewicz, Peter M. (1987). The "men in black" experience and tradition: Analogues with the traditional devil hypothesis. *Journal of American Folklore, 100*(396), 148–160. doi:10.2307/540919

18. HathiTrust. (n.d.). About. Retrieved October 29, 2019, from https://www.hathitrust.org/about

19. International Association for Near-Death Studies. (2019). Journal of Near-Death Studies. Retrieved October 29, 2019, from https://iands.org/research/publications/journal-of-near-death-studies.html

20. Drinkwater, Ken, Dagnall, Neil, & Bate, Lauren. (2013). Into the unknown: Using interpretative phenomenological analysis to explore personal accounts of paranormal experiences. *Journal of Parapsychology, 77*(2), 281–294.

21. Society for Psychical Research. (2018). Journal of the Society for Psychical Research. Retrieved November 7, 2019, from https://www.spr.ac.uk/publications-recordings/journal-society-psychical-research

22. Paranthropology. (n.d.). Retrieved November 7, 2019, from http://paranthropologyjournal.weebly.com/

23. Oxford University Press. (2019). Sociology of Religion. Retrieved November 7, 2019, from https://academic.oup.com/socrel/pages/About

24. Baker, Joseph O., Bader, Christopher D., & Mencken, F. Carson. (2016). A bounded affinity theory of religion and the paranormal. *Sociology of Religion, 77*(4), 334–335.

25. Eaton, Marc A. (2015). "Give us a sign of your presence": Paranormal investigation as a spiritual practice. *Sociology of Religion, 76*(4), 389–390.

26. Supernatural Studies Association. (n.d.). About the association. Retrieved November 14, 2019, from https://www.supernaturalstudies.com/home

27. Bekavac, Luka. (2018). Spectra of transcommunication: A survival study after Raudive and Derrida. *Supernatural Studies, 5*(1), 12–13.

28. Discover. (n.d.). About the magazine. Retrieved November 14, 2019, from http://discovermagazine.com/magazine/about

29. Bhattacharjee, Yudhijit. (2012). Paranormal psychologist. *Discover, 33*(2), 52–58.

30. Phelan, Matthew. (2019). The casual observers. *Popular Science, 291*(3), 10–11.

31. American Association for the Advancement of Science. (2019). About science and AAAS. Retrieved November 14, 2019, from https://www.sciencemag.org/about/about-science-aaas?_ga=2.144028913.559877453.1573768825-485187692.1573768825

Chapter Ten

The UK's Intimate History with the Paranormal

Magic, Case Studies from the Society for Psychical Research, Special Collections, and Notable Paranormal Locations

In this chapter, I provide an overview of paranormal collections, hotspots, magical practices, and paranormal inquiry in the United Kingdom. Any conversation about the paranormal is remiss without a chapter dedicated entirely to the United Kingdom, since, as we know by now, the history of paranormal research can be traced directly back to our friends across the pond. Additionally, I insert a bit more "magic" in this chapter by providing an overview of magical practices in the United Kingdom—an area of the world that has a long and rich history of folk magic and practices that continue to this day. It is so entwined in the fabric of this region that any discussion of any paranormal subtopic would be remiss without even the most basic reference to this fact.

To facilitate the discussion in this chapter, some seminal works provided a ready font of information, and I encourage readers to consult these for more information. Renée Haynes's 1982 overview of the history of the Society for Psychical Research (SPR) and Owen Davies's work *The Haunted: A Social History of Ghosts* help craft a large portion of the discussion in this chapter. These works help us understand both the sociological and folk history of magic and the paranormal alongside the scientific inquiries that cropped up in the late nineteenth century. In chapter 2, I outlined the history of the SPR, and while I include them in this chapter as well, it is only to highlight some unique and fascinating tales from their timeline.

In addition to the history of magic and notable cases of the SPR, I also include an overview of additional societies and collections concerning the paranormal in the UK. At the end of this chapter I include some brief discussions of paranormal hotspots located across the UK. Throughout this work I reference multiple peoples and events that emerge from the UK, so it should come as no surprise that this area of the world is steeped in magic. By the end of this chapter I hope readers have a better understanding of the long and intimate history that the UK has had (and continues to have) with the magical and the paranormal.

THE MODERN WORLD OF GHOSTS

British author and scholar Owen Davies, in his investigation of the modern social history of ghosts in the UK, tells us that England is a "ghost-ridden nation,"[1] and that early rationales for ghostly encounters were rooted in moral vengeance. Davies tells of a woman who, upon attempting to write her stepson out of a will, was terrorized by the specter of her husband's first wife, the mother of the aforementioned stepson. Then there's the 1728 tale from Dorset, England, in which a boy's body was exhumed after multiple townspeople claimed to have seen his ghost. These notions of vengeful ghosts whose activities are guided by a moral compass are the result of a society guided by strong religious belief. Davies further tells us that even noted scholars who captured ghost stories and paranormal encounters were driven by an underlying need to "uphold a crumbling system of religious philosophy."[2] It wasn't until the founding of the SPR in 1882 that the narrative of paranormal experience includes ghosts that seemingly have no overt moral reason for interacting with the living.

Davies cautions us, however, from putting too much stock in the reports gathered by the SPR as its research overwhelmingly involved respondents from the middle and upper classes. In fact, very little paranormal experiences of the working class was investigated or captured by the SPR, and because of this Davies reminds us that you still see vestiges of the vengeful, moral ghost playing out in English folklore and rural beliefs even in the modern era. To be sure, changing eras bring with them new thoughtforms on phenomena, but Davies's point in this matter is a great reminder to think critically about the limitations of research—even research conducted by highly respected organizations.

Davies's work also reminds us that paranormal experiences are shaped and influenced by culture and society. For example, a notable distinction between ancient and modern ghost experiences is a gendered one. Prior to the invention of the printing press (which brought with it an enhanced amount of female readers), and prior to the rise of female mediums in the spiritualism movement, ghosts were often referred to as male. In the late 1800s, however, reports of female apparitions began to rise.

Paranormal encounters were also influenced by such seemingly mundane things as fashion and the ways in which fabric was used—such as the tradition in the 1800s of burying your loved ones in plain white sheets if you didn't have the money to pay for anything fancier. Thus the white-cloaked ghost as a stereotype of the paranormal was born, though it played out in very real ways in England. One such instance involves a thief dressing this way to intentionally scare people and ward them off as he stole, and still another time that a lawyer was beaten out of fright one night because of his white-colored clothing. In the late 1800s, reports of ghosts dressed in black started to make their way into the paranormal record and is perhaps influenced by the Victorian practice of wearing black when in mourning—a practice that, as you likely already guessed, became popular in the late 1800s.

Davies tells us that geography also affects the paranormal experience, and England is no exception. Of particular note here is the concept of liminality and borders as frequent settings of paranormal experience. These liminal places—places that are borders, or on the edge or existing between two stages—are often places where people report paranormal activity. Researchers in England, Davies informs us, who investigated paranormal encounters on rural English roads discovered that many of these encounters happened on roads that bordered two different parishes. Perhaps there is something about separation or boundary that impacts paranormal experiences? So, too, do other physical structures impact the paranormal, such as the seemingly inherent connection of an abandoned home with the paranormal or of assigning the physical location of some traumatic event a likely source of paranormal activity—battlefields, deaths, prisons, and so forth.

In terms of English religious practices that overlapped with the paranormal, an interesting overlap occurs with exorcism. This activity, likely most often connected with the Catholic Church, was instead most often performed by Protestant ministers in groups of up to twelve. More interesting, however, was the involvement of "cunning folk" who would, on occasion, be consulted in matters of banishing spirits in exorcism-like rituals. Of course, tensions between Protestant and Catholic tenets in the years surrounding the Reformation certainly helped shape paranormal beliefs in the UK. Concern over ghosts, at this time, seemed to take a backseat to concerns about witches and witchcraft, with ghosts even being thought of as the trickery of or visions sent by witches.

If you fast-forward from the Reformation about a hundred years, you see that contemporary thought on ghosts was yet again affected in the mid-1600s with the rise of Cartesianism as a school of thought. Directly challenging dominant notions of understanding the world via the senses, this new philosophy ushered in a world of materialism—or, a new world that believed knowledge was only valid if deduced through clinical, scientific measures. And though this new philosophy didn't immediately take hold in England (to be sure, it actually created a divide between philosophers who stood staunchly on either side of the debate), it signifies a shift in the timeline of paranormal cultural attitudes. Nonetheless, by the late 1700s there was a renewed interested in prophets and mystics due to the uptick of unrest and uncertainty in the English world, impacted in part by the revolutions happening in other parts of the world. Just a few years after this, the UK would be in the midst of full-blown spiritualism.

You may be asking yourself, though, "What about the current reality of paranormal thought and culture in the UK?" Rest assured, the topic of the paranormal continues to be a thriving one, as Davies tells us that "the extraordinary fact about the history of ghosts is that it is not a story of decline,"[3] and reminds us that belief in ghosts and the paranormal in the UK continues to increase with every subsequent Gallup poll on this matter. Most importantly, however, especially for our conversation here regarding the legitimacy of paranormal research, Davies tells us that these polls indicate something very important—"what the polls reveal, then, is that since the 1940s people have become less embarrassed about *expressing* their belief in ghosts."[4] He also mentions that the decline of the church as well as industrialization, urbanization, and the promotion of all things ghostly in literature and cinema help to keep the long history of the paranormal in the UK alive today. I tend to think these things assist an open-mindedness to the paranormal world that is all around us.

This is a very rapid and glancing overview of the modern history of paranormal belief in the UK and how it was shaped by the religious and cultural events of the time. This isn't to say that all things paranormal can simply be boiled down to a tidy sociological analysis, but it is nevertheless essential, especially since I don't raise these points elsewhere in this work. Understanding the ways in which our cultures and societies affect how we interpret and experience the paranormal has immense value. One could even say, as people suggest with the uptick of near-death experiences after the invention of the defibrillator, that we create opportunities for new paranormal experiences every day. In other words, the more we interact with the world around us and continue to create and invent, the more we reveal about the mysteries surrounding us. In a way, then, perhaps we are creators of the paranormal instead of passive recipients.

A BRIEF NOTE REGARDING MAGIC IN THE UK

The history of the paranormal in the UK cannot be complete without a discussion of the vast history of magical practices in this region—practices that continue to this day. Understood here through a brief discussion of cunning folk, magic in the UK is interwoven throughout British history. Scholar Davies tells us that "cunning-folk was just one of several terms used in England to describe multifaceted practitioners of magic who healed the sick and the bewitched, who told fortunes, identified thieves, induced love, and much else besides."[5] Even though the term isn't used as much today, Davies tells us, that would not have been the case in recent British history. In fact, he tells us, "two hundred years ago the majority of the population, in both town and country, would have known of at least one cunning-man or cunning-woman."[6]

Even though the term "cunning folk" appears prominently in the sixteenth century, this doesn't signify that these types of people weren't around before then. Davies reminds us that while the specific term "cunning folk" may not have been used, there indeed existed similar types of people since ancient times. For example, he states that magical remedies can readily be found in medieval manuscripts and that even the Bible references the word *pythonicos*, a word that encompasses diviners of all types, yes—even cunning folk.[7] As you might imagine, cunning folk were often subject to persecution, especially in the 1500s, even though cunning folk, Davies tells us, sometimes slipped under the punitive radar as courts and lawmakers focused on cases of witchcraft.[8] This isn't to say, of course, that cunning folk were not targeted in legislation. In the 1600s, for example, the Act of James I was "as much aimed at cunning-folk and conjurers as witches,"[9] and made it a capital offense to use divination to locate lost items or treasure, or to perform love spells. A relatively small number of cases against cunning folk made it to the courts, and Davies tells us that it is far more likely that cunning men and women were brought forth in the church-based courts—the worst punishment of which was simply excommunication. Seen as more of a moral and ethical debate between the practitioner and the church, few people instigated claims against cunning folk, as opposed to those accused of witchcraft, because cunning folk were viewed as people providing a service or a good.[10]

Specifically in England and Wales, cunning folk played a major role at helping alleviate the stressors of 1800s life in these countries. As Davies tells us in *Witchcraft, Magic, and Culture: 1736-1951*, cunning folk "existed in large numbers because many people relied on them to help them cope with a wide range of personal problems and unfulfilled desires."[11] Cunning folk were specifically consulted due to their breadth of occult knowledge. They employed various methods of addressing issues—astrology (this being a large part of their employ), divination, herbs, and so forth. In fact, cunning men and women were consulted to assist in warding against witchcraft, adding perhaps to the fact that cunning folk seemed less a target to law officials. In terms of demographics, Davies tells us that the majority of cunning folk were male farmers. Cunning women existed, to be sure, and although they are fewer in number, they employed their skills full-time, whereas cunning men were usually found engaging in this occupation after the necessary requirements of their primary occupation were completed. Tailoring their responses to each client and using a wide variety of techniques, cunning folk were consulted by people with medical ailments as recently as the early 1900s.[12]

To this day, astrologers and diviners (or, fortune-tellers) still practice in healthy numbers, and folk remedies for certain medical ailments continue to be consulted. These remnants of a more populous magical culture still play out in the social history of the United Kingdom and simply represent a changing and dynamic intersection of magic, the supernatural, and our understanding and experience of the world. Industrialization and the movement of peoples from rural to urban areas are a few factors that undoubtedly affected the future of magical practices, but Davies reminds us that the supernatural and magical is alive and well all around us—it simply wears new clothes. Instead of attributing anomalous phenomena to witches, for example, scientists study poltergeists. And while belief in fairies may be on the decline, how about the thousands of reports of alien abductions or even simply the personal belief in life beyond our planet? These are all paranormal vestiges that spring forth from the same source. Davies puts it best when he writes, "For many people today the experience of the supernatural is no longer circumscribed by the parish boundary but by the expanding universe," and further reminds us that "it is not impossible that at some point in the future, profound economic and environmental upheavals will once more create the social and cultural conditions in which once widespread beliefs and practices concerning witchcraft and magic may return."[13] And while the conversation here is brief and included to introduce the notion of magic and its relation to English culture, readers interested in learning more about cunning folk as well as the role of magic in UK history should consult any one of Owen Davies's prolific monographs on this topic.

FASCINATING TALES FROM THE SCIENTIFIC PIONEERS

Throughout this work I analyze the paranormal from a relatively scientific lens. I make the argument, though, that we need to question our standard notions of credibility and the stereotypes surrounding what it means for something to be worthy of an academic inquiry. While this might seem radical to some, especially given that I apply this to topics many consider to be on the fringe of acceptable reason, I want to include a bit more whimsy in this chapter, and so I provide here some intriguing cases from the files of the SPR. Some of these cases are quite innocent, like the woman who felt a stabbing pain in her thumb at the exact moment that her husband was involved in a crushing hand accident miles away. Or like the gentleman whose dog appeared in his dream to inform him that he was in danger, only to discover a few days later the body of his deceased dog in a waterway.[14]

Still other cases are a bit more . . . curious. Consider the tale of church official J. B. Phillips who chatted with SPR researchers about the time he was visited by the apparition of author C. S. Lewis, who informed him that "it's not so difficult as you think, you know."[15] This apparently happened twice, and on each occasion, Lewis was dressed in red tweed—offering a little more whimsy to this encounter. Lewis isn't the only literary celebrity gracing the case files of the SPR. Rudyard Kipling's own mother, in fact, was once a participant in a seance that got so lively the table began to rock and shake so violently that one participant had to leap atop it to get it to quit rocking.[16] Then there's the tale of the giant rabbit that was seen roaming about a Cambridge home occupied by a professor and his family. The professor kept note of the sightings, and SPR members observed that they topped out in the thirties, at which point it seemed the family had simply come to accept that their residence came with a peculiar mascot.[17] There is no follow-up to this case of the mysterious giant hare, and I suppose one can only hope it's hopping around its usual haunts still.

The case files of the SPR also reveal how paranormal experiencers sometimes took matters into their own hands to test phenomena. One such case involves a haunting in the Pittville Circus neighborhood of Cheltenham, England. Residents of a home in this neighborhood encountered an apparition of a weeping woman dressed in black. The apparition would float around the dwelling, so one afternoon, residents decided to set up their own tests. However, the woman seamlessly glided straight through trip wires made of fabric and, on one occasion, passed through a line of people who created a barrier in front of her.[18]

Automatic writing is another phenomenon found in the writings of the SPR. Well-known researcher Frederic W. H. Myers had a friend who became interested in learning more about this ability. This person first began practicing automatic writing in the dark until she developed impulses to write, at which point she would stop and let the pen flow seamlessly onto the paper. She recounts that she would have no memory of inscribing words onto the paper. In one instance she recorded the location of a private document belonging to Eleanor Sidgwick—a document in Sidgwick's home that she had misplaced and forgotten about. Rudyard Kipling appears yet again in the SPR's case files as they recall the automatic writing abilities displayed by his sister Alice. Alice displayed automatic writing in handwriting different than her own, and she even at one point suggested an international experiment on automatic writing when she vacationed in India. Before she left, she suggested that she and another automatic writer sit down at the same day and time once a week, each focusing mentally on the other, and try to intuit messages or accuracies. In one such instance, the England-based automatic writer wrote about a painting that, unbeknownst to her, Alice had been seated in front of during her session.[19]

Edmund Gurney, Frederic W. H. Myers, and Frank Podmore's book *Phantasms of the Living* contains some equally astonishing cases of psychical phenomena, and is a compendium of accounts given to them and other members of the SPR. One section of this two-volume work involves spontaneous paranormal encounters that affect more than one sense. In other words, encounters that involve both sight and sound or some other combination of the senses. One such case involved a Mrs. Leaworthy of Devon, who harbored a sea captain after his crew was rescued when their ship, *L'Orient*, got caught up in a storm off the English coast. The captain, as he recuperated at Mrs. Leaworthy's home, told her that he had an ominous feeling that something was wrong with his wife back home. When explaining why he felt this way, he stated that just before the storm hit his ship, he saw his wife standing before him and that she spoke to him and said not to grieve for her. Feeling rather anxious about the meaning of this vision, he sent a letter home alerting her of what happened to his ship but also inquiring about her health. Unbeknownst to the captain, his wife had indeed passed away the same day his ship sunk, though his friends and family chose to inform him otherwise until he arrived back home.[20]

Gurney and his colleagues tackle additional experiences of precognition, but one interesting portion of their work deconstructs the notion that all apparitions are merely by-products of hallucinations. They note that while a vast majority of ghostly sightings are experienced by one person in a singular event, there are cases of multiple people experiencing the same thing collectively, thereby throwing into question the assumption that all sightings are simply hallucinations originating in the mind of the experiencer. One such case involves three men (two cousins and a friend) who all collectively heard a disembodied voice calling out the last name of the cousins. They remarked and agreed that it sounded oddly like the voice of their colleague Captain Clayton. Thinking it odd, they brushed it off as a strange coincidence until the next morning when they received word that Captain Clayton had died in an accident.[21]

Readers interested in more strange tales from the case files of the SPR should seek out Renée Haynes's 1986 work *The Society for Psychical Research, 1882–1982: A History* and any number of the publications written by Gurney, Myers, Sidgwick, and more.

UNIVERSITIES, ORGANIZATIONS, AND COLLECTIONS

In addition to the Society for Psychical Research, there are other organizations within the UK that study the paranormal, some of which are affiliated with universities. One such organization is the Koestler Parapsychology Unit located within the psychology department of the University of Edinburgh in Scotland. Researcher and author Dr. Caroline Watt, a noted parapsychologist and author of the recent publication *Parapsychology: A Beginner's Guide*, is the current chair of this department. The Koestler Parapsychology Unit, according to its website, studies "the possible existence of psychic ability," "anomalous experiences and belief in the paranormal," and "historical and conceptual issues in parapsychology."[22] Though the website mentions that the department was formally created in 1985, a history of this organization highlights that parapsychology courses were offered as early as 1962. From the website, you can find an overview of the major research areas that are studied. Within these sections, Dr. Watt includes hyperlinks to notable studies published on these subjects. Furthermore, and of particular note to researchers interested in methods and/or replicating studies themselves, there is an entire section of its website dedicated to listing its current experiments. This section, labeled the "Study Registry," lists its current inquiries, such as one study that looks at traits and characteristics of experienced remote viewers and another study investigating the links between hormones during pregnancy and precognitive abilities.[23]

Seemingly far more universities in the UK offer courses and studies on the paranormal than their counterparts in the United States. This likely isn't surprising as the UK is, after all, the modern birthplace of the scientific inquiry into the paranormal, and its cultural fabric seems more intimately connected with the paranormal as well. In addition to the Koestler Parapsychology Unit, students can take courses and study the paranormal (mainly via parapsychology) at institutions such as: the University of London, Cardiff Metropolitan University, the University of the West of England, the University of Derby, the University of Greenwich, the University of Hertfordshire, Lancaster University, Manchester Metropolitan University, the University of Northampton, and the University of York.[24]

A non-university organization based out of the UK is the Association for the Scientific Study of Anomalous Phenomena (ASSAP). From its beginnings in 1981, this organization seeks to investigate the paranormal through a dedicated adherence to scientific methods and procedures while keeping up to date with the latest investigative and scientific theories. Its membership averages around three hundred people, and the authors John and Anne Spencer whom I referenced earlier in this work, were once affiliated with this organization. Other members include people who are also associated with the SPR. From the ASSAP's website, we learn that it researches psychical topics like extrasensory perception and even ghosts, as well as phenomena it labels as "Fortean," which includes cryptozoology, ufology, and more.[25] The website includes links to investigations and reports that the association has compiled along with references to its own research. Furthermore, it also includes articles that discuss practical matters for anyone interested in paranormal research, such as tips and techniques for conducting your own investigations, how to evaluate eyewitness reports, and more. One interesting facet of this organization is that it maintains a small library of paranormal-related works as well. Anyone interested in learning more about how modern ghost-hunting groups in the UK conduct investigations or anyone wanting to learn more about modern English hauntings may wish to visit this website for more information.

One interesting and unique addition to this list is the Museum of Witchcraft and Magic located in Cornwall. Its mission is to "represent the diversity and vigour of magical practice respectfully, accurately and impartially through unique, entertaining and education exhibitions, drawing upon cutting-edge scholarship along with the insights of magical practitioners."[26] Its website offers a robust catalog where you can view high-quality images of many of the items in its collection. This museum contains carvings, photos, books, letters, drawings, paintings, and much more on all types of magic and witchcraft-related topics. The categories that are available to browse by are almost overwhelming and include topics such as chaos magic, necromancy, tarot, and superstitions. You can even view a blog on the website, which is full of interesting subject matter like the folklore and superstitions surrounding witches in the Yorkshire area of England and even a discussion of Aleister Crowley's banned lectures, highlighted during Banned Books Week in 2019.[27]

The Museum of Witchcraft and Magic is one place where you can view special collections related to the paranormal, but there are others as well. The Society for Psychical Research has two physical locations where visitors can access materials such as journal publications, books, magazines, and audio files. The first location, the Vernon Mews Library of London, is where you can locate journal publications and a vast array of books and magazines and other assorted materials curated by the SPR on various paranormal topics.[28] On the SPR's website, in fact, you can search the library's catalog and even download an eighty-page PDF that lists the manuscripts housed in this library. The second location is an archival collection housed at the Cambridge University Library. This collection is exponentially larger and is where you can find thousands of books on the paranormal and all sorts of primary and secondary sources from the history of the SPR, including objects from its studies, and also including a notable collection of research on "time slips" by SPR member Andrew MacKenzie. MacKenzie studied this phenomenon referred to as time slips—an experience during which someone encounters something seemingly out of its time and place. This archival collection may not be as easily accessible as the SPR's library in London, but the website does note that a document from the SPR can help grant access to this collection.[29]

Another notable collection is available at the University of London's Senate House Library. The Harry Price Library of Magical Literature is a collection of materials that range from 1472 to modern day. Specifically, there are "nearly 13,000 books, pamphlets and periodical titles, some rare, on all aspects of magic: conjuring . . . witchcraft and the occult, prophecies, abnormal phenomena such as ghosts, mediums and spiritualism, scientific phenomena . . . and psychical research."[30] Psychical researcher Harry Price donated the items in this collection himself; visitors to the University of London can view this collection that contains works from around the world. Some of the works include five different editions of the *Malleus Maleficarum*; a 1584 edition of the *Discoverie of Witchcraft* in which one can obtain a great deal of information on the thoughts and attitudes in London on topics such as witchcraft, alchemy, and more; and even fifteen different editions of the prophecies of Nostradamus.[31]

The University of London has other collections that may be of interest to readers. The Wohl Library at the Institute of Historical Research contains a notable collection of information on witchcraft trials and accusations in the United Kingdom—particularly courtroom cases from the fourteenth and fifteenth centuries. Additionally, there are resources on witchcraft in Scotland and even some on the Salem, Massachusetts, witch trials located in this collection, such as a notebook of the Reverend Samuel Parris.[32] Still another organization located within the University of London, the Warburg Institute, contains research and items of interest to paranormal researchers. According to its website, the Warburg Institute is "one of the world's leading centres for studying the interaction of ideas, images and society" and "is dedicated to the survival and transmission of culture across time and space, with a special emphasis on the afterlife of antiquity."[33] At the Warburg Institute, you can find items such as thermographs recording temperatures and readings occurring during séances and detailed reports on the expenses for various psychical investigations. Specifically, one of the core collections of this institute is devoted to resources on astrology, divination, prophecy, and alchemy through the ages.[34]

NOTABLE PARANORMAL LOCATIONS IN THE UK

Armed with an understanding of the history of paranormal research, the cultural fabric of magic in the UK, and an overview of selected organizations and collections that feature the paranormal, an exploration of some notable paranormal hotspots perfectly rounds out this section dedicated to the UK. Even if you didn't know a single paranormal factoid about the UK, its long and rich history would likely lead you to assume that there are a number of locations filled with tales of paranormal activity. In this section, I highlight a few notable locations that are part of the paranormal tapestry of the UK. Many of these locations you can still visit today.

For our first stop on the paranormal hotspot tour, we travel to the Tower of London. Aside from being the very first ghost story that I remember reading about, the Tower of London has left its mark on countless visitors through the years. The website Haunted Rooms tells us that the Tower of London, which was built in 1078, is "one of the most haunted places in the U.K."[35] Perhaps the most famous ghost said to roam the Tower is that of Queen Anne Boleyn, who was beheaded on the tower's lawn in 1536. People have reported seeing her wander the grounds of this historic site, near where her execution likely took place. Another ghost involves an unapproved marriage between William Seymour and Arbella Stuart. The marriage, having not been approved by King James I, put a target on both William's and Arbella's backs. William was able to escape the scandal, but Arbella was captured and taken to the tower, where people surmise that she was murdered. Her ghost is reported to roam the halls of the Queen's House building on the tower grounds. Perhaps the most tragic tale involves two young boys who were sent to the tower to live out their days after being declared illegitimate heirs. While they graced the grounds with their playful antics they soon disappeared, and while nobody technically knows what happened to them, the skeletons of two male children were later discovered on the property. Visitors report seeing these young boys in white nightgowns roaming the grounds.[36]

Many of us have at least heard about the Tower of London, even if we don't specifically know that it's a paranormal hub in the United Kingdom. Let's move away from the traditional paranormal locations and dive into some perhaps lesser-known accounts—lesser known that is, to an American audience. One such tale comes from Northern Ireland and is referred to as the Cooneen Ghost House, a case that was even featured on an episode of the BBC show *Northern Ireland's Greatest Haunts*. In the early 1900s this home was occupied by the Murphy family, who soon began experiencing extreme poltergeist activity. The family reported that pillows would fly out from under their heads and that clothes left lying on a bed would suddenly appear as if someone was wearing them, only to collapse back into a heap when light was shone upon them. Phantom knocking, described as the beating of horse hooves, and incidents of people being shoved and kicked all occurred at this location as well.[37]

Another prominent paranormal case is that of the Borley Rectory in England. Noted psychical researcher and author Harry Price investigated this location in 1929. Price became most noted, in fact, for his investigation of Borley Rectory that spanned from 1929 until its fiery demise in 1939 as well as for participating in the first live broadcast conducted during an investigation.[38] Initial reports of the Borley Rectory involve the apparition of a nun roaming the building and grounds. The nun, in the folklore surrounding this case, was said to be a former lover of a monk who once lived at the rectory. In addition to the nun, a family who lived at the rectory regularly heard phantom footsteps and phantom doorbell sounds, and witnessed messages scrawled on the building's walls not attributed to anyone living or visiting the location.[39] It was at this point that Harry Price was called in to investigate; after his investigations, he even went on to publish a book about his experiences in 1940. In this work, titled *The Most Haunted House in England: Ten Years' Investigation of Borley Rectory*, Price outlines the eyewitness testimony of those who experienced paranormal encounters throughout the years at the rectory and recounts his own personal paranormal experiences. One interesting chapter, in fact, discusses a seance that he and a few other members held one evening at the rectory, during which they experienced strange rapping noises that seemingly corresponded with their entreaties for answering yes or no questions. During the seance, Price believed they contacted the former rector of the location and further describes this experiment in detail.[40]

The National Trust is a great source for further information on haunted locations across the UK. The National Trust is an organization that was created in 1895 with the explicit goal of maintaining the historic locations of the UK for future generations to visit and enjoy.[41] It openly embraces the paranormal history that abounds in its locations, and its website is a veritable treasure trove of information on scores of locations boasting eerie activity. One of these locations is Felbrigg Hall, an estate in Norfolk founded in the early eleventh century. In 1809, a fire broke out in the library of the house, and resident William Windham III rushed in to rescue the burning books. Tragically, he died from his wounds shortly thereafter, and his ghost has been seen by visitors ever since, though he is more likely to appear when a certain magical assortment of titles is placed on a table—a conjuring library list, if you will.[42]

Another tale from the archives of the National Trust concerns the Treasurer's House, a town house located in Yorkshire that boasts having the oldest ghosts in the UK. The home, built atop an old Roman road, is the site where visitors have reported seeing apparitions believed to be Roman soldiers. Most sightings occur in the cellars—a place that would have been closest to the original Roman road, interestingly. A notable experience comes from a man who was installing a new water heater one afternoon in the cellars of Treasurer's House. Toiling away, he was suddenly startled by the blasting of a trumpet and the apparition of a Roman soldier leading a horse and a trail of about twenty other soldiers down the hall. Rushing upstairs, he was greeted by the caretaker of the home who took one look at him and asked if he had just seen the ghostly Romans. Interestingly, the young man's story was attacked by skeptics, who clung to the small detail of the apparitions carrying round shields. Up to this point in the historical record, Romans were thought to have exclusively carried square shields; however, years later historians discovered that one group of Romans from the York area were markedly different from their peers in the fact that they carried round shields.[43]

So far in this chapter we've learned about some paranormal locations in England and Northern Ireland, but what about Wales and Scotland? Let's not forget about these remaining countries that help round out our discussion on the haunts of the UK. In Cardiff, Wales, there resides Castell Coch, also referred to as the "Red Castle," or the fairy-tale castle. Nestled in the woods of the Fforest Fawr, Castell Coch was built around the ruins of a thirteenth-century fortress by architect William Burges and funded by the Marquess of Bute—a man with endless pockets of money and who was, at the time, considered the wealthiest man in the world.[44] Spectral tales at this famous castle tell of a ghostly soldier who is seen hovering at the foot of people's beds and how the original Welsh owner of the ruins once turned two of his employees into stone eagles in order to guard treasure buried deep in the walls of the castle—a treasure rumored to remain hidden to this day.[45] Of course, Castell Coch isn't the only castle rumored to be inhabited by ghostly residents. Other castles in Wales house their own apparitions, such as Gwydir Castle, in which a young woman believed to have been murdered roams the halls to this day, leaving a rotten stench in her wake. Or like Chirk Castle, which features a woman in black Victorian garb ascending a staircase, and regular accounts of visitors being touched and grabbed by phantom hands. And then there's Margam Castle, which was once an abbey in the eleventh century and is hailed as the UK's most haunted castle. At Margam Castle the ghost of an old gamekeeper isn't too keen on tourists—in fact, he's been known to chuck a stone or two at curious visitors. When visitors aren't dodging the assaults of the old gamekeeper, they can hear the spectral laughter of children echoing down the hallways.[46]

When people think of Scotland and the paranormal, they likely jump immediately to visions of the Loch Ness Monster. While certainly a prominent tale of the strange and wonderful world of Scotland, Nessie isn't the only paranormal tale that emerges from Scotland. Mary King's Close, for example, is said to be the most haunted street in all of Scotland. An alleyway off Edinburgh's famed "Royal Mile," Mary King's Close was once entirely bricked up during the Plague. The ghostly vision of a young girl is often seen wandering this alleyway, which interestingly is located not too far away from Greyfriars Cemetery where gravediggers once dug up the bodies of Plague victims to pillage their possessions.[47] Speaking of Edinburgh, a notable paranormal hub is Edinburgh Castle, home to more than one ghost, including that of a headless boy, thought to be the ghost of a drummer boy who would alert the castle residents of impending danger. In northern Scotland, Culloden Moor is said to be haunted by the ghosts of men who died in battle in 1746; these men are often seen near their cairns, or stones marking the spot where they died.

While this is a brief overview that merely introduces some of the notable paranormal locations across the United Kingdom, I hope the references included in this chapter help motivate readers to take a deeper dive into this topic. There are a myriad of resources on the topic of the paranormal in the UK, many of which can be found in the annotations of this work. Regardless of your reasons for seeking more information on the paranormal, I hope you never lose that sense of magic that is woven intimately throughout this topic. Treat the paranormal with as much academic vigor as you'd like, but remember to enjoy the ride.

NOTES

1. Davies, Owen. (2007). *The haunted: A social history of ghosts.* Hampshire, England: Palgrave Macmillan, 1.
2. Ibid., 8.
3. Ibid., 241.
4. Ibid.
5. Davies, Owen. (2003). *Cunning-folk: Popular magic in English history.* London, England: Hambledon and London, vii.
6. Ibid.
7. Ibid., viii–x.
8. Ibid., 6–7.
9. Ibid., 8.
10. Ibid., 13–15.
11. Davies, Owen. (1999). *Witchcraft, magic, and culture: 1736–1951.* Manchester, England: Manchester University Press, 214.
12. Ibid., 215–221.
13. Ibid., 295.
14. Haynes, Renée. (1982). *The Society for Psychical Research 1882–1982: A history.* London, England: Macdonald, 46–47.
15. Ibid., 55.
16. Ibid., 61.
17. Ibid., 56.
18. Ibid., 56.
19. Ibid., 67.
20. Gurney, Edmund, Myers, Frederic W. H., & Podmore, Frank. (1886). *Phantasms of the living: Volume two.* London, England: Trubner, 579–580. Retrieved December 11, 2019, from https://archive.org/details/phantasmsoflivin02gurniala
21. Ibid., 174.
22. Watt, Caroline. (n.d.-a). Home. Koestler Parapsychology Unit. University of Edinburgh. Retrieved December 10, 2019, from https://koestlerunit.wordpress.com/
23. Watt, Caroline. (n.d.-b). Registered studies. Koestler Parapsychology Unit. The University of Edinburgh. Retrieved December 10, 2019, from https://koestlerunit.wordpress.com/study-registry/registered-studies/

24. Parapsychological Association. (2019). United Kingdom. Retrieved December 10, 2019, from https://www.parapsych.org/articles/34/39/united_kingdom.aspx
25. Association for the Scientific Study of Anomalous Phenomena. (n.d.). About us. Retrieved December 10, 2019, from http://www.assap.ac.uk/newsite/htmlfiles/About.html
26. Museum of Witchcraft and Magic. (2017). Visit. Retrieved December 11, 2019, from https://museumofwitchcraftandmagic.co.uk/visit/
27. Museum of Witchcraft and Magic. (2017). Blog. Retrieved December 11, 2019, from https://museumofwitchcraftandmagic.co.uk/news/
28. Society for Psychical Research. (2018). Libraries and archives. Retrieved December 10, 2019, from https://www.spr.ac.uk/about/libraries-and-archives
29. Society for Psychical Research. (2018). Cambridge archives. Retrieved December 11, 2019, from https://www.spr.ac.uk/cambridge-archives
30. University of London: Senate House Library. (n.d.-a). Harry Price Library of Magical Literature. Retrieved December 11, 2019, from https://london.ac.uk/senate-house-library/our-collections/special-collections/printed-special-collections/hpl
31. University of London: Senate House Library. (n.d.-b). Rare books and periodicals. Retrieved December 11, 2019, from https://london.ac.uk/senate-house-library/our-collections/special-collections/printed-special-collections/hpl/rare-books-and-periodicals
32. Wohl Library. (2017, September 5). The history of witchcraft in the IHR Library's collections [Blog post]. Retrieved December 11, 2019, from https://blog.history.ac.uk/2017/09/the-history-of-witchcraft-in-the-ihr-librarys-collections/
33. Warburg Institute, University of London: School of Advanced Study. (2018). The Warburg Institute. Retrieved December 11, 2019, from https://warburg.sas.ac.uk/
34. University of London. (n.d.). Archives and manuscripts. Retrieved December 11, 2019, from https://archives.libraries.london.ac.uk/results; Warburg Institute, University of London: School of Advanced Study. (2018). Library. Retrieved December 11, 2019, from https://warburg.sas.ac.uk/library-collections/library
35. Haunted Rooms. (2019). The Tower of London, London. Retrieved December 11, 2019, from https://www.hauntedrooms.co.uk/the-tower-of-london-ghosts
36. Ibid.
37. McCarra, Darren. (n.d.). The Cooneen ghost. Retrieved December 11, 2019, from http://mccarra.co/cooneen-ghost/
38. Davies, *The Haunted*, 95–96.
39. Haunted Rooms. (n.d.). Borley Rectory Essex—Was it the most haunted house in England? Retrieved December 11, 2019, from https://www.hauntedrooms.co.uk/borley-rectory-most-haunted-house
40. Price, Harry. (1940). *The most haunted house in England: Ten years' investigation of Borley Rectory*. London, England: Longmans, Green, 41–43.
41. National Trust. (n.d.-a). About the National Trust. Retrieved December 11, 2019, from https://www.nationaltrust.org.uk/features/about-the-national-trust
42. National Trust. (n.d.-c). A haunted library and a bookish ghost. Retrieved December 11, 2019, from https://www.nationaltrust.org.uk/features/a-haunted-library-and-a-bookish-ghost
43. National Trust. (n.d.-b). By the look of you, you've seen the Romans! Retrieved December 11, 2019, from https://www.nationaltrust.org.uk/features/by-the-look-of-you-youve-seen-the-romans
44. Llywodraeth Cymru Welsh Government. (2019). Castell Coch: Partners in fantasy. Retrieved December 11, 2019, from https://cadw.gov.wales/more-about-castell-coch
45. Visit Wales. (2019). Haunted Wales. Retrieved December 11, 2019, from https://www.visitwales.com/info/travel-trade/itineraries/haunted-wales-5-day-itinerary
46. Ibid.
47. McCallion, Rachel. (2014, August 14). Top 11 spooky places to visit in Scotland. Scotland.org. Retrieved December 11, 2019, from https://www.scotland.org/features/top-11-spooky-places-to-visit-in-scotland

Bibliography

Abbott, Karen. (2012, October 30). The Fox sisters and the rap on spiritualism. Smithsonian.com. Retrieved August 13, 2019, from https://www.smithsonianmag.com/history/the-fox-sisters-and-the-rap-on-spiritualism-99663697/
Academy for Spiritual and Consciousness Studies (n.d.-a). About ASCI. Retrieved June 11, 2019, from http://ascsi.org/overview/
Academy for Spiritual and Consciousness Studies. (n.d.-b). The Journal of ASCSI. Retrieved November 7, 2019, from https://ascsi.org/the-journal-of-ascsi/
Adamnan, Saint. (1905). *Life of Saint Columba (Columb-Kille) A.D. 521–597: Founder of the monastery of Iona and first Christian missionary to the pagan tribes of North Britain* (Wentworth Huyshe, Trans.). London, England: Routledge.
Alexander, Skye. (2017). *The modern witchcraft book of tarot: Your complete guide to understanding the tarot.* Avon, MA: Adams Media.
Aliens found in Ohio? The "Wow!" signal. (2010). *Weekend Edition Saturday.* NPR. Retrieved April 8, 2019, from Gale Literature Resource Center.
Alvarado, Carlos S. (2018). Eleanor Sidgwick (1845–1936). *Journal of Parapsychology, 82*(2), 127–131.
Alvarado, Carlos S. (2018, April 8). William Crookes. In *PSI encyclopedia.* Society for Psychical Research. Retrieved August 14, 2019, from https://psi-encyclopedia.spr.ac.uk/articles/william-crookes
American Association for the Advancement of Science. (2019). About science and AAAS. Retrieved November 14, 2019, from https://www.sciencemag.org/about/about-science-aaas?_ga=2.144028913.559877453.1573768825-485187692.1573768825
American Psychological Association. (2019). Journal of Abnormal Psychology. Retrieved October 29, 2019, from https://www.apa.org/pubs/journals/abn/
Amy's Crypt. (2018, April 16). The story behind Salem's haunted Witch House [Blog post]. Retrieved July 14, 2019, from https://amyscrypt.com/salem-witch-house/
Archive of the Afterlife. (n.d.). Welcome. Retrieved July 15, 2019, from https://archive-afterlife.weebly.com/
Arment, Chad. (2004). *Cryptozoology: Science and speculation.* Landisville, PA: Coachwhip.
Association for the Scientific Study of Anomalous Phenomena. (n.d.). About us. Retrieved December 10, 2019, from http://www.assap.ac.uk/newsite/htmlfiles/About.html
Association for the Study of Esotericism. (2020). What is esotericism? (2020). Retrieved January 9, 2020, from http://www.aseweb.org/?page_id=6
Atlantic University. (2018). Faculty. Retrieved June 12, 2019, from https://www.atlanticuniv.edu/admin-faculty/faculty/?submit=1&program=0&page=2

Atlantic University. (2019). *2019 academic catalog*, page 27. Retrieved June 12, 2019, from https://www.atlanticuniv.edu/media/12617/2019-au-catalog.pdf

Atwater, P. M. H. (1998). Aftereffects of near-death states. International Association for Near-Death Studies. Retrieved April 20, 2019, from https://iands.org/ndes/about-ndes/common-aftereffects.html

Atwater, P. M. H. (2003). Our tiniest near-death experiencers: Startling evidence suggestive of a brain shift. *Journal of Religious and Psychical Research, 26*(2), 86–97. Retrieved April 20, 2019, from EBSCOhost.

Aveni, Anthony. (1996). *Behind the crystal ball: Magic, science, and the occult from antiquity through the New Age*. New York, NY: Times Books.

Baker, Joseph O., Bader, Christopher D., & Mencken, F. Carson. (2016). A bounded affinity theory of religion and the paranormal. *Sociology of Religion, 77*(4), 334–358.

Barrett, William F. (1917). *On the threshold of the unseen: An examination of the phenomena of spiritualism and of the evidence for survival after death* (2nd ed.). London, England: Kegan Paul, Trench, Trubner.

Beck, Roger. (2007). *A brief history of ancient astrology*. Malden, MA: Blackwell.

Bekavac, Luka. (2018). Spectra of transcommunication: A survival study after Raudive and Derrida. *Supernatural Studies, 5*(1), 9–32.

Bernard (Joseph Pierre) Heuvelmans. (2002). In *Contemporary Authors Online*. Detroit, MI: Gale in Context: Biography. Retrieved August 14, 2019.

Bhattacharjee, Yudhijit. (2012). Paranormal psychologist. *Discover, 33*(2), 52–58.

Bielefeld University Library. (2019). What is BASE? Retrieved November 27, 2019, from https://www.base-search.net/about/en/index.php

Bigfoot Discovery Project. (n.d.). Retrieved July 15, 2019, from https://www.bigfootdiscoveryproject.com/

Blakeslee, Sarah. (2004). The CRAAP test. *Loex Quarterly, 31*(3), 6–7. Retrieved May 13, 2019, from https://commons.emich.edu/cgi/viewcontent.cgi?article=1009&context=loexquarterly

Blumenthal, Ralph, & Kean, Leslie. (2019, January 15). "Project Blue Book" is based on a true UFO story. This is it. *The New York Times*. Retrieved March 28, 2019, from https://www.nytimes.com/2019/01/15/arts/television/project-blue-book-history-true-story.html

British Columbia Scientific Cryptozoology Club. (2019). About. Retrieved June 11, 2019, from https://www.oberf.org/index.html

Brown, Alan. (2011). *Ghosts along the Mississippi River*. Jackson: University Press of Mississippi.

Brown, Roberta S., Brown, Lonnie E., & Tucker, Elizabeth. (2010). *Spookiest stories ever: Four seasons of Kentucky ghosts*. Lexington: University of Kentucky Press.

Carlton, Eric. (2000). *The paranormal: Research and the quest for meaning*. Burlington, VT: Ashgate.

Cocconi, Giuseppe, & Morrison, Philip. (1959, September 19). Searching for interstellar communications. *Nature*, pp. 844–846.

Coleman, Loren. (2001). Bernard Heuvelmans (1916–2001). The Cryptozoologist: Loren Coleman. Retrieved August 14, 2019, from http://www.lorencoleman.com/bernard_heuvelmans_obituary.html

Combs, Allan, & Holland, Mark. (1990). *Synchronicity: Science, myth, and the trickster*. New York, NY: Paragon House.

Coral Elsie Lorenzen. (2001). In *Contemporary Authors Online*. Detroit, MI: Gale in Context: Biography. Retrieved August 14, 2019.

Crair, Ben. (2018). Call of the wild man. *Smithsonian, 49*(5), 11–13. Retrieved April 17, 2019, from EBSCOhost.

Cryptozoologist: Loren Coleman. (2012). Who is Loren Coleman? Retrieved August 14, 2019, from http://lorencoleman.com/who-is-loren-coleman/

Cryptozoology and Paranormal Museum. (n.d.). About. Retrieved July 15, 2019, from https://crypto-para.org/about/

Dalton, Kathy S., Morris, Robert L., & Delanoy, Deborah L. (1996). Security measures in an automated Ganzfeld system. *Journal of Parapsychology, 60*(2), 129–147.

Daugherty, Greg. (2019, June 5). Meet J. Allen Hynek, the astronomer who first classified UFO "close encounters." History.com. Retrieved August 15, 2019, from https://www.history.com/news/j-allen-hynek-ufos-project-blue-book

Davenport, Jad. (2002, January–February). Rocky horror: The haunting legacy of Stephen King's *The Shining* looms over Colorado's Stanley Hotel. *Book*. Retrieved from Gale Literature Resource Center.

Davies, Owen. (1999). *Witchcraft, magic, and culture: 1736–1951*. Manchester, England: Manchester University Press.

Davies, Owen. (2003). *Cunning-folk: Popular magic in English history*. London, England: Hambledon and London.

Davies, Owen. (2007). *The haunted: A social history of ghosts*. Hampshire, England: Palgrave Macmillan.

Dendle, Peter. (2006). Cryptozoology in the medieval and modern worlds. *Folklore, 117*(2), 190–206. doi:10.1080/00155870600707888

Discover. (n.d.). About the magazine. Retrieved November 14, 2019, from http://discovermagazine.com/magazine/about

Divination. (2019). In *Oxford English Dictionary*. Oxford University Press. Retrieved May 21, 2019, from https://www.oed.com/view/Entry/56121?redirectedFrom=divination#eid

Drinkwater, Ken, Dagnall, Neil, & Bate, Lauren. (2013). Into the unknown: Using interpretative phenomenological analysis to explore personal accounts of paranormal experiences. *Journal of Parapsychology, 77*(2), 281–294.

Duggan, M. (2020). Julia Mossbridge. In *Psi encyclopedia*. London, England: Society for Psychical Research. Retrieved January 8, 2020, from https://psi-encyclopedia.spr.ac.uk/articles/julia-mossbridge

Duke University Libraries. (2009). Guide to the Parapsychology Laboratory Records, 1893–1984. Retrieved June 10, 2019, from https://library.duke.edu/rubenstein/findingaids/paralab/

Earls, Stephanie. (2016, October 31). Colorado's Stanley Hotel offers plenty of haunted tales: Reputation was earned before Stephen King's arrival. *The Gazette* [Colorado Springs, CO]. Retrieved March 26, 2019.

Eaton, Marc A. (2015). "Give us a sign of your presence": Paranormal investigation as a spiritual practice. *Sociology of Religion, 76*(4), 389–412.

EBSCO. (n.d.-a). Academic Search Premier: Magazines and journals. Retrieved October 25, 2019, from https://www.ebscohost.com/titleLists/aph-journals.htm

EBSCO. (n.d.-b). America: History and life. Retrieved October 25, 2019, from https://www.ebsco.com/products/research-databases/america-history-and-life

EBSCO. (n.d.-c). SocINDEX. Retrieved October 25, 2019, from https://www.ebsco.com/products/research-databases/socindex

Edmund Gurney. (2001). In *Encyclopedia of occultism and parapsychology*. Detroit, MI: Gale in Context: Biography. Retrieved August 14, 2019.

Eghigian, Greg. (2014, November 13). The psychiatrist, the aliens, and "going native." *Psychiatric Times, 31*(11), 1–3. Retrieved April 8, 2019, from EBSCOhost.

Eghigian, Greg. (2015, December 6). Making UFOs make sense: Ufology, science, and the history of their mutual mistrust. *Public Understanding of Science, 26*(5), 612–626. Retrieved April 8, 2019, from Sage Journals.

Eranos Foundation. (n.d.). Who we are: History and meaning of ERANOS. Retrieved August 20, 2019, from http://www.eranosfoundation.org/history.htm

Expedition: Bigfoot! The Sasquatch Museum. (2016). About us. Retrieved July 15, 2019, from https://www.expeditionbigfoot.com/about

FBI Records: The Vault. (1947, July 8). Roswell UFO: Part 1 of 1. Retrieved January 8, 2020, from https://vault.fbi.gov/Roswell%20UFO/Roswell%20UFO%20Part%201%20of%201/view

Feikert-Ahalt, Clare. (2012, October 31). Revealing the presence of ghosts. *In Custodia Legis: Law Librarians of Congress*. Retrieved July 15, 2019, from https://blogs.loc.gov/law/2012/10/revealing-the-presence-of-ghosts/

Frederic William Henry Myers. (2001). In *Encyclopedia of occultism and parapsychology*. Detroit, MI: Gale in Context: Biography. Retrieved August 14, 2019.

Franz Anton Mesmer. (2019, May 19). In *Encyclopaedia Britannica*. Retrieved August 13, 2019, from https://www.britannica.com/biography/Franz-Anton-Mesmer

Ganzfeld experiment. (n.d.). In *Wikipedia*. Retrieved May 14, 2019, from https://en.wikipedia.org/wiki/Ganzfeld_experiment

Gentry, Glenn W. (2007). Walking with the dead: The place of ghost walk tourism in Savannah, Georgia. *Southeastern Geographer, 47*(2), 222–238.

Ghost City. (2020). The haunted Mercer-Williams House. Retrieved January 6, 2020, from https://ghostcitytours.com/savannah/haunted-places/haunted-houses/mercer-williams-house/

Ghost Club. (2012). The Ghost Club. Retrieved August 19, 2019, from http://www.ghostclub.org.uk/

Gordon, Avery F. (2008). *Ghostly matters: Haunting and the sociological imagination*. Minneapolis: University of Minnesota Press. ProQuest eBook Central. Retrieved March 23, 2019.

Gurney, Edmund, Myers, Frederic W. H., & Podmore, Frank. (1886). *Phantasms of the living: Volume one*. London, England: Rooms of the Society for Psychical Research.

Gurney, Edmund, Myers, Frederic W. H., & Podmore, Frank. (1886). *Phantasms of the living: Volume two*. London, England: Trubner, 579–580. Retrieved December 11, 2019, from https://archive.org/details/phantasmsoflivin02gurniala

Hanks, Michele. (2019). Haunted objects: English paranormal investigation and the material mediation of doubt. *Nova Religio: The Journal of Alternative & Emergent Religion, 22*(4), 60–74.

Harry Price. (n.d.). In *Psi encyclopedia*. Society for Psychical Research. Retrieved December 20, 2019, from https://psi-encyclopedia.spr.ac.uk/articles/harry-price

HathiTrust. (n.d.). About. Retrieved October 29, 2019, from https://www.hathitrust.org/about

Haunted Rooms. (n.d.). Borley Rectory Essex—Was it the most haunted house in England? Retrieved December 11, 2019, from https://www.hauntedrooms.co.uk/borley-rectory-most-haunted-house

Haunted Rooms. (2019). The Tower of London, London. Retrieved December 11, 2019, from https://www.hauntedrooms.co.uk/the-tower-of-london-ghosts

Haunted Savannah. (2020). Haunted Sorrel Weed House. Retrieved January 6, 2020, from http://savannahitc.com/haunted-savannah/haunted-savannah/haunted-sorrel-weed-house/

Haynes, Renée. (1982). *The Society for Psychical Research 1882–1982: A history*. London, England: Macdonald.

Headaches as you age. (2017, June 1). *Mayo Clinic Health Letter, 35*(6).

Herrera, Chabeli. (2019, March 19). The UFO community still believes: And science is starting to listen. *The Orlando Sentinel*. Retrieved March 26, 2019.

Heuvelmans, Bernard. (1995). *On the track of unknown animals* (3rd ed.) (Richard Garnett, Trans.). London, England: Kegan Paul International.

Hillary, Edmund. (1960, January 24). Abominable—and improbable? *The New York Times*. Retrieved April 14, 2019, from Historic *New York Times*, ProQuest.

Historic Tours of America. (2018). The most haunted cemeteries in Savannah. Retrieved January 6, 2020, from https://www.ghostsandgravestones.com/savannah/haunted-cemeteries

Houran, James, Laythe, Brian, O'Keeffe, Ciaran, Dagnall, Neil, Drinkwater, Kenneth, & Lange, Rense. (2019). Quantifying the phenomenology of ghostly episodes: Part I—Need for a standard operationalization. *Journal of Parapsychology, 67*(2), 25–46. doi:10.30891/jopar.2019.01.03

How yellow fever turned New Orleans into the city of death. (2018, October 31). [Interview with Kathryn Olivarius]. *All Things Considered*. NPR. Retrieved March 26, 2019, from Gale Literature Resource Center.

Hutton, R. H. (1885). The Metaphysical Society: A reminiscence. In *The Nineteenth Century*, the Huxley File compiled by C. Blinderman & D. Joyce from Clark University. Retrieved May 21, 2019, from https://mathcs.clarku.edu/huxley/comm/Hutton/Hut-Meta.html

Huyghe, Patrick. (1979, October 14). U.F.O. files: The untold story. *The New York Times*. Retrieved March 27, 2019.

Idaho State University. (2019). Faculty. Retrieved December 18, 2019, from https://www.isu.edu/biology/people/faculty---professors/jeffrey-meldrum/
Incorporated Society for Psychical Research. (2018). Glossary. Retrieved April 21, 2019, from https://www.spr.ac.uk/research/glossary
Institute of Noetic Sciences. (2019). IONS: About. Retrieved July 30, 2019, from https://noetic.org/about/
International Association for Near-Death Studies. (2019). About IANDS. Retrieved April 20, 2019, from https://iands.org/about/about-iands27.html
International Association for Near-Death Studies. (2019). Journal of Near-Death Studies. Retrieved October 29, 2019, from https://iands.org/research/publications/journal-of-near-death-studies.html
International Cryptozoology Museum. (n.d.). History of the ICM. Retrieved July 14, 2019, from http://cryptozoologymuseum.com/history-of-the-icm
International Cryptozoology Museum. (n.d.). Mission & vision. Retrieved July 14, 2019, from http://cryptozoologymuseum.com/mission-vision
ITHAKA. (2019). The Journal of American Folklore. Retrieved October 29, 2019, from https://www.jstor.org/journal/jamerfolk
Jacquesvallee.net. (2019). Jacques Vallée. Retrieved December 29, 2019, from https://www.jacquesvallee.net/
J. B. Rhine: American Parapsychologist. (2019, February 16). In *Encyclopaedia Britannica*. Retrieved July 31, 2019, from https://www.britannica.com/biography/J-B-Rhine
John Wiley & Sons. (2019). Overview. Retrieved October 29, 2019, from https://onlinelibrary.wiley.com/page/journal/20448295/homepage/productinformation.html
Jones, Marie D. (2007). *PSIence: How new discoveries in quantum physics and new science may explain the existence of paranormal phenomena*. Franklin Lakes, NJ: New Page Books.
Kneeland, Timothy W. (2008, July). Robert Hare: Politics, science, and spiritualism in the early republic. *Pennsylvania Magazine of History and Biography, 132*(3), 245–260.
Krantz, Grover S. (1992). *Big footprints: A scientific inquiry into the reality of Sasquatch*. Boulder, CO: Johnson Books.
Kripal, Jeffrey J. (1999, Fall). "The visitation of the stranger": On some mystical dimensions of the history of religions. *Cross Currents, 49*(3), 367–386.
Kripal, Jeffrey J. (2014). Better horrors: From terror to communion in Whitley Strieber's *Communion* (1987). *Social Research: An International Quarterly, 81*(4), 897–920.
Kripal, Jeffrey J. (2018). Jeffrey J. Kripal: Life. Retrieved August 15, 2019, from https://jeffreyjkripal.com/life/
Kripal, Jeffrey J. (2019). *The flip: Epiphanies of mind and the future of knowledge*. New York, NY: Bellevue Literary Press.
LeRose, Chris. (2001, October). The collapse of the Silver Bridge. *West Virginia Historical Society Quarterly, 15*(4). Retrieved July 14, 2019, from http://www.wvculture.org/history/wvhs/wvhs1504.html
Lewis, James R. (2000). *UFOs and popular culture: An encyclopedia of contemporary myth*. Santa Barbara, CA: ABC-CLIO.
Library of Congress. (n.d.). *Collection: Nathan W. Daniels diary and scrapbook*. Retrieved July 15, 2019, from https://www.loc.gov/collections/nathan-w-daniels-diary-and-scrapbook/about-this-collection/
Llywodraeth Cymru Welsh Government. (2019). Castell Coch: Partners in fantasy. Retrieved December 11, 2019, from https://cadw.gov.wales/more-about-castell-coch
Long, Jeffrey, & Long, Jody. (2019). Near-Death Experience Research Foundation. Retrieved June 10, 2019, from https://www.nderf.org/index.htm
Long, Jeffrey, & Long, Jody. (2019). Out of Body Experience Research Foundation. Retrieved June 11, 2019, from https://www.oberf.org/index.html
Long, Jeffrey, & Perry, Paul. (2010). *The science of near death experiences*. New York, NY: HarperCollins.
Loxton, Daniel, Prothero, Donald R., & Shermer, Michael. (2013). *Abominable science! Origins of the Yeti, Nessie, and other famous cryptids*. New York, NY: Columbia University Press.

Magee, Glenn Alexander. (Ed.). (2016). *The Cambridge handbook of Western mysticism and esotericism*. New York, NY: Cambridge University Press.

Magic. (2019). In *The Oxford English Dictionary*. Oxford University Press. Retrieved May 21, 2019, from https://www.oed.com/view/Entry/112186?redirectedFrom=magick#eid

Maher, Michaeleen. (2015). Ghosts and poltergeists: An eternal enigma. In Etzel Cardeña, John Palmer, & David Marcusson-Clavertz (Eds.), *Parapsychology: A handbook for the 21st century*. Jefferson, NC: McFarland.

Maher, Michaeleen C., & Hansen, George P. (1992). Quantitative investigation of a reported haunting using several detection techniques. *Journal of the American Society for Psychical Research, 86*(4), 347–374.

Martelle, Scott. (2006, December 6). Ray Wallace, 84, took Bigfoot secret to grave—Now his kids spill it. *Los Angeles Times*. Retrieved April 17, 2019, from https://www.latimes.com/archives/la-xpm-2002-dec-06-me-wallace6-story.html

McCallion, Rachel. (2019, August 14). Top 11 spooky places to visit in Scotland. Scotland.org. Retrieved December 11, 2019, from https://www.scotland.org/features/top-11-spooky-places-to-visit-in-scotland

McCarra, Darren. (n.d.). The Cooneen ghost. Retrieved December 11, 2019, from http://mccarra.co/cooneen-ghost/

McCorristine, Shane. (n.d.). About me. Retrieved December 20, 2019, from https://www.shanemccorristine.net/

McCorristine, Shane. (2011). William Fletcher Barrett, spiritualism, and psychical research in Edwardian Dublin. *Estudio Erlandeses, 6*(6), 39–53.

McPherson, Joyce. (2016, April). Reconciling Doyle's paradox: Sherlock Holmes and the work of the Society for Psychical Research. *VIJ: Victorians Institute Journal*, 1–9.

Meldrum, Jeff. (2016). Sasquatch & other wildmen: The search for relict hominoids. *Journal of Scientific Exploration, 30*(3), 355–373.

META Lab. (2019). The META Lab at UCSB. Retrieved May 14, 2019, from https://labs.psych.ucsb.edu/schooler/jonathan/

Miles, Tiya. (2015). Goat bones in the basement: A case of race, gender, and haunting in old Savannah. *South Carolina Review, 47*(2), 25–36.

Miscellaneous: Committee for the Scientific Investigation of Claims of the Paranormal. 1977–1978. TS Box 797, Folder 15, Item 1219, Years of expansion, 1950–1990: Series 3: Subject files: Freedom of belief, expression, and association, 1939–1988. Mudd Library, Princeton University. *American Civil Liberties Union Papers, 1912–1990*. Retrieved October 25, 2019, from Gale Primary Sources.

Mossbridge, Julia. (2017, June 23). Do you wonder about your PsiQ? Institute of Noetic Sciences. Retrieved January 8, 2020, from https://noetic.org/blog/do-you-wonder-about-your-psiq/

Mossbridge, Julia A., & Radin, Dean. (2018). Precognition as a form of prospection: A review of the evidence. *Psychology of Consciousness: Theory, Research, and Practice, 5*(1), 78–93.

MUFON: Mutual UFO Network. (n.d.). Welcome to MUFON. Retrieved April 8, 2019, from https://www.mufon.com/

Museum of Witchcraft and Magic. (2017). Blog. Retrieved December 11, 2019, from https://museumofwitchcraftandmagic.co.uk/news/

Museum of Witchcraft and Magic. (2017). Visit. Retrieved December 11, 2019, from https://museumofwitchcraftandmagic.co.uk/visit/

National Trust. (n.d.-a). About the National Trust. Retrieved December 11, 2019, from https://www.nationaltrust.org.uk/features/about-the-national-trust

National Trust. (n.d.-b). By the look of you, you've seen the Romans! Retrieved December 11, 2019, from https://www.nationaltrust.org.uk/features/by-the-look-of-you-youve-seen-the-romans

National Trust. (n.d.-c). A haunted library and a bookish ghost. Retrieved December 11, 2019, from https://www.nationaltrust.org.uk/features/a-haunted-library-and-a-bookish-ghost

Noakes, Richard. (2004). The "bridge which is between physical and psychical research": William Fletcher Barrett, sensitive flames, and spiritualism. *History of Science, 42*(4), 419–464.

Noakes, Richard. (2004). *Entry on William Fletcher Barrett.* Chicago, IL: Chicago University Press, 2. Retrieved July 31, 2019, from https://ore.exeter.ac.uk/repository/handle/10871/15939
North American Bigfoot Center. (2019). The museum. Retrieved July 14, 2019, from https://northamericanbigfootcenter.com/museum
O'Connell, Mark. (2017). *The Close Encounters man: How one man made the world believe in UFOs.* New York, NY: HarperCollins.
Oxford University Press. (2019). Sociology of Religion. Retrieved November 7, 2019, from https://academic.oup.com/socrel/pages/About
Pandarakalam, James Paul. (2017). Understanding introvertive visions and extrovertive apparitions. *Journal for Spiritual and Consciousness Studies, 40*(2), 127–139.
Paperity. (n.d.). About. Retrieved May 14, 2019, from https://paperity.org/about/
Paranormal. (2019). In *Merriam-Webster.* Retrieved August 26, 2019, from https://www.merriam-webster.com/dictionary/paranormal
Paranormal. (2019). In *Oxford English Dictionary.* Oxford University Press. Retrieved August 26, 2019, from https://www.oed.com/view/Entry/137554?redirectedFrom=paranormal#eid#eid#eid
Paranthropology. (n.d.). Retrieved November 7, 2019, from http://paranthropologyjournal.weebly.com/
Parapsychological Association. (2019). Carlos Alvarado. Retrieved August 19, 2019, from https://www.parapsych.org/users/carlos/profile.aspx
Parapsychological Association. (2019). Convention history. Retrieved June 10, 2019, from https://www.parapsych.org/section/23/convention_history.aspx
Parapsychological Association. (2019). Harvey Irwin. Retrieved August 19, 2019, from https://www.parapsych.org/users/hirwin/profile.aspx
Parapsychological Association. (2019). History of the Parapsychological Association. Retrieved April 22, 2019, from https://www.parapsych.org/articles/1/14/history_of_the_parapsychological.aspx
Parapsychological Association. (2019). James Houran. Retrieved August 15, 2019, from https://parapsych.org/users/jhouran/profile.aspx
Parapsychological Association. (2019). United Kingdom. Retrieved December 10, 2019, from https://www.parapsych.org/articles/34/39/united_kingdom.aspx
Parapsychological Association. (2019). What is the Parapsychological Association? Retrieved April 22, 2019, from https://www.parapsych.org/articles/1/1/what_is_the_parapsychological.aspx
Parapsychology. (2019). In *Oxford English Dictionary.* Oxford University Press. Retrieved April 21, 2019, from https://en.oxforddictionaries.com/
Peabody Essex Museum. (n.d.). The Phillips Library. Retrieved July 14, 2019, from https://www.pem.org/visit/library
Phelan, Matthew. (2019). The casual observers. *Popular Science, 291*(3), 10–11.
Porter, Darwin, & Prince, Danforth. (2007). *Frommer's portable Savannah* (3rd ed.). Hoboken, NJ: Wiley.
Price, Harry. (1940). *The most haunted house in England: Ten years' investigation of Borley Rectory.* London, England: Longmans, Green.
ProQuest. (n.d.). PsycARTICLES. Retrieved October 25, 2019, from https://www.proquest.com/products-services/psycarticles-set-c.html
ProQuest. (2019). About ProQuest Dissertations and Theses Global. Retrieved November 27, 2019, from https://search.proquest.com/pqdtglobal/productfulldescdetail?accountid=11654
Radin, Dean. (2018). *Real magic : Ancient wisdom, modern science, and a guide to the secret power of the universe.* New York, NY: Harmony Books.
Radin, Dean. (2019). Biography. Retrieved July 30, 2019, from http://www.deanradin.org/
Regal, Brian. (2008). Amateur versus professional: The search for Bigfoot. *Endeavor, (32)*2, 53–57.
Regal, Brian. (2016). Bigfoot or Sasquatch. In Christopher R. Fee & Jeffrey B. Webb (Eds.), *American myths, legends, & tall tales: An encyclopedia of American folklore. Vol. 1: A– F.* Santa Barbara, CA: ABC-CLIO.

Reincarnation. (n.d.). In *Merriam-Webster's Online Dictionary*. Retrieved April 21, 2019, from https://www.merriam-webster.com/dictionary/reincarnation

Rhine, J. B. (1937). *New frontiers of the mind: The story of the Duke experiments*. New York, NY: Farrar & Rinehart.

Rhine Research Center. (2019). About the Rhine Research Center today. Retrieved June 10, 2019, from https://www.rhine.org/who-we-are/rhine-today.html?start=1

Rhine Research Center. (2019). Museum. Retrieved July 15, 2019, from https://www.rhine.org/what-we-do/rhine-newsletter/86-who-we-are/rhine-today/106-museum.html

Rhine Research Center. (2019). What is the Rhine. Retrieved May 14, 2019, from https://www.rhineonline.org/about-us

Richet, Charles. (1923). *Thirty years of psychical research: Being a treatise on metaphysics*. New York, NY: Macmillan.

Rojcewicz, Peter M. (1987). The "men in black" experience and tradition: Analogues with the traditional devil hypothesis. *Journal of American Folklore, 100*(396), 148–160. doi:10.2307/540919

Ruffle, Libby. (2017, May). Vessels of the gods. *History Today, 67*(5), 50–61.

Russell Targ. (n.d.). In *Psi encyclopedia*. Society for Psychical Research. Retrieved December 19, 2019, from https://psi-encyclopedia.spr.ac.uk/articles/russell-targ

Saybrook University. (2019). Ph.D. in Psychology: Consciousness, Spirituality, and Integrative Health Specialization. Retrieved May 14, 2019, from https://www.saybrook.edu/areas-of-study/humanistic-clinical-psychology/phd-psychology/consciousness-spirituality-and-integrative-health-specialization/

Schoch, Robert M. (2018, January 1). The Wow! Reconsidered signal. *Atlantis Rising Magazine*, pp. 24, 26, 61–62. Retrieved April 8, 2019, from EBSCOhost.

Schoch, Robert M., & Yonavjak, Logan. (2008). *The parapsychology revolution: A concise anthology of paranormal and psychical research*. New York, NY: Penguin.

Schultz, Bart. (2004). *Henry Sidgwick—Eye of the universe: An intellectual biography*. Cambridge, England: Cambridge University Press.

Seale-Collazo, James. (2012). Charisma, liminality, and freedom: Toward a theory of the everyday extraordinary. *Anthropology of Consciousness, 23*(2), 181.

SETI Institute. (n.d.). FAQ: What is the SETI Institute? Retrieved April 2, 2019, from https://www.seti.org/faq#seti1

SETI Institute. (2019). Mission. Retrieved June 10, 2019, from https://www.seti.org/about-us/mission

SETI Institute. (2019). SETI. Retrieved June 10, 2019, from https://www.seti.org/seti-institute/Search-Extraterrestrial-Intelligence

Shiah, Yung-Jong, Chang, France, Tam, Wai-Cheong Carl, Chuang, Shen-Fa, & Yeh, Lun-Chang. (2013). I don't believe but I pray: Spirituality, instrumentality, or paranormal belief? *Journal of Applied Social Psychology, 43*(8), 1704–1716. doi:10.1111/jasp.12125

Shuker, Karl. (Ed.). (n.d.). *The Journal of Cryptozoology*. Retrieved June 10, 2019, from http://www.journalofcryptozoology.com/

Sidgwick, Arthur, & Sidgwick, Eleanor M. (1906). *Henry Sidgwick: A memoir*. London, England: Macmillan.

Skinner, Doug. (n.d.). John A. Keel: A brief biography. Retrieved July 31, 2019, from https://www.johnkeel.com/?page_id=21

Slavoutski, Sergei. (2012). Is the reincarnation hypothesis advanced by Stevenson for spontaneous past-life experiences relevant for the understanding of the ontology of past-life phenomena? *International Journal of Transpersonal Studies, 31*(1), 83–96.

Society for Psychical Research. (2018). About the SPR. Retrieved June 10, 2019, from https://www.spr.ac.uk/about-spr

Society for Psychical Research. (2018). Cambridge archives. Retrieved December 11, 2019, from https://www.spr.ac.uk/cambridge-archives

Society for Psychical Research. (2018). Deborah Delanoy. Retrieved August 15, 2019, from https://www.spr.ac.uk/about/people/deborah-delanoy

Society for Psychical Research. (2018). Journal of the Society for Psychical Research. Retrieved November 7, 2019, from https://www.spr.ac.uk/publications-recordings/journal-society-psychical-research
Society for Psychical Research. (2018). Libraries and archives. Retrieved December 10, 2019, from https://www.spr.ac.uk/about/libraries-and-archives
Society for Psychical Research. (2018). Our history. Retrieved June 10, 2019, from https://www.spr.ac.uk/about/our-history
Sommer, Andreas. (2014, December). Psychical research in the history and philosophy of science: An introduction and review. *Studies in History and Philosophy of Biological and Biomedical Sciences, 48*, 38–45.
Stafford, Betty. (2014). Is reincarnation true? The research of Ian Stevenson. *Journal for Spiritual and Consciousness Studies, 37*(1), 33–37.
Steiger, Brad, & Steiger, Sherry. (2006). *Conspiracies and secret societies*. Detroit, MI: Visible Ink Press.
Strand, Clark. (2008). *Waking up to the dark*. New York, NY: Spiegel & Grau.
Strieber, Whitley, & Kripal, Jeffrey J. (2016). *The super natural: Why the unexplained is real*. New York, NY: Jeremy P. Tarcher.
Supernatural. (2019). In *Merriam-Webster*. Retrieved August 26, 2019, from https://www.merriam-webster.com/dictionary/supernatural
Supernatural Studies Association. (n.d.). About the association. Retrieved November 14, 2019, from https://www.supernaturalstudies.com/home
TANC Lab. (n.d.). Home. Retrieved May 14, 2019, from http://tanclab.org/ .
Targ, Russell. (2014). Russell Targ: Brief bio. Retrieved June 4, 2019, from http://www.espresearch.com/russell/
Targ, Russell. (2015, April 14). The reality of ESP: A physicist's proof of psychic abilities. *Watkins Mind, Body, Spirit*. Retrieved May 28, 2019, from https://www.watkinsmagazine.com/the-reality-of-esp-a-physicists-proof-of-psychic-abilities
Traveling Museum of the Paranormal & Occult. (2018). About the museum. Retrieved July 14, 2019, from http://paramuseum.com/about/
Traveling Museum of the Paranormal & Occult. (2018). The dark mirror. Retrieved July 14, 2019, from http://paramuseum.com/pieces/the-dark-mirror/
Traveling Museum of the Paranormal & Occult. (2018). Hoodoo coffin nail. Retrieved July 14, 2019, from http://paramuseum.com/pieces/voodoo-coffin-nail/
Traveling Museum of the Paranormal & Occult. (2018). The idol of nightmares [Billy]. Retrieved July 14, 2019, from http://paramuseum.com/pieces/idol-nightmares-billy/
Turner, Victor. (1969). *The ritual process: Structure and anti-structure*. Chicago, IL: Aldine Publishing Company.
Ukpokolo, Isaac E. (2012). Memories in photography and rebirth: Toward a psychosocial therapy of the metaphysics of reincarnation among traditional Esan people of southern Nigeria. *Journal of Black Studies, 43*(3), 289–302. Retrieved April 21, 2019, from JSTOR.
University of London. (n.d.). Archives and manuscripts. Retrieved December 11, 2019, from https://archives.libraries.london.ac.uk/results
University of London: Senate House Library. (n.d.-a). Harry Price Library of Magical Literature. Retrieved December 11, 2019, from https://london.ac.uk/senate-house-library/our-collections/special-collections/printed-special-collections/hpl
University of London: Senate House Library. (n.d.-b). Rare books and periodicals. Retrieved December 11, 2019, from https://london.ac.uk/senate-house-library/our-collections/special-collections/printed-special-collections/hpl/rare-books-and-periodicals
University of Virginia Division of Perceptual Studies. (2019). Rector and visitors of the University of Virginia. Retrieved May 14, 2019, from https://med.virginia.edu/perceptual-studies/
U.S. National Archives and Records Administration. (n.d.-a). Vermont: Records projects. Retrieved July 15, 2019, from https://www.archives.gov/nhprc/projects/states-territories/vt.html
U.S. National Archives and Records Administration. (n.d.-b). What is the National Archives and Records Administration? Retrieved July 15, 2019, from https://www.archives.gov/about

van Gennep, Arthur. (1960). *The rites of passage.* Chicago, IL: University of Chicago Press.
Victorian Popular Culture. (n.d.). Nature and scope—Spiritualism, sensation, and magic. Retrieved October 21, 2019, from http://www.victorianpopularculture.amdigital.co.uk/Introduction/NatureAndScope/Spiritualism
Victorian Popular Culture. (2019). Introduction to Victorian popular culture. Retrieved October 25, 2019, from http://www.victorianpopularculture.amdigital.co.uk/
Views of monster lessen skepticism. (1934, April 22). *The New York Times.* Retrieved April 14, 2019, from Historic *New York Times*, ProQuest.
Visit Historic Savannah. (n.d.). Sorrel-Weed House. Retrieved January 6, 2020, from https://www.visit-historic-savannah.com/sorrel-weed-house.html
Visit Savannah. (2020). Bonaventure Cemetery. Retrieved January 6, 2020, from https://www.visitsavannah.com/profile/bonaventure-cemetery/6129
Visit Wales. (2019). Haunted Wales. Retrieved December 11, 2019, from https://www.visitwales.com/info/travel-trade/itineraries/haunted-wales-5-day-itinerary
Wahbeh, Helané, Radin, Dean, Mossbridge, Julia, Vieten, Cassandra, & Delorme, Arnaud. (2018). Exceptional experiences reported by scientists and engineers. *Explore: The Journal of Science & Healing, 14*(5), 329–341. doi:10.1016/j.explore.2018.05.002
Warburg Institute, University of London: School of Advanced Study. (2018). Library. Retrieved December 11, 2019, from https://warburg.sas.ac.uk/library-collections/library
Warburg Institute, University of London: School of Advanced Study. (2018). The Warburg Institute. Retrieved December 11, 2019, from https://warburg.sas.ac.uk/
Watkins Mind, Body, Spirit. (2016). About. Retrieved May 29, 2019, from https://www.watkinsmagazine.com/about
Watt, Caroline. (n.d.-a). Home. Koestler Parapsychology Unit. University of Edinburgh. Retrieved December 10, 2019, from https://koestlerunit.wordpress.com/
Watt, Caroline. (n.d.-b). Registered studies. Koestler Parapsychology Unit. University of Edinburgh. Retrieved December 10, 2019, from https://koestlerunit.wordpress.com/study-registry/registered-studies/
William James. (1998). In *Encyclopedia of world biography online.* Detroit, MI: Gale in Context: Biography. Retrieved August 14, 2019.
Willow Creek–China Flat Museum: Bigfoot Country. (2019). Home. Retrieved July 14, 2019, from http://bigfootcountry.net/
Witch House. (n.d.). Witch House: History. Retrieved July 14, 2019, from https://www.thewitchhouse.org/
Wohl Library. (2017, September 5). The history of witchcraft in the IHR Library's collections [Blog post]. Retrieved December 11, 2019, from https://blog.history.ac.uk/2017/09/the-history-of-witchcraft-in-the-ihr-librarys-collections/
Zaleski, Carol. (1988). *Otherworld journeys: Accounts of near-death experience in medieval and modern times.* New York, NY: Oxford University Press.
Zdrenka, Marco, & Wilson, Marc Stewart. (2017, Spring). Individual difference correlates of psi performance in forced-choice precognition experiments: A meta-analysis (1945–2016). *Journal of Parapsychology, 81*(1), 9–32. Retrieved June 4, 2019, from EBSCOhost.

Index

AAS. *See* American Association for the Advancement of Science
Academy for Spiritual and Consciousness Studies (ASCSI), 105, 110n20, 239
American Association for the Advancement of Science (AAAS), 54, 108, 248, 278n31, 295
Archive of the Afterlife, 116, 127n7
Arment, Chad, 30, 47n131, 188–189
ASCSI. *See* Academy for Spiritual and Consciousness Studies
Association for the Study of Esotericism, 108, 111n37
astrology, 38, 41, 48n178, 156, 208, 269, 283, 296; history of, 38; research involving, 158, 160, 163, 208, 210–211, 269–272
Atwater, P. M. H., 27, 46n113, 46n115, 203, 264

Barackman, Cliff, 118
Barrett, William Fletcher, 22, 46n89, 56, 57, 64n32, 64n33, 64n35, 296
BCSCC. *See* British Columbia Scientific Cryptozoology Club
Bigfoot, 30, 32, 34–36, 37, 47n148, 48n161, 48n168, 127n14, 127n15, 127n16, 127n19, 189, 191, 193–195, 255, 266, 268, 269, 296, 297, 300, 301, 304; museums, 116, 118, 119. *See also* Bluff Creek; Gimlin, Bob; Krantz, Grover S.; Patterson, Roger; relict hominoid; Sasquatch
Bluff Creek, 34–36
Borley Rectory, 178, 290, 294n39, 294n40, 298. *See also* Price, Harry
British Columbia Scientific Cryptozoology Club (BCSCC), 107, 110n26

Cardeña, Etzel, 63, 63n3, 140, 242, 300
Center for Research on Consciousness and Anomalous Psychology (CERCAP), 63, 242
Center for UFO Studies, 60
CERCAP. *See* Center for Research on Consciousness and Anomalous Psychology
clairvoyance, 1, 20, 22, 58, 59, 107–108, 125, 131, 217, 235
Cocconi, Giuseppe, 15, 17, 45n54
Coleman, Loren, 60, 65n58, 65n59, 116, 145, 146, 189–190, 296
consciousness, xviin2, 20, 22, 23, 26, 46n96, 47n122, 58, 63, 104–106, 110n13, 110n20, 137, 140, 183, 184, 203, 204, 205, 206, 207, 208, 220, 225, 239, 242, 244, 258, 259, 262–264, 277n13, 277n14, 300, 301, 302, 303. *See also* near-death experience
credibility, xiii, xiv–xvi, xxvi, xxviii, 80, 81, 83–99, 147; components of, 90–93; of scholarly and non-scholarly/popular

305

sources, 93–94
Crookes, William, 54, 64n28, 142
cryptozoology, 30–38, 47n130, 47n131, 59, 60, 287; museums, 116, 118, 119, 120, 127n4, 127n5, 127n18; research involving, 145–148, 188–196, 265–269; scientific organizations, 107, 110n26, 110n28. *See also* Bigfoot; Coleman, Loren; Heuvelmans, Bernard; Keel, John; Krantz, Grover S.; Loch Ness monster; Meldrum, Jeff; Mothman; relict hominoid; Sanderson, Ivan T.; Sasquatch
Cryptozoology and Paranormal Museum, 119, 127n18
cunning folk, 41, 269; in the United Kingdom, 157, 213, 215, 281, 283–284

Delanoy, Deborah, 63, 66n69, 296
divination, 3, 38, 39, 41, 124, 283; history of, 38–41, 157, 208, 216–217, 283; methods of, 131, 156, 157–158, 168, 208; psychological connection, 271–272; research involving, 156–157, 157–158, 158, 208–210, 209–210, 269–272. *See also* astrology; magic; tarot
Duke University, xiii, 22, 59, 238, 242; parapsychology lab, 102–104, 105, 108, 110n11, 118, 185. *See also* parapsychology; Rhine, J. B.

Edinburgh, Scotland, 244, 287, 292, 293n22, 293n23
electronic voice phenomena (EVP), xxiii, 239
England, 122, 136, 138, 141, 157, 175, 177, 178, 196, 213, 215, 216, 245, 252, 264, 272, 280, 281, 283, 285, 288, 290, 292, 293n1, 293n5, 294n39, 294n40. *See also* Borley Rectory
ESP. *See* extrasensory perception
EVP. *See* electronic voice phenomena
Expedition: Bigfoot! The Sasquatch Museum, 119, 120
extrasensory perception, xiii, 20, 22, 23, 59, 103, 105, 125, 180, 183, 185, 186, 222, 240, 258, 287

folklore, 24, 30, 34, 37, 41–42, 47n130, 47n148, 138, 139, 169, 235, 240, 277n16, 277n17, 280, 288; and cryptozoology, 145, 148, 189, 190, 191, 195, 265, 269; and ufology, 202, 254
Fort, Charles, 222, 224–225
Fox sisters, 21, 53–54, 64n20, 179
Friedman, Stanton, 149, 199, 253

Ganzfeld experiment, 23, 63, 66n70, 94–96, 97, 99n10, 239, 296, 298
ghosts, 6–12, 7, 20, 44n18, 44n23, 44n26, 44n30, 44n33, 123, 128n23, 293n1, 298; belief in, 41–42; research involving, 56–57, 62, 63n3, 65n66, 130–137, 174–179, 250–252; types of, 6; and United Kingdom, 280–282, 284–286, 289–293, 293n1, 294n35, 294n37, 294n42
Gimlin, Bob, 36, 118, 190, 194
Gordon, Avery, 6, 44n17
Gurney, Edmund, 56, 58, 64n10, 65n46, 181–182, 286, 293n20, 297

hauntings, 6–12, 44n17, 44n22, 285, 287; notable locations, United Kingdom, 289–293; notable locations, United States, 6–12; research involving, 62, 81n1, 130–137, 174–179, 250–252
Hermeticism, 41, 108, 160, 164, 208, 209, 212–213, 217, 218, 219, 223, 275
Heuvelmans, Bernard, 30–31, 47n138, 60, 65n57, 65n58, 192, 268, 296
Hill, Betty and Barney, 13, 123, 199
Himalayas, 3, 32, 38, 146, 195, 266; Yeti, 32, 48n155, 195
Houran, James, 62, 65n65, 65n66, 176, 237, 250, 298, 301
Hynek, J. Allen, 15, 60, 65n56, 198, 199–200, 201, 202, 254, 255, 297. *See also* ufology

IANDS. *See* International Association for Near-Death Studies
Institute for the Study of Religious and Anomalous Experience (ISRAE), xxii, xxiii
Institute of Noetic Sciences (IONS), 61, 62, 65n60, 65n68, 225, 299, 300

International Association for Near-Death Studies (IANDS), 27, 46n112, 46n113, 203, 242, 277n19, 299
International Cryptozoology Museum, 60, 116, 127n4, 127n5, 190. *See also* Coleman, Loren
IONS. *See* Institute of Noetic Sciences
ISRAE. *See* Institute for the Study of Religious and Anomalous Experience

James, William, 58, 65n47, 304
Jung, Carl, xiii, 156, 159, 221, 223–224, 270

Keel, John, 59, 65n51, 151, 193, 200, 302. *See also* Mothman
Krantz, Grover S., 37, 47n136, 193–194, 194, 196, 268
Kripal, Jeffrey, 2, 4–5, 43n6, 44n14, 44n16, 62, 65n63, 65n64, 225, 226, 258, 299, 303

libraries, xxviii; and access to paranormal research, 73–78, 80
Library of Congress, 122
liminality, xiv–xvi, xviin2, 183, 281
Loch Ness monster, 33–34, 60, 129, 147
Long, Jeffrey, 25, 106, 203, 205. *See also* near-death experience
Lorenzen, Coral, 59, 65n53

magic, 38–41, 48n183, 48n185, 61, 108, 141, 225–226, 238, 277n1; in the United Kingdom, 283–284, 288–289, 293n5, 293n11, 294n26; research of magical practices, 156–170, 210–219, 269–272, 273–276
Meldrum, Jeff, 32, 34, 47n146, 194, 226n4, 266–267, 300
Mesmer, Franz, 52–53, 64n13, 125, 223
mesmerism, 51, 52–53, 125, 159
Metaphysical Society, 51, 64n4
Moody, Raymond, 25, 27, 203, 206, 207
Morrison, Philip, 15–17, 45n54
Mossbridge, Julia, 23, 46n96, 62, 65n62, 65n67, 65n68
Mothman, 59, 116, 117, 129, 193, 200, 255; museum, 116
MUFON. *See* Mutual UFO Network

Mutual UFO Network (MUFON), 17, 45n60, 248, 253
Myers, Frederic W. H., 2, 56, 57–58, 64n10, 65n43, 181–182, 256, 285–286, 293n20
mysticism, 38–41, 48n186, 58, 62, 108; research involving, 159, 161–162, 162–161, 163, 208, 211, 261–262

National Archives, 121, 127n20, 127n21
NDERF. *See* Near-Death Experience Research Foundation
near-death experience, 24–28, 40, 42, 46n100, 46n115, 63, 106, 110n24, 282, 296, 299, 304; research involving, 130, 154–155, 203–206, 206–204, 261–264. *See also* Atwater, P. M. H.; Long, Jeffrey; Moody, Raymond; NDERF; OBERF; Stevenson, Ian
Near-Death Experience Research Foundation (NDERF), 25, 106, 110n24, 205, 299
Nessie. *See* Loch Ness monster
New Orleans, 10–12; LaLaurie mansion, 10, 11; Magnolia mansion, 11
North American Bigfoot Center, 118, 127n14
Northern Ireland, 290, 292

OBERF. *See* Out of Body Experience Research Foundation
occult, 39–41, 48n183, 117, 127n8, 135, 144, 283, 289; research involving, 161, 165, 166, 168–170, 177–174, 209–219, 223, 270, 271, 273–276. *See also* divination; Hermeticism; magic; mysticism
Ohio State Radio Observatory, 17; Wow! signal capture, 17, 45n58, 45n59
oracle, 3, 131; in divination practices, 38, 153, 208, 209, 210; in Greek history, 3, 38. *See also* divination
Out of Body Experience Research Foundation (OBERF), 106, 110n25

paranormal, 1–41; cultural biases of, 3, 4–5; history of research involving, 49–55; prominent contemporary researchers, 59–63; prominent historical researchers, 56–58; timeline of historical ideology, 52–55; traditional definitions, 1–3; and the United Kingdom, 279–293

paranormal investigation, 67–81; logistics and techniques, 68–71

paranormal research, 220–226; gathering primary and secondary research, 71–81, 94–99; keyword cloud, 95–96; and library access, 73–78, 80; primary source examples, 113–115, 122–126

Parapsychological Association, 22, 46n90, 46n91, 62, 65n65, 107, 110n29, 171n4, 179, 242, 294n24

parapsychology, 19–24, 45n71, 63n3, 64n36, 103–104, 110n11; history of, 21–24; *Journal of Parapsychology*, 62, 63, 95, 102, 242–243, 250, 251, 252, 256, 258, 259, 260, 261; notable researchers, 59, 62–63; research into, 139–144, 179–188, 256–261. *See also* clairvoyance; Duke University; extrasensory perception; precognition; psychokinesis; telekinesis

Patterson, Roger, 36, 118, 190, 194

Peabody Essex Museum, 115, 127n1

Pearce, Hubert, 103

precognition, 2, 20, 23–24, 46n96, 62, 87, 88, 102, 104, 107, 185, 188, 247, 257, 260, 286, 300

Price, Harry, 175, 178, 226n2, 289, 290, 294n30

primary research, 71–72, 79, 230; examples, 113–126

Project Blue Book, 14–15, 16, 45n51, 60, 121, 199, 200, 202, 296

Project Sign, 14–15, 60, 199

psychical research. *See* parapsychology

psychokinesis, 20, 22, 23–24, 62, 72, 107, 134, 142, 180, 183, 184, 185, 186–187, 242, 257, 259. *See also* telekinesis

Radin, Dean, 23, 39, 43, 46n96, 48n185, 61, 63n1, 65n62, 176, 203, 225

reincarnation, 20, 24, 27–29, 47n119, 47n122, 47n129, 105, 233, 239, 243, 248; research involving, 104, 106, 142, 154–155, 159, 183, 204, 204–207, 208, 220. *See also* Stevenson, Ian

relict hominoid, 32, 47n146, 266–267. *See also* Bigfoot; cryptozoology; Meldrum, Jeff; Sasquatch

remote viewing, 2, 23, 107, 159, 180–181, 187–188, 245, 258. *See also* Targ, Russell

Rhine, J. B., 22, 59, 65n49, 102–104, 107, 110n2, 118, 125, 142, 168, 184–187, 299. *See also* Duke University

Rhine, Louisa, 185–186

Rhine Education Center, 102, 104, 105, 107

Rhine Research Center, 109n1, 110n18, 118–119, 127n17, 137, 242, 245

Richet, Charles, 52–55, 64n11, 142, 186, 232

Salem, Massachusetts, 115, 127n3, 269. *See also* Peabody Essex Museum; Salem witch trials; Witch House

Salem witch trials, 115, 289; primary source research, 126

Sanderson, Ivan T., 195, 266, 268

Sasquatch, 32, 34–37, 47n136, 47n146, 47n148, 119, 120, 127n19, 146, 191, 193–195, 196, 266, 268. *See also* Bigfoot; cryptozoology; Krantz, Grover S.; Sanderson, Ivan T.; Meldrum, Jeff

Savannah, 8–10; Bonaventure Cemetery, 10; Mercer-Williams house, 9; Sorrel-Weed house, 9

Search for Extraterrestrial Intelligence (SETI), 15–17, 45n56, 79, 106, 199, 248, 254

secondary research, 72

SETI. *See* Search for Extraterrestrial Intelligence

Shipton, Eric, 32, 195

Sidgwick, Eleanor, 51, 56–57, 64n36, 285

Sidgwick, Henry, 56–57, 64n38, 64n39, 108

Society for Psychical Research (SPR), 21, 46n81, 51–52, 56–58, 64n10, 66n69, 103, 108, 110n32, 111n33, 133, 135, 140, 175, 177, 178, 184, 235, 236, 256, 277n6, 278n21, 279, 284–286, 288, 294n28; history of, 21, 46n81, 51–52, 182; *Journal of the American Society for Psychical Research*, 241; *Journal of*

the Society for Psychical Research, 244; seminal figures, 56–58
spiritualism, 21–22, 46n89, 53–54, 57–58, 64n20, 64n25, 64n32, 64n33, 121–122, 124, 137, 144, 157–159, 159, 168, 175, 177–174, 178, 179, 213, 216, 229, 238, 274, 277n1, 280, 281, 289
SPR. *See* Society for Psychical Research
Stanley Hotel, 12, 44n36, 44n37
Stevenson, Ian, 28–29, 47n119, 47n122, 104, 142, 155, 204–207
Swedenborg, Emanuel, 206, 211

Targ, Russell, 23, 84–87, 99n2, 99n4, 187, 226n3. *See also* remote viewing
tarot, 38, 39, 48n182, 156, 157, 157–158, 163, 166, 209, 210, 219, 272, 288, 295
telekinesis, 20, 186
Tower of London, 290, 294n35
Traveling Museum of the Paranormal & Occult, 117, 127n8, 127n11, 127n12, 127n13

UAP. *See* unidentified aerial phenomena
UFO. *See* unidentified flying object
ufology, 13–19, 45n61, 59–60, 287; research involving, 148–151, 196–202, 252–255; Roswell, 13, 44n40, 153, 199, 234, 297. *See also* Hill, Betty and Barney; Hynek, J. Allen; Project Blue Book; unidentified flying object
unidentified aerial phenomena (UAP), 124, 252. *See also* unidentified flying object

unidentified flying object (UFO), 13–18, 16, 43n5, 44n40, 45n44, 45n60, 45n61, 45n67, 59–60, 65n53, 65n56, 79, 114, 121, 149–151, 167, 169, 193, 196–216, 222–223, 224, 233, 234, 236, 240, 245, 248, 252–255, 296, 297, 298, 299, 301. *See also* Hill, Betty and Barney; Hynek, J. Allen; Mutual UFO Network; Project Blue Book; ufology; unidentified aerial phenomena
United Kingdom, 133, 217, 279–293; magical practices, 215, 283–284; paranormal history, 280–282, 284–286; paranormal hotspots, 133, 289–293; universities and special paranormal collections, 287–289. *See also* cunning folk; Society for Psychical Research
universities engaged in paranormal research, 102–104. *See also* Duke University

Vallée, Jacques, 202, 226n5, 255

Wales, U.K., 215, 283, 292, 294n44, 294n45
Walton, Travis, 14
Waverly Hills Sanatorium, 8
West Virginia, 59, 116–117, 127n6, 151, 193. *See also* Keel, John; Mothman
Willow Creek-China Flat Museum, 118, 127n15
Witch House, 115, 127n2, 127n3

Zener, Karl, 22, 102, 103, 238

About the Author

Courtney M. Block is the reference, instruction, and user engagement Librarian at Indiana University Southeast in New Albany, Indiana. She received her master of library science from Indiana University, Bloomington, in 2010 and has worked in both public and academic libraries, helping build communities through service and scholarship. She is a member of the Institute for the Study of Religious and Anomalous Experience, a nonprofit paranormal research organization in southern Indiana. An advocate of challenging the status quo whenever possible, Courtney has conducted research into library/librarian stereotypes, social media as a way to mitigate library anxiety, and the role of servant leadership as a model for libraries. She has presented her research both nationally and internationally, at conferences such as UX in Libraries, the Pop Culture Association, and IDEAL. Her lifelong love of the paranormal is shared with her mom, and on any given weekend you might find them checking out a local haunt. Her favorite cryptid is Bigfoot, but Mothman is a close second.

www.ingramcontent.com/pod-product-compliance
Lightning Source LLC
Chambersburg PA
CBHW032017230426
43671CB00005B/113